RACE RELATIONS

Current Perspectives

EDGAR G. EPPS

University of Chicago

WINTHROP PUBLISHERS, INC.

Cambridge, Massachusetts

Library of Congress Cataloging in Publication Data

Epps, Edgar G   1929-   comp.
     Race relations: current perspectives.

     Includes bibliographical references.
     1. United States — Race question.   I.   Title.
E184.A1E66   301.45'1'0420973   72-13002
ISBN 0-87626-744-4

ii

Dedication

My indebtedness to my students and colleagues is gratefully acknowledged. They may not recognize their contributions as they are expressed here, but I have learned much from many challenging discussions. I also wish to acknowledge the generosity of the publishers and scholars who have graciously permitted me to reprint their works in this volume. Finally, I am grateful to Kathryn H. Cotton and Celia H. Jefferson for their assistance in collecting materials and preparing the manuscript.

Acknowledgements

J. Milton Yinger, "Recent Developments in Minority and Race Relations," *Annals of the American Academy of Political and Social Science*, Vol. 378 (July, 1968), pp. 130–145. By permission of the Publisher and the author.

L. Paul Metzger, "American Sociology and Black Assimilation: Conflicting Perspectives," *The American Journal of Sociology*, Vol. 76 (January, 1971), pp. 627–647. Reprinted by permission of the author and the University of Chicago Press.

John D. McCarthy and William L. Yancey, "Uncle Tom and Mr. Charlie: Metaphysical Pathos in the Study of Racism and Personal Disorganization," *The American Journal of Sociology*, Vol. 76 (January, 1971), pp. 648–672. Reprinted by permission of the authors and the University of Chicago Press.

"The Slave Plantation: Background to Present Conditions of Urban Blacks" by Roy Simon Bryce-Laporte is reprinted from *Race, Change and Urban Society*, Vol. 5, URBAN AFFAIRS ANNUAL REVIEWS, edited by Peter Orleans and William Ellis, pp. 257–284, by permission of the Publisher, Sage Publications, Inc.

Francesco Cordasco and Rocco G. Galatioto, "Ethnic Displacement in the Interstitial Community: The East Harlem Experience," *Phylon*, Vol. 31 (Fall, 1970), pp. 302–312. Reprinted by permission of *Phylon* and the authors.

Joan W. Moore, "Colonialism: The Case of Mexican Americans," *Social Problems*, Vol. 17, No. 4 (Spring, 1971), pp. 463–472. Reprinted with permission of the author and The Society for the Study of Social Problems.

Marshall Sklare, "Intermarriage & Jewish Survival," *Commentary*, Vol. 49 (March, 1970). Reprinted from *Commentary*, by permission. Copyright © 1970 by the American Jewish Committee.

Audrey James Schwartz, "The Culturally Advantaged: A Study of Japanese-American Pupils," *Sociology and Social Research*, Vol. 55 (April, 1971), pp. 341–353. Reprinted by permission of *Sociology and Social Research* and the author.

D. Y. Yuan, "Voluntary Segregation: A Study of New York Chinatown," *Phylon*, Vol. 24 (Fall, 1963). Reprinted by permission of *Phylon*.

Alvin Poussaint and Carolyn Atkinson, "Black Youth and Motivation," in *The Black Scholar*, Vol. 1, No. 5 (March, 1970), pp. 43–51. Reprinted by permission of The Black World Foundation, Sausalito, California, and the authors.

Robert Staples, "The Myth of the Black Matriarchy," in *The Black Scholar*, Vol. 1, No. 3–4 (January-February, 1970), pp. 8–16. Reprinted by permission of The Black World Foundation, Sausalito, California, and the author.

Edwin Harwood and Claire C. Hodge, "Jobs and the Negro Family: A Reappraisal," *The Public Interest*, No. 23 (Spring, 1971) pp. 125–131. Copyright © 1971

National Affairs, Inc. Reprinted by permission of *The Public Interest* and the authors.

Ulf Hannerz, "Roots of Black Manhood: Sex, Socialization and Culture in the Ghettos of American Cities," *TRANS-action*, October, 1969. Copyright © October, 1969 by *TRANS-action*, Inc., New Brunswick, New Jersey.

Virginia Heyer Young, "Family and Childhood in a Southern Negro Community." Reproduced by permission of the American Anthropological Association from *American Anthropologist*, Vol. 72, No. 2, 1970.

Sidney Kronus, "Some Neglected Aspects of Negro Class Comparisons," *Phylon*, Vol. 31 (Winter, 1970), pp. 359–371. Reprinted by permission of *Phylon* and the authors.

Edgar G. Epps, "Sex Differences in Attitudes Toward Black Consciousness and Integration Among Southern Black College Students." Presented at the Annual Meeting of the Southern Sociological Society, Atlanta, Georgia, April, 1970 (revised).

Robert Blauner, "Internal Colonialism and Ghetto Revolt," in *Social Problems*, Vol. 16, No. 4 (Spring, 1969), pp. 393–408. Reprinted by permission of the author and The Society for the Study of Social Problems.

Charles V. Hamilton, "The Silent Black Majority," in *The New York Times Magazine*, May 10, 1970. Copyright © 1970 by The New York Times Company. Reprinted by permission.

Andrew Hacker, "Civil War." Adapted from *The End of the American Era* by Andrew Hacker. Copyright © 1970 by Andrew Hacker. Reprinted by permission of the author and Atheneum Publishers. Appeared originally in *The New York Times Magazine*.

Barbara A. Sizemore, "Separatism: A Reality Approach to Inclusion?", Chapter 12, *Racial Crisis in American Education*, 1969, R. L. Green, ed., pp. 249–279. Reprinted by permission of Follett Educational Corporation, Chicago, Illinois, and the author.

Cedric Clark, "The Concept of Legitimacy in Black Psychology." Copyright © 1972 by Cedric Clark. Reprinted by permission of the author.

Walter W. Stafford and Joyce Ladner, "Comprehensive Planning and Racism." Reprinted by permission of the *Journal of the American Institute of Planners*, Vol. 35, No. 2 (March, 1969).

Fred J. Cook, "Mayor Kenneth Gibson Says—'Wherever the Central Cities are Going, Newark is Going to Get There First,'" *The New York Times Magazine* (July 25, 1971). Copyright © 1971 by the New York Times Company. Reprinted by permission.

Contents

3. INSTITUTIONAL PERSPECTIVES: EFFECTS OF RACISM ON BLACK AMERICANS

A. Sociological Perspectives on the Black Family / 163

B. Perspectives on the Political Process and Black Americans / 259

Introduction

The decade of the 1960's encompassed both the student sit-ins which featured prominently in the non-violent phase of the Civil Rights Revolution and the urban violence of Watts, Newark, and Detroit. Sometimes called the beginning of the Black Revolution, it was during the summer of 1966 that "Black Power" became a household phrase. The most militant voices in the black community were no longer those of the non-violent protest leaders; the leaders of SNCC and later the Black Panthers became the spokesmen for militance and Black nationalism. Perhaps the most important of the recent developments in American race relations is the emerging sense of group pride that is increasingly expressed by all racial minorities. The call for Black Power has been echoed by calls for Chicano Power and Red Power. Racial minorities are emphasizing group identity based on the positive aspects of their cultural heritages. The articles in this collection represent an attempt to provide the student with readings that express the effects of recent developments in race relations on the works of scholars writing in this area.

The concept of race relations as used in this book usually refers to patterns of interaction between Black Americans and White Americans. However, it more accurately refers to relations between White Americans and other nonwhite minorities as well. Most texts and books of readings in race relations attempt to introduce students to the total range of minority-majority problems both in the United States and in other nations. In my opinion, a single course cannot do justice to the variety of minority experiences in this country. Nor can it hope to cover race and ethnic relations in other countries adequately. Faced with this conclusion, it seems preferable to focus this collection of essays on the experiences of the largest racial minority in the United States.[1] American minorities

---

[1] By racial minorities, I mean those groups that, in social usage, are considered to be members of non-white racial populations. Milton Gordon has used the terms racial and quasi-racial groups to refer to Negroes, Indians, Mexican-Americans, and Puerto Ricans ("Assimilation in America: Theory and Reality," in *Minorities in a Changing World*, Milton L. Barron, ed. (New York, Alfred A. Knopf, Inc., 1967), p. 412). Oriental Americans can also be included in the category of racial minorities.

are currently concerned with self-determination based on their own unique experiences and the goals derived from shared experiences. Each racial minority is deserving of systematic treatment in its own right. It would be presumptuous for me, or for other students of race relations, to assume that the experiences and goals of one group can be generalized to apply to other groups. This book emphasizes readings which will help explain the processes which operate to keep Black Americans in a subordinate position in American society.

The book is divided into three sections. The first section consists of articles concerned with the way sociologists approach the study of race relations. The second section includes articles treating the experiences of non-black minority groups in American society. The last section is devoted to articles that analyze the effects of institutionalized racism on the life styles and life chances of Black Americans. This final section contains the largest proportion of articles and is divided into two sub-sections focusing on the family, and political processes and institutions.

By concentrating on the experiences of Black Americans, the editor has narrowed the focus of this book to such an extent that other minorities receive comparatively little consideration. Section Two consists of selections describing selected experiences of other racial and cultural minorities. These selections are included to provide the student with an opportunity to see how other groups have responded to problems of discrimination, segregation, and societal pressures that deny the legitimacy of non-Anglo or non-Christian cultures. The intent is to demonstrate that the Black Experience differs from the experiences of other groups rather than to emphasize similarities. However, the reader cannot help but be impressed by the many similarities in patterns of discrimination as well as in group reactions to discrimination.

Traditionally, American society has been willing to accept culturally different peoples if such people were willing to become acculturated and lose their cultural distinctiveness. At the same time, the American social system has maintained economic, educational, political, and legal systems which discriminate against those who are culturally or physically different.

Racial minorities may become acculturated, but they cannot lose their physical distinctiveness. Therefore, they cannot follow the pattern of European ethnics and "disappear" into the mainstream. Black Americans also carry the burden of an American heritage which includes enslavement and legal segregation—a burden which they share with no other American ethnic group. The experience of slavery and its aftermath continues to play a significant role in the problems facing Black Americans today in the rural South and in the urban ghetto.

European ethnics, including Jewish Americans, are differentiated by culture rather than by genetic or assumed racial differences.

Sociologists have tended to take the view that successful assimilation of racial and ethnic groups into the mainstream culture is almost inevitable. We know, however, that no racial minority has ever been assimilated into the American mainstream and that the process is largely incomplete for ethnic minorities as well. This assimilationist bias in sociology has been associated with a fondness for gradualistic approaches to social change in the area of race relations.[2] Thus, sociologists were slow to acknowledge the possibility of changing race relations through either legal action or direct protest although they tended to prefer the former to the latter. There was also very limited recognition of the vital role minority group members themselves play in the reformulation of race relations.

Most analyses of race relations in the United States have been conceptualized within the framework of an "order" model of society. In this framework, ethnic and racial minorities are viewed as "deviant" groups which must adjust to the institutionalized norms of society. A competing theoretical framework, the "conflict" model, emphasizes the roles of power and social conflict as they interact in the process of social change.[3] The approach used in this book is more congruent with the conflict model than with the order model. Although articles written from both viewpoints are included, the focus is on the historical and social processes associated with changes in race relations in America. The conflict approach also allows us to give full value to the efforts of minority groups to effect change in their own positions relative to other groups in our analysis of race relations.

The increased militancy of Black Americans has resulted in the recognition of the national character of American race conflict. It is no longer possible, as it was in the past, to view the "race problem" as a "southern problem." There is also an increasing awareness that the race problem is primarily a "white problem" rather than a black problem. In other words, there is a race problem in America because there is racism in America: individual and institutional racism. The first type consists of overt acts of discrimination or violence by individuals. "The second type is less overt, far more subtle, less identifiable in terms of specific individuals committing the acts. But it is no less destructive of human life."[4]

[2] See the article by L. Paul Metzger on "American Sociology and Black Assimilation" in this volume for a more detailed discussion of this trend. The same point is made by John Horton in his discussion of "Order and Conflict Theories of Social Problems as Competing Ideologies," *American Journal of Sociology,* 71 (May, 1966), pp. 701–13.

[3] John Horton, *Ibid.*

[4] Racism is defined as the practice of making decisions and policies on considerations of race which result in subordinating a racial group and maintaining control over that group. The emphasis is on the *consequences* of racial practices rather than the

Institutional racism is a greater problem than individual racism because the former is a necessary condition for the latter: individual racism must have an institutional framework. Without institutional support, individual racial prejudices would have little more importance than individual food preferences; deviance from the cultural norm would be considered an eccentricity rather than a social problem. The fact is that institutionalized racism encourages behavior which is detrimental to the welfare of blacks even when the white persons involved are not aware of the racial implications of their behavior. Therefore, in spite of the tolerant attitudes expressed by many young people, especially college students, they are caught up in a system which makes it almost mandatory for them to live their lives in a manner which supports racial discrimination in housing, education and interpersonal relations. An understanding of race relations, therefore, requires an understanding of the institutional framework within which racial interaction takes place.

---

intentions of the actors involved. This definition and the definition of individual and institutional racism are based on the book by Stokely Carmichael and Charles V. Hamilton, *Black Power: The Politics of Liberation in America* (New York: Random House, 1967), pp. 3–4.

1.
Theoretical Perspectives

The four articles in the first section were selected because they provide different perspectives on the study of race relations. The first article is essentially a "state of the art" paper which tells us what events and trends in race relations were considered important in the late 1960's and how social scientists interpreted these phenomena. The remaining articles in this section were selected because they represent new perspectives. Each article in its own way asks the reader to look at racial phenomena in a manner which will permit him to formulate new hypotheses that may challenge much of the traditional wisdom in the field.

The first selection, by J. Milton Yinger, provides the reader with a brief overview of the field of minority and race relations as it is treated in most sociologically-oriented textbooks. Yinger describes significant events and movements including both legal changes and protest movements. He points out that research and theory in race relations are becoming more rigorous, but that most studies remain on a descriptive level. One of the more important shifts in scholarly interest is the turning away from studies of "the prejudiced personality." The shift away from the "Mark of Oppression" type of study, which focused on emotional problems of blacks that are attributable to racial discrimination, is also noted and indicates that scholars are beginning to pay attention to the "strengths" of victimized groups. Yinger also summarizes studies of the degree to which minorities are integrated into or segregated from the major institutions of American society; he concludes with a description of the civil rights movement.

Yinger's treatment of the "range of usages of Black Power" can be useful for the student who finds himself confused by the many individuals and groups who differ in goals and political strategies, but who nevertheless have found it useful to embrace Black Power. In his discussion of the *Civil Rights Commission Report*, however, Yinger leaves out the important distinction between individual and institutional racism. His conclusion, that there is a need for a careful examination of racism as a system, is hardly debatable, however.

The remaining articles in this section are examples of the efforts of scholars to reconceptualize theory and research in race relations. Metzger argues that the theme of the eventual assimilation of the racial and ethnic minorities of the United States has been a recurrent preoccupation of American sociology. He examines some of the major arguments which have appeared in the sociological literature in support of the assimilationist view and questions the validity of the assumption that assimilation is the inevitable outcome of racial interaction in America. He concludes that a perspective which takes into account the social forces generating ethnicity as well as those favoring assimilation is necessary for an accurate and relevant analysis of the role of ethnic and racial groups in American life.

McCarthy and Yancey question the widely held assumption that Black Americans are very likely to experience "crisis of identity" and to exhibit low self-esteem. Their review of empirical studies suggests that the evidence in support of the "Mark of Oppression" hypothesis is shaky at best and that traditional arguments require rethinking. These authors also present a series of alternative perspectives which suggest hypotheses that conflict with those derived from the traditional position. Their approach leads McCarthy and Yancey to question the assumption that Black Americans accept the biased evaluations of whites and therefore develop negative self-images. They suggest, in fact, that poor blacks respond with strength to oppression. This article also implies that there may be positive psychological value in the development of a strong sense of black group identity. As Metzger has pointed out in the previous article, theories which attribute positive outcomes to the strengthening of ethnicity are relatively rare in American sociology.

The final article in this section, "The Slave Plantation: Background to Present Conditions of Urban Blacks," by Bryce-Laporte, stresses the institutional nature of the slave plantation and the effects of this "total institution" on the historical development of race relations in America. This article also features what is a recurring theme in many of the selections included in this collection: the challenge of the Black Revolution to traditional scholarship. In some instances, the challenge is concerned with correcting the omissions of earlier scholars; in others, the emphasis is on shifting the perspective of the researcher from viewing the problem through the eyes of the dominant group (white perspective) to seeing the problem through the eyes of the oppressed (black perspective). The most important contribution of Bryce-Laporte's article is its emphasis on the historical nature of the current racial situation. Current patterns of race relations are inextricably rooted in the history of American social institutions. One of the most pervasive

of these institutions was the plantation system which has left a
permanent mark on present-day institutions. As Bryce-Laporte puts it,
"The urban condition of most black people, the ghetto, must be studied
for its retentions, parallels, and departures from the slave plantation."
White conceptions of Black Americans and the institutionalized system
by which blacks are subjugated cannot be understood unless they are
related to the background of slavery. This focus on the unique aspects
of the Black American's struggle for equality provides a perspective for
comparison with the experiences of other minorities described in
Section Two.

Recent Developments in Minority and Race Relations

J. MILTON YINGER

In minority and race relations, event has piled on event and commentary on commentary in such profusion in the last five years that this brief review can only sketch the highlights.[1] Our commission is to examine scholarly developments within the discipline, but this will entail some attention to the major upheavals and transformations that have powerfully focused scholarly attention. Although we shall deal only with the United States, the problems under study are of world-wide significance, and attention to the minority and race relations of other societies has begun to attract the attention of scholars more fully than in the past.[2] In many parts of the world, relatively stable arrangements are breaking up, demanding both study and social action. Throughout most of Southeast Asia, the status of the "overseas Chinese" is being redefined. Pressures against persons of Indian descent in the nations of East Africa are not only reshaping intergroup relations in those lands but promoting restrictive immigration policies in Great Britain. Efforts to remove the disabilities of the "untouchables" in India are, in some instances, being met with violence. South Africa's apartheid policy grows in rigor in the face of international censure. In light of these references, which could be multiplied, it is wise to stress the fact that the examination of minority and race relations is of international significance.

[1] I shall deal almost wholly with material from the last five years, and that only illustratively, for many topics will have to be neglected in this brief review. For references and commentary on material previous to 1963, see Milton M. Gordon, "Recent Trends in the Study of Minority and Race Relations," THE ANNALS, Vol. 350 (November 1963), pp. 148–156; and George E. Simpson and J. Milton Yinger, *Racial and Cultural Minorities*, third ed. (New York: Harper and Row, 1965).

[2] Illustrative publications of the last few years include George DeVos and Hiroshi Wagatsuma, *Japan's Invisible Race: Caste in Culture and Personality* (Berkeley and Los Angeles: University of California Press, 1967); "Color and Race," *Daedalus*, Vol. 96 (Spring 1967), whole issue; Guy Hunter, *Southeast Asia: Race, Culture, and Nation* (New York: Oxford University Press, 1966); Pierre L. van den Berghe, *South Africa: A Study in Conflict* (Middletown: Wesleyan University Press, 1965); Philip Mason (ed.), *India and Ceylon: Unity and Diversity* (New York: Oxford University Press, 1967).

DEMOGRAPHIC TRENDS

From 1790 until 1940, the nonwhite population of the United States fell from about one-fifth of the total to about one-tenth. Since 1940, the trend has been slightly reversed, so that, at the present time, nearly one-eighth is nonwhite, with the majority of these being Negro. (Out of 200 million people in the country, 21.5 million are Negro.) More importantly, the Negro population has moved with great speed from farm to city and from South to North. Two-thirds live in metropolitan areas (in fact, one-third live in our twelve largest cities), and fewer than half live in the states of the Old Confederacy. If present trends continue, within a decade several of our largest cities will join Washington, D.C., on the list of cities with a majority of Negro citizens. As the population urbanizes, more and more of the migrants come from other cities, not from depressed farm areas, and tend to be of higher educational and income levels than the resident Negro population in the cities into which they move.[3] This trend can be of great significance to questions of their adjustment and their influence in cities.

Another demographic trend of long-run significance for American society has been influenced by the 1965 revisions of the immigration laws.[4] The quota provisions that have been in effect since 1924 were designed both to reduce the total number of immigrants and to guarantee that the great majority would come from northern and western Europe. Since immigration from the quota countries was reduced from an average of about 500,000 per year during the first quarter of the twentieth century to an average of about 100,000 during the second quarter, with Great Britain, Ireland, and Germany being most heavily represented, there is no doubt that the law produced the intended results. It also produced, however, some unintended results: it may have slowed the growth of the economy; it complicated our foreign relations, particularly with the nations of Asia; and it opened up new sources of migration, especially from Mexico, Puerto Rico, and the rural South of the United States. It could be argued that the Quota Control Act of 1924 powerfully supported the civil rights movement, forty years later, by vastly encouraging the migration of Negroes to cities.

The 1965 law removes the controversial and discriminatory national quota provisions from our immigration policy. Nations outside the Western Hemisphere are now assigned 170,000 a year, on a first-come, first-served basis, with no nation being allowed more than 20,000 of the total. (There

---

[3] See Karl Taeuber and Alma Taeuber, *Negroes in Cities* (Chicago: Aldine, 1965); see also Philip M. Hauser, "Demographic Factors in the Integration of the Negro," *Daedalus*, Vol. 94 (Fall 1965), pp. 847–877.

[4] For a general review of immigration, see E. P. Hutchinson (ed.), *The New Immigration*, THE ANNALS, Vol. 367 (September 1966).

are various family and occupational preferences as well.) For the first time, a limit has been placed on the number of immigrants permitted from the nations of the Western Hemisphere. The total is not to exceed 120,000 per year, but no national limitations have been added.

Although the law does not go into full effect until July 1, 1968, its influence has already been felt, with Italy, Nationalist China, Portugal, and Greece sending large numbers in fiscal 1967. It is estimated that in fiscal 1969 these countries, and perhaps others, will each be sending a full 20,000. It is too early to guess what unexpected results may also flow from this revision of the laws governing immigration; but on the basis of past experience, we must suppose that various unanticipated economic, political, and social consequences—some of them fortunate, some unfortunate—will certainly flow from the revisions.

THEORY AND METHOD

Before examining some of the substantive areas in the study of minority and race relations, let me note briefly the developments in modes of approach. There has been no radical departure from earlier approaches during the last five years, but there has been an acceleration of the trend toward more rigorous research. This can be seen, in part, in the call for a more formal statement of a theory of intergroup relations, as expressed, for example, in H. M. Blalock's *Toward a Theory of Minority-Group Relations.*[5] He stresses the need for much more precise statement of the problems under investigation, accurate measurement, attention to the system properties of discrimination, and more powerful mathematical tools for the study of that system. A second trend is the formalization of a comparative approach. There have been many studies in the past which have reviewed a variety of situations according to some standard outline, but seldom have the comparisons been based on a rigorously designed analytic structure. With the growth in interest in race relations around the world, we can expect increased attention to systematic comparative research.[6] On the research level, we find more careful and theoretically sophisticated applications of survey methods[7] and some extension of genuinely experimental methods.[8]

[5] H. M. Blalock, *Toward a Theory of Minority-Group Relations* (New York: John Wiley and Sons, 1967). See also J. Milton Yinger, *Toward a Field Theory of Behavior* (New York: McGraw-Hill, 1965), chap. xi.

[6] For a good beginning, see Pierre L. van den Berghe, *Race and Racism: A Comparative Perspective* (New York: John Wiley and Sons, 1967).

[7] For example, Robin M. Williams, Jr., with J. P. Dean and E. A. Suchman, *Strangers Next Door* (Englewood Cliffs, N.J.: Prentice-Hall, 1964); Gary T. Marx, *Protest and Prejudice: A Study of Belief in the Black Community* (New York: Harper and Row, 1967); and, on a smaller scale, Frank R. Westie, "The American Dilemma: An Empirical Test," *American Sociological Review*, Vol. 30 (August 1965), pp. 527–538.

[8] See, for example, Irwin Katz, *et al.*, "The Influence of Race of the Experimenter and

The great bulk of scholarly work, however, remains on a descriptive level, guided by, but not vigorously derived from, a generally stated theoretical orientation.

MAJOR AREAS OF CURRENT SCHOLARLY INTEREST

A large share of the research produced during the last five years can be classified under four broad headings: the social psychology of prejudice and discrimination, pluralism, minority and race relations in the major institutions, and the civil rights movement—including studies of urban riots and Black Power. These are not analytically precise categories, but they form a convenient outline for a commentary on a wide range of materials.

The Social Psychology of Prejudice and Discrimination

During the 1950's, no topic was more thoroughly examined than this one. *The Authoritarian Personality*[9] both symbolized and precipitated research on this theme; and it was followed by scores of studies designed to test, to extend, or to overthrow its conclusions. There has been less work on this topic in recent years. This is probably not so much because its major problems have been reasonably well solved as because the crises associated with the intergroup aspects of race relations have commanded our attention more powerfully in the last few years than the personal or interpersonal aspects. In part, however, it may be fair to say that the personality approach to prejudice and discrimination has been assimilated into a larger theory, which requires simultaneous attention to situational factors. Research on the personality factors in the prejudices of majority-group members is now focused, to an important degree, on the task of studying the complex of *interacting* factors that may produce hostility toward outgroups.[10]

Instructions upon the Expression of Hostility by Negro Boys," *The Journal of Social Issues*, Vol. 20 (April 1964), pp. 54–59; and, for a methodological report on an experiment in progress, J. Milton Yinger, Kiyoshi Ikeda, and Frank Laycock, "Treating Matching as a Variable," *American Sociological Review*, Vol. 32 (October 1967), pp. 801–812.

[9] T. W. Adorno, *et al.*, *The Authoritarian Personality* (New York: Harper and Row, 1950).

[10] See, for example, Ralph Epstein and S. S. Komorita, "Childhood Prejudice as a Function of Parental Ethnocentrism, Punitiveness, and Outgroup Characteristics," *Journal of Personality and Social Psychology*, Vol. 3, No. 3, 1966, pp. 259–264; D. D. Stein, J. A. Hardyck, and M. B. Smith, "Race and Belief: An Open and Shut Case," *Journal of Personality and Social Psychology*, Vol. 1, No. 4, 1965, pp. 281–289; Robert Coles, "Northern Children under Desegregation," *Psychiatry*, Vol. 31 (February 1968), pp. 1–15; Yinger, *op. cit.*; and Muzafer Sherif, *In Common Predicament: Social Psychology of Intergroup Conflict* (Boston: Houghton Mifflin, 1966).

Research on personality aspects of minority status has been more extensive in the last few years, strongly encouraged by the decisive effects of the civil rights movement. There has been careful documentation of the crushing effects of segregation and discrimination, but also powerful demonstration of resiliency and adaptiveness in the face of severe stress. The negative part is well stated by Kenneth Clark:

> It is now generally understood that chronic and irremediable social injustices corrode and damage the human personality, thereby robbing it of its effectiveness, of its creativity, if not its actùal humanity. . . Racial segregation, like all other forms of cruelty and tyranny, debases all human beings—those who are its victims, those who victimize, and in quite subtle ways, those who are merely accessories.[11]

Current work is documenting, however, more than personality damage. The unreservedly pessimistic view of such an earlier work as *The Mark of Oppression: A Psychological Study of the American Negro*, by Abram Kardiner and Lionel Ovesey,[12] is sharply qualified by studies of artistic creativity, politically effective organization, and healthy responses to the crises of desegregation. This last has been documented by Robert Coles' psychiatric studies of the ways in which Negro children have handled the stresses of school desegregation. In many cases, the anxiety has been severe, and there has doubtless been psychological damage in some instances, but the more common response has been a growth of self-confidence and a realistic adaptation to stress.[13]

Pluralism

Both opposition to and support for integration in American society continue to promote discussion of pluralism. In most commentaries, two

[11] From Kenneth Clark, *Dark Ghetto* (New York: Harper and Row, 1965), p. 63. See also Thomas F. Pettigrew, *A Profile of the Negro American* (Princeton, N.J.: D. Van Nostrand, 1964); Thomas F. Pettigrew (ed.), "Negro American Personality," *Journal of Social Issues* (whole issue), Vol. 20 (April 1964); and Eugene B. Brody and R. L. Derbyshire, "Prejudice in American Negro College Students," *Archives of General Psychiatry*, Vol. 9 (December 1963), pp. 619–628. These scholarly works are reinforced by several important "action" books that deserve careful study: Malcolm X, *The Autobiography of Malcolm X* (New York: Grove Press, 1965); Claude Brown, *Manchild in the Promised Land* (New York: The Macmillan Company, 1965); and Frantz Fanon, *The Wretched of the Earth* (New York: Grove Press, 1963). Oscar Lewis has added to his earlier works documenting the personality effects of "the culture of poverty" a graphic portrayal of life among deprived Puerto Rican families, on that island and in New York. See *La Vida* (New York: Random House, 1966).
[12] Abram Kardiner and Lionel Ovesey, *The Mark of Oppression: A Psychological Study of the American Negro* (New York: W. W. Norton, 1951).
[13] See Robert Coles, *Children of Crisis: A Study of Courage and Fear* (Boston: Little, Brown, 1967); see also, H. A. Nelson, "The Defenders: A Case Study of an Informal Police Organization," *Social Problems*, Vol. 15 (Fall 1967), pp. 127–147.

questions are mixed: How pluralistic is America? And how pluralistic ought it to be? These are primordial questions among Jews, many of whom feel caught between opposite problems: anti-Semitism, on the one hand, and the danger of loss of group cohesion and identity on the other. Virtually all signs point to a significant reduction in anti-Semitism during the last generation, although residual elements, sometimes tied to conservative Christian views, must not be overlooked.[14] The larger concern at the present time is the threat of loss of group identity in a progressively more favorable environment. As a scholarly problem, the issue becomes: What are the conditions under which a religio-ethnic minority group maintains, or fails to maintain, its distinctiveness? Will residential, economic, and educational intermingling—now becoming more and more common—undermine the solidarity of the group, or will they merely shift the grounds on which that solidarity is based? Formal and informal American policy may have shifted from "Anglo-Conformity," to "the melting pot," to "pluralism," to use the classification suggested by Milton Gordon,[15] but the effects of social change may work in a contrary direction. That structural assimilation of Jews into the economic, political, and educational life of the nation is proceeding quite rapidly, no one can doubt. Whether this is prologue to cultural assimilation is more problematic. The viability of ethnic subcultural systems in a mobile, affluent society with a relatively low level of prejudice has yet to be fully tested. Two recent studies document both the vulnerability and the toughness of the Jewish ethnic group.[16] The conditions under which one of these qualities outweighs the others have yet to be specified in terms of a general theory.

In recent years, developments among Negroes raise the question of pluralism in a different way. The dominant value among American Negroes has been integrationist. Somewhat paradoxically, in face of modest successes in integration, some racial and religious movements, some intellectuals, and, probably, some part of the mood of a great many

[14] See Charles Glock and Rodney Stark, *Christian Beliefs and Anti-Semitism* (New York: Harper and Row, 1966); and Charles H. Stember *et al.*, *Jews in the Mind of America* (New York: Basic Books, 1966).

[15] See Milton Gordon, *Assimilation in American Life* (New York: Oxford University Press, 1964); see also Nathan Glazer and Daniel P. Moynihan, *Beyond the Melting Pot* (Cambridge, Mass.: M.I.T. Press and Harvard University Press, 1963); and J. Milton Yinger, *A Minority Group in American Society* (New York: McGraw-Hill, 1955), chap. vi.

[16] See Marshall Sklare and Joseph Greenblum, *Jewish Identity on the Suburban Frontier* (New York: Basic Books, 1967) and Benjamin Ringer, *The Edge of Friendliness: A Study of Jewish-Gentile Relations* (New York: Basic Books, 1967). For a study of a racial ethnic group, see Stanley L. M. Fong, "Assimilation of Chinese in America: Changes in Orientation and Social Perception," *American Journal of Sociology*, Vol. 71 (November 1965), pp. 265–273.

individual Negroes have become pluralistic, even isolationist. The hopes aroused by a little integration have so far outrun the facts, that bitterness and loss of faith in the system have mounted. These have combined with a growing racial pride to increase a pluralistic emphasis: We do not want to integrate, some Negroes are saying. All we want is justice and equality; then we'll live our own lives. It seems likely, although it would be difficult to document, that this point of view has grown stronger in the last five years. It remains for research to specify more precisely the conditions under which it will continue to grow or to begin to fade away.[17]

Minority and Race Relations in the Major Societal Institutions

Study of the degree to which minorities are integrated into or segregated from the major institutions of a society has been a significant part of the scholarly work of race relations specialists for a long time. This interest has continued to be important during the last five years.

The economy. Most of the study of economic institutions has been descriptive and action-oriented: that is, the effort has been to state precisely what the economic situation of minorities is, what the trends are, and what changes are needed to produce greater equality of opportunity. From various indicators, it seems clear that for the Negro population, if not for all minorities, the decade 1953–1963 was a period of little or no economic improvement. The preceding fifteen years had produced greater gains in income, both relatively and absolutely, than any previous such period in American history; thus, the leveling off of the gains about 1953 was experienced as particularly frustrating. Using median family income as an index, we may note that gains among the Negro population were from about 30 percent of white income in 1930 to 53 or 54 percent in 1953. For a decade after that, there was little change; and then slow improvement began again, reflecting the continued strength of the economy, strong governmental efforts, the beginning of serious attention to discrimination by white businessmen, and the continued pressures of the civil rights movement. By 1966, median Negro family income was 58 percent of median white family income.[18]

The last several years have seen a small but steady upgrading of the average job level of Negro workers. For example, in 1966, 6 percent were in professional and technical jobs, compared with 4 percent in 1960; there

[17] See Simpson and Yinger, *op. cit.*, pp. 176–178; and Charles Keil, *Urban Blues* (Chicago: University of Chicago Press, 1966).

[18] U.S., Bureau of Labor Statistics, *Social and Economic Conditions of Negroes in the United States* (Washington, D.C.: U.S. Government Printing Office, 1967); see also A. M. Ross and Herbert Hill (eds.), *Employment, Race, and Poverty* (New York: Harcourt Brace Jovanovich, 1967); and *Fortune* (January 1968: "A Special Issue on Business and the Urban Crisis").

were small gains in teaching, medical, clerical, managerial, and other white-collar jobs. Attention to these gains in income and job level should not, of course, lead us to forget that very large differences remain, that improvement since 1953 has been slight.[19]

Several other aspects of the economic situation have received attention from students of minority and race relations. We shall mention only three, noting again that most commentary on them is descriptive of the current scene rather than analytic: government economic policy, labor unions, and housing. Since 1945, there has been a steady increase in the number of states with fair-employment-practices laws. Twenty-one states, with 60 percent of the nation's population (45 percent of the nonwhite population) now have such laws. A federal Equal Employment Opportunity Commission was established by the 1964 Civil Rights Act, covering all workers in interstate commerce (operationally defined as those work situations with more than twenty-five employees) or those involving the use of federal funds. It is difficult to measure the influence of these laws, since they enter a scene rapidly changing because of other forces as well. Their most stringent enforcement procedures are seldom used; practices clearly in violation of their provisions continue to exist; yet the legal redefinition of what constitutes fair employment practice is generally regarded as one of a series of interacting influences that are slowly transforming the employment situation for minority workers.[20]

There has been little shift in the labor union situation in the last several years. Industrial unions continue to be substantially open, although much less so in the South than in the North, and not without subtle discriminatory procedures among their members on the basis of race. Many craft unions continue to be highly segregated and discriminatory, even though the last official barriers to integration were removed in 1963. In the last few months, some slight changes are visible, largely as a result of mounting pressure from the federal government: refusal to release federal funds for construction until contractors have demonstrated nondiscriminatory practices in hiring, governmentally sponsored apprentice programs, and continued investigation of union practices by the Equal Employment Opportunities Commission are among the indications that discrimination

---

[19] See Otis D. Duncan, "Discrimination against Negroes," THE ANNALS, Vol. 371 (May 1967), pp. 85–103; see also Fernando Penalosa and E. C. McDonagh, "Social Mobility in a Mexican-American Community," *Social Forces*, Vol. 44 (June 1966), pp. 498–505; and Patricia C. Sexton, *Spanish Harlem: Anatomy of Poverty* (New York: Harper and Row, 1965).

[20] See Paul H. Norgren, "Fair Employment Practice Laws—Experiences, Effects, Prospects," in Ross and Hill (eds.), *loc. cit.*, pp. 541–570; see also Leon Mayhew, *Law and Equal Opportunity: A Study of the Massachusetts Commission against Discrimination* (Cambridge, Mass.: Harvard University Press, 1968).

in the craft unions is beginning to be put under some pressure. So far, however, these procedures have produced little effect on actual employment opportunities for Negroes in the skilled crafts.[21]

In the field of housing, there has been no scholarly equivalent, in the last five years, to the multivolume study of the Commission on Race and Housing, published in 1960.[22] There has been consistent attention, however, particularly in the various reports of the United States Commission on Civil Rights and in a variety of scholarly studies.[23] No clear trend is discernible in the contemporary scene. Negroes continue to move into the central cities in substantial numbers, increasing both concentration and segregation. But there are some countercurrents, and there is also need for some distinctions among types of housing situations. At least five situations can be distinguished, for which causes and consequences are not identical: (1) segregated, nonwhite ghettos, often the product of a conflict-laden "invasion" of an area of white residence, and largely characterized by poverty, overcrowding, and discrimination; (2) public housing, some integrated, some segregated; (3) the occasional purchase of a home by a nonwhite family in an established middle- or upper-class white neighborhood; (4) new communities, established by private contractors, working within limits set by the capital and mortgage markets, public attitudes, and legal possibilities; and (5) nonwhite suburbs, the product of a growing middle and upper class in the context of a basically segregated situation.

Public attention is largely concentrated on the first of these situations, which, in fact, probably involves the largest number of persons. But full understanding of the housing situation requires attention to the other four situations as well. They are growing in importance, and the time may not be far away when trends in these sectors of the housing market will be of greater significance than trends in the ghettos. The latter are supported by poverty, prejudice, and the pull of some sense of community. Policies and practices both of private builders and of governments have sustained

[21] See John E. Hutchinson, "The AFL-CIO and the Negro," in Ross and Hill (eds.), *loc. cit.*, chap. xv; Thomas O. Hanlon, "The Case Against the Unions," *Fortune* (January 1968), pp. 170–173, 188–190; F. Roy Marshall and V. M. Briggs, Jr., *The Negro and Apprenticeship* (Baltimore: Johns Hopkins Press, 1967).

[22] The central volume was Davis McEntire, *Residence and Race* (Berkeley and Los Angeles: University of California Press, 1960).

[23] In addition to the annual reports of the Civil Rights Commission, see Taeuber and Taeuber, *op. cit.*; L. K. Northwood, *Urban Desegregation: Negro Pioneers and Their White Neighbors* (Seattle: University of Washington Press, 1965); Charles Abrams, "The Housing Problem," *Daedalus*, Vol. 95 (Winter 1966), pp. 64–76; Eunice Grier and George Grier, "Equality and Beyond: Housing Segregation in the Great Society," *Daedalus*, Vol. 95 (Winter 1966), pp. 77-106. (The Fall 1965 and Winter 1966 issues of *Daedalus* are devoted solely to articles on "The Negro American," and deserve careful study.)

the ghetto. But in the last five years, there has been an acceleration of trends supporting both dispersal and integration: by 1967, twenty-one states and a number of cities had fair housing practices laws. As this is written (April 10, 1968), the national Congress has just passed such a law. Equally important, federal policy has shifted, from active support of segregation, to troubled ambiguity, to fairly forthright opposition wherever federal funds or powers are involved. In the summer of 1967, the Pentagon began to wield a powerful economic sanction over landlords around some military bases: only those who adopted a nondiscriminatory policy would be on the approved list for the families of men in the service. The entry of some labor unions into the mortgage market and as builders of housing for their members; the activity of a few church groups both in promoting integrated housing as a value and in backing some projects; the increased economic and political power of minorities; the active efforts of a few private builders in the field of integrated housing; and a general shift toward a more liberal attitude, as reflected in public opinion polls on housing—all of these trends, though presently less powerful than the forces promoting central city ghettos, are keeping the housing situation in 1968 more fluid and unpredictable than it is generally seen to be. Which of the trends will prevail depends, of course, on underlying economic and political processes which set the context for housing decisions to an important degree.

Politics. In the last five years, the first Negro was elected to the United States Senate since Reconstruction days (1966); two large cities elected Negro mayors (Cleveland and Gary, 1967); several other Negro mayors have been elected by city councils; and a Negro candidate for Congress in Mississippi, although defeated, received nearly twice as many votes in a primary election (1968) as the total of Negro registrants in the state a few years earlier. These are illustrative of the direct political gains from the rapid increase in Negro voters, the result of a twenty-year trend which was accelerated by the 1964 Civil Rights Act and a great many private efforts. Indirect effects are generally regarded as more important than the elections won. Candidates must now, in many areas, vie for minority votes. There are nearly three million Negro registrants in the South (there were 250,000 in 1944), and nearly four million in the North. Slowly, we begin to see more jobs for Negroes, more participation on juries, more services, and more influence on policy decisions in those areas where they vote in large numbers. Their participation changes the nature of the campaigns, with moderates having a greater chance to win. Since Negroes make up only 8 percent of the registered voters, and an even smaller proportion of the economic and organizational power involved in politics, their increased political participation has produced no major transformation of status, but it has added a strong weapon to the civil rights campaign.

Scholarly studies of these political trends include both general examina-
tions of the consequences of minority participation and studies of particular areas and specific elections.[24] It is clear from these studies that the
changes of the last two decades have been primarily of the traditional
variety, with Negroes able to play balance-of-power politics and to enter
into various coalitions. The total result, however, has not been to break
decisively the patterns of discrimination to which they are subjected.
In this context, sentiment grows for new and different patterns of political
activity, for example, ghetto-based ideological groups that stay outside
the main parties, trying, by means of the solidarity of purpose and the
intensity of their group feeling, to bargain with those in power for major
concessions. It remains to be seen whether this conflict-oriented approach
to politics will become more important and whether it will prove to be
effective. It seems likely to increase, along with in-the-party bargaining,
and the mixture may be more powerful politically than either strategy
alone.

Related to the study of politics, and to several other topics, is the
examination of minorities in the Armed Forces. With three and a third
million men under arms, military service continues to be a decisive part
of the national scene. Approximately 9 percent of the men in the service
are Negroes, but only 2 percent of the officers—a reflection of residual
discrimination, poorer preparation, and less seniority. As of mid-1967,
11 percent of the troops in Vietnam were Negro, and they had experienced 15 percent of the combat deaths, indicating their greater representation among combat infantrymen, their greater readiness to volunteer
for various special forces, and the greater likelihood of their re-enlisting
for additional tours of duty.

With hundreds of thousands of returned servicemen now part of the
civilian population in minority communities, their military experience and
their treatment upon return has become an important fact of national
life. Many had steadier and higher income in the service than before (or
perhaps afterward); some were trained in a skill which they could not
have obtained in civilian life; they lived in relatively nonsegregated
situations, with new patterns of expectation being generated; and, probably most important, hundreds of thousands of Negro and white troops
have experienced the dangers and tragedies of combat together, with
powerful effects on their attitudes. There has been no major, systematic

[24] For representative studies, see James Q. Wilson, "The Negro in Politics," *Daedalus,*
Vol. 94 (Fall 1965), pp. 949–973; Jack Walker, "Negro Voting in Atlanta, 1953–1961,"
Phylon, Vol. 24 (Winter 1963), pp. 379–387; Everett C. Ladd, Jr., *Negro Political
Leadership in the South* (New York: Cornell University Press, 1966); Irving Horo-
witz and Louis and Martin Liebowitz, "Social Deviance and Political Marginality:
Toward a Redefinition of the Relation between Sociology and Politics," *Social Prob-
lems,* Vol. 15 (Winter 1968), pp. 280–296.

attempt to assess the consequences of these facts; but there is substantial agreement, among those who have studied the situation, on the accumulated judgment of earlier work: Shared military experience, particularly on the battlefield, reduces prejudice; the substantial integration of the armed forces of the United States has produced a major pressure toward civilian integration by shaping the attitudes and increasing the skills of Negro servicemen; and the military institution itself, because of its massive influence on the economy, on manpower use, and on public policy, vitally affects race relations—primarily toward integration in the last several years.[25]

The family. We shall discuss only one aspect of the large topic of minority-group family patterns, an aspect that has received major attention in the period under review. Increases in the number of Negroes on welfare rolls and a higher rate of illegitimacy have focused attention on the stresses experienced by Negro families. This attention was powerfully increased, in March 1965, by the appearance of a government document entitled *The Negro Family: The Case for National Action.*[26] Its thesis can be stated in these terms: "At the heart of the deterioration of the fabric of Negro society is the deterioration of the Negro family." The interpretation of causes was sympathetic, namely, that the weakness is rooted in slavery and has been nourished by a century of discrimination and segregation, but the assertion of the fact of deterioration was relatively unqualified.

"The Moynihan Report," as it came to be called, precipitated a great deal of political and scholarly controversy.[27] We shall be concerned only with the latter. Few critics denied the basic set of facts with which the report was concerned; but several stressed the need for seeing them in the context of other facts, and many believed that different interpretations were more adequate. One might synthesize the arguments of several critics in these terms: The Moynihan Report emphasized socialization to a subculture, resulting in deviant tendencies.[28] Its critics emphasized the

25 See, for example, C. C. Moskos, "Racial Integration in the Armed Forces," *American Journal of Sociology,* Vol. 72 (September 1966), pp. 132–148.
26 Daniel P. Moynihan and Paul Barton, *et al., The Negro Family: The Case for National Action* (The Moynihan Report), U.S. Department of Labor, Office of Policy Planning and Research (Washington, D.C.: U.S. Government Printing Office, 1965).
27 See Lee Rainwater and William L. Yancey, *The Moynihan Report and the Politics of Controversy* (Cambridge, Mass.: The M.I.T. Press, 1967).
28 See G. S. Goldberg, "The Moynihan Report and Its Critics," *IRCD Bulletin,* Vol. 2 (May 1966), whole issue; Herbert Gans, "The Negro Family: Reflections on the Moynihan Report," *Commonweal,* Vol. 83, October 15, 1965, pp. 47–51; William Ryan, "Savage Discovery," *The Nation,* Vol. 201, November 22, 1965, pp. 380–384; A. C. Hill and F. S. Jaffe, "Negro Fertility and Family-Size Preferences: Implications for Programming of Health and Social Services," in Talcott Parsons and Kenneth Clark (eds.), *The Negro American* (Boston: Houghton Mifflin, 1966), pp. 205–224; and Rainwater and Yancey, *op. cit.*

pathological structure within which the family was forced to exist. These two perspectives have different implications for policy: one suggests a need to change individual tendencies and family patterns; the other implies a need to transform drastically the situations with which they are forced to cope. The latter point is illustrated by Gans when he writes that "it may well be that instability, illegitimacy, and matriarchy are the most positive adaptations possible to the economic conditions which Negroes must endure."[29] For the Negro male, to be itinerant and rootless may be the best way to maintain self-respect under the sharply discriminatory conditions he faces.

We need to be certain that all necessary controls for class, education, recency of move to the city, and other relevant variables have been made before we see the facts as signs of a peculiarly Negro pathology. There is also need to note that the problem of Negro illegitimacy is more visible because of the greater difficulty in placing Negro infants for adoption and the practice of recording mulatto children as Negro even though one parent is Caucasian. Furthermore, if one is to speak of a comparative Negro-white family pathology, it is essential that the nature of the pathology be specified. Is it only out-of-wedlock births, or does it involve a complex of factors—premarital coitus, differential availability of contraceptives, rates of induced abortion, and unreported out-of-wedlock births? Whites probably use precipitate marriage more readily as a way of avoiding an illegitimate birth. All of these points together would not eliminate the central thesis of the Moynihan Report—that many Negro families are caught in a cycle of illegitimacy-poverty-inadequate socialization. These points do, however, qualify the thesis in important ways and point to different policy requirements.

Education. Ethnic and racial minorities in American society have widely differing experiences in education. On the one hand, those of Chinese or Japanese descent and Jews have higher levels of education, as measured by the median school years completed and the percentages with college degrees, than the white Christian majority. On the other hand, Indian, Puerto Rican, Mexican, and Negro Americans are seriously disadvantaged in education. Most scholarly work in the last few years has focused on the problems of Negro education and the controversies surrounding efforts to integrate the schools. Once again, we can only illustrate the issues being studied in this complex field of interest.

In the last five years, the United States has witnessed the paradoxical fact that the pace of school integration has picked up somewhat in the South while schools in the North have probably become more segregated. Federal pressure on Southern schools has increased during the last three years; and now over 90 percent of the school districts of the states

[29] Gans, *op. cit.,* p. 49.

formerly maintaining segregated schools have either desegregated or submitted acceptable plans. Between 25 and 30 percent of Negro children in these states now go to school with white children. Every public college in the region is in compliance with legal requirements. Although not all have Negro students, there are over 35,000 Negro students in formerly all-white colleges and universities, including substantial numbers in schools where, only a few years ago, there were strong battles to keep them out. Despite these facts, it is a mistake to forget that the South is still characterized by massive school segregation.

In the North, complete segregation is less commonly the rule, but in most cities a majority of Negro children go to schools where they make up a large proportion of the student body. Note, for example, the percentage of Negro children who go to schools 90 to 100 percent Negro in the following cities: Gary, 90 percent; Chicago, 89 percent; Cleveland, 82 percent; Buffalo, 77 percent; Detroit, 72 percent; Milwaukee, 77 percent.[30] In most instances, these percentages represent increases over the first decade. They demonstrate that, in spite of a variety of programs to promote integration—without which an even more sharply segregated pattern would exist—Northern schools have not been able to cancel out two powerful forces: the flight of whites to the suburbs and the growth of private-school enrollments (largely white).

In face of these facts, some scholars, public officials, parents, and educators are beginning to ask—even if they had formerly supported integration: Should we not devote our energies toward improving schools throughout our cities, particularly those in the ghettos, and set aside, at least for a time, the effort to integrate them? The central scholarly study of this problem, the Coleman Report, comes to a different conclusion.[31] The authors review the facts of segregation; they demonstrate that, on the average, minority children go to poorer, more crowded schools; and they show that the children in most racial minorities, Orientals excepted, fall progressively behind national norms as they go into higher grades. Most important, however, they show that the quality of school attended is of greatest importance, in terms of performance, for those pupils from the most disadvantaged backgrounds. In particular, a setting that gives them some sense of control over their own lives promotes higher aspirations and performance; and for the Negro children,

[30] See U.S., Commission on Civil Rights, *Racial Isolation in the Public Schools*, Vol. I (Washington, D.C.: U.S. Government Printing Office, 1967), p. 7.

[31] See James S. Coleman, *et al.*, *Equality of Educational Opportunity* (Washington, D.C.: U.S. Government Printing Office, 1966). For commentaries, see R. A. Dentler, "Equality of Educational Opportunity—A Special Review," *Urban Review*, Vol. 1 (December 1966), pp. 27–29; and R. C. Nichols, "Schools and the Disadvantaged," *Science*, Vol. 154, (December 9, 1966), pp. 1312–1314. See also the two volumes on *Racial Isolation in the Public Schools, op. cit.*

this sense of control is increased when they attend schools with large proportions of white children. Integrated schools, they argue, strengthen school performance.

Perhaps the most common argument against this position is along this line: Substantial segregation of schools is inevitable under present circumstances; major efforts to desegregate will only speed up the flight of white families to the suburbs and to private schools. Attention should be focused, therefore, on the improvement of ghetto schools, leaving integration to a later period. The reply to this argument is likely to be: Our experience shows that "quality ghetto schools" cannot be obtained. Both for political reasons and for reasons based on our knowledge of the sources of motivation and aspiration to learn, segregated schools will remain poorer learning environments.[32] The evidence seems to this writer to support the latter view. The two goals of improving ghetto schools in various ways, while promoting integration, need not be mutually exclusive; but the latter should not be sacrificed in an unrealizable independent effort to obtain the former. If this position is taken, the need is to seek for new programs to extend the presently inadequate efforts to promote integration. In the last ten years, we have discovered that only small gains can be obtained by the redrawing of school lines, consolidating two schools, token amounts of busing, and other small-scale efforts to promote integration. Successful integration in the years ahead will depend upon the extensive use of downtown-suburb collaboration; the development of school parks; perhaps, the building of consolidated business-education-residential complexes that will draw in a variety of classes and races; and much more persuasive use of federal funds and federal power to encourage local programs and to support the complementary tasks of housing and job integration.[33]

[32] See the "debate" in the *New Republic:* Joseph Alsop, "No More Nonsense about Ghetto Education," *New Republic,* July 22, 1967, pp. 18–23; Robert Schwarts, Thomas Pettigrew, and Marshall Smith, "Fake Panaceas for Ghetto Education: A Reply to Joseph Alsop," *Ibid.,* September 23, 1967, pp. 16–19; Joseph Alsop, "Ghetto Education," *Ibid.,* November 18, 1967, pp. 18–23; Robert Schwarts, Thomas Pettigrew, and Marshall Smith, "Is Desegregation Impractical?", *Ibid.,* January 6, 1968, pp. 27–29. See also A. H. Passow, Miriam Goldberg, and A. J. Tannenbaum (eds.), *Education of the Disadvantaged* (New York: Holt, Rinehart and Winston, 1967).

[33] A number of recent books about ghetto schools that are not scholarly studies but sharp critiques are valuable for the student of contemporary education. For example, Jonathan Kozol, *Death at an Early Age* (Boston: Houghton Mifflin, 1967); Nat Hentoff, *Our Children Are Dying* (New York: Viking Press, 1966); John Holt, *How Children Fail* (New York: Pitman, 1964); Peter Schrag, *Voices in the Classroom* (Boston: Beacon Press, 1965). That there are educational problems other than those produced in the ghetto is well shown by Murray L. Wax, *et. al.,* "Formal Education in an American Indian Community," *Social Problems,* Vol. 11 (Spring 1964, Supplement).

The Civil Rights Movement

For a quarter of a century, students of minority and race relations have been examining the breakup of America's patterns of segregation and discrimination. The movement has evolved through a number of stages, with different strategies, different participants, and different levels of conflict. Somewhat arbitrarily, one might suggest that 1944–1954 was the constitutional stage, marked at the beginning by a Supreme Court ruling against white primaries and at the end with a Court ruling against school segregation. The next stage might be called the decade of nonviolent but active protest. Federal laws and additional court decisions were important, but the decisive events were related to the entrance of large numbers of deprived people directly into the struggle. One might mark the beginning with the Montgomery bus boycott, 1955, and the end by the March on Washington, 1963, in which 210,000 persons, Negro and white, joined Martin Luther King in proclaiming: "I have a dream" of a society without discrimination and prejudice. We are now in the midst of a third stage, which can well be called the Black Power period. Impatience among Negroes has mounted, despite—or, indeed, because of—the important gains. Resistance has mounted among some whites. Established action groups are affirming: We must push harder; change must be much more rapid. New action groups are declaring: Only self-reliance is appropriate; the white world is throwing us crumbs; it is stalling; therefore we must organize Black Power. And the most frustrated, having lost all confidence in the system, have been drawn into violence.

I shall deal only with this last, the Black Power, stage. In light of the speed of changes in strategy and goals in the last twenty-five years, it would be foolish to regard this as a final pattern. Ten years from now, it may look as "outmoded" as the "pre-Montgomery" pattern of mild constitutional reform. This is not to suggest that the 1970's will witness an even higher level of conflict and violence, that escalation of the conflict is inevitable, for the course of events depends upon the national response to the present crisis. So far, we have experienced a fairly standard "revolutionary" sequence, with small gains engendering large hopes—and the gap between gains and hope creating the context in which further change proceeds. If the seeds of major change that have already been planted can be nourished and brought to fruition in the next several years, this Black Power period will prove to be the peak of conflict, followed by more constructive rebuilding. If lack of imagination, inertia, unwillingness to pay a large price for an even larger gain, and distraction by other problems prevent effective action, the nation may be faced by mounting tragedy.

Scholars have been so busy simply trying to observe the constantly shifting facts that few major, systematic studies are available. Much of the material for the student, in fact, is found in the steady stream of reports in newspapers, in several journals of news and opinion, in government reports, and in the writings of participants and interpreters of the Black Power movement.[34]

The term "Black Power" clearly has no denotative meaning in current discussions, whether used by those participating in the movement or by those seeking to understand it. The conflict element which characterizes all of its varieties spills over, on the one hand, into violence (which is not a synonym for conflict), and, on the other, into activities permitting, even seeking, white support, but rejecting white management. The key variable determining an individual's or a group's location along this range is degree of faith that the national system is capable of change. One might describe the range of usages as follows.

1. At one extreme are those who say: Violence is a necessary method; self-segregation is desirable. Since the system is incapable of improvement, it must be destroyed. The rhetoric of this group suggests that they seek, not equality but black dominance. "Separate and dominant" is the manifest, if not the deeper, underlying message of such a spokesman as H. Rap Brown.

2. In the center are those who believe that effective action demands the organization of exclusively black groups designed to attack inequality by the use of political, economic, and, if need be, violent weapons. There is little interest in co-operation with white persons or with moderate Negro organizations. "Equal but separate" might be thought of as the slogan of this segment of the Black Power movement, epitomized by Stokely Carmichael.

3. On the moderate side of the Black Power movement are those who continue to see value in the political process, but regard it as much too slow. Civil disobedience, in the Gandhi sense, is a major strategy. Their organiza-

---

[34] In addition to several sources already cited, the following may illustrate what is a veritable flood of material: William Brink and Louis Harris, *Black and White: A Study of U.S. Racial Attitudes Today* (New York: Simon and Schuster, 1967); U.S. National Advisory Commission on Civil Disorder, *Report of the National Advisory Commission on Civil Disorders* (New York: Grosset and Dunlap, 1968)—as of this writing, the official government publication is not yet available; Lewis M. Killian takes a pessimistic view in *The Impossible Revolution* (New York: Random House, 1968); Martin Luther King, Jr., *Why We Can't Wait* (New York: New American Library, 1964); Nathan Wright, Jr., *Black Power and Urban Unrest* (New York: Hawthorn Books, 1967); Stokely Carmichael and Charles V. Hamilton, *Black Power: The Politics of Liberation in America* (New York: Random House, 1967); Whitney M. Young, Jr., *To Be Equal* (New York: McGraw-Hill, 1964); Bayard Rustin, " 'Black Power' and Coalition Politics," *Commentary*, Vol. 42 (September 1966), pp. 35–40; David Danzig, "In Defense of 'Black Power,' " *Commentary*, Vol. 42 (September 1966), pp. 41–46; Arnold M. Rose (ed.), *The Negro Protest*, THE ANNALS, Vol. 357 (January 1965); Christopher Lasch, "The Trouble with Black Power," *The New York Review of Books*, Vol. 10, No. 4, Feb. 29, 1968, pp. 4–14. In addition, it should be noted that the already cited books by Malcolm X, Claude Brown, and Frantz Fanon have become powerful symbols of the Black Power movement.

tions are dominated by Negroes, but co-operation with whites is accepted and sought. "Integrated and equal *now*," Martin Luther King is saying.[35]

The more violent aspects of Black Power can be seen as a combination of anger (now spilling over, with the removal of the inhibitions imposed by our earlier rigid patterns) and of escapism (the cost, in improved performance, of integration being seen as high), plus the search for personal dignity. On the surface, Black Power seems to be blatantly antiwhite. At a deeper level, it can be interpreted as an attack on the lack of self-respect that is so difficult for Negroes to escape in a society that has treated them so shabbily: "From now on we can expect the militants in the movement to be more concerned with emboldening timid Negroes than with reassuring timid whites."[36]

The National Advisory Commission on Civil Disorders makes a related point:

> The Black Power advocates of today consciously feel that they are the most militant group in the Negro protest movement. Yet they have retreated from a direct confrontation with American society on the issue of integration and, by preaching separatism, unconsciously function as an accommodation to white racism. Much of their economic program, as well as their interest in Negro history, self-help, racial solidarity and separation, is reminiscent of Booker T. Washington. The rhetoric is different, but the ideas are remarkably similar.[37]

If this interpretation is correct, the threat of violence and serious disruption of the nation can be removed, not by trying to repress the Black Power movement but by attacking the causes: the sense of hopelessness and the frustration aroused in a seriously deprived group living in an affluent society.

Some of this hopelessness is expressed in what appears to be the senseless and random violence of riots. The *Report of the National Advisory Commission on Civil Disorders* is a very effective rebuttal of the conspiracy interpretation of the riots. It also exposes the rumors, the exaggerations, and the distortions that have been part of the public image of the disorders, focusing attention, instead, on the overwhelmingly difficult problems of life in the ghetto.

---

[35] The present tense of this verb was made tragically inaccurate a few days after it was written. Whether the death of Martin Luther King will decisively mark the end of the "Montgomery period" and the heightening of the level of conflict, or will jolt that nation into the enormous efforts and changes that equality demands, remains uncertain.

[36] Bruce Detwiler, "A Time to Be Black," *New Republic*, Vol. 155, September 21, 1966, p. 21; see also Joseph S. Himes, "The Functions of Racial Conflict," *Social Forces*, Vol. 45 (September 1966), pp. 1–10.

[37] National Advisory Commission on Civil Disorders, *op. cit.*, pp. 11–12.

The Commission concludes: "Our nation is moving toward two societies, one black, one white—separate and unequal." "White racism is essentially responsible for the explosive mixture which has been accumulating in our cities since the end of World War II."[38] These statements seem to me to be overly simple as analysis, however useful they may be in the social struggle of the day. The first statement disregards the several ways in which the nation has been integrating in the last generation, even while it has been becoming more segregated in other ways. There are countercurrents. The problem is to determine which are the stronger and more likely to prevail under given policies and trends. The second statement, which tends to lodge a kind of "guilt" with the white population, is no more adequate as a guide to analysis. It has been criticized by many persons for its alleged failure to place blame, at least partly, on rioters themselves. That is not its weakness in my judgment. The difficulty is not that the report fails to spread the blame, but that it does not go far enough in its search for causes. White racism is a fact, but it also requires explanation. It is an intervening, not an independent, variable. We are not served by continuing a rhetoric of praise and blame, simply shifting the burden to a new guilty party. The need is for a careful examination of racism as a system, isolating its causes in the life conditions, the training, and the fears and hopes of various parts of the population. Only then will we be in a position to modify the system effectively.

American Sociology and Black Assimilation: Conflicting Perspectives

L. PAUL METZGER

INTRODUCTION

The failure of sociologists to anticipate and direct their research attention to new developments in American race relations during the 1960's has been acknowledged by Hughes (1963) and Pettigrew and Back (1967,

[38] *Ibid.*, pp. 1, 10. For a vivid description of the Watts riot that makes the same point, see Robert Conot, *Rivers of Blood, Years of Darkness* (New York: Bantam Books, 1967); see also Anthony Oberschall, "The Los Angeles Riot of August 1965," *Social Problems,* Vol. 15 (Winter 1968), pp. 322–341; and for a systematic study of many riots, see Stanley Lieberson and A. R. Silverman, "The Precipitants and Underlying Conditions of Race Riots," *American Sociological Review,* Vol. 30, (December 1965), pp. 887–898.

pp. 714–16). Rossi (1964, pp. 125–26) noted that "it is sadly ironic that as the pace of change in race relations stepped up in the past four years, the volume of social science research has declined during the same period." With the exception of projects sponsored by the federal government—most notably, the so-called Coleman and Moynihan reports (Coleman 1966; Rainwater and Yancey 1967)—significant in terms of their potential impact on national policy but resting on the theoretical foundations of an earlier period of basic research (Tumin 1968, pp. 118–19), the picture Rossi sketched remains relatively unchanged; his call for research into the black movements, the political aspects of racial change, and the role of ethnicity in American life has been met by only a handful of sociologists. Despite two recent studies by Bell (1968) and Levy (1968), the civil rights movement of the early sixties remains largely uncharted by sociologists. Similarly, the Black Power and nationalist movements which succeeded it, as distinct from the earlier Muslim movement (about which there are able accounts by Lincoln [1961] and Essien-Udom [1962]), remain virtually *terra incognita* within the sociological profession.

As an explanation for this failure, Hughes suggests that the concern with professionalism among sociologists has impaired their capacity to empathize with the movements of lower strata; Pettigrew and Back (1967, p. 706) refer to the timidity of foundations, the obstacles placed in the way of race-relations research by diehard white segregationists, and "a sociological bias in race relations toward studying the static and segregation-making elements." It is the thesis of this paper that the failure can be attributed in part to the theoretical framework through which most American sociologists have viewed race relations in the United States. This framework, it is believed, rests essentially on the image of American society which has been set forth by American liberalism, wherein the minority problem is defined in the narrow sense of providing adequate, if not equal, opportunity for members of minority groups to ascend as individuals into the mainstream culture. America, in this view, is the land of opportunity through competitive struggle in the marketplace; it can, and will, provide opportunities for all to gain just rewards for their individual merit. (American liberalism differs with American conservatism largely over the issue of whether the opportunities already present are adequate and takes its reformist cast from its recognition that they are not.)

Sociologists, by and large, have accepted this image of Horatio Alger in the Melting Pot as the ideal definition of American society. Although they have repeatedly documented the discrepancy between social reality and cultural myth in America, they have also taken the view that the incorporation of America's ethnic and racial groups into the mainstream culture is virtually inevitable. (Similar tendencies can be discerned in the field of social stratification, according to Pease, Form, and Rytina 1970.) Successful assimilation, moreover, has been viewed as synonymous with equality of opportunity and upward mobility for the members of minority groups; "opportunity," in this system, is the opportunity to discard one's ethnicity and to partake fully in the "American Way of Life"; in this sense, assimilation is viewed as the embodiment of the democratic ethos.

The convergence of liberal and sociological thought in the area of race relations is striking and raises serious questions about the "value-free" character of sociological inquiry in this area.[1] This is particularly the case since the equation of assimilationist with democratic values in minority-majority relations is by no means universal even within Western culture (Schermerhorn 1959). The right of national self-determination has played a significant role in the liberal-democratic movement in Europe, and as Myrdal (1944, p. 50) noted, "the minority peoples of the United States are fighting for status in the larger society; the minorities of Europe are mainly fighting for independence from it."

Equally remarkable, perhaps, is the fact that assimilationist values, with their connotations of elitism and a monocultural society, have come under as little attack as they have from either liberal or radical social criticism in the United States. The philosophy of democratic cultural pluralism has had, in fact, able spokesmen in America, most notably during the period of World War I (Bourne 1964) and the twenties (Kallen 1924), but the issue of ethnic pluralism has not been a central preoccupation of the American Left until the recent emergence of the Black Power movement. This can be traced, perhaps, to the ascendancy in the thirties of Marxian modes of thought in Left circles and the resulting preoccupation with economic and political questions, on one hand, and working-class solidarity, on the other.

The aim of this paper is to examine some of the major arguments which have appeared in the sociological literature in support of the view that the outcome of race relations in the United States will be the integration or assimilation[2] of the Negro into the American mainstream. The wide-

---

[1] Horton (1966) has stated that "the liberal tendency of American sociology . . . is particularly marked in the sociological analysis of the Negro question. . . . The liberal fate of minorities, including Negroes, is basically containment through socialization to dominant values" (pp. 707–8). He goes on to argue that "contemporary liberalism . . . is a variant of conservative order theory" (p. 707).

[2] The terms "integration" and "assimilation" are not necessarily synonymous. Integration, especially as it was used in the fifties, can have the limited meaning of "desegregation" (particularly de jure) and, sociologically, need not be followed by assimilation in the usual sense of cultural merger. Most sociologists have seemingly assumed, however, that desegregation would be followed by the gradual movement of blacks into mainstream American culture, and that racial characteristics would

spread and uncritical acceptance of these arguments by sociologists, it is believed, has contributed heavily to the void in race-relations research which has been noted above, as well as to the tendency to regard black-nationalist movements as "extremist" (Glazer and Moynihan 1963, p. 78), "escapist" (Morsell 1961, p. 6), and essentially deviant-pathological phenomena.[3] It will be pointed out that some of the components of a revised perspective on American race relations can already be found within the sociological literature and that a new perspective will include (1) abandoning the idea that racial assimilation in the form of gradual absorption of black Americans into the middle-American mainstream is necessarily either inevitable or desirable from the standpoint of demo-cratic values, (2) a recognition that forces producing ethnicity as well as forces favoring assimilation are operative in American society today and that a realistic analysis of the ethnic and racial situation will take both into account, (3) a more balanced view of "black pluralism" (Killian 1968, p. 135) than has thus far appeared in the work of most sociologists. In short, it is argued that a rethinking of the theory of eventual assimila-tion will open up prospects for a more pertinent and realistic assessment of minority problems, particularly race problems, in the United States.

The arguments favoring eventual assimilation will be grouped under two headings: (1) those which rest on assertions about the nature of the dominant white American society, (2) those which rest on assertions about the nature of minority groups and experience within this society.

ARGUMENTS FROM THE NATURE OF THE
DOMINANT WHITE SOCIETY

Central to the view of those sociologists who have taken the position that racial assimilation is the key to the American racial problem are certain beliefs about the nature of modern society in general, and Ameri-can society in particular, which imply that prejudice, discrimination, and racist institutions are incompatible with the major features of modern social organization and hence will eventually "wither away." These assertions have taken various forms, but the common thread running

gradually lose their significance as determinants of social status and identity, and it is this assumption which is called into question here (see also Gordon 1964, pp. 246–47). The tendency for sociologists to use the two terms interchangeably is apparent in the writings of Hauser (1966*a*, 1966*b*).

3 For a different view, see Gregor (1963, p. 431), who writes that "Negro proletarian radicalism has stood, largely mute, beyond the pale of American intellectual life." An effective rationale for the study of such movements has been made by Record (1956).

through them has had several consequences: (1) the liberal optimism of most sociologists with respect to the possibility of peaceful and orderly change in the direction of racial integration,[4] (2) the belief that the major locus of institutional racism lay in the South, as a kind of underdeveloped area, the modernization of which would remove most of the institutional supports of racism; (3) the belief that vestigial remains of racism in the urbanized and industrialized North would disappear as the educational, economic, and occupational status of both blacks and whites improved in the direction of greater affluence and security for all. Clearly, this perspective ill equipped sociologists for the racial crises of the sixties, a period of rapid economic growth and high prosperity which nonetheless witnessed heightened racial tension, urban ghetto violence on an unprecedented scale, and marked racial polarization (National Advisory Committee on Civil Disorders 1968).[5]

[4] Even in the sixties, after the appearance of solidly organized white resistance in the South (Vander Zenden 1959*a*, 1959*b*, 1965) sociologists gave voice to this optimism in uninhibited terms. Rose, for example, wrote (1965, p. 7) "there could be no doubt that the races were moving rapidly toward equality and desegregation by 1964. . . . The change had been so rapid . . . that this author ventures to predict—if current trends continue—the end of all legal segregation and discrimination to a mere shadow in two decades. These changes would not mean that there would be equality between the races within this time . . . but the dynamic social forces creating inequality will, if the present trends continue, be practically eliminated in three decades."

[5] The emergence of the black movement in the sixties and the racial crises which followed forced sociologists to acknowledge, ex post facto, the resistance of American society to racial integration. They were quick to apply the retrospective wisdom that social change entails strain and conflict and that racial conflict may have positive functions (Himes 1966). Mounting black pressure was accounted for, again ex post facto, by an application of reference-group theory in the form of the notion of "relative deprivation" (Pettigrew and Back 1967, pp. 694–96). It should be noted that insofar as this theory assumes that the black movement is the product of actual *gains* made by blacks since World War II, it is open to question since the extent of black gains, especially vis-à-vis whites, in this period is not clear. On the negative side, for example, residential segregation increased in American cities between 1930 and 1960 (Hauser 1966*b*, pp. 76–77), and there was virtually no change in the ratio of nonwhite to white family income between 1947 and 1964 (Fein 1966, p. 122). Moynihan points out (1966, p. 189) that the acknowledged growth of the black middle class may not be accompanied by improvement in the condition of the black lower-class majority and, in *The Negro Family: The Case for National Action,* claims that the black family is in a state of decline (Rainwater and Yancey 1967). Wright (1967), citing comparative data from the U.S. Census, disputes the notion of the rapid socioeconomic advance of the Negro since World War II. Finally, Wilhelm and Powell (1964) find the roots of the black movement not in Negro advance, but *retrogression:* "With the onset of automation, the Negro is moving out of his historical state of oppression into uselessness. . . . He is being removed from economic participation in white society"; and his nascent nationalism constitutes a "quest for identity" (pp. 3–6). In short, the theory of relative deprivation as an account of black unrest has yet to be adequately tested.

Robert E. Park and the Race Relations Cycle

In 1926, one of the most famous and influential statements of the theory of eventual assimilation was made by Robert E. Park (1950, pp. 149–50): "In the relations of races there is a cycle which tends everywhere to repeat itself. . . . The race relations cycle which takes the form . . . of contacts, competition, accommodation and eventual assimilation, is apparently progressive and irreversible. . . . Racial barriers may slacken the tempo of the movement, but cannot change its direction. . . . The forces which have brought about the existing interpenetration of peoples are so vast and irresistible that the resulting changes assume the character of a cosmic process." The universality and inevitability of this "cosmic process" along with other formulations of race-relations cycle theories have long since been questioned by many sociologists,[6] but the acceptance of some form of melting-pot theory as descriptive of American society has been strongly maintained nonetheless.[7]

An ambiguity with respect to Park's (1950) views on the eventual assimilation of the American Negro should be noted. In 1913, for example, he wrote:

> Under conditions of secondary contact, that is to say, conditions of individual liberty and individual competition, characteristic of modern civilization, depressed racial groups *tend to assume the form of nationalities* [italics mine]. A nationality, in this narrower sense, may be defined as the racial group which has attained self-consciousness, no matter whether it has at the same time gained political independence or not. . . . The fundamental significance of the nationality movement must be sought in the effort of subject races to substitute, for those supplied to them by aliens, models based on their racial individuality and embodying sentiments and ideals which spring naturally out of their own lives. . . . In the South . . . the races seem to be tending in the direction of a biracial society, in which the Negro is gradually gaining a limited autonomy. [pp. 219–20]

Frazier (1947, p. 269) noted that even up to "about 1930, Park's sociolog-

---

[6] Berry (1958, pp. 128–49) provides a useful and critical survey of Park and others' cycle theories. Etzioni (1959) presents a systematic critique of Park's views in the context of his review of Wirth's *The Ghetto* (1928). He points out that there is no a priori reason for regarding assimilation as the inevitable outcome of culture contact, and that Park's theory, because it fails to specify the temporal span of and conditions producing each phase, can accommodate any observation and hence is untestable.

[7] For a statement of the theory of the "triple melting pot," which presents the case for the disappearance of the ethnicity of the white immigrant groups within the wider structure of American religious pluralism (itself compromised by the ecumenical movement and a shared commitment to the "American Way of Life" as a quasi-religious ideal), see Herberg (1955, particularly chap. 2).

ical theory in regard to race relations did not go beyond the thesis of a bi-racial organization." Hence, if Park believed in the eventual assimilation of races in the United States, his attention as an observer in the contemporary situation was strongly focused on the emergence of a black "national consciousness." Insofar as he regarded the growth of such a consciousness as a stage in the process leading to eventual assimilation, however, his cycle theory can be regarded as one of the more potent influences in the direction of viewing assimilation as a natural and inevitable process in the evolution of modern society.[8]

An American Dilemma

If Gunnar Myrdal (1944) was critical of the "do-nothing (laissez faire)" presuppositions which he detected in the work of American sociologists (including Park) and the subsequent tendency of the latter to "ignore practically all possibilities of modifying—by conscious effort—the social effects of the natural forces" (p. 1050), his classic opus remained very much within the assimilationist tradition. The author of *An American Dilemma* wrote that "we assume it is to the advantage of American Negroes as individuals and as a group to become assimilated into American culture, to acquire the traits held in esteem by the dominant white Americans" (p. 929).[9]

Myrdal discerns no structural impediment in American society to the realization of an assimilationist program: the race problem is a moral problem "in the heart of the American" (p. xlvii); and "America is free to choose whether the Negro shall remain her liability or become her opportunity" (p. 1022). This decidedly nonsociological approach to the problem is justified, according to Myrdal, because "there is evidently a strong unity in this nation and a basic homogeneity and stability in its valuations. Americans . . . have something in common: a social ethos, a political creed. It is difficult to avoid the judgment that this 'American Creed' is the cement in the structure of this great and disparate nation" (p. 1). Furthermore, "the conquering of color caste in America is Amer-

[8] The fact that an earlier generation of American sociologists did not regard the assimilation of the American Negro as anything like an immediate prospect and viewed the emergence of a sense of collective unity as an outcome of the Negro's status in American society is apparent in E. B. Reuter's *The American Race Problem* (1927). In chap. 16, Reuter traces the history of, and analyzes the "growth of race consciousness," and concludes that "the continued growth of a Negro nationalistic spirit in America is perhaps inevitable" (p. 429).

[9] It is to the credit of Myrdal that he recognized that this assumption was indeed a "value premise" (p. 929) and not the statement of a "natural force" or an "inevitable social process." This distinction frequently is blurred in the sociological literature, as, for example, when Herberg (1955, p. 23) writes that the "perpetuation of ethnic differences is altogether out of line with the logic of American reality." This "logic" would seem to amount to little more than the power of an entrenched social myth.

ica's own innermost desire. . . . The main trend in its history is the gradual realization of the American Creed" (p. 1021).[10] The creed is carried, Myrdal believed, by the "huge institutional structures" of the society, through which "a constant pressure is brought to bear on race prejudice, counteracting the natural tendency for it to spread and become more intense. . . . The ideals thereby gain fortifications of power and influence in society. This is a theory of social self-healing that applies to the type of society we call democracy" (p. 80).

Despite his hortatory tone and his call for national planning, social legislation, and social engineering on the part of an enlightened leadership, however, Myrdal had relatively few concrete suggestions for policy with respect to the race problem beyond his faith in the power of concerted educational effort (pp. 48–49) to break down the already-crumbling walls of the "caste beliefs and valuations" which he believed lay at the heart of white racism.[11] The race problem would be solved simply by moving the society further in the course on which it was already set—that of welfare capitalism—which would require no major reorganization of its economic and political institutions. In the process, the South, as the major locus of the racial problem and "itself a minority and a national problem" (p. 1010), would take its place in the mainstream of the American polity.[12]

At the level of social determinants, Myrdal suggested that the forces of modernization in the South—industrialization, urbanization, the spread of literacy—were themselves powerful mechanisms for the elimination of racism in America. This theme frequently recurs in the post-

[10] For a critique of Myrdal's view that the "strain toward consistency" produced by the psychological and moral discomforts of the dilemma is a major motive force in the direction of realization of the American creed, see Medalia (1962).

[11] In his emphasis on beliefs and attitudes, Myrdal's analysis had an affinity with the social psychological interpretation of race relations which has been so pronounced in American social science. Blumer (1958b) refers to this interpretation as the "prejudice-discrimination axis" and characterizes it as follows: "It rests on a belief that the nature of relations between racial groups results from the feelings and attitudes which these groups have toward each other. . . . It follows that in order to comprehend and solve problems of race relations it is necessary to study and ascertain the nature of prejudice" (p. 420). It is probable that the search for the determinants of prejudice and discrimination in attitudinal sets, personality structure, or role-specific behavior has inhibited the development of a social structural perspective on race relations in American sociology. The work of Lohman and Reitzes (1952, 1954) offered some corrective, but the lead they offered has not been followed.

[12] Ralph Ellison (1966, pp. 298–99) writes that "An American Dilemma . . . sponsored by a leading capitalist group . . . is the blueprint for a more effective exploitation of the South's natural, industrial, and human resources. . . . In the positive sense, it is the key to a more democratic and fruitful usage of the South's natural and human resources; and in the negative, it is the plan for a more efficient and subtle manipulation of black and white relations—especially in the South."

Myrdal writings on race, and is especially emphasized by Arnold Rose (1956, p. 75): "The conditions which led to the development of the caste system in the nineteenth century are no longer with us. . . . New forces have arisen which make the caste system increasingly less desirable and useful to the dominant white group in the South or any other section of the country: These include industrialization, automation, the leadership of the United States in the free Western world, rising educational levels among both whites and Negroes. . . . These changes . . . *have made a mere hollow shell of tradition*" (italics mine).[13]

Hence, the belief that racism is incompatible with the major features of modern social organization has roots which go far deeper than Myrdal's liberal optimism and ethical-philosophical idealism. It is, in fact, rooted in what is perhaps the major theme of modern sociological theory —the shift in Cooley's terms, from "primary" to "secondary" relations as the basis of social order.

The Sociological Tradition

In the course of their presentation of the case for the inevitability of desegregation, Simpson and Yinger (1959, p. 389) note that "in the approach to desegregation that we are taking, one can perceive a major recurring theme of sociological theory. Here is Sir Henry Maine's idea of the shift from status to contract. Here is an illustration of the perceptiveness of Simmel's work . . . concerning the influence of a money economy. Here is much of Toennies and Weber and Durkheim. Parsons and others who use the structural-functional approach have caught this fundamental orientation in such a way as to make it more readily applicable to such . . . problems as the one with which we are concerned."[14]

Thus, it is no surprise that Parsons (1966, p. 739) states that the major theoretical reason for asserting that conditions are ripe in America for

[13] Similar statements can be found in Simpson and Yinger (1954, 1958, 1959) and Rose (1965). The hypothesis that urbanization constitutes a major impetus to racial integration and equalization has been challenged on theoretical grounds by Killian and Grigg (1966) and Howard and Brent (1966); Blalock (1959) found little support for it in an analysis of Southern census data and comments that "urbanization in the South has at least in part taken a form which is compatible to that developed in certain colonial territories. . . . It is . . . entirely possible that as the South continues to urbanize, at least in the early stages . . . nonwhites may remain in the most unskilled positions. . . . A constant or even an increasing gap may be maintained" (pp. 147–48).

[14] Greeley (1964), a proponent of the view that the ethnic group, which he defines as a "semi-gemeinschaft collectivity" (p. 108), remains a significant element in modern social structure, suggests that the gemeinschaft-gesellschaft tradition poses a "danger that sociologists, impressed with the tremendous increase in gesellschaft, would rule out the possibility of the survival of gemeinschaft, at least beyond the level of the nuclear family" (p. 107).

the full "inclusion" of the Negro is that "the universalistic norms of the society have applied more and more widely. This has been true of all the main bases of particularistic solidarity, ethnicity, religion, regionalism, state's rights, and class. . . . Today, more than ever before, we are witnessing an acceleration in the emancipation of individuals of all categories from these diffuse particularistic solidarities." Whether phrased in terms of the Parsonian pattern variables, the older formulations of Durkheim, Cooley, or Toennies, or Myrdal's American Creed, it is clear that this tradition of sociological theory views ethnicity as a survival of primary, quasi-tribal loyalties, which can have only a dysfunctional place in the achievement-oriented, rationalized, and impersonal social relationships of the modern, industrial-bureaucratic order.

That the tenets of this theoretical tradition necessarily imply the inevitable disappearance of "particularistic solidarities," however, has been put to a major theoretical test in the recent work of Van den Berghe (1967). Rather than assuming, with the Myrdal-Parsons school, that race relations per se tend to disappear in gesellschaftlike societies, he asserts that they merely shift their form from "paternalistic" to "competitive." In the latter case, there is declining contact between racial castes, segmentation into ghettos, and economic competition between racial groups. Although Van den Berghe (1967) asserts that racial cleavages in competitive societies "constitute one of the major sources of strain and disequilibrium in such systems" (p. 30), he makes no judgment as to their ultimate disappearance and states that a possible outcome is the "Herrenvolk democracy . . . in which the exercise of power and suffrage is restricted, *de facto* and often *de jure*, to the dominant group" (p. 29).

Van den Berghe's formulation is one of the few attempts in the literature to link the persistence of racial cleavages in competitive modern societies to the essential structure of such societies, and thus represents a major theoretical departure from the tradition discussed in this section. It is a departure which permits the description of America as a "socially pluralistic" society along racial lines despite its *cultural* homogeneity (pp. 34–36), which views racial cleavage and conflict as inherent in the nature of competitive society (pp. 30–31) and sees racism[15] as central to, rather than a "hollow shell" within, the Western cultural tradition (pp. 11–18). As such, it provides a perspective for the analysis of racial consciousness and conflict which is lacking in the orthodox Myrdal-Parsons schema.

---

[15] Van den Berghe defines racism as "any set of beliefs that organic, genetically transmitted differences are intrinsically associated with the presence or absence of certain socially relevant abilities or characteristics" (p. 11).

White Gains and White Resistance

Mounting white resistance, North and South, to the black movement in the sixties forced sociologists to reassess the role of racism in the American social fabric, and, in doing so, they have introduced (or reapplied) concepts which echo Van den Berghe's theoretical analysis. Killian (1968), for example, in *The Impossible Revolution?* writes that "the theme of white supremacy has always been an integral and pervasive feature of the American system" (p. 16)[16] and adds, "it is the challenge to white dominance that will require the greatest adjustment in the social order and that provides the greatest revolutionary potential" (p. 22). By virtue of his exclusion from a "white man's country" (p. 26), the black, says Killian, is "in the process of becoming an ethnic group" (p. 137), a development which is a radical challenge to the assimilationist ideal in America and which, hence, is fraught with the potential for a revolutionary confrontation.

The notion that specifiable "gains" accrue to whites by virtue of the subordination of blacks was introduced by Dollard (1937) and suggests that white resistance to racial change rests on something more than cultural lag or Myrdalian moral schizophrenia. As such, it is a valuable corrective to the notion that racism is "dysfunctional" or "deviant" within the wider culture. Heer (1959) and Glenn (1963, 1965, 1966) have offered both theoretical and empirical support for this notion, and Glenn writes: "Negro-white antagonism in the United States is and will long remain a matter of realistic conflict. Negroes cannot advance without the loss of traditional white benefits and it is unlikely that most of the whites who benefit . . . will willingly allow Negro advancement. This is not to say that race prejudice and social discrimination are strictly or even largely an expression of economic rationality [1966, p. 178] . . . nor should the many known and possible dysfunctions of discrimination be overlooked. However . . . the tradition of discrimination against Negroes apparently receives continuous reinforcement from the present self-interests of the majority" (1963, pp. 447–48). To the extent, however, that the theory of white gains conceives of white resistance in terms of benefits to individuals, or categories of individuals, it tends to find its place within a social psychological rather than a social structural perspective. Hence, there is not, as yet, a systematic exploration by American sociologists of the possibly latent and positive functions of racism in sustaining the "equilibrium" of the American social system.

[16] Westie (1965, pp. 537–38) also notes that "a wealth of sociological evidence suggests that in many social situations in America, it is not the person who behaves in a prejudiced manner who is deviant, but rather, the non-prejudiced person who refuses to discriminate. . . . People with no dilemma in Myrdal's sense seem to experience another type of dilemma; a conflict between their endorsement of democratic action and yet another normative system, which exists in the majority of American local

Summary

Two perspectives on the features of modern society as they bear on the question of racial assimilation have been presented here. The first, which has occupied the place of a conventional orthodoxy in American sociology since World War II, takes the position that racism is a carry-over from the past which is bound to wither and decay and that, as a consequence, the gradual assimilation of the races can be expected. In the sense that the American creed is viewed as normatively constituent of American society, this perspective suggests a consensus model of racial change and relegates the stresses and strains of the process to a secondary place, as a kind of by-product of inevitable and healthful social trends—the rearguard response of a dying tradition. The second perspective suggests that racism is integral in American society, that it is central to the culture and interests of the white majority, and that its breakdown will only occur through a protracted process of social conflict and at least some degree of restructuring of the existing institutional arrangements of the society. The gradual emergence of the elements of such a perspective can be noted in the sociological literature in the sixties, although there is little doubt that the first perspective continues to hold sway as a kind of official orthodoxy within the sociological establishment (see, e.g., Parsons 1966, Hauser 1966a, and Pettigrew 1969). An earlier prototype of the second perspective has been present in the Marxian analysis of the race problem.[17]

The affinity of these two perspectives with liberal and radical ideological stances, respectively, on the race problem is apparent (Horton 1966). Our purpose here, however, is neither to claim more abstract-truth value for one or the other (although we believe that the credibility of the first has been seriously put to the test by the racial events of the sixties) nor to condemn both on grounds of their ideological "contamination."[18] Like

communities; the system which says that one ought to be prejudiced and ought to discriminate."

[17] For an effective, if neglected, analysis of American race relations in the Marxian tradition, see Cox (1948). As noted above, Marxism failed to supply a corrective to the assimilationist bias of both American social science and American social criticism. In fact, the overall impact of Marxian thought has been to relegate ethnicity to the status of "false consciousness"; national and ethnic sensibility is viewed as an outgrowth of the culture of capitalism and as a stratagem of the bourgeoisie for dividing and weakening the working-class movement. For the orthodox Marxist, minorities and minority problems, as such, will disappear with the cessation of class oppression. The strengths of the Marxian interpretation of racism lie in its linking of this pattern to the total structure of the society of which it is a part and its insistence that the race problem has determinants in the economic institutions and the struggle for power and privilege in the society. The viable elements of the Marxian perspective can be retained even as the simplistic account of the race problem as a reflex of the class struggle has been, correctly, rejected.

[18] We agree with Horton (1966, p. 713) when he writes that "the error of the sociolo-

many sociological theories, these perspectives are schema which serve to point to differing aspects of a complex and probably contradictory reality. What is problematic, we believe, is the overwhelming acceptance, until recently, of the assimilationist perspective among sociologists and the claim that it is supported by social science evidence (Pettigrew 1969) in a way in which the second perspective—which can be referred to as "pluralistic"—is not. In our view, neither the accumulated evidence of social science research nor developments in American race relations in the sixties can support this view. Moreover, the acceptance of the assimilationist perspective has played a large role in shaping the direction of empirical research on race relations[19] and in inhibiting the development of research efforts pertinent to the last decade. Beyond pointing to the ideologically liberal presuppositions which have permeated this perspective, the further specification of factors which can account for its acceptance is a problem in the sociology of knowledge, which is beyond the scope of this paper.

ARGUMENTS FROM THE NATURE OF AMERICAN MINORITY GROUPS

If sociologists who have favored the assimilation-integration perspective have taken a benign view of the capacity and willingness of American society to achieve racial assimilation, they have also supported their position through a common set of assumptions about American minorities in general and blacks in particular. These assumptions can be stated as follows: American minorities (especially blacks) desire assimilation into mainstream America. As far as the white ethnic immigrant groups are concerned, there have been no insuperable obstacles in either their sociocultural characteristics or their ideologies which have prevented their assimilation; in this respect, their most relevant traits have been those which they shared with lower-class groups in American society as a consequence of their having entered the society at the lower rungs of the class hierarchy. They have shared the majority commitment to the American creed, and the rate of their assimilation is directly proportional to their access to the socializing agencies of the dominant culture. The conventional position on the assimilation of white ethnics was well stated by Warner and Srole (1945, p. 295) when they wrote: "The future of American ethnic groups seems to be quite limited; it is likely that they will be quickly absorbed. When this happens, one of the great epochs of American history will be ended, and another, that of race, will begin" (p. 295).

gist is not that he thinks politically and liberally about his society, but that he is not aware of it."

[19] The main trends of this research prior to the 1960's have been thoroughly summarized in the invaluable papers of Drake (1957) and Blumer (1958*b*).

With the exception of the distinctiveness of his castelike position in the South and his unique visibility, the position of the Negro, it has been believed, is similar. In the words of Kristol (1966), "the Negro today is like the immigrant yesterday," and if his special history and status in American society have subjected him to unusually severe barriers to full participation, his absorption can be expected nonetheless. The remainder of this section will discuss some questions which arise concerning this view of black assimilation in the light of the recent reassessment by social scientists of the assimilation process and the nature of black culture in American society.

The Assimilation of White Ethnic Immigrants

If the assimilation of blacks is predicated on the analogy of their position with that of the white ethnic groups, serious problems arise if the assimilation of the latter has been, in fact, much less extensive than has been commonly supposed. Such is the conclusion of recent analyses of ethnicity in American society. As early as fifteen years ago, Glazer (1954, p. 172) noted that a kind of ethnic consciousness, part "nostalgia" and part "ideology," was observable among the descendants of immigrant groups, which consciousness performs "some functions, and even valuable functions, in American life." Gordon (1964) distinguishes between structural assimilation (participation in the dominant society at the primary group level) and acculturation (acquisition of the culture of the dominant group). He argues that the latter process has been rapid on the part of minorities in American society, but that the former has not and will remain limited for the foreseeable future (except in the "intellectual sub-society"). In the sense that primary social participation for most people remains limited by ethnic boundaries, the United States, argues Gordon, can be described as structurally pluralistic along ethnic, racial, and religious lines. Glazer and Moynihan (1963) note the differential response and resistance of diverse minorities to Americanizing influences and state that the ethnic group is more than a survival of traditional immigrant culture; it is, they claim, a product of the impact of American life on such culture, a "new social form" (p. 16). They go beyond Gordon in emphasizing the ethnic influence in secondary (occupational, political) as well as primary spheres. Greeley (1969, p. 7) doubts that even the acculturation process has been as thorough as Gordon claims and has called for (1964) a reassessment of the ethnic group as a source of identity, interest-group formation, and subcultural differentiation in American society.

In view of the emphasis placed by these writers on ethnicity in contemporary American society, it is surprising, perhaps, that they have not explicitly addressed themselves to a reassessment of the assimilation-integration perspective as it applies to the Black American. If the white minorities have legitimately preserved an ethnic identity, should not the blacks propose to do the same? In this connection, the views of these writers are squarely in the assimilationist tradition. Glazer and Moynihan (1963, p. 52), for example, write that "it is not possible for Negroes to view themselves as other ethnic groups viewed themselves . . . because the Negro is only an American, and nothing else. He has no values and culture to guard and protect." In a similar vein, Gordon (1964, p. 114) writes of the black community that "dual social structures are created solely by the dynamics of prejudice and discrimination rather than being reinforced by ideological commitment of the minority itself." Both these studies, in short, are concerned with the survival or transformation of *prior* ethnic identities in America rather than with the generation of *new* ones, or, in Singer's (1962) terms, "ethnogenesis." Moreover, they fail to raise the question of what the meaning and content of racial assimilation can be in a society which remains ethnically plural. In the words of Harold Cruse (1967, p. 9), "Although the three main power groups— Protestants, Catholics, and Jews—neither want nor need to become integrated with each other, the existence of a great body of homogenized, inter-assimilated white Americans is the premise for racial integration. Thus, the Negro integrationist runs afoul of reality in pursuit of an illusion, the 'open society'—a false front that hides several doors to several different worlds of hyphenated Americans."

The Problem of Black Culture

If the American Negro has been considered "100 percent American" by sociologists, the divergence of his culture from the middle-class norm has at the same time been heavily examined and documented. The prevailing sociological view was stated by Myrdal (1944, p. 928): "American Negro culture is not something independent of general American culture. It is a distorted development, or a pathological condition of the general American culture." The view that the race problem is a white man's problem here becomes coupled with the view that the black has been unable to create an authentic subculture in America, owing to his oppression and powerlessness, and, hence, that his condition is to be diagnosed as one of a pervasive social pathology.

It is beyond the scope of this paper to review the reassessment of this perspective which is currently under way in the social sciences, but two observations can be made. First, this reassessment, no doubt stimulated by the efforts of black intellectuals (e.g., Ellison 1966; Cruse 1967) to question the "social pathology" interpretation of black culture, has been mainly evident in the work of the so-called urban anthropologists rather than that of sociologists. Their application of ethnographic techniques to the study of the culture of the black ghetto contrasts with the usual practice of sociologists of compiling statistical indexes of social disorganization. Particularly notable in this respect have been the works of Keil (1966) and Hannerz (1969), as well as the theoretical attack mounted by Valentine (1968) on the theory of the "culture of poverty." Recent essays by Blauner (1969) and McCarthy and Yancey (1971) make an overdue shift of sociological attention in this direction. Ellison's (1966, p. 302) comment that "in Negro culture, there is much of value for America as a whole. What is needed are Negroes to take it and create of it the un-created consciousness of their race" might well serve as a major leitmotiv of this reassessment on the part of both the scholarly and the black communities.

Second, the sociological emphasis on the pathologies of the black community produced a tendency among sociologists in the sixties to view the major barriers to racial integration as residing in the sociocultural characteristics of the black minority itself rather than in the racism of the dominant society. Whether phrased in the form of demographic characteristics (Hauser 1966b)[20] or the social disorganization which is believed to spring, in part, from these and, in part, from the "heritage" of prejudice and discrimination (rather than from the current institutional functioning of the society itself), these views have harmonized nicely with the benign orthodox analysis of American society outlined earlier. They have led to considerably less optimistic prognoses for the rapid assimilation of the Negro than were characteristic of the fifties (e.g., Broom and Glenn 1965, pp. 187–91) and have led to charges, especially on the part of black activists, that social scientists were simply providing a new apologia for the racial status quo in America. In any case, the view that black culture contains positive elements that can form the basis of a black ethnic consciousness which can and should be preserved is a challenge of major dimensions to the orthodox sociological image of the black community and black culture in America.

Note on the Caste Hypothesis

Through the work of Dollard (1937), Davis, Gardner, and Gardner (1941), and Warner (1936), the concept of caste became, during the forties, an almost standard tool for the analysis of American race relations. The caste hypothesis acknowledged that the race problem could not be regarded as merely another instance of the minorities problem in the United States, owing to the unique position of the Negro in the overall system of stratification. Moreover, at least in the statement of Warner, the caste hypothesis viewed racial development (especially in the South) as tending toward "parallelism" (Warner 1936, p. 235), or, in

---

[20] The hypothesis that there is a direct correlation between economic discrimination and Negro population increase has been put to empirical test by Blalock (1956) and Glenn (1963), whose data do not clearly support it.

Park's terms, a "biracial society." Within the conventional sociological literature, then, there has been available a conceptual framework which was not assimilationist in its premises but which has not been adequate to account for or foresee the racial crisis of the past decade.

Several reasons for the failure of the caste hypothesis in this respect can be noted. First, it described a system of racial accommodation in which the permanent status subordination of the black caste was believed to lie in a system of folkways and mores which both castes accepted as inevitable and unalterable. Hence, it was attacked by both Myrdal (1944) and Cox (1948) for failing to take into account the dynamic forces which were altering the traditional Southern pattern of "race etiquette," for exaggerating the extent of black compliance with this system, and for neglecting the role of force and violence in maintaining it. Second, the thesis of a biracial society was incompatible with the liberal-assimilationist ethos and (if only implicitly) was rejected by those sociologists who shared this ethos and feared the possibility—which Warner, in his 1936 statement, neglected—of the interracial conflict which was latent in a structure of caste parallelism. Finally, the caste concept was applied, even by the Warner school, largely to the South; hence it was compatible with the view of the Northern Negro as the "new immigrant" whose problems, in their essentials, were no different from those of the earlier white immigrants whose assimilation was proceeding apace.

An urgent need in the current analysis of American race relations is a conceptual framework which recognizes as the caste hypothesis does, the unique status of the black in America but which views this status, as the caste hypothesis does not, as a dynamic force with the potential for transforming the black community and black personality in the direction of becoming a major-change agency in American society. Singer's (1962, p. 423) concept of "ethnogenesis . . . the process whereby a people, that is, an ethnic group, comes into existence" remains the major effort along these lines in American sociology.

CONCLUSION

Three major conclusions emerge from this survey of the role of the assimilation-integration perspective in the study of American race relations:

1. The belief that racial assimilation constitutes the only democratic solution to the race problem in the United States should be relinquished by sociologists. Beyond committing them to a value premise which compromises their claim to value neutrality, the assimilationist strategy overlooks the functions which ethnic pluralism may perform in a democratic society. Suggestions as to these functions are found in the writings of Gordon (1964, pp. 239–41), Greeley (1964; 1969, pp. 23–30), and Etzioni (1959, pp. 260–62). The application

of this perspective to the racial problem should result in the recognition that the Black Power and black nationalist movements, to the extent that they aim at the creation of a unified and coherent black community which generates a sense of common peoplehood and interest, are necessarily contrary neither to the experience of other American minorities nor to the interests of black people. The potential for racial divisiveness—and in the extreme case, revolutionary confrontation—which resides in such movements should also be recognized, but the source of this "pathological" potential should be seen as resting primarily within the racism of the wider society rather than in the "extremist" response to it on the part of the victimized minority.

2. To abandon the idea that ethnicity is a dysfunctional survival from a prior stage of social development will make it possible for sociologists to re-affirm that minority-majority relations are in fact group relations (Blumer 1958a) and not merely relations between prejudiced and victimized individuals. As such, they are implicated in the struggle for power and privilege in the society, and the theory of collective behavior and political sociology may be more pertinent to understanding them than the theory of social mobility and assimilation. Although general theories of minority-majority relations incorporating notions of power and conflict can be found in the writings of sociologists (e.g., Schermerhorn 1964; Lieberson 1961), it is only recently, in the work of Killian (1968) and Oppenheimer (1969), that such perspectives have found their way into sociologists' analyses of the American racial situation.

3. To abandon the notion that assimilation is a self-completing process will make it possible to study the forces (especially at the level of cultural and social structure) which facilitate or hinder assimilation or, conversely, the forces which generate the sense of ethnic and racial identity even within the homogenizing confines of modern society. On the basis of an assessment of such forces, it is certainly within the province of sociological analysis to point to the possibilities of conscious intervention in the social process (by either the majority or the minority group) to achieve given ends and to weigh the costs and consequences of various policy alternatives. These functions of sociological analysis, however, should be informed by an awareness that *any* form of intervention will take place in a political context—that intervention itself is in fact a political act—and that the likelihood of its success will be conditioned by the configuration of political forces in the society at large. Without this awareness—which is nothing more than an awareness of the total societal context within which a given minority problem has its meaning—sociological analysis runs a very real risk of spinning surrealistic fantasies about a world which is tacitly believed to be the best of all possible worlds. Whether the call of sociologists for racial assimilation in American society as it is currently organized will fall victim to such a judgment remains to be seen.

REFERENCES

Bell, Inge Powell. 1948. *CORE and the Strategy of Non-Violence.* New York: Random House.

Berry, Brewton. 1958. *Race and Ethnic Relations*. New York: Harper & Row.

Blalock, H. M., Jr. 1956. "Economic Discrimination and Negro Increase." *American Sociological Review* **21** (October): 584–88.

———. 1959. "Urbanization and Discrimination." *Social Problems* **7** (Fall): 146–52.

Blauner, Robert. 1969. "Black Culture: Myth or Reality?" In *Afro-American Anthropology*, edited by Norman E. Whitten, Jr. and John F. Szwed. New York: Free Press.

Blumer, Herbert. 1958*a*. "Race Prejudice as a Sense of Group Position." *Pacific Sociological Review* **1** (Spring): 3–7.

———.1958*b*. "Research on Racial Relations: The United States of America." *International Social Science Bulletin* **10** (1): 403–47.

Bourne, Randolph S. 1964. *War and the Intellectuals: Collected Essays, 1915–19*, edited by Carl Resek. New York: Harper & Row.

Broom, Leonard, and Norval D. Glenn. 1965. *Transformation of the Negro American*. New York: Harper & Row.

Coleman, James S., et al. 1966. *Equality of Educational Opportunity*. Office of Education, United States Department of Health, Education, and Welfare (OE 38001). Washington, D.C.: Government Printing Office.

Cox, Oliver C. 1948. *Caste, Class, and Race*. New York: Doubleday.

Cruse, Harold. 1967. *The Crisis of the Negro Intellectual*. New York: Morrow.

Davis, Allison, Burleigh B. Gardner, and Mary R. Gardner. 1941. *Deep South*. Chicago: University of Chicago Press.

Dollard, John. 1937. *Caste and Class in a Southern Town*. New Haven, Conn.: Yale University Press.

Drake, B. St. Clair. 1957. "Recent Trends in Research on the Negro in the United States." *International Social Science Bulletin* **9** (4): 475–94.

Ellison, Ralph. 1966. *Shadow and Act*. New York: New American Library.

Essien-Udom, E. U. 1962. *Black Nationalism: The Search for Identity in America*. Chicago: University of Chicago Press.

Etzioni, Amitai. 1959. "The Ghetto: A Re-evaluation." *Social Forces* **37** (March): 255–62.

Fein, Rashi. 1966. "An Economic and Social Profile of the Negro American." In *The Negro American*, edited by Talcott Parsons and Kenneth B. Clark. Boston: Houghton Mifflin.

Frazier, E. Franklin. 1947. "Sociological Theory and Race Relations." *American Sociological Review* **12** (June): 265–70.

Glazer, Nathan. 1954. "Ethnic Groups in America." In *Freedom and Control in Modern Society*, edited by Morroe Berger, Theodore Abel, and Charles H. Page. New York: Van Nostrand.

Glazer, Nathan, and Daniel Patrick Moynihan. 1963. *Beyond the Melting Pot: The Negroes, Puerto Ricans, Jews, and Irish of New York City*. Cambridge, Mass.: M.I.T. Press.

Glenn, Norval D. 1963. "Occupational Benefits to Whites from Subordination of Negroes." *American Sociological Review* **28** (June): 443–48.

———. 1965. "The Role of White Resistance and Facilitation in the Negro Struggle for Equality." *Phylon* **26** (June): 105–16.

———. 1966. "White Gains from Negro Subordination." *Social Problems* **14** (Fall): 159–78.

Gordon, Milton. 1964. *Assimilation in American Life*. New York: Oxford University Press.

Greeley, Andrew M. 1964. "American Sociology and the Study of Immigrant Ethnic Groups." *International Migration Digest* **1** (Fall): 107–13.

———. 1969. *Why Can't They Be Like Us?* New York: Institute of Human Relations Press.

Gregor, A. James. 1963. "Black Nationalism: A Preliminary Analysis of Negro Radicalism." *Science and Society* **27** (Autumn): 415–32.

Hannerz, Ulf. 1969. *Soulside*. New York: Columbia University Press.

Hauser, Philip M. 1966a. "Next Steps on the Racial Front." *Journal of Intergroup Relations* **5** (Autumn): 5–15.

———. 1966b. "Demographic Factors in the Integration of the Negro." In *The Negro American*, edited by Talcott Parsons and Kenneth B. Clark. Boston: Houghton Mifflin.

Heer, David M. 1959. "The Sentiment of White Supremacy: An Ecological Study." *American Journal of Sociology* **64** (May): 592–98.

Herberg, Will. 1955. *Protestant, Catholic, and Jew*. New York: Doubleday.

Himes, Joseph. 1966. "The Functions of Racial Conflict." *Social Forces* **45** (September): 1–16.

Horton, John. 1966. "Order and Conflict Theories of Social Problems as Competing Ideologies." *American Journal of Sociology* **71** (May): 701–13.

Howard, Perry, and Joseph Brent III. 1966. "Social Change, Urbanization, and Types of Society." *Journal of Social Issues* **22** (January): 73–84.

Hughes, Everett C. 1963. "Race Relations and the Sociological Imagination." *American Sociological Review* **28** (December): 879–90.

Kallen, Horace. 1924. *Culture and Democracy in the United States*. New York: Boni & Liveright.

Keil, Charles. 1966. *Urban Blues*. Chicago: University of Chicago Press.

Killian, Lewis M. 1968. *The Impossible Revolution?* New York: Random House.

Killian, Lewis M., and Charles Grigg. 1966. "Race Relations in an Urbanized South." *Journal of Social Issues* **22** (January): 20–29.

Kristol, Irving. 1966. "The Negro Today is Like the Immigrant Yesterday." *New York Times Magazine*, September 11, p. 50.

Levy, Charles J. 1968. *Voluntary Servitude: Whites in the Negro Movement*. New York: Appleton-Century-Crofts.

Lieberson, Stanley. 1961. "A Societal Theory of Race and Ethnic Relations." *American Sociological Review* **26** (December): 902–10.

Lincoln, C. Eric. 1961. *The Black Muslims in America.* Boston: Beacon Press.

Lohman, J. D., and D. C. Reitzes. 1952. "Note on Race Relations in Mass Society." *American Journal of Sociology* **58** (November): 240–46.

———. 1954. "Deliberately Organized Groups and Racial Behavior." *American Sociological Review* **19** (June): 342–44.

Medalia, Nahum Z. 1962. "Myrdal's Assumptions on Race Relations: A Conceptual Commentary." *Social Forces* **40** (March): 223–27.

Morsell, John A. 1961. "Black Nationalism." *Journal of Intergroup Relations* **3** (Winter): 5–11.

Moynihan, Daniel Patrick. 1966. "Employment, Income, and the Ordeal of the Negro Family." In *The Negro American,* edited by Talcott Parsons and Kenneth B. Clark. Boston: Houghton Mifflin.

Myrdal, Gunnar. 1944. *An American Dilemma.* New York: Harper & Bros.

Oppenheimer, Martin. 1969. *The Urban Guerrilla.* Chicago: Quadrangle Books.

Park, Robert E. 1950. *Race and Culture.* Glencoe, Ill.: Free Press.

Parsons, Talcott. 1966. "Full Citizenship for the Negro American?" In *The Negro American,* edited by Talcott Parsons and Kenneth B. Clark. Boston: Houghton Mifflin.

Pease, John, William Form, and Joan Rytina. 1970. "Ideological Currents in American Stratification Literature." *American Sociologist* **5** (May): 127–37.

Pettigrew, Thomas F. 1969. "Racially Separate or Together?" *Journal of Social Issues* **25** (January): 43–69.

Pettigrew, Thomas F., and Kurt W. Back. 1967. "Sociology in the Desegregation Process: Its Use and Disuse." In *The Uses of Sociology,* edited by Paul F. Lazarsfeld, William H. Sewell, and Harold L. Wilensky. New York: Basic.

Rainwater, Lee, and William L. Yancey. 1967. *The Moynihan Report and the Politics of Controversy.* A Trans-Action Social Science and Public Policy Report. Cambridge, Mass.: M.I.T. Press.

Record, Wilson. 1956. "Extremist Movements Among American Negroes." *Phylon* **17** (March): 17–23.

Report of the National Advisory Commission on Civil Disorders. 1968. New York: Bantam.

Reuter, Edward B. 1927. *The American Race Problem.* New York: Crowell.

Rose, Arnold. 1956. "Intergroup Relations vs. Prejudice: Pertinent Theory for the Study of Social Change." *Social Problems* **4** (October): 173–76.

———. 1965. "The American Negro Problem in the Context of Social Change." *The Annals* **357** (January): 1–17.

Rossi, Peter. 1964. "New Directions for Race Relations Research in the Sixties." *Review of Religious Research* **5** (Spring): 125–32.

Schermerhorn, R. A. 1959. "Minorities: European and American." *Phylon* **20** (June): 178–85.

———. 1964. "Toward a General Theory of Minority Groups." *Phylon* **25** (September): 238–46.

Simpson, George E., and J. Milton Yinger. 1954. "The Changing Pattern of Race Relations." *Phylon* **15** (December): 327–46.

———.1958. "Can Segregation Survive in an Industrial Society?" *Antioch Review* **18** (March): 15–24.

———. 1959. "The Sociology of Race and Ethnic Relations." In *Sociology Today*, edited by Robert K. Merton, Leonard Broom, and Leonard S. Cottrell, Jr. New York: Basic.

Singer, L. 1962. "Ethnogenesis and Negro Americans Today." *Social Research* **29** (Winter): 419–32.

Tumin, Melvin M. 1968. "Some Social Consequences of Research on Racial Relations." *American Sociologist* **4** (May): 117–23.

Valentine, Charles A. 1968. *Culture and Poverty*. Chicago: University of Chicago Press.

Van den Berghe, Pierre L. 1967. *Race and Racism: A Comparative Perspective*. New York: Wiley.

Vander Zenden, James. 1959*a*. "Desegregation and Social Strains in the South." *Journal of Social Issues* **15** (4): 53–60.

———. 1959*b*. "A Note on the Theory of Social Movements." *Sociology and Social Research* **44** (September–October): 3–8.

———. 1965. *Race Relations in Transition: The Segregation Crisis in the South*. New York: Random House.

Warner, W. Lloyd. 1936. "American Caste and Class." *American Journal of Sociology* **32** (September): 234–37.

Warner, W. Lloyd, and Leo Srole. 1945. *The Social Systems of American Ethnic Groups*. New Haven, Conn.: Yale University Press.

Westie, Frank R. 1965. "The American Dilemma: An Empirical Test." *American Sociological Review* **26** (August): 527–38.

Wilhelm, Sidney M., and Elwin H. Powell. 1964. "Who Needs the Negro?" *Transaction* **1** (September–October): 3–6.

Wirth, Louis. 1928. *The Ghetto*. Chicago: University of Chicago Press.

Wright, Nathan. 1967. "The Economics of Race." *American Journal of Economics and Sociology* **26** (January): 1–12.

Uncle Tom and Mr. Charlie: Metaphysical Pathos in the Study of Racism and Personal Disorganization

JOHN D. McCARTHY and WILLIAM L. YANCEY

This essay presents a critical examination of the vast literature concerning the psychological state of the Negro American. The basic hypothesis that Negro Americans are very likely to experience "crisis of identity" and exhibit negative self-esteem will be questioned. After a brief description of the prevailing view of the psychological state of the Negro American, we will review the major theoretical statements explaining the assumed low self-esteem and crisis of identity experienced by black Americans. The third section of the essay reviews empirical research revealing a considerable amount of ambiguity over, if not directly challenging, currently held assumptions. In the concluding section we will present a series of alternative propositions which we will suggest should be considered in light of the ambiguous data presented in section three.

PROVIDING SCIENTIFIC CREDIBILITY FOR A STEREOTYPE

The assumption that the Negro American suffers debilitating effects from the psychological stresses that result from his caste position in American society finds wide support in both the popular and the scholarly literature. Other terms are employed as substitutes for self-esteem and crisis of identity but few authors challenge the thesis. For instance, Kenneth Clark (1965) says: "The effective use of the potential power of the Negro masses and the ability of Negro leaders to discipline and mobilize that power for constructive social change may well be determined by the ability of a critical mass of Negroes to control their ambivalence toward themselves and to develop the capacity for genuine and sustained respect for those Negroes who are worthy of confidence and respect" (p. 197). He is clearly comparing what might be with the actual state of affairs. Negro political mobilization is seen as inhibited by ambivalence toward self.

Silberman (1964), in his widely known work, *Crisis in Black and White*, states the position in this manner: "The Negroes' demand for recognition is a crucial part of the struggle to overcome the devastation that the past three hundred fifty years have wrought on Negro personality. The apathy, the aimlessness, the lack of interest in education that characterize the Negro lower classes, and the crisis of identity that afflicts Negroes of all classes, stem from their sense of dependence and powerlessness—their conviction that 'Mr. Charlie' controls everything, Negro leaders included, and that he has the cards stacked so that Negroes can never win" (p. 198).

In *The Negro in America,* Rose (1948) attributes not only problems of self-esteem of the Negro American to majority pressures, but also the totality of the deviation of the black community from middle-class white standards to majority prejudice and discrimination. He says, "The instability of the Negro family, the inadequacy of educational facilities for Negroes, the emotionalism in the Negro church, the insufficiency and unwholesomeness of Negro recreational activity, the excess of Negro sociable organizations, the narrowness of interest of the average Negro, the provincialism of his political thinking, the high Negro crime rate, the cultivation of the arts to the neglect of other fields, superstition, personality difficulties, and other 'characteristic' traits are mainly forms of social ill-health, which, for the most part, are created by caste pressures" (p. 294).

Pettigrew's review of the literature on Negro American psychology reaches similar conclusions. He (1964) writes: "The personality consequences of this situation can be devastating—confusion of self-identity, lowered self-esteem, perception of the world as a hostile place, and serious sex-role conflicts" (p. 25), but cautions that all Negroes in the United States do not respond to the caste situation in the same manner. He outlines three major responses to oppression: moving toward, moving against, and moving away from the oppressor (p. 27). It is revealing that Pettigrew's review of this literature suggests that for each alternative response, psychopathological behavior of one form or another is evident (pp. 27–48).

Few authors challenge this general thesis, though one does encounter a few tentative challenges. Coles (1964) questions the generalizability of the assumptions when he writes, "Though in no way do I deny what Kardiner and Ovesey have called 'the mark of oppression,' it remains equally true that alongside suffering I have encountered a resilience and an incredible capacity for survival" (p. 348).

Erikson (1966), discussing the application of the concept of identity to race relations, issues less than a strong challenge when he writes:

Again, the literature abounds in descriptions of how the Negro, instead, found escape into musical or spiritual worlds, or expressed his rebellion in compromise of behavior now viewed as mocking caricatures, such as obstinate meekness, exaggerated child likeness, or superficial submissiveness. And yet, is "the Negro" not often all too summarily and all too exclusively discussed in such a way that his negative identity is defined *only* in terms of his defensive adjustments to the dominant white majority? Do we (and can we) know enough about the relationship of positive and negative elements *within* the Negro personality and *within* the Negro community? This alone would reveal how negative is negative and how positive, positive. [p. 155]

For the most part, however, there is a rather clear consensus: the black man's life and personality are disorganized as a result of white prejudice and discrimination.

In their various attempts to demonstrate the negative consequences of caste victimization, social scientists have, in their description of the Negro American, unwittingly provided scientific credibility for many white-held stereotypes of the Negro. There have been, no doubt, important political and ideological reasons for such a position, and as Rainwater (1966) has noted, social research has attempted to "demonstrate that responsibility for the disadvantages Negroes suffer lies squarely upon the white caste which derives economic, prestige, and psychic benefits from operation of the system" (p. 174).

Indeed, the argument that psychological disabilities result from prejudice and discrimination did play an important part in the evidence presented to the U.S. Supreme Court preceding the 1954 school desegregation decision. It is our contention, however, that such a view has found wide support as much because it complemented political strategy as because it was based upon solid evidence. If the description is a distortion of the social facts, as we argue, then it has probably had the negative consequence of reinforcing the syndrome which it suggests exists.

EXPLANATIONS OF A STEREOTYPE

While there is general agreement about the psychological state of the Negro, there is some underlying debate as to whether the negative self-esteem of the Negro stems principally from being placed in the role of "Negro," as Pettigrew (1964) emphasizes, or whether it derives principally from the negative evaluation of others that in turn leads to a development of a "Negro role," as Kardiner and Ovesey (1951) suggest. Nevertheless, the broad theoretical perspective developed by Cooley, Mead, and Sullivan has been the major rationale buttressing many of the explanations of lower self-esteem and identity crisis. A third frequently occurring mode of explanation, sometimes difficult to separate from the first two, is that of the interaction of caste and class. We will discuss the three perspectives in order.

The Consequences of Uncle Tom

The application of the first perspective has been relatively straightforward. Since his arrival in the United States, the Negro has been a member of a powerless minority. The powerful white majority demanded

that the Negro play the Uncle Tom role, characterized by obsequious-
ness. At times such a role was necessary for physical survival, and it
normally produced more of what little could be gained from the white
oppressor. But this behavior was for white consumption only. Among
other Negroes another "truer" role was manifest. Such disparate behavior, however, according to this perspective, creates problems resulting in confusion and a crisis of identity. It may also produce self-hatred
among some Negroes who attempt unsuccessfully to resist the Uncle
Tom role.

Stanley Elkins (1959), in drawing the analogy between the concentration camp and American slavery, presents a clear use of the role-per-
sonality perspective. He notes that the expectations of the pervasive and
dependent roles of the prisoner and the slave were exacting. Within
these narrow boundaries developed the role of the childlike "Sambo"
among American slaves which did not exist in Latin America or in
Africa. Elkins suggests that while such a role was perhaps difficult for
the arriving slaves to learn, before Emancipation the Sambo role was
fully institutionalized. With Emancipation the move from "slave" to
"accommodating Negro" under Jim Crow apparently was not a difficult
transition.

John Dollard's (1937) description of the accommodated Southern
Negro is similar to Elkins's description of Sambo. Dollard writes: "If the
reader has ever seen Stepin Fetchit in the movies, he can picture this
type of character. Fetchit always plays the part of a well-accommodated
lower-class Negro, whining, vacillating, shambling, stupid, and moved
by very simple cravings" (p. 257). Although Dollard's research was
carried out in the 1930's, such a view remains viable. For example,
Pettigrew (1964) notes that "being a Negro in America is less of a racial
identity than a necessity to adopt a subordinate social role. The effects
of this 'Negro role' are profound and lasting. Evaluating himself by the
way others react to him, the Negro may grow into the servile role; in time
the person and the role become indistinguishable. The personality consequences of the situation can be devastating—confusion of self-identity,
lower self-esteem, perception of the world as a hostile place, and serious
sex-role conflicts" (p. 25).[1]

---

[1] The straightforward connection between the structural position of Southern Negroes
and the role of "accommodating Negro" is, Dollard suggests, more problematic than
that suggested by Pettigrew. Even in "Southerntown," where there were relatively
few alternatives available for the Negro, Dollard found variation in the degree to
which accommodation was accepted. Lower-class Negroes and those with less education, that is, those who had "least access to a divergent conception of the Negro's
place in American society," were more likely to accept accommodation (1937, p. 256).
Conversely, the more cosmopolitan Negroes—those not limited to white Southerners
as a source of identity and esteem—who had been exposed to alternative conceptions

Dollard (1937) takes issue with a simple correspondence between the Negro's role and personality by pointing out that the role the Negro reveals to whites should not be taken as his only or "real" self. The Uncle Tom role is but a facade used to manipulate the oppressor and reveals little of the "true self" of the oppressed (see also Elkins 1959; Odum 1910).

It is problematic whether such an adaptation has positive or negative consequences for personality organization. Bettelheim's (1943) research in concentration camps indicates that in extreme situations there are negative personality consequences. Dollard's (1937) description of the accommodating Negro suggests that accommodation is fraught with dangers for the personalities engaged in it: "Accommodation involves the renunciation of protest or aggression against the undesirable conditions of life, and the organization of the character so that protest does not appear, but acceptance does. It may come to pass in the end that the unwelcomed force is idealized, that one identifies with it and takes it into the personality; it sometimes even happens that what is at first resented and feared is finally loved" (p. 255).

Pettigrew (1964) reasons similarly concerning the effects of maintaining such a dual identity when he says, "Negroes may handle tense interracial situations by attempting to separate their true selves from their role as 'Negro.' Allport points out that this mechanism actually involves a mild dissociation; one is 'himself' with other Negroes but transforms his behavior to meet the expectations of prejudiced whites. Some such dissociation occurs in the acting out of many social roles, but the intensity of racial role-playing renders this type of dissociation especially dangerous. Carried to extremes, it culminates in mental disorder" (p. 29).

Thus it is suggested that the development of a public facade by the accommodating Negro does not result in a successful separation of self from role, but a confusion over what constitutes self and a lack of understanding and acceptance of self, since he is unable to effectively maintain a dual identity without impairment.

Self-Identity through Interaction

A second perspective, following the emphasis of Kardiner and Ovesey (1951), suggests that the crisis of identity and loss of self-esteem derive largely from the images of himself which the Negro receives from the white community: the self emerges through interaction with significant others. Developing self-identity and self-esteem depends not merely upon

of "the Negro" were less likely to accept the role and identity provided by Southern whites.

objective social characteristics, but also upon the judgment of these characteristics by relevant others.

Again, the application of this theoretical position to the situation of the Negro American has been straightforward. Observers have assumed that Negroes view whites as significant others: the views of whites, who believe in Negro inferiority and act upon such beliefs, directly affect Negro self-identity and self-esteem. "Consciously or unconsciously," writes Pettigrew, "Negroes accept, in part, these assertions of their inferiority" (p. 9). Beyond the subjective evaluations and images held by whites it is also argued that differences in schools, housing, employment, and income are used as criteria for self-evaluation and identity (Proshansky and Newton 1968).

Kardiner and Ovesey (1951) state: "This central problem of Negro adaptation is oriented to discrimination he suffers and the consequences of this discrimination for the self-referential aspects of his social orientation. In simple words, it means that his self-esteem suffers (which is self-referential) because he is constantly receiving an unpleasant image of himself from the behavior of others" (p. 302). They suggest that in order to maintain "internal balance and to protect himself from being overwhelmed by it [the Mark of Oppression] [the Negro] must initiate restitutive maneuvers in order to keep functioning—all quite automatic and unconscious" (p. 303). A major consequence of these defensive measures is the development of a social facade; the Uncle Tom role develops not because the Negro is placed in that role by whites, but rather as an adaptive strategy to protect the self from negative evaluations. In a word, the dual personality of the Negro is seen as a solution to personality-identity problems rather than a cause as the first perspective suggests.[2]

Rainwater (1966), in a recent analysis of the lower-class Negro family, employs a similar theoretical perspective. Although he suggests a different locus of relevant evaluations, he arrives at similar conclusions. While Clark, Kardiner and Ovesey, and others have argued that the images Negroes receive from white society are the major determinant of low self-esteem, Rainwater suggests that white discrimination and prejudice are but the secondary cause of the Negroes' poor identity formation. A closer examination reveals that Negroes victimize Negroes. He writes: "In short, whites, by their greater power, create situations in which Negroes do the dirty work of caste victimization for them" (p. 175). Further, "at least in the urban North the initial development of racial

[2] Kenneth Clark's thesis in *Dark Ghetto* (1965) is very similar to this position, though it stems from observation of Northern, urban, lower-class Negroes. Clark suggests similar personality consequences resulting from negative evaluation by others.

identity in these terms has very little directly to do with relations with whites" (p. 204).

Rainwater views the family as the major source of identity. Out of the lower-class family, particularly the unstable one, he says, comes a "weak and debased person, who can expect only partial gratification by less than straight-forward means" (p. 206).

It is argued that through the socialization process, as it takes place within the unstable family and the lower-class neighborhood peer group, negative identities develop, since both parents and peers regularly present the individual with derogatory evaluations.[3]

The second perspective, then, stresses negative self-evaluation over "crisis of identity," though both perspectives agree on negative self-evaluation. The perspectives differ with respect to whether the Uncle Tom role is a cause or consequence of the assumed negative self-evaluation.

The Interaction of Caste and Class

While, in general, the literature reviewed here stresses the issues of *caste* over those of socioeconomic class, few authors have ignored the question of the degree to which caste is exacerbated and/or confounded by class (see Dollard 1937; Kardiner and Ovesey 1951; Davis and Dollard 1940; Rohrer and Edmonson 1960; Pettigrew 1964). Here we will review several positions which stress the interaction of caste and class factors in explaining the negative self-image presumed to be prevalent in the Negro American community.

The first variant on this theme stresses the role of economic marginality which results from caste victimization. The two consequences of such marginality seen as most important are female-headed families and jobs which lack any measure of prestige, both of which are seen as producing, though by different processes, a negative view of the self.

The relatively high frequency of female-headed families among Negroes, sometimes termed matrifocality, is seen to be perpetuated by the marginal economic position of the Negro adult male. The occupations available to the unskilled Negro man normally lack the security and income necessary to maintain a household. Further, such jobs (as, for example, waiter, cook, orderly, dishwasher, etc.) are seen by some to carry a feminine connotation (Proshansky and Newton 1968). Despite the lack of job opportunities available, the Negro male is still under the

---

[3] Rainwater's general thesis need not be limited to black families. Indeed, if it is the unstable family and the hostile world of the slum peer group that provide the significant others who in turn are the sources of such an identity, to the degree that these characterize other lower-class communities similar identities should be developed. In Rainwater's terms, "To a certain extent these same processes operate in white lower-class groups, but added for the Negro is the reality of blackness" (p. 204).

general societal prescription that he fulfill his function as provider, so he must work if he is to be evaluated positively as a man and father. The marginal employment situation results in his inability to fulfill his role as male head of household, and is said to result in a serious loss of self-esteem. Proshansky and Newton (1968) summarize much of this literature with the statement that "his predicament may take the form of a 'self-fulfilling prophecy.' He is told that he is 'no good' and 'irresponsible' and to some extent he internalizes these judgments which in turn influence his actions. When he fails, no one is surprised" (p. 205). Erikson (1966), exploring this issue, suggests that, particularly in an industrial setting, such imbalance "may, indeed, become the gravest factor in personality disorganization" (p. 167).[4] Finally, this pattern is said to produce even more dire consequences for his children if the male leaves the household unit. Pettigrew (1964) provides us with a relevant review of research indicating that the specific link between poverty and personality development takes place in the family. These studies suggest that children raised in broken families are more likely to be hedonistic, less accurate in predicting time, less socially responsible, less oriented toward achievement, more prone toward delinquency, and are likely to manifest problems of sex-role identity (pp. 17–19). Thus, the institutional arrangements of slavery and Jim Crow are said to have been replaced by racial and economic marginality that now function as major forces which produce the loss of self-esteem and personality crisis of the adult male and the pathological character of the socialization process in female-headed households.

While the focus upon class factors in this literature normally means attention to the Negro's marginal economic circumstances, Frazier (1957) in his controversial classic, *Black Bourgeoisie*, attends to the peculiar situation of the middle-class Negro, thereby avoiding the implications of economic marginality. Frazier's study is consistent with the general tendency of this literature to characterize the Negro as pathological, no matter what his circumstances, by suggesting that the black bourgeoisie is ambivalent about identification with the "Negro masses" and responds by a flight into a world of "make believe" based upon emulation of the white middle class. "Since the world of make-believe cannot insulate the

---

[4] The traditional literature suggests that Jim Crow was directed more at the Negro male rather than the Negro female. Black women are said to be allowed more freedom, suffer less discrimination, and are provided more opportunities than black men. As a consequence, Negro men are said to have lower self-esteem than Negro women. While this argument has no implications for racial differences in self-esteem among women, the arguments presented earlier hold for females as well as males. Given the cultural prescriptions relating employment to male authority and the male role, one expects to find a similar sexual difference among lower-class whites, that is, underemployed men should have lower self-esteem than their female counterparts.

black bourgeoisie completely from the world of reality, the members of this class exhibit considerable confusion and conflict in their personalities" (p. 25). So Frazier rejects the argument that the marginal economic circumstances of the Negro American are responsible for his personality difficulties. Cultural marginality coupled with the unique situation of economic security among an oppressed people produce similar personality consequences.

SOME EVIDENCE

In this section we bring research evidence to bear upon the traditional arguments and hypotheses, but first several prefatory comments are in order. First, we must ask: very likely compared with whom? If we compare the self-hatred of any social grouping with an ideal personality state—as the neo-Freudians are fond of doing—we can do nothing more than find what we seek—a discrepancy. We hold with Campbell (1957) that any meaningful scientific evidence involves at least one formal comparison, and we do not believe that a comparison between an observed state of affairs and an ideal state of affairs meets the criteria of formal scientific comparison.

Let us very briefly examine some evidence which does not meet our criteria of formal comparison in order to demonstrate the dangers of accepting conclusions based upon such evidence. Kardiner and Ovesey, in their work, *The Mark of Oppression* (1951), draw generalizations concerning the effects of prejudice and discrimination from twenty-five intensive case studies of Negro Americans. The only obvious comparison being made by the authors is between the twenty-five subjects' assessed personality states and some ideal of personality structure. The authors do, of course, make an informal comparison. Having treated a number of white patients in therapy, a racial comparison is implicit, but it is certainly not systematic. One of the many conclusions drawn from this evidence by the authors is that the social definition of blackness in American society is in some measure responsible for the self-hatred and lack of esteem within this sample. After intensive review of Kardiner and Ovesey's case-study material, Rohrer and Edmonson (1960) conclude that only seven of the cases examined exhibit self-hatred and consequent lack of self-esteem. Further, they note that five of these cases had undergone previous therapeutic experience. Whether or not the self-hatred evidenced by any of the subjects is a result of prejudice and discrimination must also remain in doubt in the absence of a formal comparison.

In addressing the hypothesis of black self-hatred with a formal comparison, a number of possibilities present themselves. One might compare self-hatred among black Americans with self-hatred among black Africans or black Europeans. The literature surveyed above would predict greater prevalence of self-hatred among black North Americans than among black South Americans or Africans, but the possibility also exists that Americans are more prone to self-hatred than Africans (Elkins 1959). The racial comparison within the United States appears most meaningful to us, however, so the following review will attend only to evidence which makes the racial comparison with regard to relevant variables.

We would prefer to have systematic evidence of the type outlined above on self-esteem, self-hatred, and ambiguous identity, but very little exists. Therefore, it becomes necessary to broaden the range of indicators which will be accepted as pertinent to the prevailing literature. We shall also accept anomie, mental disorder, suicide, and alcoholism as indicators of personal disorganization. Acceptance of such indicators involves a number of assumptions which may not be warranted. On the other hand, all appear to represent personal disorganization, and there is evidence that they possess at least some measure of common variance (see Rushing 1968; Vanderpool 1969).

Self-Esteem

There is extensive evidence suggesting that black children become aware of differences in skin color very early in their development. Negro children have been shown to prefer white dolls to brown dolls (Clark and Clark 1958; Goodman 1952) and to assign brown dolls to poorer housing and inferior roles (Radke and Trager 1950). Most of the authors who report this evidence are cautious in interpreting such findings, but reviewers of this literature have been rather free in concluding that this evidence suggests self-doubt, self-hate, and identity problems (see Berelson and Steiner 1964). It is a rather long jump in our opinion, however, from racial awareness, preference for white dolls, and assignment of inferior roles to brown dolls to self-hatred on the part of such children. There are a number of plausible explanations for such findings which have nothing to do with self-hatred. Personality ratings accompanying one piece of research in this tradition demonstrate that the Negro children were more cheerful, more curious, more inclined toward leadership, kinder, and more sensitive (Goodman 1952)—hardly picturesque of rampant self-hatred. In our opinion the evidence embodied in this literature is open to various interpretations, especially since much of it does not make a racial comparison (see Greenwald and Oppenheim 1968). We do not argue that the interpretation commonly made is necessarily incorrect. It may be correct, but the evidence remains inconclusive.

Is there any evidence which is more directly to the point for black and white children? A series of studies carried out by Baughman and Dahlstrom (1968) provides evidence at variance with the conclusions commonly drawn from the research on Negro and white children. The results of interviews with Negro and white eighth graders in a rural Southern community are worth quoting:

> When we turn to the self-concepts of these children, their interview statements about themselves are markedly positive. This is particularly true for the Negro children, a fact that is at variance with the widely accepted belief that the self-esteem of the Negro is inevitably damaged, even at an early age. The Negro children in our sample, for instance, much more frequently reported themselves as being popular with their peers than the white children did. Also, there was a tendency for more Negro than white children to say that they were *very* satisfied being the kind of person they were. In addition, significantly more Negro than white children described their home life as being happier than that of the average child. Clearly, if the self-concepts of these Negro children have been unduly damaged, this fact is not reflected in their interview statements about themselves, nor in the educational and vocational aspirations which they report for themselves (and which they seem optimistic about realizing). [p. 462]

Further, Morris Rosenberg (1965), summarizing ethnic groups' differences in self-esteem, concludes, "We see that Negroes, who are exposed to the most intense, humiliating, and crippling forms of discrimination in every institutional area, do not have particularly low self-esteem" (p. 57). This finding is particularly noteworthy since the Negroes in Rosenberg's sample represent the lowest socioeconomic status group, but are about average on his measure of self-esteem.

Two other studies which purport to measure self-concept of Negro and white youth based upon national samples of youth of high school age present evidence which is at variance with the traditional conception of racial differences in self-esteem. These studies are both concerned with academic achievement. The measures of self-concept might better be termed "academic self-concept." Coleman et al. (1966) report that "responses to these questions [concerning academic self-concept] do not indicate differences between Negroes and whites" (p. 281). McDill, Meyers, and Rigsby (1966), examining a matched sample of Negro and white youth of high school age, demonstrate that Negroes display a higher average self-esteem score than the white sample.

Finally Rosenberg reports the use of his self-esteem scale in another context involving the racial comparison with adults. He reports that a colleague "found among attendants [in a mental hospital], who are the lowest ranking nursing personnel, Negroes had higher self-esteem than whites, according to our scale" (p. 63). In interpreting this evidence, he says, "In this middle Atlantic city, the job of attendant is a relatively good job for a Negro but a very poor position for a white. Self-esteem may be more a matter of one's position within one group than the rank of the group in relation to other groups" (p. 63).

It is interesting to note the impact of the traditional argument concerning race and self-esteem when one finds authors uncovering what is apparently negative evidence. Rosenberg is apparently surprised, while McDill et al. (1966) challenge the validity of the measure and resort to intellectual gymnastics in order to reinterpret negative evidence into the traditional argument: "High self-esteem on the part of Negroes is a defense mechanism against discrimination" (chap. 10, p. 16).

Mental Disorder

Much of the evidence addressed to racial differences in the personal pathologies is based upon data gathered by care agencies. Consequently, such evidence can only give us indications of incidence, while the traditional arguments predict differences in prevalence. Furthermore, in light of the systematic work demonstrating differential response with regard to race by the various agencies of the legal system in the United States (Pettigrew 1964), evidence based upon such official reactions to the so-called personal pathologies requires extreme caution.

Pettigrew (1964), in reviewing the state of knowledge on racial differences in mental disorders, concludes that the Negro psychosis incidence rate is higher than the comparable white rate. The only study cited by Pettigrew, however, which takes into account both public and private first admissions, demonstrates that the white incidence rate is higher (Jaco 1960). This suggests caution in the interpretation of data concerning racial differences in incidence rates for psychosis based only upon first admissions to public hospitals. Pettigrew concludes that neurosis incidence rates for first admissions to state hospitals demonstrate that the white rate is higher than the Negro rate. He admits that both the survey and the admissions evidence support a view that for certain disorders the Negro incidence rate may be lower than the white rate (p. 77).

To avoid accepting incidence rates as indicators of prevalence, we might use sample survey techniques. There are problems, however, with adopting such a research strategy. Relatively few persons exhibit severe mental disorders. A study employing such a strategy, carried out by Pasamanick et al. (1964), attempted to estimate prevalence rates of psychoses, psychoneuroses, and psychophysiologic, autonomic, and visceral disorders based upon clinical evaluations of a subsample of a larger sample of the population of Baltimore. Though Pasamanick and his coinvestigators found that the nonwhite (almost totally Negro) prevalence rate for each of these diagnosed disorders was startlingly below the white rate, the total number of cases upon which the rates were based for all of the disorders was eighty-six. The total number of nonwhites so diagnosed, then, was a small proportion of this number, so the possibility remains strong that such rates are highly unreliable, especially for the nonwhite population.

A final research strategy which attempts to assess prevalence of mental disorder is the use of paper and pencil tests in sample surveys which have been previously validated on normal and diagnosed populations. Dohrenwend (1966), reviewing attempts to assess the prevalence of treated as well as untreated psychological disorders in this manner, reports eight studies which make a racial comparison, though without rigorous socio-economic status controls. Four of the studies he reviews show higher rates of disorder for whites and four show higher rates of disorder for Negroes. Dohrenwend's own study, carried out in the Washington Heights section of New York City, does not demonstrate differences in psychological disorder between his Negro subsamples and his Jewish and Irish subsamples. With income controlled, the pattern of differences reported by Dohrenwend between his Negro and Irish samples is suggestive, though the differences are not large. For respondents who have a family income of $5,000 a year or less, the Irish respondents are more likely to report symptoms of psychological disorder, while among respondents who have a family income of more than $5,000 a year the Negro respondents are more likely to report such symptoms.

Again it is our opinion that this evidence here suggests rethinking, rather than acceptance, of the traditional arguments on racial differences in personal organization. Again we find attempts by authors investigating racial differences in psychological disorder attempting to explain away what appear to be negative findings. Dohrenwend appeals, though in rather convincing fashion, to problems of measurement rather than accepting the evidence as he finds it.

Suicide

The nonwhite suicide rate in the United States is consistently far below the comparable white rate (Gibbs 1966; Labovitz 1968). This fact is normally explained as Pettigrew (1964) explains it: "Negro American aggression is more often turned outward in the form of homicide than inward as suicide" (p. 78). Such an explanation, in its most simple form, as stated here, seems no more than a description of a state of affairs once the proponent accepts the assumption that suicide and homicide are different forms of aggression stemming from the same causal conditions (see Henry and Short 1954).

We concede that many would regard including mention of racial differences in suicide rates here as somewhat tenuous, though there are a number of commentators on the etiology of suicide who argue that self-degradation is an important factor in explaining individual suicide (Kilpatrick 1968). Finally, there is some indication that individual suicide is related to a number of the other personal pathologies under discussion here (Rushing 1968).

The differences between the white and the nonwhite suicide rate hold up under sex, age, socioeconomic status control (*Suicide in the United States*, 1967; Rushing 1968; Labovitz 1968).[5] The pattern of differences with class controlled, however, is suggestive and deserves some note here. Two studies demonstrate that the differences between the white and nonwhite suicide rates are greater at the lower socioeconomic level than they are at the higher socioeconomic levels. That is, though affluent nonwhites are less likely than affluent whites to commit suicide, the difference at this socioeconomic level is less than the difference when both groups are poor. For instance, Maris (1969) demonstrates that for Cook County, Illinois, for the years 1959–63, among males, the higher the socioeconomic status level the smaller the difference in suicide rate between whites and nonwhites. Rushing (1969) presents standard mortality rates for suicide for 1950 among males in the United States, and his data show the same pattern.

Alienation and Anomia

Sociologists have developed a large body of empirical work with the concepts of alienation and anomia. This is not the place to engage in a discussion of the distinction between the concepts, but it is fair to say that, at least empirically, they have been shown to have some overlap and are in practice used somewhat interchangeably. There are a large number of measures which are highly relevant to the comparison we are interested in making here (Nettler 1957).

The evidence making a racial comparison on measures of anomia or alienation remains ambiguous. For instance, Middleton (1963) reports results for a small Florida community which reveal, controlling for years of education completed, that Negroes are more alienated than whites. Killian and Grigg (1962), on the other hand, report data for two southeastern communities, one with a population of 300,000 and one with a population of less than 3,000, which show no differences in anomia for the urban sample and large differences for the rural sample. Killian and Grigg used a composite measure of social position in making the comparisons, and where the differences obtained, Negroes were more likely to be alienated. Kornhauser, Mayer, and Sheppard (1956), in a study of the voting behavior of labor union members in Detroit, had occasion to examine racial differences in anomia. Though the data are not presented for the racial comparison, and no socioeconomic status control is introduced, they report that Negroes have high anomia ratings in just about the same proportion as do the whites. Finally, Brink and Harris (1966, p. 135) conclude,

---

[5] A recent monograph by Hendin (1969) presents evidence indicating that in New York City the rate of nonwhite suicides is about equal to the white rate.

after discussing data from a number of recent national surveys making comparisons between poor blacks and whites, that "the net result is that low-income whites feel quite hopelessly caught up in the forgotten backwash of society." This evidence certainly casts some doubt upon the traditional assumptions with regard to racial differences in alienation.[6]

Alcoholism

Let us conclude our brief review of evidence concerning racial differences in the so-called personal pathologies with a brief mention of alcoholism. In an excellent review of the available work concerning such differences, Sterne (1967) concludes that the evidence reveals a higher rate of alcoholism among Negroes than among whites. As with mental illness rates, however, the bulk of this empirical work is based upon subjects who have come to the attention of care agencies, and Sterne shows that data drawn from official agencies are not altogether unanimous in demonstrating higher rates for Negroes. On the other hand, death rates from cirrhosis of the liver are much higher for whites (Rushing 1969). Again, this evidence lacks consistency with respect to a conclusion concerning the racial comparison.

Finally, Rushing's (1969) data on alcoholism show that, with occupation controlled, the smallest differences between white and nonwhite males occur among the professional and managerial groups, while the white rate far exceeds the nonwhite rate in the lower prestige occupational categories.

Though we have ranged beyond direct measures of self-esteem, we believe that the evidence reviewed is pertinent to the central hypotheses of the traditional literature. It seems obvious to us that the evidence is highly ambiguous. Both defenders and attackers of the traditional view of the personal disorganization of the Negro American can find support in this body of evidence. The evidence is generally of less than desirable quality, which allows a proponent to dismiss negative evidence on methodological grounds in many instances.

DERIVING SOME ALTERNATIVE HYPOTHESES

Since we are convinced that at best the traditional view is only partially supported by the existing evidence, and further that the effects of the black experience in its present and historical forms are far more complicated than has normally been assumed, we offer several counterhypotheses here. We feel that such an exercise is useful in that it suggests crucial tests: such counterhypotheses require for their dismissal evidence which more clearly supports the traditional hypotheses.

[6] This research makes premature such exchanges as that between Coleman (1964) and Gordon (1965) based upon assumed racial differences in alienation.

Following the work of Morris Rosenberg (1965) and Stanley Coopersmith (1967), we will view self-esteem as an evaluative attitude toward
the self.

Coopersmith (1967) suggests that relative evaluations are important
antecedents or determinants of self-esteem. He notes, in his summary of
prior theoretical statements concerning self-esteem, four principal factors:
"(1) The amount of *respectful, accepting and concerned treatment* that
the individual receives from significant others in his life. (2) Our *history
of successes* and the status and position we hold in the world. (3) Experiences are interpreted and modified in accord with the individual's
values and aspirations. (4) The individual's *manner of responding to de-
valuation*" (p. 37). We suggest that these factors are the very assumptions
employed by those authors reviewed in the second section of this paper.
Indeed, it is Mead, Cooley, and Sullivan, among others, whom Coopersmith is summarizing (pp. 29–36). We propose such factors here as
guidelines, as we discuss the position of the Negro in the United States.
So, as is evident, we do not propose adopting a radically different theoretical approach to these issues. We will suggest that with only minor altera-
tions such factors produce conflicting hypotheses concerning the self-
esteem of the Negro American.

Respectful Treatment

The literature on Negro self-esteem has for the most part followed
Kardiner and Ovesey's assumption that Negroes accept white definitions
of themselves.

In contrast to this assumption, research by social psychologists indicates rather clearly that the sources of evaluation important for self-
identity are individuals occupying social positions quite similar to ego
(Pettigrew 1967). This suggests that Negroes, rather than using whites,
would be most likely to use other Negroes as sources of identity
and esteem, for a number of reasons; the reality of de facto segregation
being one of the most important.[7] Rainwater's (1966) research on lower-

---

[7] We have phrased the traditional arguments and our own in group terms. We have
spoken and will speak of Negroes and whites, and have attended to evidence in the
form of relevant group rates. We do not mean to imply that all Negroes, or whites for
that matter, find themselves in similar social circumstances or respond to the same
circumstances in exactly the same manner. We recognize, in fact we insist, that the
variables under discussion *are* variables. Consequently, when we make the statement
that Negroes are highly likely to use the evaluations of other Negroes as sources of
identity and self-esteem, we would expect a great deal of variation here within the
Negro subgroup depending upon the constellation of other variables such as region,
class, relative size of Negro and white population within a geographic area, and the
like. Consequently, we would predict very different sources of evaluation and consequences for self-esteem for the Negro living in a small North Dakota town working as
a store clerk and his counterpart in Harlem. The same would be true for the black

class Negroes complements the social psychological literature in his suggestion that it is the family and peer group that are the principal sources of self-identity. He suggests that it is the broken family and the expressive system of the corner peer group that are the principal causes of low self-esteem and crises of identity. He goes on to suggest that, except for the negative definition of black skin, the same processes of identity formation should take place among lower-class whites who are in similar social and economic positions. Disregarding the definition of black skin, and assuming different sources of relevant evaluation, the application of the self-through-interaction thesis leads to a different conclusion concerning the self-esteem of black Americans.

Therefore, *to the degree that Negroes do not use biased white evaluators in developing a self-evaluation, the process of development of self-identity within the black community will parallel the developmental process in the white community*, and to that degree, when social class is controlled, *Negroes and whites should not differ in levels of self-esteem.*[8]

Success and Values

Coopersmith (1967) notes that self-evaluations stemming from one's experiences are judged as successes or failures depending on one's values and aspirations (p. 37). Consequently we cannot infer self-evaluation directly from an objective reading of success and failure; we must put such a history into a context of values and aspirations. This point only becomes relevant when it is not assumed that the American cultural structure can be characterized by one dominant set of values about which there is a high degree of consensus.

One can make a distinction between a group of authors who argue that American society is characterized by a set of common values and a second group who stress distinct subcultural value systems.

The first group of writers has assumed that society is integrated by a common system of values and that all members are more or less aware of and committed to these values. Parsons (1953), for example, assumes that

high school teacher, educated at a state university in the Northeast and teaching in the Northeast compared with the black individual educated at a predominantly black state university in the South and teaching at a predominantly black high school in the rural deep South. After comparing such group rates, of course, the burden of such an explanation rests upon demonstrating within group differences as the hypothesis, with respect to social group rates, is certainly consistent with a number of other explanations. While not denying within-group or between-community differences, we stress racial-group differences here in response to the phrasing of traditional arguments.

[8] The degree to which blacks employ whites as significant others ought to vary directly with informal contact with whites. Though such contacts may be selective, it might be hypothesized that variation in contact is negatively related to self-esteem.

a common value system underlies the system of stratification. He writes: "Stratification *in its valuation aspect*, then, is the ranking of units in a social system in accordance with the standards of the common value system" (p. 93). Merton's (1957) statement on anomie articulates this position with its assumption that most Americans are aware of and committed to a value system epitomized in the American Dream. Such a perspective allows one to make direct inferences regarding self-evaluation from an individual's objective successes and failures.

The second group of theorists has assumed that American society is composed of a number of autonomous and conflicting subcultures. Perhaps the strongest statement of this position was made by Miller (1958) who wrote concerning lower-class culture: "There is a substantial segment of present-day American society whose way of life, values, and characteristic patterns of behavior are the product of a distinctive cultural system which might be termed 'lower class'" (see also Davis 1946; Lewis 1961; Becker 1963). This perspective allows one to argue that the distinct values developed within the lower class can provide alternative criteria for success and contribute to positive self-evaluation, hence blunting middle-class definitions of failure and evaluations of such failure.

It should also be noted that the literature we have been questioning has assumed that the conflict which has characterized the relationship between white and black Americans has resulted in disorganization and disintegration within the Negro community (Coser 1956; Williams 1947). We suggest, following the arguments of Lewin (1948), Myrdal (1944, pp. 1766–67), and more recently Himes (1966), that, on the contrary, racial conflict and isolation have resulted in a measure of cohesion and solidarity among Negro Americans. If conflict has had such consequences, then it should function to sharpen variant value systems. There is some evidence indicating that Negroes generally, and especially working- and lower-class Negroes, have developed life-styles that reflect relatively autonomous and cohesive subcultures (Keil 1966; Billingsley 1968; Valentine 1968; Hannerez 1969).

Following those who suggest that class is the crucial variable necessary to isolate such value subcultures, one would predict that the lower class would be least likely to accept the dominant definitions of success and worthiness. Recognizing the effects of racial conflict, however, suggests that lower-class whites should be more vulnerable to dominant definitions than lower-class blacks (see Dahrendorf 1959, pp. 189–93). Middle-class blacks should be more likely than lower-class blacks to accept the dominant value system. Following this line of reasoning, we suggest that middle-class whites should be most highly committed to the dominant value system and lower-class blacks should be least committed. We would suggest, then, that the possibilities for variant value subcultures would be greatest among the black lower class[9] and smallest among the white middle class, falling somewhere between the two extremes.

If, in fact, success and failure are translated into self-evaluation within a context of values and aspirations, and variant subcultures provide alternative criteria of success and failure, then there are avenues to credible and high self-esteem that do not depend upon the dominant value configuration. *Lower-class blacks will manifest higher self-esteem than lower-class whites, and middle-class blacks will manifest lower self-esteem than middle-class whites.*

Responses to Evaluation

The subcultural explanation comes close to implying that members of subcultures are neither influenced by nor aspire to the values of the dominant culture. Recent literature describing the poor suggests that the required structural autonomy for the development of an autonomous subculture does not exist in an industrial-urban society. That is to say, it is unlikely for a group of people, no matter how limited their resources, to be totally unaware of and unaffected by the larger community.[10] By this view, both the black poor and the white poor encounter the criteria of worth expressed by more affluent Americans. Rather than asking how such negative evaluations harm individuals who are subject to them, we ask how one defends himself in the face of them.

Here we are following Merton (1957), who asks, "When are relatively slim life-chances taken by men as a normal and expectable state of affairs which they attribute to their own personal inadequacies and when are they seen as the result of an arbitrary social system of mobility, in which rewards are not proportioned to ability?" (p. 240).

Cloward and Ohlin (1960) argue that persons who ascribe their failure to the social system attack the system and become alienated from it to

[9] Though we are led to make this argument on theoretical grounds, we are somewhat skeptical of it on empirical grounds. The research on educational aspirations of black and white youth indicates that black adolescents are at least as likely and probably more likely to accept dominant definitions of educational success (see Proshansky and Newton 1968, pp. 196–202). On the other hand, viewing the above argument in developmental terms may mean that this evidence does not contradict the position. We have neglected to confront the developmental aspects of self-evaluation in discussing racial differences here. In so doing, we do not mean to imply that we do not recognize the crucial importance of such aspects in developing an explanation of racial differences in self-evaluation. The traditional literature, under review, stresses the factors affecting adult self-evaluation; so, too, have we. The more theoretical work on self-esteem, though, stresses the early adolescent period, suggesting development of a stable self-evaluation during this period. These two emphases conflict in their interpretation of the implications of the educational aspiration data for social differences in adult self-evaluation.

[10] There may be some exceptions to this position for the United States as reflected in communities in isolated Appalachian areas.

some degree. "The individual who locates the source of his failure in his own inadequacy, on the other hand, feels pressure to change himself rather than the system. Suffering from a loss of self-esteem, he must either develop mechanisms that will protect him from these feelings of personal inadequacy or work toward eliminating them by developing greater personal competence. By implication, then, attributing failure to one's own faults reveals an attitude supporting the legitimacy of the existing norms" (p. 112). One response to failure results in negative self-evaluation or low self-esteem; the second results in a withdrawal of loyalty from conventional structures and has no apparent effect on self-esteem.[11] Under what structural conditions are persons who fail likely to respond to such failure by blaming the system rather than themselves? Cloward and Ohlin suggest two conditions: (1) When there is a "discrepancy between institutionally induced expectations (as distinct from aspirations) and possibility of achievement, which produces a sense of unjust deprivation." (2) When there are "highly visible barriers to the achievement of aspirations, which give rise to feelings of discrimination" (p. 113).

The position of the lower- and working-class Negro in America is obviously characterized by these conditions. Thus Myrdal (1944) noted several decades ago: "The standard explanation of Negro failures, and the only one publicly accepted, is to place the responsibility upon the caste system and whites who uphold it. . . . As the Negro protest is rising and is becoming popularized, the view becomes more and more widespread that white oppression and caste deprivation are to be blamed and not Negro inferiority" (p. 759). Traditionally, white prejudice and discrimination have been quite open and have become more subtle as the articulation of the system-blame position has become more widespread. On the other hand, lower-class whites possess a far less well-articulated view with which to reinterpret negative evaluations, and barriers to success for lower-class whites are less visible. Poor white reaction to governmental efforts made in response to black protest may be the beginnings of such a coherent view, however (see Brink and Harris 1966). The implications of such a view for self-evaluation of the individual black man are made explicit by Myrdal (1944), when he says, "It preserves self-respect and does not necessarily damage ambition" (p. 759).

The system-blame reinterpretation of failure and negative evaluation should not be as likely an option for the middle-class black, however. In spite of discrimination he has achieved some measure of success within the dominant value framework. Acceptance of the system-blame perspective should be more difficult since it suggests that he could not be successful if it held (see Rytina, Form, and Pease 1970). Consequently, we suggest

11 See Elton Jackson's (1962) interpretation of his data on status inconsistency, symptoms of stress, and political attitudes for a complementary position.

that the system-blame explanation does not function as well in defending middle-class blacks from negative evaluation. We are again led to the proposition that *lower class blacks should exhibit higher self-esteem than lower-class whites, but middle-class blacks should exhibit lower self-esteem than middle-class whites.*

In this section we have developed three theoretical perspectives in contrast to the traditional view. As we have stated above, the burden of these views rests upon the explanation of within-group differences, as a number of arguments presented result in similar predictions of racial differences by class level. Given the ambiguity of the evidence reviewed, we believe that each of these perspectives ought to be subjected to empirical test.

POLICY IMPLICATIONS

Let us conclude by discussing for a moment the possible political implications of the alternative perspectives we have outlined above, since, we believe, political implications have always been relevant to the emphases in this literature. Both segregationists and black militants may find solace in these perspectives, which can be stated to support either ideological position. The segregationist might say, "You see, segregation is good for them," implying that there are also positive consequences of segregation. The black militant will, no doubt, appreciate our analysis of the traditional literature as at best stereotyped, and commend our suggestion that poor blacks respond with strength to oppression.

In either case, the public policy implication of the alternative views of Negro self-esteem presented here stands in sharp contrast to the traditional hypotheses of Negro self-hatred and pathology. Valentine (1968) argues strongly and quite convincingly that academic poverty experts and liberal intellectuals in general view the cultural adaptations of the poor, especially the Negro poor, as pathological. The adaptations which the poor make to their circumstances are viewed from a middle-class perspective, which easily leads to characterization of these adaptations as unhealthy, destructive of human potential, and physically damaging (see also Rodman 1964). The political thrust of such "race" research, then, combined with what appears to be a rather consistent view of the poor as pathological, may account for the plausibility of the standard view of Negro self-hatred. It has been politically acceptable to denigrate the poor, especially the Negro poor, if the burden has been placed upon the white majority for the hypothesized state of affairs.

Yet, as the controversy surrounding the "Moynihan Report" clearly indicates, a description that suggests Negroes, or the poor in general, are pathological, even though plausible given the social and economic constraints under which they live, implicitly suggests that the problems that characterize these groups may be attacked, not only on the institutional level, but also on the individual and family level. Martin Luther King, Jr. (1967), commenting on the pathologies normally associated with the Negro family, identifies the political ambiguities inherent in the traditional position. He writes: "As public awareness increases there will be dangers and opportunities. The opportunities will be to deal fully rather than haphazardly with the problem as a whole—to see it as a social catastrophe and to meet it as other disasters are met with an adequacy of resources. The dangers will be that the problem will be attributed to innate Negro weaknesses and used to justify neglect and rationalize oppression" (p. 404).

If empirical evidence supports an alternative description and explanation of racial differences in self-esteem, then institutional change rather than individual psychiatric or welfare services should be the primary focus of public policy aimed at amelioration of the consequences of racism.

REFERENCES

Baughman, E. Earl, and W. Grant Dahlstrom. 1968. *Negro and White Children.* New York: Academic.

Becker, Howard S. 1963. *Outsiders.* New York: Free Press.

Berelson, Bernard, and Gary A. Steiner. 1964. *Human Behavior.* New York: Harcourt Brace Jovanovich.

Bettelheim, B. 1943. "Individual and Mass Behavior in Extreme Situations." *Journal of Abnormal and Social Psychology* 38: 417–52.

Billingsley, Andrew. 1968. *Black Families in White America.* Englewood Cliffs, N.J.: Prentice-Hall.

Brink, William, and Louis Harris. 1966. *Black and White.* New York: Simon & Schuster.

Campbell, Donald T. 1957. "Factors Relevant to the Validity of Experiments in Social Settings." *Psychological Bulletin* 54: 297–312.

Clark, Kenneth B. 1965. *Dark Ghetto: Dilemmas of Social Power.* New York: Harper & Row.

Clark, Kenneth B., and Mamie P. Clark. 1958. "Racial Identification and Preference in Negro Children." In *Readings in Social Psychology,* edited by Eleanor E. Maccoby et al. New York: Holt, Rinehart & Winston.

Cloward, Richard A., and Lloyd E. Ohlin. 1960. *Delinquency and Opportunity.* Glencoe, Ill.: Free Press.

Coleman, James S. 1964. "Implications of the Findings of Alienation." *American Journal of Sociology* 70: 76–78.

Coleman, James S., Ernest Q. Campbell, Carol J. Hobson, James McPartland, Alexander Mood, Frederic D. Weinfeld, and Robert L. York. 1966. *Equality of Educational Opportunity.* Washington, D.C.: Government Printing Office.

Coles, Robert. 1964. *Children of Crisis.* Boston: Little, Brown.

Coopersmith, Stanley. 1967. *The Antecedents of Self-Esteem*. San Francisco: Freeman.

Coser, Lewis. 1956. *The Function of Social Conflict*. Glencoe, Ill.: Free Press.

Dahrendorf, Ralf. 1959. *Class and Class Conflict in Industrial Society*. Stanford, Calif.: Stanford University Press.

Davis, Allison. 1946. "The Motivation of the Underprivileged Worker." In *Industry and Society*, edited by W. F. Whyte. New York: McGraw-Hill.

Davis, Allison, and John Dollard. 1940. *Children of Bondage*. New York: Harper & Row.

Dohrenwend, Bruce P. 1966. "Social Status and Psychological Disorder: An Issue of Substance and an Issue of Method." *American Sociological Review* **31** (February): 14–34.

Dollard, John. 1937. *Caste and Class in a Southern Town*. Garden City, N.Y.: Doubleday and Anchor Books.

Elkins, Stanley. 1959. *Slavery*. Chicago: University of Chicago Press.

Erikson, Erik H. 1966. "The Concept of Identity in Race Relations: Notes and Queries." *Daedalus* **95** (Winter): 145–71.

Frazier, E. Franklin. 1957. *Black Bourgeoisie*. Glencoe, Ill.: Free Press.

Gibbs, Jack P. 1966. "Suicide." In *Contemporary Social Problems*, edited by R. K. Merton and R. A. Nisbet. 2d ed. New York: Harcourt Brace Jovanovich.

Goodman, Mary Ellen. 1952. *Race Awareness in Young Children*. Cambridge, Mass.: Wesley.

Gordon, Daniel N. 1965. "A Note on Negro Alienation." *American Journal of Sociology* **70**: 477–80.

Greenwald, Herbert J., and Don P. Oppenheim. 1968. "Reported Magnitude of Self-Misidentification among Negro Children—Artifact?" *Journal of Personality and Social Psychology* **8**: 49–52.

Hannerez, Ulf. 1969. "The Rhetoric of Soul: Identification in Negro Society." In *The Making of Black America*, edited by August Meier and Elliott Rudwick. New York: Atheneum.

Hendin, Herbert. 1969. *Black Suicide*. New York: Basic.

Henry, A. F., and J. F. Short, Jr. 1954. *Suicide and Homicide*. Glencoe, Ill.: Free Press.

Himes, Joseph S. 1966. "The Functions of Racial Conflict." *Social Forces* **45** (September): 1–10.

Jackson, Elton. 1962. "Status Consistency and Symptoms of Stress." *American Sociological Review* **27** (August): 469–80.

Jaco, E. Gartley. 1960. *The Social Epidemiology of Mental Disorders*. New York: Russell Sage Foundation.

Kardiner, Abram, and Lionel Ovesey. 1951. *The Mark of Oppression: Explorations in the Personality of the American Negro*. New York: Norton.

Keil, Charles. 1966. *Urban Blues*. Chicago: University of Chicago Press.

Kilpatrick, Elizabeth. 1968. "A Psychoanalytic Understanding of Suicide." In *Suicide*, edited by Jack P. Gibbs. New York: Harper & Row.

Killian, Lewis M., and Charles M. Grigg. 1962. "Urbanism, Race, and Anomia." *American Journal of Sociology* 67: 661–65.

King, Martin Luther, Jr. 1967. "Civil Rights and the Negro Family." In *The Moynihan Report and the Politics of Controversy*, edited by Lee Rainwater and W. L. Yancey. Cambridge, Mass.: M.I.T. Press.

Kornhauser, Arthur N., Albert J. Mayer, and Harold L. Sheppard. 1956. *When Labor Votes*. New York: University Books.

Labovitz, Sanford. 1968. "Variation in Suicide Rates." In *Suicide*, edited by Jack P. Gibbs. New York: Harper & Row.

Lewin, Kurt. 1948. *Resolving Social Conflicts*. New York: Harper & Row.

Lewis, Oscar. 1961. *The Children of Sanchez*. New York: Random House.

McDill, Edward L., Edmund D. Meyers, Jr., and Leo Rigsby. 1966. *Sources of Educational Climates in High Schools*. Department of Social Relations. Baltimore, Md.: Johns Hopkins University.

Maris, Ronald W. 1969. *Social Forces in Urban Suicide*. Homewood, Ill.: Dorsey.

Merton, Robert K. 1957. *Social Theory and Social Structure*. Glencoe, Ill.: Free Press.

Middleton, Russell. 1963. "Alienation, Race and Education." *American Sociological Review* 28: 973–77.

Miller, Walter. 1958. "Lower Class Culture as a Generating Milieu of Gang Delinquency." *Journal of Social Issues* 8: 5–19.

Myrdal, Gunnar. 1944. *An American Dilemma*. 2 Vols. New York: Harper & Row.

Nettler, Gwynn. 1957. "A Measure of Alienation." *American Sociological Review* 22 (December): 670–76.

Odum, Howard. 1910. "Social and Mental Traits of the Negro." *Studies in History, Economics and Public Law* 37: 551–65.

Parsons, Talcott. 1953. "A Revised Analytical Approach to the Theory of Social Stratification." In *Class, Status and Power*, edited by R. Bendix and S. M. Lipset. New York: Free Press.

Pasamanick, Benjamin, Dean W. Roberts, Paul W. Lemkau, and Dean B. Krueger. 1964. "A Survey of Mental Disease in Urban Population: Prevalence by Race and Income." In *Mental Health of the Poor*, edited by Frank Reissman et al. New York: Free Press.

Pettigrew, Thomas F. 1964. *A Profile of the Negro American*. Princeton, N.J.: Van Nostrand.

———. 1967. "Social Evaluation Theory: Convergences and Evaluations." *Nebraska Symposium on Motivation*, edited by David Levine. Lincoln: University of Nebraska Press.

Proshansky, Harold, and Peggy Newton. 1968. "The Nature and Meaning of Negro Self-Identity." In *Social Class, Race and Psychological Development*, edited by Martin Deutsch, Irwin Katz and Arthur R. Jensen. New York: Holt, Rinehart & Winston.

Radke, Marian J., and Helen G. Trager. 1950. "Children's Perception of the Social Roles of Negroes and Whites." *Journal of Psychology* 29: 3–33.

Rainwater, Lee. 1966. "Crucible of Identity; the Negro Lower-Class Family." *Daedalus* 95, no. 1 (Winter): 172–216.

Rodman, Hyman. 1964. "Middle-Class Misconceptions about Lower-Class Families." In *Blue Collar World*, edited by A. B. Shostak and William Gomberg. Englewood Cliffs, N.J.: Prentice-Hall.

Rohrer, John H., and Munro S. Edmonson. 1960. *The Eighth Generation Grows Up*. New York: Harper & Row.

Rose, Arnold. 1948. *The Negro in America*. New York: Harper & Row.

Rosenberg, Morris. 1965. *Society and the Adolescent Self-Image*. Princeton, N.J.: Princeton University Press.

Rushing, William A. 1968. "Individual Behavior and Suicide." In *Suicide*, edited by Jack P. Gibbs. New York: Harper & Row.

Rytina, Joan Huber, William H. Form, and John Pease. 1970. "Income and Stratification Ideology: Beliefs about the American Opportunity Structure." *American Journal of Sociology* 75: 703–16.

Silberman, Charles E. 1964. *Crisis in Black and White*. New York: Random House.

Sterne, Muriel W. 1967. "Drinking Patterns and Alcoholism among American Negroes." In *Alcoholism*, edited by David J. Pittman. New York: Harper & Row.

Suicide in the United States: 1950–1964. 1967. Washington, D.C.: Government Printing Office.

Valentine, Charles A. 1968. *Culture and Poverty*. Chicago: University of Chicago Press.

Vanderpool, James A. 1969. "Alcoholism and Self Concept." *Quarterly Journal of Studies in Alcoholism* 30 (March): 59–77.

Williams, Robin. 1947. *The Reduction of Intergroup Tensions*. SSRC Bulletin no. 57, New York.

The Slave Plantation: Background to Present Conditions of Urban Blacks

ROY SIMON BRYCE-LAPORTE

THE BLACK PRESENT AND THE SLAVE PAST

It is generally agreed upon that the largest number of blacks to come to the United States since 1619 came from Africa directly or by way of the Caribbean. They came as slaves and the most common setting in which they lived, worked, and died was the slave plantation. It can be generally agreed upon, therefore, that the slave plantation constitutes the contextual base-line necessary for arriving at a *fuller understanding*[1] of the behavioral, institutional, and communal development problems of black people in the United States as well as other parts of the New World. This recognition led Wagley to juxtapose against the terms Euro- and Indo-America the term Plantation America (Rubin 1960: 3–5). And, it was none other than E. Franklin Frazier, known for his vehement attacks on the Herskovitsian contention of African survivals, who argued that Plantation America was indeed interchangeable as a term with Negro America, inasmuch as the principal historical influence on New World black culture was indeed the plantation (Rubin 1960: v).

The reference to the slave plantation past as genesis of black problems, black perspectives, and black behavioral patterns is not limited to scholars. Activists, black and white, have made similar claims. Malcolm X, the celebrated black nationalist martyr, and one of the most successful mobilizers of urban black masses, made repeated pleas for an understanding of slavery, if the present-day plight of black people was to be understood. The people in the street in time of greatest crisis, anxiety, and under-organization (i.e., riots) have been known to offer as the on-the-scene reason for their actions "to get Mister Charlie [Whitey] off our backs." The language may be contemporary ghetto talk or grass roots rhetoric, but the sentiments and consciousness behind it are historical, sociological, and point to a persistent problem for black people in America since the beginning of black slavery.

While the organizational-residential context under which blacks were found yesterday may have been the slave plantation, today it is the urban

---

[1] We use the term "fuller understanding" to indicate knowledge which transcends the questions of persistence and functions of social behavior to include process, meaning, and origin as well. Such knowledge is not derivable from traditional synchronic and rigid studies, but must result from historical, comparative, and intuitively creative humanism as well (see Evans-Pritchard, 1951: 58–62; Smith, 1962).

ghetto. Whether the shift from past to present, rural to urban, or planta-tion to ghetto had serious consequences for the life chances, the institu-tional and political-economic development, and the life style and culture of black people, is a question deserving serious sociological study. Whether the contentions of scholars and the charges of activists are valid or correct demand empirical examination. As such, these mandates fall within the scope of what C. Wright Mills (1959) called "sociological imagination"—a history-conscious and problem-derived sociology. This approach requires a sociological understanding of the earliest conditions and problems under which blacks lived before any sociological, historical, psychological, or humanistic sense can be made of their present situation.

It is indeed questionable whether presently available data and empirical technique of the social sciences and history could yield with any precision new and significant information on the nature of relationship between the slave plantation background and present-day conditions and behavior of black Americans. To do so requires information on millions of black, often alien, oppressed, and illiterate souls, spread over one-third of the United States, over the last three hundred fifty years. Merton (1957: 8–9) has warned against premature reaction of sociologists to the demands of their problem-oriented colleagues and problem-ridden public for sociological study and action on such overwhelming problems. His warning was not against ethical or political action per se, but rather against engaging in premature, futile action in light of the stage of development of sociology itself. In other words, Merton advocated a scientific priority of "appro-priate" method and knowledge accumulation over problem resolution. This is in line with his premise that the former will determine, in the final analysis, how much the latter can be accomplished. His position here dif-fers fundamentally from that of Mills (1959: 125–126), who gives prior-ity to public issues and advocates that methods should not limit the choice of problem but largely evolve from the effort to solve such problems. Yet it is by the sociologically imaginative use of what Merton calls "middle-range theorizing"—the effort to pull together theory and fact by way of intermediate levels of formalized derivations and conceptualizations—that the slave plantation, a phenomenon of the past, can be described in sociologically useful terms (Marsh 1964).

American slavery and the slave plantation have been studied for a long time by historians, most of whom pursued their study of the peculiar insti-tution in the ideographic tradition of their field. Stanley Elkin's *Slavery* (1963) represented an important departure from this tradition, in some ways a controversial breakthrough, when he pursued the analogy between the American slave system and the Nazi concentration camp as institu-tionalized systems of closure and totalitarianism which had similar effects on the personality, family, organization, leadership, forms of associational or collective behavior of their inmates—slaves and prisoners-of-war. Sociologically speaking, various questions can be raised about the assumptions and implication of Elkins' work (see Bryce-Laporte 1968; Lane 1971). Notwithstanding, his conceptualization of the slave plantation as a closed and total system is of extreme sociological and political importance. Sociologists have been giving increasing attention to such closed, all-embracing organizations. They refer to them as total institutions. However, there have been few indications that sociologists recognized the slave plantation as a total institution[2] (Bryce-Laporte 1969: 2–8; Yetman 1970).

Sociologically speaking, the visualization of the slave plantation as a total institution permits a shift in its study from that of a peculiar institution to that of a peculiar type of institution. Further, it permits the slave plantation to be studied as a level of social organization about which there is a growing bibliography (Goffman 1961: 123–124). Such a visualization opens the door toward the scholarly discussion of the validity of the historical depth of black problems, black perspectives, and black patterns of behavior which have come to characterize the rhetoric of black nationalism. This research could begin to uncover new dimensions of the condition and quality of urban life for the majority of black people in the United States today, and to evaluate and give meaning to the various ways in which blacks have tried to change those conditions. But, before these potentials can be pursued, the plantation must be treated in terms which will overcome its datedness and peculiarity, as a subject matter, and which will reveal its relevance to present-day concerns.

THE SLAVE PLANTATION AS A TOTAL INSTITUTION

The term total institution is associated principally with Erving Goffman (1961: xiii) who defined it as "a place of residence and work where a large number of like-situated individuals cut off from the wider society for an appreciable period of time, together lead an enclosed, formally administered round of life." Scott Greer (1955) makes the distinction between social organization, the regulatory form of human social behavior, and the social organizational unit, a collective recognized for its specific combination of human social roles and relation. The American slave plantation was both. While it had features of both community and instrumental-formal organization, it was neither. Rather, it shared most of the peculiarities that distinguish other total institutions from these two forms. At the same time it could have been differentiated from other total institutions in terms of its uniqueness or specificity. As a dynamic structure these bases of differentiation and uniqueness were not static, but underwent changes and thus

2 This was evident in the enthusiastic manner in which the late Horace Cayton responded to my own decision to pursue such a study. It would, he felt, create a new vista for viewing the slave plantation.

differed over time (Bryce-Laporte 1968; Edgerton and Sabagh 1962: 263–270; Etzioni 1961; Hillery 1963; Thompson 1959: 26–36).

On the level of purposes and ends, the slave plantation enjoyed similar, though not necessarily the same, specificities as other total institutions. The primary extrinsic goal of the slave planters was economic profit, but it was economic for prestigious rather than capitalistic interests (Genovese 1966a: 28–31). Thus, prestige, aggrandizement, and power over other men was the primary intrinsic goal of the slave plantation, as is common among total institutions. Ownership and management of the slave plantation and immunity from slavery were bases of prestige. Akinness to those who owned was a basis of prestige and aggrandizement. Such prestige and aggrandizement were gained at the expense of others who were owned or managed, were not immune to slavery, or were more akin to slaves.

The specialized instrumental responsibility of the slave plantation was commercial agriculture. Its other instrumental responsibility was the custody of a segment of the population perceived of as unusually different. This latter responsibility is a universal service-function among total institutions, even though all "unusually different" segments are not viewed as negative. They may be unusually "good" (i.e., religious men), or they may be unusually "bad" (i.e., dangerous criminals). They are in some common-sense terms, however, not conceived of or treated as "equals" with the rest of the "normal" world.

The condition in the United States was one of great access to land and limited access to free, exploitable labor. The slave population allowed, on the one hand, the maximum exploitation of slaves as producers of profit, or, perhaps more accurately, income derived from commercial agriculture, and later, commercial breeding. At the same time it allowed for maximum confinement, containment, and control of these slaves who were so "different" (unequal) and socially undesired by the larger society. It must be recalled that the early non-Hispanic colonizers of the United States were not motivated by the zeal of extending empire and converting or colonizing people. Rather, they came as minorities to America in flight from what they perceived as corrupted or constraining conditions, in hope of establishing religious and political utopias based on homogeneity (Handlin 1958; Morgan 1958). Thus, not the Indians but their lands were seen as frontiers, and Africans were seen as human tools rather than human targets of frontier development. The physical and cultural differences and distance between Africans and Anglos gave cause and were conducive to the establishment of the slave plantation as a custodial institution (Jordan 1969; Szasz 1970: 123–139). The rural setting and economic orientation of the colonizers were conducive to the establishment of the slave plantation as a commercial, agricultural organization; in other words, a formal-instrumental institution.

Black slavery was supported by advocates and arguments. The proslavery arguments which covered a wide range were neither inconsistent collections of thoughts nor a mere repertoire of rationalizations. They were assertions by the society and its planter class of the various purposes or ends of the slave system (McKitrick 1963; Wish 1961). Even though the assertions were inaccurate and injurious to the Africans and Negroes, these arguments were components of the ideology of the South and its conception of Africans and Negroes qua laborers, citizens, and human beings. These arguments were aspects of a theory of human nature, in this case a psychology and ideology which justified and stipulated the treatment of slaves (Goffman 1961: 129–180; Kardiner and Ovesey 1962: 42–47). They fit almost perfectly Goffman's (1961: 5) typology of total institutions by which he categorizes their specialized service-function to the larger society:

> (1) those established to care for persons felt to be both incapable and harmless; (2) those to care for persons felt to be incapable but unintended threats to the community; (3) those established to protect the community against those who are intended threats to its welfare; (4) those established to pursue some worklike and instrumental task. . . .

Another level of comparable specificities between the slave plantation and other total institutions involves external relations, especially with the larger society. The history of the slave plantation in the United States indicates that it endured for almost three hundred years and as it did, it evolved internally as well as in its external relations. Limitations on its endurance and involvement were imposed by the peculiar historical, physical, geographical, and social constraints in which it was located. Hence, not only was the slave plantation never totally static, it was never totally isolated or totally independent of its larger habitat. Its history, then, is one of variation in interdependence, and consonance with the larger southern society (Thompson 1959; Genovese 1966a).

The American plantation was at the start a rather dependent, circumscribed, and noninfluential organization. It was formed and charged in the beginning as an instrument of the colonial, economic, and governmental bureaucracy. Its hold on its inmates was temporary and limited. In time it developed power, potentiality for exchange, scope, and pervasiveness. Its highest level of development was reached when it became a producer of cash crops, having great land resources which its instrumental specialization—extensive commercial agriculture—also demanded.

During the period of American political independence and democratization and the discontinuance of regular market relations with Europe, the importance of the custodial and specialized service-functions of the slave plantation were underplayed. Manumission increased and the slave trade was declared illegal. At that time the slave plantation was losing its custodial and specialized service-functions; it was approaching a more rehabilitative and communal model. These developments were short-lived and finally reversed with new demands for American cotton now being refined with the recently invented cotton gin. Then, external recruitment of slaves was resumed, and antislave trading laws were ignored. When external recruitment proved inadequate and insufficient to meet the demands, internal recruitment, external retention, and status ascription were reemphasized. Thus, the custodial services were reinstated anew and an ideology of difference and therefore need for control were revived.

The period of reassertion or reemergence of the slave plantation was one which witnessed the broadening of the scope of control to embrace the slave's entire life (not just all activities at a given time in life). It was a period marked by the increase in power and pervasiveness of the slave plantation over the slave society and the men who populated it. Planters dominated the politics and economics of the South, directed policies in their own self-interest, and defended that interest to the point of war. The pervasiveness of the slave plantation extended to freeman, runaway slave, and paroled slave even in locations as far as the West and the North, as well as cities of the South. It affected the treatment they received, the laws legislated against them, and threatened their security and freedom.

To the extent that the above plantation was impermeable, it gave to its slaves more material security and benign or paternal treatment than the freemen and runaways of the rural South experienced. This increased the pervasiveness and saliency of the plantation over its inmates, inasmuch as it may have led to their cherishing physical comfort or security over freedom. To the extent that the plantation was permeable, it reflected the basic status differences and theory or psychology of human nature held by the larger society about slaves, and treated them as inferior beings who could be exploited, contained, and suppressed. The pervasiveness of the slave plantation regimen was quite evident in the frontier and antebellum cities where the restriction of slaves and even of free blacks by symbolic barriers, such as Jim Crow laws, very much resembled plantation standards.

Another level of comparable specificities which the slave plantation shared with total institutions includes contextual features represented by its structure, processes, and inherent paradoxes and dilemmas. By and large, the slave plantation was characterized by a coercive-alienative control-compliance structure. Given its profit-making goal, such a control-compliance structure was incongruent. From Weber through Etzioni, sociologists have recognized that the most effective employer-employee relationship in profit-making organizations is one of manipulation and calculation with interjection of human relationships. The slave plantation (like most total institutions) was likely incongruent for another reason: its dual goal or orientation (Etzioni 1961). Prestige, the universal intrinsic goal, rivaled and undercut profit-making (Genovese 1966a). In addition, the slave plantation shared other structural features or concomitants of total institutions. These included a single authority structure headed by the master or his surrogate, often an overseer, and the rigid stratification and segregation of slaves and management. Also included were various institutionalized structural modes of impositions and deprivations which differentiated the two segments and discriminated against the slaves—imposition of residence and occupational roles, generalization of status, regimented schedule of activities, deprivation of privacy, power, property, free movement, indigenous primary organization, cultural development, and role repertoire.

The context represented by the slave plantation also included a set of interrelated operations and practices which were part of the overall rationale for the successful and smooth running of the estate. Among these were recruitment, socialization and mortification, a privilege-punishment system, tension-release, rehabilitation and aggrandizement, discharge, stigmatization, and so on. Many of these processes were mutually exclusive or inherently incompatible and thus, together with the other levels of complexities, created various dilemmas and paradoxes for the slave plantations, as is true of other total institutions.

The dilemmas of custody versus rehabilitation and of mortification versus aggrandizement (Edgerton and Sabagh 1962: 263–272; Etzioni 1961; Tittle and Tittle 1965: 216–221) were very closely related in the case of the slave plantation. Comparable to other total institutions, the conflict experienced by the slave plantation in regard to these two dilemmas was light. In establishments where discharge is common and thus confinement is not indefinite, the issue of how much to stress custodial stringency over rehabilitation becomes a very serious issue. Similarly, in establishments where inmates are derived basically from external sources and are likely to be returned to such sources, the judicious balancing between mortification and aggrandizement becomes a problematic matter. These conditions were true for the plantation only in colonial days.

In the heyday of the slave plantation, however, custody was generally perpetual, inmate status was ascriptive, recruitment and selection criteria were internal, and physical discharge took the form of death or escape. Moreover, the tasks and roles required of slaves by the plantation regimen were generally rudimentary and routinized. Thus, there was no great urge for intensive socialization or rehabilitation programs outside of the case of newly arriving Africans or former free Negroes or city slaves. Likewise, the issue of mortification versus aggrandizement was academic for slaves other than the cases just mentioned. That is not to say that the dilemmas did not exist or that problems did not emerge. The fact that slaves had to be punished for and prevented from escaping or doing harm to their managers or owners would indicate that the mortification process was not always thorough. In fact, it could only be so if slaves were killed psychologically or physically. In addition, even though slave aggrandizement tended to be pathologically limited, and false-based, it created problems of maintaining a totally conforming slave population.

A third dilemma, the humanistic-bureaucratic dilemma, is not unknown to most formal-instrumental organizations or to communities or societies with bureaucratic orientations. However, it perhaps was more strongly felt on the slave plantation than most other total institutions (Moore 1941: 191–201). The slave plantation attempted more than any other total institution to view and treat its inmates as subhuman property. On the other hand, the slave plantation came closest perhaps, among many though not all total institutions, to acknowledging the equality in essence (not in status) between inmates and staff, particularly by its sponsorship and participation in family formation among slaves, and between them and managers or owners. The moral, ethical, and emotional sensitivities, and the feelings of attachment and commitment associated with the family, particularly with women and children, were more than the closedness and cruelty of the slave plantation could contain. It is true that the sponsoring of family formation and limited recognition of slave families were largely efforts to perpetuate the slave plantation and assure an internal and reliable source of recruitment. But it is also true that these practices brought out of slaves their human qualities and drew out of other men a degree of action, attention, and attentiveness that men reserve only for other men. Such practices represent the kinds of concerns and involvement which beset institutions whose work is people (Goffman 1961: 74–92). Thus the statement by U. B. Phillips (1963: 217) that: "All in all, the slave regime was a curious blend of . . . tyranny and benevolence, of antipathy and affection."

A last level of comparable specificities between the slave plantation and other total institutions is the behavior of inmates. From the distance of the outside observer, the context presented by the slave plantation as the slave appears is one of total and eternal closedness and control, one of exploitation, imposition, and deprivation, in which the slaves never could have a chance to consciously and deliberately act without reckoning with the staff and standards of the slave plantation. Even if this picture has been exaggerated, the presence of the slave plantation did have a great impact on and saliency for the slaves' behavior. While it should not be doubted that the behavior of slaves may have had some impact and saliency for the staff and standards of the plantation in return, it seems futile to deny that the behavior of slaves, especially the sustained, overt, collective-organized behavior, had to be very adjustive and truncated. Slave behavior was comprised of varying efforts, some in submission to the dictates of the plantation and others in defense against it. The circumstances of the slaves, especially those on large plantations, were not only different from the circumstances of the masters and free citizens, but so, too, their culture. In other words, the culture of the plantation was dual or plural, inasmuch as there were pronounced qualitative and quantitative differences in role repertoire and organization between the slave and the master classes.

The plantation staff did not promote the emergence or reemergence of roles of leaders or of organizations among the slaves which were property, protest, or power-oriented. To have permitted this would have been irrational and a direct contradiction of all the purposes or ends of the slave plantation, its ideology, and psychology of human nature, and would have threatened its entire structure as a total institution. Ownership of physical property among plantation slaves was almost nonexistent and limited to a few household supplies, extra clothing, and the crops or stocks that they raised on land assigned to them. They were neither free to purchase nor work toward purchase of durable, basic property; e.g., land, home, and the like. They were most often not able to purchase their own freedom. They could not own other persons as property or slaves and whatever claims they had over the spouses, children, and parents were largely offset, inasmuch as in legal terms they were all mere properties of the master. The pretense of ownership also reached overdetermined dimensions with some slaves, who at one and the same time acted as property and as part owner of plantation and planter (in much the same way children "own" their homes and parents).

The conditions of control, totalness, and remoteness which characterized the slave plantation of the United States made open, sustained, collective resistance among the slaves virtually impossible. Most successful resistance was individual, isolated, and rapid. Collective resistance was generally sporadic, if open, and necessarily subtle, if sustained. In other words, the very conditions which made open, sustained, collective resistance infeasible made more subtle, covert, elusive forms of group action sustainable and prevalent. The "underlife" (Goffman 1961: 199) or "covert culture" (Rose 1969: 623–630) of the slaves consisted largely of secondary adjustments and these adjustments were, in fact, subtle, elusive roles and sociocultural relations which were prevalent and sustained among them. The underlife of the slaves included, among other things, prayer meetings, spirituals, prayers, folk tales, an invisible church, and an underground escape organization. Passing as white or as free; slipping away from plantations through slave country and to free society; and the protecting of other slaves engaged in these maneuvers, represented the most daring forms of successful resistance that American slaves were able to sustain. Thus, psychological and physical flight (rather than direct fighting) became the modus operandi of American slave resistance (Bryce-Laporte 1969: 6).

Flight or escape required a different form of organization and role repertoire than would be required for open defiance. It demanded more invisible and covert bonds and called for cunning and elusive skills rather than confrontation and power. By the same token, however, such escapist actions were not sufficient to accommodate the large numbers desiring freedom. Thus, many slaves found relief in removal activities; e.g., folklore, spirituals, prayers, work songs, and in institutional ceremonies; e.g., prayer meetings, festive celebrations, and so forth. Such removal activities and institutional ceremonies had tension-releasing rather than freedom-rendering functions. They represented means of expression and rebellion rather than means of strategic revolution. Given the limitations of these expressive and escapist actions, there were occasional sporadic riots and rebellions among the slaves. However, these more aggressive forms of defiance were generally suppressed in a vicious public manner and were often followed by the tightening of custodial regulations. The failure of resistance was in part an indication of the lack of necessary organization and power for successful paramilitary rebellion. On the other hand, the failure indirectly boosted the invisible underground approach or led to sublimation of tensions in some other ways.

Few rehabilitative activities of the kind that could precipitate, or stem from, an anticipation of freedom, were permitted or promoted among slaves. Education and religion for slaves were discouraged in the earlier periods. They were encouraged as the institution began its decline around the period of the Declaration of Independence. Fear of rebellion and the reemergence of the importance and predominance of the slave plantation were accompanied by reimposition of bans on both education and religion. The rationale for discouraging these practices was neatly tied to the purpose and nature of the slave plantation. It made no sense to allow education as long as slaves were to be seen as subhumans, condemned to perpetual confinement and exploitation, and replaceable by local and foreign recruits. The nature of work on the plantation required no sophisticated training and time for such superfluous activities could be used in maintenance and production activities (Woodson 1919: 153–154).

Once banned, open education of slaves was not permitted or practiced by most planters or managers of plantations. Religion was once more permitted among the slaves only when planters were convinced that it would make slaves more placid rather than provoke unrest and instill a human awareness among them. Planters took their house slaves to services with them and often-times permitted field slaves to attend their own prayer meetings alone. Both religious practices were largely viewed as removal activities which modulated the distance, severity, tension, and formality of the slave plantation regimen with highly charged emotionalism, and, at the same time, promoted conformity and compassion.

The slave plantation regimen discouraged the founding of indigenous or autonomous primary bonds among slaves. It finally conceded some such privileges in the form of the family only when it seemed necessary for the perpetuation of the plantation and not threatening to its custodial or specialized responsibilities. In the early stages of slavery the sex ratio was imbalanced. Slaves were mostly men, separated from their traditional family, and given the sex imbalance and the barriers to interracial sex; the presence of a stable union between slaves on the level of family may have been uncommon. Over time, family or quasi-family relations among the slaves were largely of the nature of secondary adjustments—unsponsored, extralegitimate, and somewhat covert relations. As secondary adjustments, awareness and acknowledgment of them by the staff were less likely, and accommodations to allow for these unions were at first unusual and gradual.

It was, however, during the days of the larger plantation and of the abolition of the slave trade that the slave family was promoted with vigor: a behavioral pattern among inmates that is sponsored or demanded by the staff. It was now of the nature of a primary adjustment. The fact that awareness and acknowledgment of family formation among the slaves led to certain allowances and accommodations by masters and overseers, indicates that the plantation as well as the slaves underwent categorical redefinition. The direction of this change, inasmuch as it involved the total institution adjusting to its inmates, illustrated the point mentioned but left undeveloped by Goffman (1961: 188–193). The fact that the change involved promoting a family among inmates of a total institution suggests that it is as important to understand the conditions leading up to the emergence of the slave family, as it is to understand the consequences of the plantation context on such a family. The latter is too often stressed at the expense of the former.

The "sponsored" slave family was a means of providing and rearing internal recruits (Frazier 1939). It was presumed that since every member of the family was a slave he was controllable and thus the unit would not be disruptive of the larger establishment (Elkins 1963: 53–55). Consequently, the slave family was most likely truncated as a primary group, both in terms of internal roles and of institutional functions and form. This holds true using either the African or Anglo-American models of family during that time. Slave narratives suggest that this did not mean that strong bonds were not sustained among members of families separated forcibly or never permitted to relate freely. Furthermore, the strength of such bonds was reaffirmed by the risks slaves took and the routes they tramped to be near or visit their loved ones.[3] The presence of the family unearthed the self-awareness and primary group loyalties among slave families and also elicited emotional involvement and sympathetic concern for the slaves from the staff and larger society. Such expressions of humanity confounded in direct and indirect ways the impersonal, subhuman standards normally imposed on the slaves and subhuman limitations associated with them.

Over and beyond the various latent forms of behavior of the slaves, the slave plantation regimen organized and scheduled most of the activities of the slaves. A substantial part of the activities of the slaves was regimented, routinized, and closely supervised. They were the behaviors of the slaves which were most directly reflective of and determined by the context represented by the slave plantation. Such behaviors were also of the nature of what Goffman calls primary adjustments. They consisted of obedience and conformity of the slaves to the clear, premeditated, fixed mandates of the plantation regimen. It is largely in reference to these levels of behavior that Elkins (1963) seemed to conclude that the slave plantation was responsible for the predominance of the "Sambo personality"—dependence, childishness, and obedience—among American slaves. In fact, Elkins' analysis falters because he inadvertently accepts the prophecy or stereotype of the clown or Sambo as given (Allport 1958: 27). He then proceeds to explain it and to use it to chastise the system, as well as to demand a change. Elkins equivocates between self and the presentation of self, between being and acting. In so doing he contributed to the apparent verification of a stereotype which certainly is not completely accurate about the past and that has proven more harmful than useful as a ploy for correcting the present situation (see Bryce-Laporte, 1971).

Goffman clearly does not subscribe to the notion of a totally subdued or zombified self as being characteristic of inmates. Rather, he views them (inmates) as merely powerless to successfully destroy or radically transform the total institution. This powerlessness lies in the success of the total institution in containing and controlling the inmates as well as in the frailty of any collective disruptive efforts which they may be able to try against the total institution. Thus, Goffman portrays a picture of the inmates as a powerless and trapped aggregation of human beings, whose only rational recourse other than submission is escape. Other than physical escape which could mean death or suicide, Goffman (1961: 319)

---

[3] Historians are producing increasing evidence of a high percentage of two-parent households and marriages among ex-slaves during Reconstruction. While we must be careful not to generalize too extensively from these findings, they do make plausible the argument that an ethic and the bonds of family organization were already strong among all classes of blacks, even during slavery (Blassingame 1970; Guttman 1971; Robinson 1969).

accentuates various modes of subtle social acts, involved psychological mechanisms of escape, expression, and self-management which occur because of the nature of the human self. "Recalcitrance is not an incidental mechanism of defense but rather an essential constituent of the self" (see Lasch and Frederickson, 1967: 315–329). In addition, he suggests various organization inconsistencies and external contingencies which create conflict in and affect the control and efficiency of the establishment. Hence, it may be argued that there are those levels on which the totality of the total institution is not thoroughly effective; e.g., in confrontation with the selves of its inmates, in its own organizational operation with people as work, and its dependency on and permeability to the larger society (with all the latter's dynamics, conflicts, and complexities).

In Goffman's own analysis, he makes some reference to slavery and estates, but at no time concentrates on the slave plantation as a specific referent. The consequence is that his treatment of institutional-societal relationship is less developed than the first two considerations. Somehow, there is seemingly no explicit beginning and no conceivable end to a specific total institution or type, and very little discussion takes place on the stages of relations which developed between institution and society. So that, where Goffman speaks about the moral career of the inmate (i.e., preclinical, clinical, and postclinical), he treats change on the level of the individual, less on the level of the institution, and certainly not on the level of the larger social order. Even though in another context Goffman (1963) speaks about the roles of watchdog agencies and the "wise" friends and ex-inmates who protect the welfare of inmates, he does not deal with the possibility of a successful revolution by inmates; that is to say, the complete destruction of the total institution and the total elimination of structural and stigmatic legacies it often leaves behind. To leave this sociological task undone would be to fail to derive added insight from the slave plantation experience, with all its historical and dynamic uniqueness as a type of institution whose beginning and end is recorded. Such lessons for the cause of black men still affected by its normative pervasiveness should not remain unlearned.

The question can be asked, in what total institution have inmates been able to accomplish by their own actions a lasting or substantially effective revolution? That is, in what cases have inmates been able as a collective to overthrow their oppressors and destroy the custodial system, the ideology of inequality which led to its establishment, and the stigma and social restrictions which follow membership in it? Even though studies of inmate culture have shown differences in the disposition of different types of inmates toward their stay and status, none shows inmates as ordinarily defined carrying out such a successful revolution. Riots or massive demonstrations by prisoners in penitentiaries and concentration camps tend to be futile or limited beyond the expressive or spectacular level. Such actions may call attention to the adversity of their conditions, but have not directly or immediately ended in their release or the destruction of laws or penal institution. Perhaps there are cases of greater success among the religious bodies or communities which become secular as a group, but it is not known to begin with how much they had already undergone some transformation from total institutions to community in the eyes of the larger world and certainly where the label and ideology associated with their confinement are positive, their chances of losing identity are less problematic.

With reference to slavery, it is generally believed that it was the slave revolts in the Caribbean and Latin America that reached the heights worthy of being considered successful revolution. They were successful inasmuch as they represented massive, persistent, organized actions by slaves that led to various impressive arrays of autonomous states—from sovereign nations to almost closed communities. Such feats were impressive because they overcame the power and pervasiveness of the old order and supplanted it with a new order. The existence of such autonomous forms of social organization negated the myths of inequality entertained about black men and used to rationalize slavery: black slaves proved that they were able to defeat white men by force and wit; establish and defend the frontier, property, and community they gained in battle or in pursuit; and shelter and protect those persons dear to them, as well as those practices that they valued culturally. Those black men had to be accepted as men, and equals, even if reluctantly and only temporarily.

There have been many efforts made to explain the differences between North American slave resistance and those of the Caribbean and Latin America. Often these explanations beclouded the fact that there were also unsuccessful revolts, unorganized and expressive protests in the other Americas, as well; that slaves betrayed other slaves there, too; and that ex-slaves and half-breeds were often used to suppress slave revolts and runaways in proportions unknown to North America. Given the condition of slavery, especially wherever that meant being inmates, it could not be expected that slaves could succeed without a conducive outer setting— both social and environmental. Hence, it is beyond the individual or institutional level that one must turn for an adequate understanding of the form, persistence, magnitude, and impact of resistance. One must turn to the larger society, to specific times in the history of that society for insights into the relationship between the total institution and the society and the definition entertained by that society about the inmate population. In other words, the synchretic, micro-sociological approach must be combined with a historical (perhaps comparative) macro-sociological approach to yield that fuller understanding.

In the case of the United States, slaves generally lacked both the internal and external prerequisites for successful massive defiance. As we have argued in opposition to Elkins, this did not lead them (at least not all of them) to be subdued or zombified. Rather, as Goffman's approach would suggest, they were powerless and trapped, and thus more likely to be elusive than either aggressively resistant or internally submissive. In the absence of elaborate internal or external prerequisites, escape ranged from subtle social and personal modes of eluding and expression to physical escape by way of running away, suicide, or infanticide. The conditions of control in the American slave plantations, the presence of a small minority of free blacks or friendly whites, the strangeness and severity of the physical environment, and the absence of extra-institutional rivalry, prohibited massive action. Given the conditions which runaway and rebel slaves encountered in the antebellum United States, many were forced to live by concealing their real identity (passing), or by residing beyond the boundaries of the societal-legal setting in which slave planters held hegemony. Thus, in the United States much external assistance took the form of the Underground Railroad and various abolitionist and colonization movements which organized and assisted escapees and agitated for freedom. However, for the most part, outside support for inmates was weak in political power, small in number, and generally not aggressively or violently defiant in action (John Brown and his like being exceptions).

Elkins sought to demonstrate that in the case of the American slaves, not only did they not engage in massive revolutionary efforts, but that whenever they did, it was usually under the leadership of ex-slaves or freemen (in Goffman's term, wise ex-inmates). Moreover, these and other efforts by abolitionists were ineffectual in the South because of the nature of the southern antebellum society. It lacked institutional arrangements for channeling rivalry, reform, or radicalism; it was pervaded by complete consensus in favor of slavery and in opposition to any intermediate arrangements for gradually rehabilitating the slaves; and it treated all advocates of abolition and equality as subversives or outside agitators (Elkins 1963: 192–222). Moreover, planters were not merely head staff of their estates, but they formed the dominant class in their society. Proslavery interests thus permeated slave society (Genovese 1966a).

The slave plantation was, in fact, simply a regional and historical adaptation of the institutionalized embodiment of white racism which pervaded the larger society. Slavery took other forms in the urban areas and in the North, and where slavery did not exist discrimination, segregation, and exploitation did. Perhaps the most telling point was the fact that freedmen, especially in the antebellum South and the "open" West, were often deprived of a property base and frontier land on which to build communities, economic-political power, and to gain self-respect (Bittle and Geiss 1957: 147–160; Berwanger 1967; Litwack 1961; Pease and Pease 1963; Hill 1946).

Even after Emancipation and the Civil War, they were denied the acre and the mule, and, later gerrymandered from local control. They were denied land and frontier—the basic prerequisites of honor, mobility, and power in a traditional, agrarian, feudal state. Inasmuch as the country was developing a capitalistic structure, this disenfranchisement proved to be crucial in crystallizing their alienated relationship to property—the principal source of power in a capitalistic society. They were condemned as a people to be nonpropertied producers operating under tenuous imaginings of political freedom and power.

Denial of the basic material resources to which they were always attached also meant denial of the symbols and statutes through which they would have been redefined and recognized as free, equal, and competitive men by their fellow men. In the words of Frank Tannenbaum (1946) they were denied a "moral personality"; i.e., social recognition as equal men, free and equal citizens, and therefore the opportunity to prove their manhood and citizenry.

Slavery, as Tannenbaum (1946: vii) argued, is a matter of definitions of men by other men, which come to give reason and rationalization for certain institutional arrangements by which some men are differentiated, segregated, and exploited by their fellow men. Thus, the appearance and disappearance of a specific institutional context (i.e., plantation), does not necessarily lead to a change in the basic definition, but may reflect efforts to resolve conflicting pressures or regulate coalescent interests. Hence, it is as important to study the developmental history of the society, the institutional forms in which its ideologies regarding man and race are expressed at different times, the degree to which these changes in form reflect the impact of modernization rather than ideological revolution, as it is to study the nature and consequences of these contextual changes on the condition and quality of life of the "pariah group" and on their chances for real rehabilitation (full acceptance as equals).

When seen from a comparative perspective, slavery and plantation are not coterminous, each can exist independently of the other. In the United States not only was there urban slavery and other nonplantation forms of slavery, but it was noticeable particularly in the South that as certain locations became more urbanized, plantations were replaced by smaller compounds (with slave quarters and fences, nevertheless). Plantation codes were replaced by Jim Crow municipal laws, while patrollers continued to exist. In line with one notion of urbanization, city slaves had more choices, greater freedom of movement, and a more diffused authority structure, but as slaves they still had to deal with the reality of confinement. Physical closure was merely replaced by legal closure (Cash 1941: 103; Franklyn 1956: 1–9; Wade 1964: 266–270; Meier and Rudwick 1969: 14–19). What is more, the official cessation of slavery did not lead to the total redefinition of black men as equals. Van Woodward (1968) correctly referred to equality as the "deferred commitment." In Tannenbaum's view, American blacks were not permitted to shed their slavery "stigma"; what Goffman (1963) calls "spoiled identity."

The Ghetto as Legacy

The abolition of slavery and the disappearance of the slave plantation can be likened to the sudden destruction of any total institution by external sources. The afflicted are usually transferred to another total institution of the same type. That is, until their social definition or the larger society's attitudes toward the afflicted have changed, special institutions will be developed to quarantine and service them. In fact, whatever the emergency structure that is used to hold and treat them, it will then take on the identity of a specific total institutional type by virtue of its association with the afflicted; e.g., prisons for the bad, asylums for the mad, reservations for the useless, concentration camps for the dangerous and disdained.

Accordingly we should not be surprised that blacks have increasingly been quarantined into urban ghettos, disproportionately to more conventional but negatively labeled total institutions, and continue to be deprived of frontier, property, power, or community. Nor should we be surprised at the structure of these new locales. These present forms of institutionalized racism are simply indications that blacks have not undergone, in the eyes of their former masters, what Peter Berger and Thomas Luckmann (1966: 157–167) call "successful alteration"; that is, sufficient rehabilitation to be accepted fully and treated as equals. But, as pointed out, the denial of rehabilitative opportunities is perhaps as old and institutionalized as the denial of a rehabilitated status. Slavery was intended as a self-sustaining system—a vicious circle of injustice. Military and moral pressures, perhaps economic ones, militated against the persistence of slavery, and urbanization militated against the prevalence of plantations today, but underlying those new urban forms is that lingering definition of blacks as contemptuous unequals. And, built into their operations and structures, are mechanisms for maintaining and reinforcing that inequality.

The ghetto then is not simply an expression of unequal urban development or black social disorganization. It is an expression of the racial legacy of slavery, an urban adaptation of a historically racist society. The phrase "to get Mr. Charlie [Whitey, the Man] off our backs" is at minimum a recognition of that legacy. It is obviously derived from the "ole Massa" tradition of slave plantation days. And while from an objective analytic stance the ghetto as an urban condition is much more complex and diffused than the plantation, it is sociologically fruitful to speculate on the similarities and differences between the two social forms. In fact, the concern should go further to inquire as to which blacks utter such phrases and when. It is already interesting to hear them uttered at times of anxiety and desperation, for it implies a visceral, deeply felt sentiment. To the extent that under such circumstances the range extends beyond just ghetto dwellers to the wider black population, it is suggested that as an utterance of purpose and a definition of a situation, this sentiment is widely shared as well.

Compared to a plantation, the proximity of the black ghetto to the model of a total institution is less obvious but, nevertheless, it shares a number of the anticommunal characteristics of the old estate, even though slavery as such is nonexistent in the United States today. The black ghetto is not owned or managed by a single individual, but from the eyes of the black residents it is often perceived to be owned and managed by one single, exclusive group—whites. "Mr. Charlie" or "the Man" is thus a label for a collective referent with little regard for sex, age, ethnicity, or number. It is a recognition that on certain structural levels the discrete stratification of people into white dominant and black subordinate within a given urban residential context is not a crucial break from the usually smaller and more simplified plantation structure but rather an elaboration. The extrinsic objectives of the ghetto may be multiple, diffused, and less clear, but its intrinsic function is quite similar to the plantation—to legitimize differences among men in terms of superiority and acceptability of those who *can* live outside from those who *must* live within. Its specialized functions are not always as utilitarian as the plantation, but it shares the same universal functions as the plantation—to exercise custody over the different or unequal. Even though the physical boundaries are often less static than the plantation, they are always made salient in the minds of the populace. Police patrols, uncooperative taxi drivers and garbage collectors, unscrupulous real estate agents and merchants, and uninhibited black pedestrians by their activities give clues to the shift in boundary from time to time. The scope of confinement in the ghetto is felt particularly by those residents who are unemployed or for other reasons are forced to perform most of their daily activities within the local neighborhood. This saliency is even more sharply felt by those whose imaginative or intellectual faculties are not sufficiently developed to provide psychological escape from their physical confinement.

Even though urban power structures are generally viewed as more diffused and democratic than older agrarian forms, in the case of the black ghetto the power structure tends to be in fact unilaterally white and remote at its highest levels. This is still generally true notwithstanding the growing number of black mayors in American cities, particularly as it becomes clear that white suburban and rural populations, through state and county governments, maintain a stranglehold on urban development. The problems and priorities of the ghetto dwellers are often ignored or relegated to a secondary concern unless by implication the calamities they represent are thought to have far-reaching effects. Property and space are often owned by white absentee proprietors. And whether the loci of employment are local or not, unemployment tends to be high, various forms of social ills tend to prevail, and there is a proliferation of welfare and other forms of corrective or paternalistic agencies. In addition to many such agencies being nonrepresentative and substandard, they tend to be noneffective in that they neither improve the rehabilitative potential of their wards nor change the local conditions. They also tend to be ritualistic, repressive, or both. In fact, they often come to recruit, mortify, and stigmatize ghetto dwellers and, therefore, add to the justification of their continued segregation. With reference to their repressiveness, it takes various forms from outright police brutality to more subtle means of social control and cooptation. The institutional network of the ghetto thus represents a system of social control and sanction which is executed by way of coercion and control of crucial services, and is designed to stifle creative individuality, daring leadership, or viable local cooperative groupings which in any way seem likely to undermine the present relationship of the ghetto to the rest of the society, and by extension, blacks to whites.

The ghetto then represents many things not normally found in standard white or establishment-sociological literature. It is an arena of uneven confrontation of will, sentiments, and interests between two traditionally antagonistic forces—those who have achieved status, power, frontier, and community, and those whom they seek to prevent from acquiring such bases of equality (Clark 1965). Surely it is also the arena of contest and simultaneously of communion (Kaplan 1969: 164–176; Neuwirth 1969: 148–165; Pitt 1970) among blacks themselves, who, beyond the monolithic category imposed upon them by their white antagonists, comprise an array of different statuses, types, and stages of social development. But despite these internal differentiations there is a shared feeling among blacks of not having undergone a complete change of status in the eyes of white America, that their conditions have not completely changed *as a people*, even if as individuals. Thus, as *black* individuals, their acquired statuses are threatened and their individualities overlooked, especially in time of crisis.

It is this frustration, ending sometimes in futility, sometimes in a fighting mood, that such utterances express. It is a feeling of unfulfillment. For, while the ghetto has become the modern birthplace of some of the most ambitious creative schemes for self-development and self-determination in black America, it has also been the scene of some of the most telling catastrophes and fiascos. The situation is complicated further by accumulated tensions. Tension converts into distress as the immediate causes seem not solely externally derived but also stem from internal frictions and disabilities within the black population (Comer 1967: 21–27; Kramer 1970: 213–253). Thus the utterances and actions of ghetto dwellers re-

The Slave Plantation / 87

flect not simply a style of life nor preoccupation with the present problems, but rather the burdensome baggage of bondage and oppression which antedates the contemporary and the urban.

The history of the United States has been described as that of the acquisition and development of the frontiers. Some historians have declared the frontier closed since the end of the nineteenth century (Turner 1893). Elkins and McKitrick (1954: 321–353) have ably demonstrated that an important concomitant of frontier development has been local community development and participatory democracy. The history of the United States has also been described as a movement from rural to urban society. Urbanization, of which all of this is a part, is then a historical process, one that has been defined as an increase in the complexity or scale of social organization (Greer 1962: 33–66). However, urbanization is not equally experienced or shared by all people or regions of a society at the same time (Myrdal 1957). That is just part of the complexity. Another aspect of that complexity has to do with a *masking* process which accompanies urbanization, so that old issues are constantly being replaced by new issues whether they have been solved or not. Given the inequality in the society, the problems of the powerful and articulate in-groups are often attended to and solutions sanctioned over those of less powerful, inarticulate groups. In fact, given the power and interest of those who constitute the "establishment" (and I use this term broadly to include even radical white groups in the United States, who are not in power or in conformity with government but nevertheless control resources and hold privileged positions, in terms of being heard, over non-whites), the problems and priorities of black people are often submerged or redefined away from the uncomfortable and the threatening basic truths of American racism that predate and underlie urban arrangements.

It is a basic truth of American racism that blacks as a group in the United States have been deprived of frontier and its concomitants of community and participatory democracy in respectable proportions. The plantation may have had, as one of its original functions, the opening of the frontier (Gray 1933; Lynd 1967: 139), but while the slaves labored within the plantation to open that frontier, they were deprived of access to that frontier and of the opportunity to establish communities in the Plantation South. On the other hand, the notion of frontier, a more symbolic phenomenon, a sense of having to achieve, acquire, and exercise domain over something of value, must have been cherished by them in their quest to be equals in the American context. Given the racialistically instigated lag between black and white political-economic developments, it is not difficult to understand that the notion of frontier persists among blacks when it may have died or even been transformed in meaning for whites. Given the power differentiation between whites and blacks today, it is not difficult to appreciate either, that the present urban institutions are not oriented to articulate or reinforce the notions of black people over those of whites. Hence the very notions of ethnic frontier and local neighborhood which are essential for providing impetus to the movement of black people at this particular moment in their history, are issued negative values or secondary priorities by urban agencies, in contrast to the thrust of the Black Muslims, CORE, Republic of New Africa, Black Studies, the Black Academy of Arts and Letters, the Institute of the Black World, and other current expressions of nationalist domain.

The history of the United States has been described as that of waves of immigrants, each motivated by notions of frontier, which they eventually came to enjoy either as plural communities or as parts of an integrated political-economic arrangement or both (Gordon 1964; Lewis 1969). Blacks, one of the oldest immigrant groups, despite the coercive nature of their arrival to America and their brutalizing slave experience, rejected colonization as a scheme and instead chose the way of other Americans—integrated communities or homogeneous ones within a presumably larger integrated total society. Both efforts were frustrated by the two evil white twins of power and paternalism. They have been refused the alternative of equal participation in American democracy or that of establishing control over their own communities. Thus the frustration continues, and the fundamental fight for black frontier persists.

The scene of the struggle today is the ghetto—"getting Mr. Charlie off our back," "getting ourselves together," and "getting our own thing going." The very ordering of these phrases is suggestive of the mood, momentum, and direction of current black movement—from the earlier unorganized, tension-releasing rebellions of Watts, Newark, and Detroit, to the later organized community- and institution-building struggles at Ocean Hill-Brownsville, Newark, and Atlanta. The present can be history and black ghettos are the scene of the making of history by blacks in the interests of blacks.

The ghetto must be studied as frontierland which black people are trying to conquer, to develop as *their* community, to engage in participatory democracy as they seek to build and develop that community. The ghetto is not closed frontier, as establishment-historical literature would suggest. It is merely urban. It is claimed developed territory, defended by white interest groups, much more powerful and sophisticated than the red Indians of old. The drive for domain and the quest for community control by the "newly arrived" black people are repeatedly frustrated by the self-proclaimed new "natives." The contest of urban confrontation is so complex and dynamic that the underlying issues are constantly being masked by new overlays of cumulating epiphenomenal ones. The urban condition continues to be an overwhelmingly complex institutional arrangement which reflects interests intrinsically at odds with the desires of black people, but interests often distant and beyond "where black people are at."

The rhetoric of the ghetto must not be dismissed any more than the actions of its speakers. Cool talk, angry talk, crazy talk, jive. Whatever it may be called it must be looked upon with historical consciousness as existential and perceptive cues for new sociological insights on the meaning and nature of black urban behavior. The urban condition of most black people, the ghetto, must be studied for its retentions, parallels, and departures from the slave plantation. The particular behavioral and organizational nuances and limitations of ghetto people must be studied in comparison with slaves, as Malcolm X suggested. The complexity of ghetto culture must be studied in terms of a "bicultural underlife" of a people of whom most have been segregated and suppressed ever since their arrival in the continental USA (Blauner 1970: 347–366; Valentine and Valentine 1970). As such it is a set of behaviors and expectations too often unnoticed, misunderstood, and disregarded. It is pregnant with secondary adjustments and esoteric symbolism, which confound scholars and white citizens alike. The conception that white men hold today of black men and the institutionalized system by which it is expressed must be studied against the plantation past. It is only then we can begin to answer how far we have come, how much further we must go, and what means are necessary to get there. *Dig it? Then let's get with it.*

REFERENCES

Allport, G. 1958. *The Nature of Prejudice*. New York: Doubleday.

Berger, P. and T. Luckmann 1966. *The Social Construction of Reality*. Garden City, N.Y.: Doubleday.

Berwanger, E. H. 1967. *The Frontier Against Slavery*. Urbana: University of Illinois Press.

Bittle, W. E. and G. L. Geiss 1957. "Racial Self-fulfillment and the Rise of an All-Negro Community in Oklahoma." *Phylon* **18**: 247–260.

Blassingame, J. 1970. "A Social and Economic Study of the Negro in New Orleans." Ph.D. dissertation. Yale University. Unpublished.

Blauner, R. 1970. "Black Culture: Myth or Reality?" in N. Whitten and J. Szwed (eds.) *Afro-American Anthropology*. New York: Free Press.

Bryce-Laporte, R. S. 1971. "Slaves as Inmates; Slaves as Men: a Sociological Discussion of Elkins' 'Sambo' Thesis," in A. Lane (ed.) *The Debate on Slavery: Stanley Elkins and His Critics*. Urbana: University of Illinois Press.
——— 1969. "The American Slave Plantation and our Heritage of Communal Deprivation." *American Behavioral Scientist* (March–April): 2–8.
——— 1968. "The Conceptualization of the American Slave Plantation as a Total Institution." Ph.D. dissertation. UCLA. Unpublished.

Cash, M. V. 1941. *The Mind of the South*. New York: Random House.

Clark, K. 1965. *The Dark Ghetto*. New York: Harper & Row.

Comer, J. 1967. "The Social Power of the Negro." *Scientific American* **216** (April): 21–27.

Edgerton, R. and G. Sabagh 1962. "From Mortification to Aggrandizement: Changing Self-concepts in the Careers of the Mentally Retarded." *Psychiatry* **35**, 3.

Elkins, S. 1963. *Slavery: A Problem in American Institutional Intellectual Life*. New York: Grosset & Dunlap.
———— and E. McKitrick, Jr. 1954. "A Meaning for Turner's Frontier." Parts I and II. *Pol. Sci. Q.* **69**: 3 & 4.

Etzioni A. 1961. *A Comparative Analysis of Complex Organizations*. New York: Free Press.

Evans-Pritchard, E. E. 1951. *Social Anthropology*. London: Cohen & West.

Franklyn, J. H. 1956. "History of Racial Segregation in the United States," in T. Reid (ed.) *Racial Desegregation and Integration*. Annals of the Amer. Academy of Pol. and Social Sci. **34**: 1–9.

Frazier, E. F. 1960. "Introduction," in V. Rubin (ed.) *Caribbean Studies: A Symposium*. Seattle: University of Washington Press.
———— 1939. *The Negro Family in the United States*. Chicago: Chicago University Press.

Genovese, E. 1966*a*. *The Political Economy of Slavery*. New York: Random House.
———— 1966*b*. "The Legacy of Slavery and the Roots of Black Nationalism." *Studies on the Left* **6**, 6:2–36.

Goffman, E. 1963. *Stigma*. Englewood Cliffs, N.J.: Prentice-Hall.
———— 1961. *Asylums*. Garden City, N.Y.: Doubleday.

Gordon, M. 1964. *Assimilation in American Life*. New York: Oxford University Press.

Gray, L. C. 1933. *History of Agriculture in the Southern United States to 1860*, Vol. 1. Washington, D.C.: Carnegie Institute.

Greer, S. 1962. *The Emerging City*. New York: Free Press.
———— 1955. *Social Organization*. New York: Random House.

Guttman, H. (Forthcoming) *The Invisible Fact*. New York: Pantheon.

Handlin, O. 1958. "Editor's preface" in E. Morgan. *The Puritan Dilemma: The Story of John Winthrop*. Canada: Little, Brown.

Hill, M. 1946. "The All-Negro Society in Oklahoma." Ph.D. dissertation. University of Chicago. Unpublished.

Hillery, G. 1963. "Villages, Cities, and Total Institutions." *Amer. Soc. Rev.* **28**.

Jordan, W. 1969. *White Over Black: American Attitudes Toward the Negro, 1510–1815*. Baltimore: Penguin.

Kaplan, H. M. 1969. "The Black Muslims and the Negro American Quest for Communion." *British J. of Sociology* **20** (June): 164–176.

Kardiner, A. and L. Ovesey 1962. *The Mark of Oppression.* New York: World.

Kramer, J. 1970. *The American Minority Community.* New York: Thomas Y. Crowell.

Lane, A. (ed.) 1971. *The Debate on Slavery: Stanley Elkins and His Critics.* Urbana: University of Illinois Press.

Lasch, C. and G. Frederickson 1967. "Resistance to Slavery." *Civil War History* **13**.

Lewis, Sir. A. 1969. "Black Power and the American University." *Princeton University Magazine* (Spring): 8–12.

Litwack, E. 1961. *North of Slavery.* Chicago: University of Chicago Press.

Lynd, S., Jr. 1967. *Class Conflict, Slavery, and the United States Constitution.* New York: Bobbs-Merrill.

Marsh, R. 1964. "The Bearing of Comparative Analysis on Sociological Theory." *Social Forces* **43**, 2.

McKitrick, E. (ed.) 1963. *Slavery Defended.* Englewood Cliffs, N.J.: Prentice-Hall.

Meier, A. and E. Rudwick 1969. "A Strange Chapter in the Career of 'Jim Crow.'" *The Making of Black America*, Vol. II. New York: Atheneum.

Merton, R. 1957. *Social Theory and Social Structure.* Glencoe: Free Press.

Mills, C. W. 1959. *The Sociological Imagination.* New York: Grove Press.

Moore, W. 1941. "Slave Law and the Social Structure." *J. of Negro History* **26**, 2.

Morgan, E. S. 1958. *The Puritan Dilemma: The Story of John Winthrop.* Canada: Little, Brown.

Myrdal, G. 1957. *Rich Lands and Poor Lands.* New York: Harper & Row.

Neuwirth, G. 1969. "A Weberian Outline of a Theory of Community: Its Application to the 'Dark Ghetto'." *British J. of Sociology* **20** (June): 148–163.

Pease, W. H. and J. H. Pease 1963. *Black Utopia.* Madison: The State Historical Society of Wisconsin.

Phillips, U. B. 1963. *Life and Labor in the Old South.* Boston: Little, Brown.

Pitt, J. P. 1970. "The Meaning of Black Consciousness: Community or Communion?" Paper given at 55th Annual Meeting of the Assn. for the Study of Negro Life and History. Philadelphia.

Robinson, A. 1969. "The Reconstruction in Memphis." Senior essay. Yale. Unpublished.

Rose, A. 1969. "Varieties in Sociological Imagination." *Amer. Soc. Rev.* **34**.

Rubin, V. (ed.) 1960. *Caribbean Studies: A Symposium.* Seattle: University of Washington Press.

Smith, M. G. 1962. "History and Social Anthropology." *J. of the Royal Anthropological Institute* **67**, 5.

Szasz, T. S. 1970. *Ideology and Insanity*. New York: Doubleday.

Tannenbaum, F. 1946. *Slave and Citizen*. New York: Knopf.

Thompson, E., Jr. 1959. "The Plantation as a Social System." *Plantations of the New World*. Washington, D.C.: Pan American Union.

Tittle, C. and D. Tittle 1965. "Social Organization of Prisoners: an Empirical Test." *Social Forces* **43**, 2.

Turner, F. J. 1893. "The Significance of the Frontier in American History," in E. E. and F. M. (eds.) *The Early Writings of Frederick Jackson Turner*. Madison: University of Wisconsin Press.

Valentine, C. and M. L. Valentine 1970. "Blackston." Progress report of a community study on Urban Afro-America. Unpublished manuscript.

Wade, R. C. 1964. *Slavery in the Cities—The South, 1820–1860*. London: Oxford University Press.

Wagley, C. 1960. "Plantation America: A Cultural Sphere," in V. Rubin (ed.) *Caribbean Studies: A Symposium*. Seattle: University of Washington Press.

Wish, H. 1961. *Antebellum*. New York: Capricorn Books.

Woodson, C. 1919. *The Education of the Negro Prior to 1861*. Washington, D.C.: Assn. for the Study of Negro Life and History.

Woodward, V. 1968. *The Burden of Southern History*. Baton Rouge: Louisiana State University Press.

Yetman, N. 1970. "Testing Elkins' 'Sambo' Thesis: Some Preliminary Problems." Unpublished manuscript.

2.

Perspectives on Minority Experiences in America

Political scientist, Nathan Glazer, argues that "neither in America, nor elsewhere, are race and ethnicity categories so different that the processes that affect the assimilation and integration of ethnic groups change completely when groups of a different race are involved."[1] Other scholars emphasize the differences between black and other groups or between groups who have been colonized (Black Americans, Mexican Americans, Puerto Ricans, American Indians) and those who have not been colonized (European-Americans).[2] The articles in this section illustrate some of the many variations and similarities in majority-minority relations involving different racial and ethnic groups in America. The first article, taken from the Kerner Commission Report, addresses the question of how the Black Experience differs from the experiences of other groups. In addition to the background of slavery and its impact on attitudes and institutions as described in the article in Section One by Bryce-Laporte, Black Americans are faced with a relatively mature economic system and a rigidly entrenched political system. These institutions are more difficult to penetrate and more resistant to manipulation today than they were during the period when European ethnic groups were struggling to get out of the ghetto. The Commission's treatment of "cultural factors," especially with regard to family stability, needs reconsideration (see Staples' article on the matriarchy in Section Three). The question of time is also bothersome. The implication that blacks have done well in two generations ignores the generations of slaves who came before. However, while the editor disagrees with some of the interpretations in this brief article, the article nevertheless points out some of the ways in which the white

[1] Nathan Glazer, "Blacks and Ethnic Groups: The Difference, and the Political Difference It Makes," *Social Problems* 18 (Spring, 1971), p. 447.
[2] See Robert Blauner's article in this volume for an insightful analysis of the colonial model.

ethnic experience differs from the current situation facing Black Americans.

Ghetto experience is a part of the history of many ethnic groups. Although a strong argument can be made for the unique problems of the Black Ghetto (its relative permanence and its enforced rather than voluntary character), most ethnic groups have found it possible to leave the slum and find better housing as their economic conditions improved. Cordasco and Galatioto describe the "natural history" of a slum area in the tradition of the "Chicago School."[3] This article is of particular interest because it brings out several points that are often neglected in studies of race relations. First, the authors describe the pattern of succession in the slums in which each ethnic group moves out as soon as it becomes economically feasible and is replaced by a new low-status group. Second, they indicate that ethnic minorities were not very likely to "integrate" with one another even when they were all white and European. Finally, they recognize the fact that minorities often improve their own status at the expense of others less fortunate than themselves. Again the uniqueness of the black situation is obvious. Who can blacks take advantage of? Who comes after blacks in the slum succession? So far, blacks can only look forward to being replaced by demolition teams "renewing" the area or reclaiming it for middle-class whites.

The other articles in this section are concerned with the experiences of specific ethnic groups. Mexican Americans comprise the second largest racial minority in America. The article by Joan Moore describes the diversity within the group as well as some of its special problems. According to Moore, "colonialism" has been increasingly used by minority ideologues to account for their situation in the United States. Her article is an attempt to specify the concept in the case of Mexican Americans, with political participation on the elite and on the mass level illustrating the varieties of internal colonialism to which the Mexican American population has been subjected. She delineates three culture areas: New Mexico, with "classic colonialism"; Texas, with "conflict colonialism"; and California, with "economic colonialism." Factors distinguishing the three "culture areas" include ecology of settlement, historical discontinuities, and proportions of voluntary-immigrant as compared with charter-member descendents making up the Mexican American population of a specific area. The Chicano

[3] *The City,* by Robert E. Park, Ernest W. Burgess, and Roderick D. McKenzie, published in 1925, is a classical example of the early work of the University of Chicago school of urban sociology. The Chicago urban sociologists had a lasting impact on scholarly research into urban affairs. They focused on the complexities of the urban community and on the prospect of discovering patterns of regularity in its apparent confusion.

militant ideology incorporates symbols which attempt to transcend these regional and historical differences.

One major difference between the Mexican American situation and that of Black Americans is that it is possible for middle-class Mexican Americans to leave the *barrio* and become integrated into "Anglo" society in much the same way that European ethnics left the ghetto. While many do not choose to turn away from their ethnic roots, the option is still available to those who find it attractive. Black Americans have no such option available unless they are physically capable of "passing" into the white race.

The question of the extent to which a particular ethnic group has been assimilated into American society has been of concern to scholars for some time. Milton Gordon has attempted to clarify the issue by making a distinction between "structural assimilation" and "cultural assimilation."[4] Integration into the economic, political, and educational life of the nation is called structural assimilation. Integration into the social and cultural life of the Anglo-American dominant group is referred to as cultural assimilation. The former is assumed to be more readily attainable than the latter. Most ethnic groups encourage structural assimilation, but they tend to be ambivalent when it comes to cultural assimilation. Two articles in this section describe groups, Jews and Japanese, which have been successful in attaining a measure of structural assimilation, but in which there are strong forces resisting cultural assimilation.

Since moving from the slums the Jews have become a rather privileged ethnic group in American society. Educationally and occupationally, Jews, on the average, have higher status than other white Americans. They also encounter few restrictions on their housing and mobility today. Jews are, therefore, seemingly prime candidates for the melting pot since they are largely of European descent and share many cultural traditions with WASPs. Yet, there has always been a strong force within the Jewish community that resisted "assimilation." One expression of the resistance to assimilation is the attempt to maintain an endogamous marriage pattern. The article by Marshall Sklare discusses recent developments in the American Jewish Community as they relate to the question of intermarriage.

The question of group survival is also important to racial minorities, but these groups have not yet become as completely acculturated as the Jews. Thus, while the problem is less urgent at present for racial minorities, increased contact with whites in college and on the job as these groups acquire middle-class status is likely to result in increased

---

[4] Milton Gordon, *Assimilation in American Life* (New York: Oxford University Press, 1964).

intermarriage with the result that these groups may feel threatened
and attempt to develop strategies to promote endogamy. The irony is
that success in improving a group's socioeconomic status may be a
greater threat than poverty to its continued existence as a distinct group.

Japanese Americans also represent a relatively affluent minority
group. Their economic status would probably be even more favorable
if many on the West Coast had not undergone incarceration during
World War II and suffered considerable loss in property and potential
earnings as well as status in the community. Currently, whether because
of their ability to resist acculturation or because of their successful
acculturation, Japanese Americans, like Jewish Americans, are considerably above the American average in education and somewhat
above average in occupational status. At the same time, Orientals and
Jews have lower than average rates of crime and delinquency. In both
cases, ability to resist acculturation in combination with cultural
backgrounds that prepared their offspring for competition in the
American educational system have worked to the advantage of the
group. Several articles in this collection discuss the psychological effects
of racism on Black Americans and the relationship of self-esteem to
achievement. It is interesting to note here that *high* self-esteem is
positively related to achievement of Anglo pupils, but *low* self-esteem is
positively related to achievement of Japanese pupils. The same kind of
reversal applies to the concept of "locus of control." These results
support the notion that Japanese achievement is probably based on
non-Western cultural patterns that operate effectively within the
American milieu. Questions of assimilation and intermarriage are also
relevant for Japanese Americans. Although these questions are not
discussed directly in this article, one is left with the impression that the
pressures for maintaining group identity are strong.

The final article in this section analyzes the process of segregation.
The analysis is written from the viewpoint that Metzger called
"assimilationist bias." It does demonstrate that members of a group
can practice voluntary segregation (separatism, in today's rhetoric)
effectively while the majority of the group's members practice dispersion
and move toward integration into the majority society. The concept of
defensive insulation associated with the need for self-help has parallels
in some of the strategies advocated by black community leaders
(the most highly developed example of black separatism is the Nation
of Islam). Yuan's assumption that assimilation is the eventual outcome
of the conflict between Chinese Americans and whites does not allow
for the strong pressures within the Chinese community that still
encourage the preservation of Chinese culture and traditions. Efforts to
transport children from San Francisco's Chinatown to other areas of
the city to promote school integration (September, 1971) have met

strong resistance from the Chinese community. There has been a revival of Chinese parochial schools and a boycott of the public schools to protest this threat to the integrity of Chinese culture. How much of the resistance is due to Chinese Americans' adoption of American prejudices against blacks is a moot question. In any case, self-segregation is still alive in San Francisco.

Comparing the Immigrant and Negro Experience

NATIONAL ADVISORY COMMISSION ON CIVIL RIGHTS

We have . . . surveyed the historical background of racial discrimination and traced its effects on Negro employment, on the social structure of the ghetto community, and on the conditions of life that surround the urban Negro poor. Here we address a fundamental question that many white Americans are asking today: why has the Negro been unable to escape from poverty and the ghetto like the European immigrants?

THE MATURING ECONOMY

The changing nature of the American economy is one major reason. When the European immigrants were arriving in large numbers, America was becoming an urban-industrial society. To build its major cities and industries, America needed great pools of unskilled labor. The immigrants provided the labor, gained an economic foothold, and thereby enabled their children and grandchildren to move up to skilled, white collar, and professional employment.

Since World War II, especially, America's urban-industrial society has matured; unskilled labor is far less essential than before, and blue-collar jobs of all kinds are decreasing in number and importance as a source of new employment. The Negroes who migrated to the great urban centers lacked the skills essential to the new economy; and the schools of the ghetto have been unable to provide the education that can qualify them for decent jobs. The Negro migrant, unlike the immigrant, found little opportunity in the city; he had arrived too late, and the unskilled labor he had to offer was no longer needed.

THE DISABILITY OF RACE

Racial discrimination is undoubtedly the second major reason why the Negro has been unable to escape from poverty. The structure of discrimination has persistently narrowed his opportunities and restricted his prospects. Well before the high tide of immigration from overseas,

Negroes were already relegated to the poorly paid, low status occupations. Had it not been for racial discrimination, the North might well have recruited Southern Negroes after the Civil War to provide the labor for building the burgeoning urban-industrial economy. Instead, Northern employers looked to Europe for their sources of unskilled labor. Upon the arrival of the immigrants, the Negroes were dislodged from the few urban occupations they had dominated. Not until World War II were Negroes generally hired for industrial jobs, and by that time the decline in the need for unskilled labor had already begun. European immigrants, too, suffered from discrimination, but never was it so pervasive as the prejudice against color in America, which has formed a bar to advancement, unlike any other.

ENTRY INTO THE POLITICAL SYSTEM

Political opportunities also played an important role in enabling the European immigrants to escape from poverty. The immigrants settled for the most part in rapidly growing cities that had powerful and expanding political machines, which gave them economic advantages in exchange for political support. The political machines were decentralized; and ward-level grievance machinery, as well as personal representation, enabled the immigrant to make his voice heard and his power felt. Since the local political organizations exercised considerable influence over public building in the cities, they provided employment in construction jobs for their immigrant voters. Ethnic groups often dominated one or more of the municipal services—police and fire protection, sanitation, and even public education.

By the time the Negroes arrived, the situation had altered dramatically. The great wave of public building had virtually come to an end; reform groups were beginning to attack the political machines; the machines were no longer so powerful or so well equipped to provide jobs and other favors.

Although the political machines retained their hold over the areas settled by Negroes, the scarcity of patronage jobs made them unwilling to share with the Negroes the political positions they had created in these neighborhoods. For example, Harlem was dominated by white politicians for many years after it had become a Negro ghetto; even today, New York's Lower East Side, which is now predominantly Puerto Rican, is strongly influenced by politicians of the older immigrant groups.

This pattern exists in many other American cities. Negroes are still underrepresented in city councils and in most city agencies.

Segregation played a role here too. The immigrants and their descendants felt threatened by the arrival of the Negro and prevented a Negro-immigrant coalition that might have saved the old political machines.

Reform groups, nominally more liberal on the race issue, were often dominated by businessmen and middle-class city residents who usually opposed coalition with any low-income group, white or black.

CULTURAL FACTORS

Cultural factors also made it easier for the immigrants to escape from poverty. They came to America from much poorer societies, with a low standard of living, and they came at a time when job aspirations were low. When most jobs in the American economy were unskilled, they sensed little deprivation in being forced to take the dirty and poorly paid jobs. Moreover, their families were large, and many breadwinners, some of whom never married, contributed to the total family income. As a result, family units managed to live even from the lowest paid jobs and still put some money aside for savings or investment, for example, to purchase a house or tenement or to open a store or factory. Since the immigrants spoke little English and had their own ethnic culture, they needed stores to supply them with ethnic foods and other services. Since their family structures were patriarchal, men found satisfactions in family life that helped compensate for the bad jobs they had to take and the hard work they had to endure.

Negroes came to the city under quite different circumstances. Generally relegated to jobs that others would not take, they were paid too little to be able to put money in savings for new enterprises. Since they spoke English, they had no need for their own stores; besides, the areas they occupied were already filled with stores. In addition, Negroes lacked the extended family characteristic of certain European groups—each household usually had only one or two breadwinners. Moreover, Negro men had fewer cultural incentives to work in a dirty job for the sake of the family. As a result of slavery and of long periods of male unemployment afterwards, the Negro family structure had become matriarchal; the man played a secondary and marginal role in his family. For many Negro men, then, there were few of the cultural and psychological rewards of family life. A marginal figure in the family, particularly when unemployed, Negro men were often rejected by their wives or often abandoned their homes because they felt themselves useless to their families.

Although most Negro men worked as hard as the immigrants to support their families, their rewards were less. The jobs did not pay enough to enable them to support their families, for prices and living standards had risen since the immigrants had come, and the entrepreneurial opportunities that had allowed some immigrants to become independent, even rich, had vanished. Above all, Negroes suffered from segregation, which denied them access to the good jobs and the right unions, and which deprived them of the opportunity to buy real estate or obtain business loans or move out of the ghetto and bring up their children in middle-class neighborhoods. Immigrants were able to leave their ghettos as soon as they had the money; segregation has denied Negroes the opportunity to live elsewhere.

THE VITAL ELEMENT OF TIME

Finally, nostalgia makes it easy to exaggerate the ease of escape of the white immigrants from the ghettos. When the immigrants were immersed in poverty, they too lived in slums, and these neighborhoods exhibited fearfully high rates of alcoholism, desertion, illegitimacy, and the other pathologies associated with poverty. Just as some Negro men desert their families when they are unemployed and their wives can get jobs, so did the men of other ethnic groups, even though time and affluence has clouded white memories of the past.

Today, whites tend to exaggerate how well and how quickly they escaped from poverty, and contrast their experience with poverty-stricken Negroes. The fact is, among many of the Southern and Eastern Europeans who came to America in the last great wave of immigration, those who came already urbanized were the first to escape from poverty. The others who came to America from rural backgrounds, as Negroes did, are only now, after three generations, in the final stages of escaping from poverty. Until the last 10 years or so, most of these were employed in blue-collar jobs, and only a small proportion of their children were able or willing to attend college. In other words, only the third, and in many cases, only the fourth generation has been able to achieve the kind of middle-class income and status that allows it to send its children to college. Because of favorable economic and political conditions, these ethnic groups were able to escape from lower-class status to working class and lower middle-class status, but it has taken them three generations.

Negroes have been concentrated in the city for only two generations, and they have been there under much less favorable conditions. Moreover, their escape from poverty has been blocked in part by the resistance of the European ethnic groups; they have been unable to enter some unions and to move into some neighborhoods outside the ghetto because descendants of the European immigrants who control these unions and neighborhoods have not yet abandoned them for middle-class occupations and areas.

Even so, some Negroes have escaped poverty, and they have done so in only two generations; their success is less visible than that of the immigrants in many cases, for residential segregation has forced them to remain in the ghetto. Still, the proportion of nonwhites employed in white-collar, technical, and professional jobs has risen from 10.2 percent in 1950 to 20.8 percent in 1966, and the proportion attending college has risen an equal amount. Indeed, the development of a small but steadily increasing Negro middle class while the greater part of the Negro population is stagnating economically is creating a growing gap between Negro haves and have-nots.

This gap, as well as the awareness of its existence by those left behind, undoubtedly adds to the feelings of desperation and anger which breed civil disorders. Low-income Negroes realize that segregation and lack of job opportunities have made it possible for only a small proportion of all Negroes to escape poverty and the summer disorders are at least in part a protest against being left behind and left out.

The immigrant who labored long hours at hard and often menial work had the hope of a better future, if not for himself then for his children. This was the promise of the "American dream"—the society offered to all a future that was open-ended; with hard work and perseverance, a man and his family could in time achieve not only material well-being but "position" and status.

For the Negro family in the urban ghetto, there is a different vision— the future seems to lead only to a dead-end.

What the American economy of the late 19th and early 20th century was able to do to help the European immigrants escape from poverty is now largely impossible. New methods of escape must be found for the majority of today's poor.

Ethnic Displacement in the Interstitial Community: The East Harlem Experience

FRANCESCO CORDASCO and
ROCCO G. GALATIOTO

Frederick M. Thrasher's definition of a so-called interstitial community is typical of the sociological thinking of the 1920's, which was influenced strongly by the University of Chicago school headed by Park and Burgess. Thrasher, loyal to the concentric circle theory of cities, maintained that an *interstitial area,* an area that would be called today a *ghetto,* is typified by deterioration, shifting population and cultural isolation.[1] The

---

[1] See Thrasher's classic study, *The Gang* (Chicago, 1927); for general orientation, see

work of William F. Whyte and Herbert J. Gans points out that such areas
are not necessarily disorganized socially and are not deteriorating in terms
of social organization and integration;[2] indeed, the term *deterioration* is
too crude and value ridden for serious sociological purposes. Yet Thrasher
was correct in stating that slums are plagued by shifting population and
are essentially isolated from the rest of society. In these two respects, the
sociologically complex and fascinating area of the upper East Side of
Manhattan known as East Harlem is an interstitial area, or a slum. East
Harlem is and has been a poor area and has had its share of social pathology. But it is the isolation of a slum from the rest of society simply because its subculture does not conform directly to the culture patterns of
a dominant group that causes it to be known by "outsiders" as a pathological and decadent area.

East Harlem is an interesting area. Most minority groups have lived
there at one time or another; however, the ideal melting pot never melted
substantially. The immediate scope of this paper is to trace the movement
of the largest ethnic groups through this area from 1900 to 1960. These
groups are Italians, Jews, Puerto Ricans and Negroes. The aim of this
paper is to document and establish probable reasons for the change in
East Harlem from a "Little Italy" to a so-called Spanish Harlem, and
enventually to an extension of Negro Harlem. East Harlem housed during
the 1920's the largest Italian immigrant community in the United States.
We will attempt to explain and trace the growth of the Italian population
and its replacement by Puerto Ricans and Negroes, with some notice of
the Jewish subcommunity which slowly withdrew from the area.

Geographically, East Harlem is defined as the area from 96th Street
north to the Harlem River. This area is divided statistically in terms of
Health Areas, each of which is subdivided into Census Tracts.

Although culturally isolated, the area is serviced by several surface
line buses and several subways. The main subway that passes through
the area is the Lexington Avenue Line, but it must be noted that at one
time the Third Avenue "L" and the Second Avenue "L" also served the
area. There are some physical barriers that act also as social barriers: the
tracks of the New York Central Railroad run elevated from 96th Street to
110th Street along Park Avenue, and at one time they separated middle-
class Central Harlem from lower-class East Harlem. However, as Central
Harlem began to change into a Negro ghetto, the Jewish and Protestant
middle classes moved out, and today these tracks serve only as physical

David R. Hunter, *The Slums: Challenge and Response* (New York, 1964); and Marshall B. Clinard, *Slums and Community Development* (New York, 1966).
[2] *Cf.* William F. Whyte, Jr., *Street Corner Society* (Chicago, 1943, 2nd ed., 1955);
and Herbert J. Gans, *The Urban Villagers: Group and Class in the Life of Italian
Americans* (New York, 1962).

TABLE 1

Health Areas and Their Equivalent Census Tracts for East Harlem

Health Areas	Census Tracts
16	198, 196, 204, 206, 210
17	192, 194, 202
20	182, 184
21	180
22	178, 188
25	172, 174
28	160, 168
29	158, 166
30	164

barriers that separate the low-rent housing projects west of Park Avenue from the low-rent tenements on the East side that appear to be doomed because of the bulldozer ideology.[3] Another physical barrier is Mount Morris Park and there is, of course, the limiting effect of the Harlem and East Rivers.

The most important street in East Harlem is 116th Street. This has been traditionally the most desirable residential area, and it still houses what remains of the professional offices of doctors, lawyers, and brokers. This street signified to the Italian population a sort of main street— equivalent to the *il corso* of their native towns and villages. It is then not surprising that old-timers remember when their dream was to move to 116th Street where the rents were high, but where prestige was achieved. East Harlem today is predominantly Negro and Puerto Rican. A few Italians, mostly elderly, remain in some "pockets," but they are slowly disappearing. East Harlem is a typical urban slum, a kind of necessary evil that will be part of the industrial city until all discrimination and class differences are rooted out.

It is erroneous to conclude that the slum resulted from the ethnic immigrations. Anderson, in his thorough study of the history of the slum, shows that slums existed before the great ethnic immigrations. He observes that "As a social phenomenon, the slum seems to resist most attempts to abolish it. Whether opposed by movements of reform or rising land values, it only yields to change its locale or modify its appearance. This has been at least the characteristic of the slum in New York. . . .

[3] See Patricia C. Sexton, *Spanish Harlem* (New York, 1965), particularly, "The Bulldozer and the Bulldozed," pp. 35–46; and Jane Jacobs, *The Death and Life of Great American Cities* (New York, 1961). For commentary on Sexton, see F. Cordasco, "Spanish Harlem: The Anatomy of Poverty," *Phylon* (Summer, 1965), 195–96.

TABLE 2

Political District	Male	Female	Total
31	22,503	28,499	51,002
32	32,064	30,930	62,994
33	28,362	27,749	56,111
34	35,614	34,919	70,533
Totals	118,543	122,097	240,640

Whether tent or tenement, the slum in this city is as old as the segregation of the poor."[4] This is even more true today. With the building of so-called housing projects, an entire area is destroyed and many of those displaced settle in contiguous areas, thus enlarging the slum. Also, low-rent housing areas usually "become worse centers of delinquency, vandalism and general hopelessness than the slums they were supposed to replace."[5]

EAST HARLEM AT THE TURN OF THE CENTURY

A census taken by the New York Police Department in 1895 based on political districts roughly equivalent to what is today known as East Harlem released the figures shown in Table 2 above.[6]

In the period 1902–03, according to the most reliable source of ethnic enumeration, *The Report of the Tenement House Department of New York City*, East Harlem was predominantly Irish and German: "The Italians who predominate today [1930], in 1903 were in the minority. This point serves to illustrate that the Italians did not settle in East Harlem until the first decade of the new century. The nucleus of Italians was located along Second Avenue from 102nd to 116th Streets. They were more densely located in the vicinity of Thomas Jefferson Park."[7] Between 1900 and 1910, ethnic trends in East Harlem were creating an Italian subcommunity which was to become the largest Italian settlement in the United States.

[4] Nels Anderson, *The Social Antecedents of a Slum: A Developmental Study of the East Harlem Area* (unpublished Ph.D. dissertation, New York University, 1930), p. 16.
[5] Jacobs, *op. cit.*, p. 4.
[6] Reported in Salvatore Cimaluca, *The Natural History of East Harlem from 1880 to the Present* (unpublished M.A. thesis, New York University, 1931), p. 44. The significance in terms of absolute data of Table 2 is questionable because of poor enumeration, and because the political districts of the period do not correspond exactly to what is known as East Harlem today.
[7] Cimaluca, *op. cit.*, p. 46.

WHY EAST HARLEM?

Around 1900, the number of Italians who came to the United States increased steadily, but this immigration did not reach its apex until 1914.[8] Because of the economic conditions of these early immigrants (conditions aggravated by the *padrone* system),[9] they were forced to live in "pockets" of extreme poverty and squalor. The first Italian slum was in notorious Mulberry Bend of lower Manhattan. The conditions of this slum are best outlined by Jacob Riis in *How the Other Half Lives*.[10] This original "Little Italy" was so unfit for human habitation that "the only remedy was demolition."[11] In the late 1890's demolition was a rare phenomenon, and the proposal made in 1884 by the Tenement House Commission to demolish the Bend was unusual and quite courageous. After a long battle, the area was ordered evacuated and made ready for demolition by 1895.[12] But after many houses had been demolished, some people continued to live in the Bend under even worse conditions. If the qualitative terms used above to describe the Bend are too imprecise, one should turn to Riis for vital statistics which show that the Bend's rate of infantile mortality was 139.83 per thousand births, as compared to the rate for New York City as a whole of 26.27.[13] The general mortality for the Bend was 10 percent higher than for the city as a whole.[14]

It is little wonder that some Italians left this area and settled where they formed core communities that were to grow as additional immigrants joined them. As soon as these core communities were established the number of Italians living in them grew, not necessarily because of an exodus from the Bend but because of the large number of Italians who were entering the United States during this period and settling near their relatives and *paesani*. The demolition of the Bend and the moving out of Italian families who had been able to free themselves from their status of virtual indentured servants had an effect on the ethnic make-up of East Harlem. We believe that a core community was established in East Harlem which acted as a magnet in attracting others who were arriving from Italy. There is evidence that at the turn of the century there was indeed a

[8] See generally Robert F. Foerster, *The Italian Emigration of Our Times* (Cambridge, Massachusetts, 1919; reissued with an introductory Note by F. Cordasco, New York, 1968).

[9] See Marie Lipari, "The Padrone System," *Italy American Monthly* (April, 1935), 4–10.

[10] Jacob Riis, *How the Other Half Lives* (New York, 1902).

[11] Stephen Noft (ed.), *Gli Italiani di New York*. Works Projects Administration (New York, 1933), p. 14.

[12] See Jacob Riis, *The Battle With the Slum* (New York, 1902).

[13] *How the Other Half Lives*, p. 65.

[14] Riis' major writings against the tenement slums are assembled in F. Cordasco (ed.), *Jacob Riis Revisited: Poverty and the Slum in Another Era* (New York, 1968).

small Italian community in East Harlem. In talking to some old-timers, we found that some of their relatives had come from the Mulberry Street area at the turn of the century. So far we have answered why the Italians might have moved from Mulberry Bend but not why they settled in East Harlem. That in East Harlem the houses were already old and transit facilities were accessible to the area is important. It would appear to be accurate to say that East Harlem was only one of the many core communities in New York but that because it was in Manhattan where dwellings were less expensive than in newer boroughs like Brooklyn, it became a "Little Italy" by 1910.

But during the following decade a turning point was reached since East Harlem saw a total decrease of 7,224 persons between 1910 and 1920.[15] This may seem small, but it must be seen in conjunction with the fact that the influx of Italians in this area was increasing. This decrease is important sociologically since it shows that the German and Irish elements were moving out very rapidly because of the influx of Italians. This influx must have been traumatic to the older residents of the area and there is no doubt that the "there goes the neighborhood" syndrome became widespread. The Jews were a group that also responded to this pressure by moving out, and their exodus will be outlined below. During this time, the Negro population began to increase in Central Harlem and gradually squeezed out the middle-class element in this area.

By 1920, the Italian immigration had become smaller as a result of the legal curtailments of migration from eastern and southern Europe; but the moving out of the older groups from East Harlem continued and a net decrease in population is recorded. Of course, it must be noted that some more mobile Italians also left the area. Cimaluca shows that in the 1920 to 1930 period, many Italians left New York City.[16]

THE 1920–1930 PERIOD

The period 1920–1930 is characterized by a Jewish exodus, by a further drop in the total population, and by the stabilization of the Italian segment. By this time Italians were the largest group in East Harlem, and, for the first time, some Puerto Ricans—a very small number—began to settle near the northeast corner of Central Park. Another interesting development during this period was the increasing pressure that Negroes were beginning to exert eastward.

The increase in the Negro population can be dealt with first because it was the most obvious development in East Harlem. By 1931, there were

15 Cimaluca, *op. cit.*, p. 50.
16 Cimaluca, *ibid.* See, also, Noft, *op. cit.*, for Italian demographic shifts during this period.

TABLE 3

Jewish Populations in East Harlem from 1919 to 1937

1919	128,000
1923	122,000
1927	52,000
1932	15,500
1937	4,000

164,566 Negroes in East Harlem, or 38 percent of the total population. This number has continued to increase up to the present.

The most interesting ethnic population trend during this period is the decline of the Jewish population. The 1937 *Welfare Council Report* tabulated the decline.[17] (See Table 3 above.)

The decline is significant, and interesting to study in some detail. The exodus of the Jewish group is of great sociological importance insofar as it shows that when a minority group has reached a certain middle-class status it regards other minority groups as a threat to the well-being of its neighborhood. This tragic but true pattern operates among most groups and signifies, perhaps, the point at which a minority "arrives." According to the Jewish Welfare Board Study of 1931, the total Jewish population in East Harlem had decreased from a high of 213,209 in 1920, to 159,927 in 1930, a total decrease of 28 percent.[18] This study goes on to note that "The influx of Puerto Ricans (among whom there is a considerable Negro element) and Negroes into East Harlem has been a significant factor in displacing the Jewish population which is moving largely to the Bronx and Brooklyn."[19]

It may be true that the rapid Jewish exodus of the 1930's is attributable to the Puerto Ricans; but, as we have seen from Table 3, the Jewish exodus began in 1919. And, as we shall see below, the number of Puerto Ricans in the 1920's was nominal; and even in 1930 there were few Puerto Ricans in East Harlem. As an hypothesis of why the Jews moved out of this area we propose a kind of socioeconomic thesis. First, the Jews were

[17] Welfare Council of New York, *Report on East Harlem Population* (New York, 1937).

[18] Jewish Welfare Center of New York, *Study of Changes in the Population of East Harlem* (New York, 1931); see also the Center's *Supplementary Study of the Federation Settlement* (New York, 1932), and an earlier study of the Jewish Welfare Board of New York, *Preliminary Study of the Institutional Synagogue* (New York, 1924). Note a large discrepancy between the Jewish studies and the Welfare Council *Report*. The Jewish studies are probably more accurate since the Welfare Council relied on Census data where Jews were enumerated by nationality. The Jews knew who their co-religionists were.

[19] *Ibid.*, p. 1. The Jewish studies are available at the Jewish Welfare Center of New York (145 East 32nd Street, New York City).

responding to a new middle-class ethic. The 1920's had been years of prosperity and the developing Bronx was becoming increasingly attractive. Second-generation Jews, responding to the demands of the middle-class ethic, were the first to leave. The old-timers at first refused to go, but as time went on their ideas about East Harlem began to change. We have noted already in passing that at this time the Jewish population was being pushed by growing Negro Harlem from the west and on the east. This threatened the older Jewish community and the exodus to the Bronx was slowly completed. What we discern is a succession of new ethnic groups in East Harlem; Negroes and Italians pushing out Jews while Italians were in turn to be pushed out by Puerto Ricans who in turn would be pushed out by Negroes.

Although our hypothesis differs from the explanation given in the Jewish study, the wealth of information in the study is of great value. Moreover, the study is extremely useful because it outlines in detail the last large Jewish community in East Harlem. This was specifically in the area bounded by 112th Street, 98th Street, Fifth Avenue, and Third Avenue. This area in particular saw a decrease in total Jewish population from 48,000 in 1923, to 11,000 in 1930, a drop of 400 percent.[20] By 1940, most Jews had moved out of East Harlem, although many instead of selling their houses became landlords whose houses were rented to Negroes. Many of the old Jewish merchants also remained. Jews thus became the only white men accessible to Negroes, and many of the problems involving Negroes and Jews are to be explained by this fact.[21]

THE GROWTH OF THE PUERTO RICAN POPULATION

It is interesting to note Cimaluca's statement that the East Harlem area, "at the present [1930] is being invaded by Puerto Ricans; these people speak their native language which is Spanish, and they are commonly called 'spicks.' "[22] This is a most important statement because it heralds things to come. As we shall point out below, although in 1930 there was no "invasion," the term *spick* was widely used among Italians as a derogatory label for Puerto Ricans they believed to be "invading" their neighborhood. Italians, who had been called by a variety of derogatory names, for the first time could transfer some of their frustration to the Puerto Ricans, and the word *spick* was a good vehicle for this transfer. The sociological significance here is obvious. It is an observed fact

[20] *Ibid.*, pp. 1–2. *The Supplementary Study* (*op. cit.*) includes a detailed block by block account of the remnants of the Jewish Community.
[21] See generally, Nathan Glazer and Daniel Patrick Moynihan, *Beyond the Melting Pot: The Negroes, Puerto Ricans, Jews, Italians, and Irish of New York City* (Cambridge, Massachusetts, 1963).
[22] Cimaluca, *op. cit.*, p. 30.

TABLE 4

Number of Puerto Ricans in the United States at Census Dates and in 1935

Year	Number	Increase
1910	1,513	—
1920	11,811	10,298
1930	52,774	40,943
1935*	58,200	5,426

* Estimate, December 31.

that in the United States one minority tries to benefit at the expense of another—even if this benefit is purely psychological.

The growth of the Puerto Rican population in East Harlem was slow. Chenault's pioneer work, *The Puerto Rican Migrant in New York City,* is the best source of data for the study of this growth. At the time of Chenault's writing there was no separate enumeration for Puerto Ricans in the Census. Chenault cites data accumulated by the United States Department of Labor, and the above table can be constructed from the data assembled.[23]

Chenault noted, "because the movement of Puerto Ricans in the United States is technically one of internal migration, there are no legal restrictions against his [sic] coming to the United States."[24] This made the enumeration even more difficult. However, from Table 4 it was obvious that the United States was hardly being invaded by Puerto Ricans. But this term, once applied to most of the more visible groups, was to be attached to the Puerto Ricans and was to make their problems more difficult.

The bulk of the immigration from Puerto Rico into New York City came after World War II, and before the war, "the major part of the movement of Puerto Rican people took place in the decade 1920–1930."[25] We have already pointed out that this was still an insignificant migration numerically but a significant one sociologically. The Italian immigration over, the need for an exploitable "green horn" group was met by the Puerto Ricans. The Depression, with its high rate of unemployment, put an end to the demand for cheap labor after 1930; thereafter, the number of immigrants from Puerto Rico dropped and did not increase until the late 1940's, as Table 5 shows.[26]

[23] Laurence Chenault, *The Puerto Rican Migrant in New York* (New York, 1938). Considerable documentation on the Puerto Rican mainland experience is in F. Cordasco and Eugene Bucchioni, *Puerto Rican Children in the Mainland Schools: A Source Book for Teachers* (New York, 1968).
[24] Chenault, *op. cit.,* p. 53.
[25] *Ibid.,* p. 54.
[26] *Ibid.,* p. 37. Chenault constructed his table from data available in the United States Department of Labor reports.

TABLE 5

Movement of Persons Between Puerto Rico and the United States

Fiscal Year	Arrivals from Puerto Rico	Departures to Puerto Rico	Excess of: Arrivals	Excess of: Departures
1921	9,480	7,694	1,786	—
1922	6,576	7,059	—	438
1923	9,036	6,829	2,207	—
1924	11,512	7,231	4,281	—
1925	1,279	8,136	3,143	—
1926	14,055	9,212	5,243	—
1927	19,161	9,728	9,433	—
1928	17,034	10,808	6,266	—
1929	15,911	9,462	6,449	—
1930	18,617	9,290	9,327	—
1931	11,517	12,625	—	1,108
1932	9,683	10,385	—	702
1933	8,700	9,953	—	1,253
1934	11,569	7,466	4,103	—
1935	13,174	10,214	2,960	—
Total	177,304	136,092	55,198	3,501

Chenault defined the first Puerto Rican settlement as the area from 110th to 97th Streets. The increase in the number of Puerto Ricans in East Harlem caused the area to begin taking on Hispanic characteristics.

This section on the Puerto Ricans must be concluded with some additional data on other changes which were taking place in East Harlem in the 1930–1940 decade. Regarding the total population of the area, the decline that began in 1910 continued. This shows that the Puerto Ricans were unable to replace all of those who were moving out as a result of the "Puerto Rican scare" first reported by Cimaluca. East Harlem during this period remained predominantly Italian, and in 1937 the *East Harlem Study* states that, "This area houses what is probably the largest Italian colony in the Western Hemisphere and also contains a major portion of the largest Puerto Rican colony in the world."[27] This was the largest Puerto Rican colony because there were of course not many Puerto Rican colonies outside the New York area.

FROM 1950 ONWARD

At a glance, three trends characterize the period of the past 20 years. First, there is the sharp increase in the Puerto Rican element, an increase

[27] Mayor's Committee on City Planning, *East Harlem Community Study* (New York: East Harlem Council of Social Agencies, 1937), p. 16.

| Ethnic | 1950 | | 1957 | |
Composition	Total	Percentage	Total	Percentage
White	88,829	49.15	59,264	39.71
Nonwhite Non-Puerto Rican }	31,498	17.43	26,575	17.69
Puerto Rican	60,380	33.42	63,575	42.60
Total Population	180,707	100.00	149,414	100.00

* The 1950 figures are from the United States Census of 1950, the 1957 figures are from a special New York City enumeration. The table comes from the *East Harlem Town Report*, June 6, 1969, p. 2.

which gave the area the unofficial name of *Spanish Harlem*. Second, there is the disappearance of the Italian group. Only some "pockets" remain. The bulk of these inhabitants of Italian descent are older persons. They live for the most part on East 116th Street from Second Avenue to the river and along Pleasant Avenue near Thomas Jefferson Park. Third, there is the increase of the Negro population. Also, as a continuing trend, the decline in total population continues. Table 6 shows the population drop from 1950 to 1957.

According to the *Town Hall Report*, part of this drop is a result of pending housing and school construction; however, in view of the fact that this represents an almost chronic loss of population, we disagree with this report. The population loss is in keeping with a pattern of continuing decline. The area of East Harlem is in a state of decline. Furthermore, the number of old people in the population of the area is on the increase. These facts point to two important demographic factors. Foreign immigration into East Harlem is ending (we consider Puerto Ricans as foreigners in this respect). A migrant population is usually a young population, especially when the migration is from a distant place. The increasing age of the East Harlem inhabitants supports this observation. These facts, however, apply to only the white East Harlem population because the movement of Negroes into this area is largely from Central Harlem and because the number of Negroes coming from the South (technically internal migration but it can be classified as long distance migration) has declined substantially in recent years.[28]

According to a recent report made by the East Harlem Committee on Aging, "a breakdown of the white population [of East Harlem] shows 65 percent of it to be comprised of Puerto Ricans, 14 percent of Italian stock

[28] HARYOU, *Youth In The Ghetto* (New York, 1964), p. 124.

and 2 percent of various other ethnic origins."[29] The total population of the area is estimated as 170,000, of which 63 percent is white, 35 percent is Negro, and 2 percent falls under the catch-all category of "other races."[30] The report breaks down the white population in terms of age, and one interesting fact is that 11 percent of this group is 60 years old or over. This corroborates the statement above that the white population in East Harlem is becoming an old population.

Today, East Harlem looks like any other slum in New York. It has a Puerto Rican dominance, but this is slowly vanishing as the area becomes increasingly Negro. Among the whites, only the poor and the elderly remain, while the more mobile go to live elsewhere. The net effect is to make the area even poorer.

SOME SOCIOLOGICAL IMPLICATIONS

By analyzing the changes in ethnic groups in East Harlem, we have noted several sociological points that need elaboration. The most important concerns the movement of groups. One ethnic group pushes another. This shows that, no matter what the nation's ideological tenets are, the importance of ethnicity in American inter-group life cannot be denied. Robert E. Park could not have been more wrong when he formulated his "race relation cycle." He stated optimistically that "The race relation cycle . . . takes the form, to state it abstractly, of contacts, competition, accommodation, and eventual assimilation."[31] The "melting pot" concept is obvious in his thesis; but judging from the empirical reality in East Harlem, this cycle never had a chance because the cultural differences among the various groups in the area were so strong that there was no possible way for any meaningful contact and eventual accommodation to take place.[32]

This brings us to the problem of the role of contact as a conflict-reducing agent. There is little doubt that inter-group contact reduces stereotyping and misunderstanding. But if cultural forces block contact, there is no hope that the cycle can be operative. Applied to East Harlem, this

29 The East Harlem Committee on Aging, *Older People in East Harlem* (New York, Department of Labor, Migration Division, Commonwealth of Puerto Rico, 1964).
30 *Ibid.*, p. 26.
31 Robert E. Park, "The Race Relation Cycle" in Amitai and Eva Etzioni (eds.), *Social Change* (New York, 1964), p. 377.
32 Leonard Covello, principal of East Harlem's Benjamin Franklin High School for almost a quarter of a century, strove valiantly to effect community participation in the social institutions of the area (presaging the community-control conflicts presently attending the Intermediate School #201 complex in East Harlem) but without long-range success. See Leonard Covello, "A High School and its Immigrant Community: A Challenge and An Opportunity," *Journal of Educational Sociology*, IX (February, 1936), 333–46.

would mean that the various ethnic groups were and are completely isolated from each other. There is the continuing isolation and lack of understanding that are normal for any such situation, but we disagree with Sexton's analysis of the East Harlem Italian community as an example of extreme isolation. The journalistic statements made by Sexton are unfortunate and show the difficulty of studying an area as complicated as East Harlem.[33]

Another consideration is the role that each group has played in the elevation of the group just above it. It appears that a group will try to advance at the expense of a group just below it. We have already pointed out that this may have psychological rewards for a group that has been the target of discrimination and which seeks another group to which to transfer some of its frustrations. This takes us to the role of the Negro group as the "last mover." Negroes are helping push Puerto Ricans out of East Harlem. The question is who, if anybody, will push the Negroes out. It seems unlikely that another ethnic group will ever migrate in sufficient numbers to help Negroes break the vicious cycle which Myrdal calls "The Principle of Cumulation."[34] Negroes will find exits from the ghetto only through the resolve of society as a whole to break the vicious cycle.

[33] See footnote 3, *supra*.
[34] Gunnar Myrdal, "The Principle of Cumulation" in Etzioni, *op. cit.*, pp. 455–58.

Colonialism: The Case of the Mexican Americans

JOAN W. MOORE

American social scientists should have realized long ago that American minorities are far from being passive objects of study. They are, on the contrary, quite capable of defining themselves. A clear demonstration of this rather embarrassing lag in conceptualization is the current reassessment of sociological thought. It is now plain that the concepts of "acculturation," of "assimilation," and similar paradigms are inappropriate for groups who entered American society not as volunteer immigrants but through some form of involuntary relationship.[1]

The change in thinking has not come because of changes within sociol-

[1] Oddly enough it now appears that the nature of the introduction into American society matters even more than race, though the two interact. I think this statement can be defended empirically, notwithstanding the emergence of, for example, Japanese-American *sansei* militancy, with its strong race consciousness (see Kitano, 1968).

ogy itself. Quite the contrary. It has come because the minorities have begun to reject certain academic concepts. The new conceptual structure is not given by any academic establishment but comes within a conceptual structure derived from the situation of the African countries. In the colonial situation, rather than either the conquest or the slave situation, the new generation of black intellectuals is finding parallels to their own reactions to American society.

This exploration of colonialism by minority intellectuals has met a varied reaction, to say the least, but there have been some interesting attempts to translate these new and socially meaningful categories into proper academic sociologese. Blauner's (1969) article is one of the more ambitious attempts to relate the concept of "colonialism" as developed by Kenneth Clark, Stokely Carmichael and Eldridge Cleaver to sociological analysis. In the process, one kind of blurring is obvious even if not explicit: that is, that "colonialism" was far from uniform in the 19th Century, even in Africa.[2] In addition, Blauner (1969) makes explicit the adaptations he feels are necessary before the concept of colonialism can be meaningfully applied to the American scene. Common to both American internal colonialism of the blacks and European imperial expansion, Blauner argues, were the involuntary nature of the relationship between the two groups, the transformation or destruction of indigenous values, and, finally, racism. But Blauner warns that the situations are really different: "the . . . culture . . . of the (American black) colonized . . . is less developed; it is also less autonomous. In addition, the colonized are a numerical minority, and furthermore, they are ghettoized more totally and are more dispersed than people under classic colonialism."

But such adaptations are not needed in order to apply the concept fruit-fully to America's second largest minority—the Mexican Americans.[3] Here the colonial concept need not be analogized and, in fact, it describes and categorizes so accurately that one suspects that earlier "discovery" by sociologists of the Mexican Americans, particularly in New Mexico, might have discouraged uncritical application of the classic paradigms to all minorities. The initial Mexican contact with American society came by conquest, not by choice. Mexican American culture *was* well developed; it *was* autonomous; the colonized *were* a numerical majority. Further, they were—and are—less ghettoized and more dispersed than the American blacks. In fact, their patterns of residence (especially those existing at the turn of the century) are exactly those of "classic colonialism." And they were indigenous to the region and not "imported."[4]

2 For a good analysis of the variation, and of today's consequences, see the collection of papers in Kuper and Smith, 1969.

3 Mexican American intellectuals themselves have persistently analyzed the group in the conquest frame of reference. For a significant example, see Sánchez (1940).

4 "Indigenous" by comparison with the American blacks. Spanish America itself was

In at least the one state of New Mexico, there was a situation of comparatively "pure" colonialism. Outside of New Mexico, the original conquest colonialism was overlaid, particularly in the 20th century, with a grossly manipulated voluntary immigration. But throughout the American Southwest where the approximately five million Mexican Americans are now concentrated, understanding the Mexican minority requires understanding both conquest colonialism and "voluntary" immigration. It also requires understanding the interaction between colonialism and voluntarism.

In this paper I shall discuss a "culture trait" that is attributed to Mexican Americans both by popular stereotype and by social scientists—that is, a comparatively low degree of formal voluntary organization and hence of organized participation in political life. This is the academic form of the popular question: "What's wrong with the Mexicans? Why can't they organize for political activity?" In fact, as commonly asked both by social scientists and popular stereotype, the question begs the question. There is a great deal of variation in three widely different culture areas in the Southwest. And these culture areas differ most importantly in the particular variety of colonialism to which they were subjected. In the "classically" colonial situation, New Mexico, there has been in fact a relatively high order of political participation, especially by comparison with Texas, which we shall term "conflict colonialism," and California, which we shall term "economic colonialism."[5]

New Mexico.—An area that is now northern New Mexico and parts of southern Colorado was the most successful of the original Spanish colonies. At the beginning of the war between the United States and Mexico, there were more than 50,000 settlers, scattered in villages and cities with a strong upper class as well as a peasantry. There were frontier versions of Spanish colonial institutions that had been developing since 1600. The conquest of New Mexico by the United States was nearly bloodless and thus allowed, as a consequence, an extraordinary continuity between the Mexican period and the United States period.[6] The area became a territory of the United States and statehood was granted in 1912.

a colonial system, in which Indians were exploited. See Olguín (1967), for an angry statement to this effect.

[5] Of course, we are not arguing that colonialist domination—or for that matter the peculiar pattern of voluntary immigration—offers a full explanation of this complex population, or even of the three culture areas which are the focus of this paper. Mexican Americans and the history of the region are far too complexly interwoven to pretend that any analytic thread can unravel the full tapestry. For other theses, see the analyses developed in Grebler *et al.* (1970).

[6] This account draws on González (1967); Lamar (1966); Holmes (1964); and Donnelly (1947). Paul Fisher prepared a valuable analytic abstract of all but the first of these sources while a research assistant. I have used his document extensively here.

Throughout these changes political participation can be followed among the elite and among the masses of people. It can be analyzed in both its traditional manifestations and in contemporary patterns. In all respects it differs greatly in both level and quality from political participation outside this area. The heritage of colonialism helps explain these differences.

On the elite level, Spanish or Mexican leadership remained largely intact through the conquest and was shared with Anglo leadership after the termination of military rule in 1851. The indigenous elite retained considerable strength both in the dominant Republican party and in the state legislature. They were strong enough to ensure a bilingual provision in the 1912 Constitution (the only provision in the region that guarantees Spanish speakers the right to vote and hold office). Sessions of the legislature were—by law—conducted in both languages. Again, this is an extraordinary feature in any part of the continental United States. Just as in many Asian nations controlled by the British in the 19th century, the elite suffered little—either economically or politically.

On the lower-class level, in the villages, there was comparatively little articulation of New Mexican villages with the developing urban centers. What there was, however, was usually channeled through a recognized local authority, a *patrón*. Like the class structure, the *patrón* and the network of relations that sustained him were a normal part of the established local social system and not an ad hoc or temporary recognition of an individual's power. Thus political participation on both the elite and the lower-class levels were outgrowths of the existing social system.

Political participation of the elite and the *patrón* system was clearly a colonial phenomenon. An intact society, rather than a structureless mass of individuals, was taken into a territory of the United States with almost no violence. This truly colonial situation involves a totally different process of relationship between subordinate and superordinate from either the voluntary or the forced immigration of the subordinate—that is, totally different from either the "typical" American immigrant on the eastern seaboard or the slave imported from Africa.

A final point remains to be made not about political participation but about proto-political organization in the past. The villages of New Mexico had strong internal organizations not only of the informal, kinship variety but of the formal variety. These were the *penitente* sects and also the cooperative associations, such as those controlling the use of water and the grazing of livestock.[7] That such organizations were mobilized by New Mexican villagers is evidenced by the existence of terrorist groups operat-

---

[7] González (1967:64) concludes that *moradas*, or *penitente* organizations, "were found in most, if not all, of the northern Spanish settlements during the last half of the 19th Century and the first part of the 20th."

ing against both Anglo and Spanish landowners. González (1967) mentions two: one functioning in the 1890's and one in the 1920's. Such groups could also act as local police forces.

Let us turn to the present. Political participation of the conventional variety is very high compared to that of Mexican Americans in other states of the Southwest. Presently there is a Spanish American in the United States Senate (Montoya, an "old" name), following the tradition of Dennis Chavez (another "old" name). The state legislature in 1967 was almost one-third Mexican American. (There were no Mexican American legislators in California and no more than six percent in the legislature of any other Southwest state.) This, of course, reflects the fact that it is only in very recent years that Mexican Americans have become a numerical minority in New Mexico, but it also reflects the fact that organized political participation has remained high.

Finally, New Mexico is the locus of the only mass movement among Mexican Americans—the *Alianza Federal de Mercedes*, headed by Reies Tijerina. In theme, the *Alianza,* which attracted tens of thousands of members, relates specifically to the colonial past, protesting the loss of land and its usurpation by Anglo interests (including, most insultingly, those of the United States Forest Service). It is this loss of land which has ultimately been responsible for the destruction of village (Spanish) culture and the large-scale migration to the cities.[8] In the light of the importance of the traditional village as a base for political mobilization, it is not really surprising that the *Alianza* should have appeared where it did. In content the movement continues local terrorism (haystack-burning) but has now extended beyond the local protest as its members have moved to the cities. Rather than being directed against specific Anglo or Spanish land-grabbers, it has lately been challenging the legality of the Treaty of Guadalupe Hidalgo. The broadening of the *Alianza*'s base beyond specific local areas probably required the pooled discontent of those immigrants from many villages, many original land grants. It is an ironic feature of the *Alianza* that the generalization of its objectives and of its appeal should be possible only long after most of the alleged land-grabbing had been accomplished.

Texas.—Mexican Americans in Texas had a sharply contrasting historical experience. The Mexican government in Texas was replaced by a revolution of the American settlers. Violence between Anglo-American settlers and Mexican residents continued in south Texas for generations after the annexation of Texas by the United States and the consequent

---

[8] González (1967:75) analyzes the *Alianza* as a "nativist" movement, and suggests that its source is partly in the fact that *"for the first time* many elements of Spanish-American culture are in danger of disappearing" (emphasis added).

full-scale war. Violence continued in organized fashion well into the 20th
Century with armed clashes involving the northern Mexican *guerilleros*
and the U.S. Army.

This violence meant a total destruction of Mexican elite political participation by conquest, while such forces as the Texas Rangers were used
to suppress Mexican American participation on the lower status or village
levels. The ecology of settlement in south Texas remains somewhat reminiscent of that in northern New Mexico: there are many areas that are
predominantly Mexican, and even some towns that are still controlled by
Mexicans. But there is far more complete Anglo economic and political
dominance on the local level. Perhaps most important, Anglo-Americans
outnumbered Mexicans by five to one even before the American conquest.
By contrast, Mexicans in New Mexico remained the numerical majority
for more than 100 years after conquest.

Texas state politics reflect the past just as in New Mexico. Mexican
Americans hold some slight representation in the U.S. Congress. There are
two Mexican American Congressmen, one from San Antonio and one from
Brownsville (at the mouth of the Rio Grande river), one of whom is a
political conservative. A minor representation far below the numerical
proportion of Mexican Americans is maintained in the Texas legislature.

It is on the local level that the continued suppression is most apparent.
As long ago as 1965 Mexican Americans in the small town of Crystal City
won political control in a municipal election that electrified all Mexican
Americans in Texas and stirred national attention. But this victory was
possible only with statewide help from Mexican American organizations
and some powerful union groups. Shortly afterward (after some intimidation from the Texas Rangers) the town returned to Anglo control. Some
other small towns (Del Rio, Kingsville, Alice) have recently had demonstrations in protest against local suppressions. Small and insignificant as
they were, the demonstrations once again would not have been possible
without outside support, primarily from San Antonio. (The most significant of these San Antonio groups have been aided by the Ford Foundation. The repercussions in Congress were considerable and may threaten
the future of the Ford Foundation as well as the Mexican Americans in
Texas.)

More general Mexican American political organizations in Texas have a
history that is strikingly reminiscent of Negro political organization.
(There is one continuous difference: whites participated in most Negro
organizations at the outset. It is only very recently that Anglos have been
involved with Mexicans in such a fashion. In the past, Mexicans were almost entirely on their own.) Political organization has been middle class,
highly oriented toward traditional expressions of "Americanism," and ac-
commodationist. In fact, the first Mexican American political association
refused to call itself a political association for fear that it might be too

provocative to the Anglo power structure; it was known as a "civic" organization when it was formed in Texas in the late 1920's. Even the name of this group (LULAC or the League of United Latin American Citizens) evokes an atmosphere of middle-class gentility. The second major group, the American G.I. Forum, was formed in an atmosphere of greater protest, after a Texas town had refused burial to a Mexican American soldier. In recent years, increasing politicization has been manifested by the formation of such a group as PASSO (Political Association of Spanish Speaking Organizations). But in Texas, throughout the modern period the very act of *ethnic* politics has been controversial, even among Mexican Americans.[9]

California.—The California transition between Mexican and American settlement falls midway between the Texas pattern of violence and the relatively smooth change in New Mexico. In northern California the discovery of gold in 1849 almost immediately swamped a sparse Mexican population in a flood of Anglo-American settlers. Prior to this time an orderly transition was in progress. Thus the effect was very much that of violence in Texas: the indigenous Mexican elite was almost totally excluded from political participation. A generation later when the opening of the railroads repeated this demographic discontinuity in southern California the Mexicans suffered the same effect. They again were almost totally excluded from political participation. The New Mexico pattern of social organization on a village level had almost no counterpart in California. Here the Mexican settlements and the economy were built around very large land holdings rather than around villages. This meant, in essence, that even the settlements that survived the American takeover relatively intact tended to lack internal social organization. Villages (as in the Bandini rancho which became the modern city of Riverside) were more likely to be clusters of ranch employees than an independent, internally coherent community.

In more recent times the peculiar organization of California politics has tended to work against Mexican American participation from the middle and upper status levels. California was quick to adopt the ideas of "direct democracy" of the Progressive era. These tend somewhat to work against ethnic minorities.[10] But this effect is accidental and can hardly be called "internal colonialism," coupled as it was with the anti-establishment ideals of the Progressive era. The concept of "colonialism," in fact, appears most useful with reference to the extreme manipulation of Mexican immigration

[9] This discussion draws on Guzmán (1967) and Cuéllar (forthcoming).
[10] Fogelson (1967) gives a good picture of political practices which had the latent consequence of excluding Mexicans from Los Angeles politics—a fact of great importance given the very large concentrations of Mexican Americans in that city. Political impotence in Los Angeles has affected a very significant fraction of California's Mexican Americans. Harvey (1966) gives a broader picture of California politics.

in the 20th century. Attracted to the United States by the hundreds of thousands in the 1920's, Mexicans and many of their U.S.-born children were deported ("repatriated") by welfare agencies during the Depression, most notably from California. (Texas had almost no welfare provisions; hence no repatriation.) The economic expansion in World War II required so much labor that Mexican immigration was supplemented by a contract labor arrangement. But, as in the Depression, "too many" were attracted and came to work in the United States without legal status. Again, in 1954, massive sweeps of deportations got rid of Mexicans by the hundreds of thousands in "Operation Wetback." New Mexico was largely spared both waves of deportation; Texas was involved primarily in Operation Wetback rather than in the welfare repatriations. California was deeply involved in both.

This economic manipulation of the nearly bottomless pool of Mexican labor has been quite conscious and enormously useful to the development of California extractive and agricultural enterprises. Only in recent years with increasing—and now overwhelming—proportions of native-born Mexican Americans in the population has the United States been "stuck" with the Mexicans. As one consequence, the naturalization rate of Mexican immigrants has been very low. After all, why relinquish even the partial protection of Mexican citizenship? Furthermore the treatment of Mexicans as economic commodities has greatly reduced both their motivation and their effectiveness as political participants. The motivations that sent Mexican Americans to the United States appear to have been similar to those that sent immigrants from Europe. But the conscious dehumanization of Mexicans in the service of the railroad and citrus industries in California and elsewhere meant an asymmetry in relationship between "host" and immigrant that is less apparent in the European patterns of immigration. Whatever resentment that might have found political voice in the past had no middle class organizational patterns. California was structurally unreceptive and attitudinally hostile.

Thus in California the degree of Mexican political participation remains low. The electoral consequences are even more glaringly below proportional representation than in Texas. There is only one national representative (Congressman Roybal from Los Angeles) and only one in the state legislature. Los Angeles County (with nearly a million Mexican Americans) has no Supervisor of Mexican descent and the city has no Councilman of Mexican descent. Otherwise, the development of political associations has followed the Texas pattern, although later, with meaningful political organization a post-World War II phenomenon. The G.I. Forum has formed chapters in California. In addition, the Community Service Organization, oriented to local community political mobilization, and the Mexican American Political Association, oriented to state-wide political targets, have repeated the themes of Texas' voluntary association on the level of the growing middle class.

How useful, then, is the concept of colonialism when it is applied to these three culture areas? We argue here that both the nature and extent of political participation in the state of New Mexico can be understood with reference to the "classical" colonial past. We noted that a continuity of elite participation in New Mexico from the period of Mexican rule to the period of American rule paved the way for a high level of conventional political participation. The fact that village social structure remained largely intact is in some measure responsible for the appearance of the only mass movement of Mexicans in the Southwest today—the *Alianza*. But even this movement is an outcome of colonialism; the expropriation of the land by large-scale developers and by federal conservation interests led ultimately to the destruction of the village economic base—and to the movement of the dispossessed into the cities. Once living in the cities in a much closer environment than that of the scattered small villages, they could "get together" and respond to the anti-colonialist protests of a charismatic leader.

Again following this idea, we might categorize the Texas experience as "conflict colonialism." This would reflect the violent discontinuity between the Mexican and the American periods of elite participation and the current struggle for the legitimation of ethnic politics on all levels. In this latter aspect, the "conflict colonialism" of Texas is reminiscent of black politics in the Deep South, although it comes from different origins.

To apply the colonial concept to Mexicans in California, we might usefully use the idea of "economic colonialism." The destruction of elite political strength by massive immigration and the comparative absence of local political organization meant a political vacuum for Mexican Americans. Extreme economic manipulation inhibited any attachment to the reality or the ideals of American society and indirectly allowed as much intimidation as was accomplished by the overt repression of such groups as the Texas Rangers.

To return to Blauner's use of the concept of "internal colonialism": in the case of the Mexicans in the United States, a major segment of this group who live in New Mexico require no significant conceptual adaptation of the classic analyses of European overseas colonialism. Less adaptation is required in fact than in applying the concepts to such countries as Kenya, Burma, Algeria, and Indonesia. Not only was the relationship between the Mexican and the Anglo-American "involuntary," involving "racism" and the "transformation . . . of indigenous values," but the culture of the Spanish American was well developed, autonomous, a majority numerically, and contained a full social system with an upper and middle as well as lower class. The comparatively non-violent conquest was really almost a postscript to nearly a decade of violence between the United States and Mexico which began in Texas.

The Texas pattern, although markedly different, can still be fitted under a colonialist rubric, with a continuous thread of violence, suppression, and adaptations to both in recent political affairs.

The Mexican experience in California is much more complicated. Mexicans lost nearly all trace of participation in California politics. Hence, there was no political tradition of any kind, even the purely negative experience in Texas. Then, too, the relationship between imported labor and employer was "voluntary," at least on the immigrants' side. The relationships were much more asymmetrical than in the "classic colonial" case.

If any further proof of the applicability of the idea of "colonialism" were needed, we have the developing ideology of the new *chicano* militants themselves. Like the black ideologies, *chicanismo* emphasizes colonialism, but in a manner to transcend the enormous disparities in Mexican American experience. Thus one of the latest versions of the ideology reaches out to a time *before* even Spanish colonialism to describe the Southwestern United States as "Aztlán"—an Aztec term. "Aztlán" is a generality so sweeping that it can include all Mexican Americans. Mexican Americans are the products of layer upon layer of colonialism and the overlay of American influence is only the most recent. That the young ideologues or the "cultural nationalists" (as they call themselves) should utilize the symbols of the first of these colonists, the Aztecs (along with Emiliano Zapata, the most "Indian" of Mexican revolutionaries from the past), is unquestionably of great symbolic significance to the participants themselves. But perhaps of more sociological significance (and far more controversial among the participants) is the attempt to legitimate *chicano* culture. This culture comes from the habits, ideas, and speech of the most despised lower-class Mexican American as he has been forced to live in a quasi-legal ghetto culture in large Southwestern cities. These symbols are all indigenous to the United States and are neither Mexican, nor Spanish, nor even Aztec. But they *do* offer symbols to all Mexican Americans, after a widely varying experience with Americans in which, perhaps, the ideologues can agree only that it was "colonialist."

REFERENCES

Blauner, Robert. 1969. "Internal Colonialism and Ghetto Revolt." *Social Problems* **16** (Spring, 1969): 393–408.

Cuéllar, Alfred. Forthcoming. "Perspective on Politics." In Joan W. Moore with Alfredo Cuéllar, *Mexican Americans*. Englewood Cliffs, N.J.: Prentice-Hall, Inc.

Donnelly, Thomas C. 1947. *The Government of New Mexico*. Albuquerque: The University of New Mexico Press.

Fogelson, Robert M. 1967. *The Fragmented Metropolis: Los Angeles, 1850–1960*. Cambridge, Mass.: Harvard University Press.

González, Nancie L. 1967. *The Spanish Americans of New Mexico: A Distinctive Heritage*. Advance Report 9. Los Angeles: University of California, Mexican American Study Project.

Grebler, Leo *et al.* 1970. *The Mexican American People*. New York: Free Press.

Guzmán, Ralph. 1967. Political Socialization." Unpublished manuscript.

Harvey, Richard B. 1966. "California Politics: Historical Profile." In R. B. Dvorin and D. Misner (eds.), *California Politics and Policies*. Reading, Mass.: Addison-Wesley, Inc.

Holmes, Jack E. 1964. *Party, Legislature and Governor in the Politics of New Mexico, 1911–1963*. Ph.D. dissertation, Chicago: University of Chicago.

Kitano, Harry H. L. 1968. *The Japanese Americans*. Englewood Cliffs, N.J.: Prentice-Hall, Inc.

Kuper, Leo and M. G. Smith (eds.). 1969. *Pluralism in Africa*. Berkeley and Los Angeles: University of California Press.

Lamar, Howard Roberts. 1966. *The Far Southwest, 1845–1912: A Territorial History*. New Haven: Yale University Press.

Olguín, John Phillip. 1967. "Where Does the 'Justified' Resentment Begin?" New Mexico Business offprint, July 1967.

Sánchez, George I. 1940. *Forgotten People*. Albuquerque: The University of New Mexico Press.

Intermarriage & Jewish Survival

MARSHALL SKLARE

The American Jewish community is a kind of fabulous invalid whose death had long ago been predicted by the doctors in attendance but whose ongoing salubrity confounds their predictions. Contradictions, as is the case with any living organism, abound. American Jewry may be inordinately "problem"-ridden and "crisis"-beset, but its institutions, with all their attendant activities, continue to thrive. New synagogues and community centers are constantly being built, and support for Israel, financial and otherwise, remains undiminished. Enrollment in Jewish day schools shows a steady growth, and while some would dismiss this as merely a response to the deterioration of the public schools, a more positive consideration is certainly at work as well. Even the grave problem of the loss of Jewish identity among college youth is not entirely a one-sided proposition. There is a new enthusiasm for Jewish studies on the campus and it is now harder to find suitable instructors than it is to attract interested students. As for extracurricular activities, the Hillel Foundation—no longer the sole Jewish address on campus—must now compete with such organizations as Yavneh (Orthodox) and Atid (Conservative). The latest campus phenomenon, of course, are the groups dedicated to challenging the Jewish Establishment, of which the best known, thanks to its recent demonstration in Boston at a convention of the Council of Jewish Federations and Welfare Funds, is the Jewish Activist League.

But whatever significance one may attach to these developments, they are overshadowed by one persistent trend: the ever-increasing incidence of intermarriage between Jews and non-Jews. It is intermarriage which weighs more heavily than all the positive trends combined, and which calls into question the "creative survival," as the phrase has it, of the American Jewish community. That this should be so is hardly surprising, since intermarriage strikes at the very core of Jewish group existence.

What precisely is the current incidence of intermarriage? This is no easy matter to determine. Official statistics are available only for Iowa and Indiana, the two jurisdictions which ask for religion in their marriage forms; but these states have small Jewish populations which are not representative of the nation at large. The privately-conducted Jewish community surveys which have been done in some communities are a better statistical source, though such surveys have generally been confined to cities with small or middle-size Jewish populations. Unfortunately, most of these studies indicate only a cumulative rate—that is, they tell us the ratio of the intermarried to inmarried but give no figure for the current rate. Furthermore, since it is safe to assume that the intermarried are more marginal to the Jewish community than the inmarried, it is reasonable to conclude that such privately-conducted surveys underestimate the true extent of intermarriage. Finally, conclusions about the incidence of intermarriage depend to a large extent upon which survey one chooses. For example, a 1958 study of San Francisco uncovered an 18.5 percent cumulative intermarriage rate while a 1963 survey of Providence, Rhode Island indicated a 2.6 percent rate. The two communities apparently represent opposite ends of the inter-marriage spectrum.

Perhaps the best guide to the current intermarriage situation is a 1965 survey of Boston. With 185,000 Jewish residents Boston has a larger Jewish population than many other cities which have been surveyed, and the temper of its Jewish life approximates that of the giant communities where the majority of American Jews live. Boston also has a balance of old and new Jewish families, with individuals of diverse educational attainment and differing levels of sophistication, and while the city's educational and research institutions may seem to attract inter-married couples, on the other hand its well-organized Jewish community draws those who are interested in intensive Jewish living.

The Boston study reveals a cumulative rate of 7 percent. The current rate, however, may be more closely approximated through a revealing cross-tabulation of the religious composition of married couples by age of the husband. Thus we find that in cases of couples where the husband is age fifty-one and over, the incidence of intermarriage is reported at 3 percent; ages thirty-one to fifty, 7 percent; thirty and younger, 20 percent. Since the marriage-formation rate is highest in the last of these groups, it is possible to estimate the current figure for intermarriage at close to 20 percent. The statistical impressiveness of this figure—one in five—becomes even more significant when we consider the added fact that the younger the couple at the time of marriage, the greater the likelihood of their having children. It is the marital pattern of the young, then, which is determinative; not only do they marry in greater numbers than their elders, but they have a greater impact on the demographic future of the Jewish community. Furthermore, they wield an influence by example on their younger, soon-to-marry siblings and cousins. It is even possible that the marital style of those thirty and under may exert a subtle pull on their elders who are seeking to remarry after divorce or the death of a spouse.

If by 1965 one in five younger Jewish couples in Boston constituted a case of intermarriage, we can safely assume that the figure is now approaching one in four. And if this is true in so conservative a city as Boston, it must mean that intermarriage has reached large-scale proportions throughout the country as a whole. Yet, despite the gravity of the problem, the Jewish community, at any rate on the official level, has devoted little attention to the matter. Indeed, the first symposium on intermarriage sponsored by a major national Jewish organization was published only as late as 1963 (*Intermarriage and Jewish Life*, edited by Werner J. Cahnman). During the same year the *American Jewish Year Book*, the standard reference work in the field, carried *its* first article on intermarriage. (In its sixty-three previous volumes, the *Year Book* discussed the matter only once, and briefly at that, in a scant two pages.) As in other areas, it was left to a non-Jewish source to take the lead, in this instance *Look* magazine, whose famous 1964 article on the subject, somewhat flamboyantly titled "The Vanishing American Jew," stimulated a discussion that still resounds today.[1]

[1] The latest book-length study of the subject is by Louis A. Berman, a psychologist at the University of Illinois (Chicago campus). Entitled *Jews and Intermarriage: A Study in Personality and Culture* (Thomas Yoseloff, 707 pp., $12.00), it is a wide-ranging investigation which includes exhaustive footnotes and a comprehensive bibliography which will be of great assistance to future investigators.

I

Why did the American Jewish community resist confronting the issue
for so long? The answer rests in the peculiar dilemmas which intermarriage poses, and which, until the matter could no longer be avoided,
inhibited public discussion. To begin with, the vast majority of American
Jews, in a radical departure from the traditions of their matchmaking
forebears, enthusiastically subscribe to the idea of romantic love as the
basis for marriage: the final determination of a mate is the prerogative
of the child rather than the parent. Obviously, there are no problems
when a Jewish boy and a Jewish girl fall in love and decide to marry;
the parents are only affirmed in their romantic bias and, there being
no other objections to the match, can give it their wholehearted blessings.
However, should it be a question of a Jewish boy and Gentile girl (or
vice versa), the value of romantic love collides with the values of
endogamy and Jewish survival. And should the parents seek to break
up the match, they must in effect ask the young people to fall *out* of
love, to renounce values they themselves have celebrated and inculcated.

Intermarriage tends to stir up another, perhaps more fundamental
conflict, this an effect of the liberal views which American Jews hold
generally on social as well as political issues. For whatever reason—
whether prompted by traditional moral values or by their self-interest
as a minority—American Jews are strong believers in the American
creed of equality for all people "regardless of race or religion." This
conviction, of course, clashes with an equally forceful ethnocentric impulse, but, for the most part, American Jews live comfortably with such
contradictions, particularly if their children continue to marry within
the faith. The moment a question of intermarriage arises, however, these
contradictions between the belief in romantic love and equality, on the
one side, and the ethnocentric impulse, on the other, force themselves
painfully to the surface. And the issue is further complicated by the
fact that so many American Jewish parents, lacking the requisite spiritual
commitments, are in no position to offer *religious* objections to a mixed
marriage.

Moreover, as strongly as American Jews may oppose intermarriage,
many are dimly aware that such unions after all represent the logical
culmination of the quest for full equality. For widespread intermarriage
can be seen to mark the end of all those discriminatory practices which
preserve social distance between the Jew and the larger community,
which restrict opportunity, and which still leave the Jew with a feeling
of lingering inferiority. Yet the fact remains that widespread intermarriage must also inevitably raise doubts regarding the basic premise of
Jewish life—that creative Jewish survival *is* possible in a free society

(which has been almost an article of faith to the American Jew, except for a small Orthodox minority).

Given so many clashing commitments and opposing values, it is no wonder that the Jewish community was reluctant to examine the issue of intermarriage until its increasing incidence made open scrutiny unavoidable.

II

The question of intermarriage, to be sure, is not one that the Jewish community alone confronts; it is a concern shared by all minorities in the United States—at least all those who care about group survival. For such groups, intermarriage is a palpable threat, one that is felt on a collective as well as an individual basis. On the group level, it poses the obvious dangers of physical attrition; in its individual aspects, it threatens the continuity of generations within the family, the ability of family members to identify with one another, and their satisfaction with family roles.

Since American Jewry is by and large survivalist in temper, all these conditions obtain, but with variations which derive from the specific Jewish situation. The most critical relates to group size. American Jewry may be the largest Jewish community in the world, but American Jews number fewer than six million in a total population of over two hundred million; their birth-rate is lower than that of the Protestants, and considerably lower than that of the Catholics. To put the case baldly, there is no surplus Jewish population to cushion the impact of mixed marriage. For while there is still a chance that the Jewish partner in a marriage will not be lost to the group, the odds are slim that the children of the union will remain within the Jewish fold.

But even more significant is the fact that when intermarriage reaches a certain frequency it creates a measure of approval for itself. While it may still be considered somewhat unconventional, the impression is fostered that intermarriage is the inevitable wave of the future. And if intermarriage is to be regarded in this light, then individuals may find themselves under a self-generated pressure to redefine the issue from that of combatting intermarriage to that of accommodating to it. Evidence is accumulating that the most highly acculturated elements of American Jewry are now engaged in making just such a redefinition. Their pattern of accommodation has implications which strike at the very nature of Jewish identity in the modern world.

This new trend toward accommodation may be observed in any upper- or upper-middle-class neighborhood. A good example is Lakeville, the fictional name of a Midwestern suburb noted for the high level of sophistication and acculturation of its Jewish residents. Lakeville was the object of intensive investigation in 1957–1958,[2] ten years later, in 1968, a selected group of the original respondents was again interviewed, with intermarriage among the subjects of inquiry.

All those queried were convinced that the intermarriage rate had risen sharply in Lakeville and that the practice was more widespread than it had been ten years earlier. This conviction was based not on intuition or hearsay but on direct personal experience. There was scarcely a family in the group that did not have a Gentile son- or daughter-in-law, or a nephew, niece, or cousin married to a non-Jew. Some unusual evidence of the extent of intermarriage was provided by one respondent— admittedly an extreme case—who had developed his own private intermarriage poll, based on the wedding invitations he and his wife received from Jewish relatives and friends: in only 50 percent of the invitations were both bride and groom Jewish. (He called the slitting open of the envelope "the moment of truth.") As for attitudes toward intermarriage, they run the gamut from full approval to outright disapproval. But even those who fall into the latter category are "soft" on the issue: though they tell their children that they will not accept such a marriage, they admitted when pressed that they were not prepared to face an estrangement between themselves and their children over intermarriage.

Jewish parents in present-day Lakeville, those with young children at any rate, still make some of the same attempts as were common in the past to head off the chance of exogamous unions on the part of their offspring. Almost without exception they send their children to the religious schools of the local synagogues (Lakeville is predominantly Reform), hoping that Jewish education, even in the form of Sunday schools, will produce Jewish commitment; and they place great stock in Confirmation, as well as in Bar and Bat Mitzvah—those adolescent *rites de passage* which have become so significant a part of American Jewish life.

A decade ago parents found it useful to follow up such educational endeavors with discussions with their maturing youngsters which stressed what, in our earlier study, we called the "discord approach." This consisted, essentially, of mental-health arguments, which emphasized the point that the marital relationship is fraught with enough difficulties without introducing yet another potential disharmony, such as a mate of a different faith. Enlightened people, it was conceded, have the right to freedom of marital choice, but wisdom dictates that the choice be a fellow Jew, for the wages of intermarriage are unhappiness. Advocacy of the view that exogamy would result in marital pathology was a safe

[2] See Marshall Sklare and Joseph Greenblum, *Jewish Identity on the Suburban Frontier*, Basic Books, 1967.

way of expressing the desire for Jewish survival while at the same time avoiding the appearance of ethnocentrism. Our latest interviews, however, reveal that there is a growing sense of unreality about the "discord approach." Nor could it be otherwise. Not only is intermarriage an everyday occurrence in present-day Lakeville, but so too is the reality of *successful* intermarriage. Furthermore, every child in the community has examples available to him of inmarriages which are not doing all that well.

Whatever the reality behind the "discord approach" even a decade ago, its use suggested a determined effort to combat intermarriage and a belief that the battle against intermarriage could be won (though, to be sure, with inevitable casualties). The most striking change in present-day Lakeville is the erosion of confidence—particularly among the more acculturated Reform Jews—in that belief. This is why the struggle is now viewed not as a matter of prevention but increasingly, on the part of the parent, as a matter of accommodation to the inevitable. In fact, one encounters parents who are more concerned about themselves than about their children. Their concern centers around how they will act should one of their children present them with an incipient case of intermarriage.

The key phrase here is "to act intelligently," that is, not lapse into hysterics but place reason before emotion and judge the prospective son- or daughter-in-law by the same standards one would use if he or she were Jewish. Most Lakeville parents today are agreed that under no circumstances must they set up a situation which will alienate them from their children, not even under the provocation of an intermarriage; and they look to their own mental wellbeing as well as their children's. One woman respondent, for example, related how her sister had worked herself into such a state of frenzy over a daughter's intermarriage that she required psychiatric treatment. Appalled by her sister's behavior, she resolved that should she ever find herself in a similar situation she would act differently. Fate soon presented her with the opportunity—a Gentile son-in-law of her own—and she passed the test with flying colors.

But when all is said and done, when all the accommodations have been made and all the social realities accepted, how is the parent to handle that most unsettling of all factors, the blow to his self-esteem? For after all, a child who marries out of the faith appears to be telling the parent that he has not succeeded in forging a close enough psychic identification between himself and his child to insure that the latter will choose a mate of identical background, thus reproducing the parents' own marriage. Inasmuch as it is not easy to admit to failure as a parent, the following responses are now commonly encountered in Lakeville.

The first might be described as the guilt-shifting ploy. Here the burden of responsibility, instead of being shouldered by the parents, is laid at the door of the synagogue, whose spiritual leaders and educators have clearly failed in *their* task ("If only the Sunday School teachers had been more competent." "If only the rabbi had been more inspiring."). The psychological mechanism, of course, is familiar and requires little further elaboration.

The second response, whose roots can also be traced to parental guilt and to damaged self-esteem, takes the form of trying to make the best of an unfortunate situation by somehow legitimating the marriage. For the parents of Lakeville this means that the ceremony must be performed by a rabbi.[3] It is not that they question the validity, legal or otherwise, of a civil wedding (heretofore the traditional recourse for mixed couples), but in the new Lakeville there are certain urgent psychological (as well as social) requirements that only a religious ceremony, with a rabbi in attendance, can satisfy. In general, the son or daughter about to embark on the intermarriage is inclined to go along with the parents.[4]

This, however, is by no means the end of the story. As the parents soon discover, it is not all that simple to find a rabbi who will do the job, even in permissive Lakeville. Indeed, it turns out that the rabbis of all of the four Reform congregations which serve the community refuse to officiate at mixed weddings. Many highly acculturated Jews in Lakeville consider their behavior outrageous, as indicated by the heat, passion, and dismay which characterize their comments on the matter: "The rabbis don't hesitate to officiate at a marriage between a Jewish boy and a Jewish girl in which the boy may be of the lowest character, or the girl a tramp. By what right then do they refuse to officiate at a marriage where the Gentile fulfills the highest aspiration of the Jewish moral code?" Not only are the rabbis accused of lack of ethical sensitivity, but it is even charged that they are uninterested in Jewish survival: "If the rabbis are truly interested in preserving Jewish religion, they should welcome mixed couples. By sending them away the rabbis close the door to their eventual conversion or to their raising the children as Jews." And

[3] A Reform rabbi, that is. Orthodox and Conservative rabbis will not officiate at mixed weddings. Neither will most Reform rabbis, as we shall see; but in the case of the Orthodox and Conservative rabbis, the abstention is based on an overall adherence to the corpus of Jewish religious law. Reform rabbis do not feel themselves under the same obligations.

[4] One would expect that the parents of the Gentile partner would object to a Jewish religious ceremony and hold out for either a civil ceremony or even a church wedding. But surprisingly enough (and this can be taken as an index of some sort to the changes that have occurred in American society), in many instances the wishes of the Jewish parents are respected. The non-Jewish bride or groom may even be enthusiastic about the idea, regarding the rabbi's blessing of the union as conferring special distinction.

one respondent even maintained that the reason for the rabbis' refusal was the fear of "getting into trouble" with their colleagues in the "rabbis' union."

But a genuine need finds its proper satisfaction: if the four "bad" rabbis of Lakeville will not perform the marriage, there is a "good" Reform rabbi serving a neighboring suburb who will. This rabbi, who comes to the rescue of distraught parents, and who, according to one of the respondents, does "a land-office business," is as competent as his more traditional-minded colleagues. To the uninstructed, he may appear suspect. One Lakeville matron who was forced to seek out his services was afraid he would turn out to be a "second-class" rabbi with dubious credentials; she was delighted to discover that he could perform as impressive a ceremony as the rabbis she knew in Lakeville. Because of the decision of this rabbi, the good life in Lakeville includes the phenomenon of intermarriage with rabbinical sanction.

III

The first known instance of a rabbi officiating at a marriage between a Jew and a Gentile—the groom was Jewish and the bride Christian—took place in Leipzig in 1849. The rabbi was Samuel Holdheim, one of the founders of Reform Judaism in Germany, and his wedding sermon on that landmark occasion is worth noting, underscoring as it does the attraction which the idea of intermarriage has exerted for Jews in the modern age.

Intermarriage, according to Holdheim, a staunch universalist in the best 19th-century tradition, is the "ideal marriage," an expression of man's noblest spiritual impulses. When two young people of different faiths plight their troth, they do nothing less than affirm that we are all children of the "one Father who created us all"; this represents the true religion, and the young couple its highest exemplars. Holdheim went on to take issue with the "discord approach" (which even then, apparently, was used to discourage intermarriages), maintaining that those who would believe that intermarriages run the risk of marital disharmony only show their small faith in the redeeming power of love: "Men misconstrue the omnipotence of love and consider love only a weak twig which must be bound to the pole of faith in order to resist the winds and storms of life. . . . However, love, as the highest moral force, stands by itself, entirely alone, and does not require a common faith for its support." Clearly Holdheim regarded intermarriage as the wave of the future, as the harbinger of a better world, where Jew and Gentile, quite literally, would lie down together, very much like the lamb and the lion in Isaiah's eschatological vision of togetherness, a world where tolerance and mutual understanding would replace the antagonisms engendered by separatism. A world, in short, where the Jew might prosper.

Intermarriage might be all that Holdheim claimed for it—and other Reform rabbis of the period and after shared his optimism—but there still remained the nagging question of the survival of the Jewish people and the Jewish religion. Even Reform rabbis who desired the brotherhood of man under the fatherhood of God realized that intermarriage must invariably lead to Jewish dissolution. It was this awareness which prevented Reform from an outright endorsement of intermarriage and which prompted the famous statement of David Einhorn, a leading American 19th-century Reform rabbi and no less a proponent of Classical Reform than Holdheim: "Each intermarriage drives a nail in the coffin of Judaism." In 1909, the Central Conference of American Rabbis (CCAR), the association of Reform rabbis (or the "rabbis' union," as our disgruntled respondent called it), passed a resolution on the controversial subject which has stood to the present day: ". . . [intermarriages] are contrary to the Jewish tradition and should therefore be discouraged by the American Rabbinate." The vagueness of the term "discouraged" satisfied both the pro- and anti-intermarriage factions since it could be interpreted to mean all things to all Reform rabbis. On the one hand, the resolution went on record as voicing the collective objection to intermarriage; on the other hand, since it merely "discouraged" but did not proscribe, it left room for each rabbi to decide for himself what course to follow. Moreover, the imprecision of the wording made it possible for the rabbis who performed intermarriages to set conditions of their own devising, should they so choose, e.g., exacting a promise from the couple that they would raise their children as Jews, or that the non-Jewish partner would convert to Judaism at a later date. Nor did the resolution prevent those more traditionally-minded rabbis from making an exception to their no-intermarriage rule when they felt that circumstances warranted it.

This permissiveness notwithstanding, the majority of Reform rabbis were not inclined to officiate at mixed weddings. Reluctance increased during the 30's and 40's when Classical Reform, with its sweeping universalistic emphasis, so at variance with the events of the day, came under wide attack and the position generally called Neo-Reform grew in strength. Neo-Reform, more traditionalist in outlook, advocated a strengthening of ties with the larger Jewish community which, at least with respect to marriage, observed Jewish religious law. Some Reform rabbis continued to perform intermarriages, but the practice fell into disrepute.

Until recently it all worked out reasonably well. There was, we might say, an "arrangement." The majority of the CCAR membership, with the approval of the Reform laity, stuck by their guns in refusing to officiate at intermarriages, but when approached to do so, a Reform rabbi could always refer the applicants to a colleague who had no compunctions in the matter. He might not always approve of his more "liberal" colleague's action, yet he rarely hesitated to make the referral; it was a way of getting off the hook and of pleasing everybody. As for the rabbis who performed these marriages, they tacitly accepted their deviant status, but continued to do what they felt they had to. The system worked to everyone's satisfaction and even grew to include Reform laymen who were part of the referral grapevine.

So long as it all stayed within reasonable bounds, statistically speaking, and so long as the parties involved acknowledged intermarriage as deviant, the larger Jewish community could afford to look aside. If some rabbis were performing marriages which had no standing in Jewish religious law, well, that was *their* responsibility; so long as the Jewish collectivity was not being made to suffer unduly, there was no need to take action. And if some couples thought that their marriages were Jewishly valid and considered their children Jewish (in cases where the wife was Gentile[5]), well, they were simply mistaken. Every now and then the lapses permitted by Reform were taken to task by Orthodox and Conservative spokesmen; however, the CCAR resolution was always on hand to silence the critics. Periodically, an Orthodox rabbi would propose the establishment of a Jewish family register so that there would be no ambiguity about who was Jewish and who not, but the idea was never taken up. By and large, a kind of status quo prevailed.

IV

But this state of affairs was not to last. The increase in the incidence of intermarriage has brought with it an increase in the number of Jewish parents who want a Jewish ceremony for their intermarrying child. Hence the increase in the number of interfaith couples seeking the services of a rabbi, and a consequent increase in the number of "intermarrying" rabbis. Furthermore, these rabbis are no longer content to remain underground, as it were. Aware of the changing attitudes of their congregants, they have grown more aggressive, refusing to concede any rabbinic inferiority. Indeed, they maintain that by their conduct they are actually fulfilling a higher rabbinic function than their tradition-minded colleagues, since their cooperation tends to "save" couples who might otherwise turn away from the Jewish community; nor, as alleged, is it they who are responsible for spreading assimilation but their op-

[5] In Jewish law only the child of a Jewish *mother* is regarded as Jewish. The child of a Jewish father and a non-Jewish mother must convert in order to be recognized as a Jew in the eyes of Jewish law. The current controversy in Israel over "who is a Jew" revolves in part around these legal requirements.

posites, who by their intransigence drive many Jews away from Judaism. The rabbinic crossfire has grown so heavy in some instances that it is not unusual to find the permissive contingent accusing the stricter faction of "insincerity" and "hypocrisy," of donning a false cloak of respectability ("If our colleagues really disagree with us, then why do they continue to make referrals?"; and more bitterly: "Why do they expect *us* to wash their dirty linen for them?").

The effect of all this has been the emergence of an effort to affirm the bona fides of the rabbis who perform intermarriages; the effort has been spearheaded by David Max Eichhorn, a retired Reform rabbi who spent most of his active career as an official of the National Jewish Welfare Board, where he was connected with the military chaplaincy. Eichhorn had been widely known in earlier years as a proponent of the view that Judaism should engage in a more active program of proselytizing among non-Jews. Recently, however, he has shifted his energies from the cause of conversion to the legitimation of intermarriage.

Eichhorn opened his campaign by polling the approximately 1,000 members of the CCAR on whether or not they officiate at mixed weddings. There were eighty-nine affirmative replies. To this number Eichhorn added the names of twenty or so who had not bothered to answer but of whose position he knew, and he concluded that: ". . . one may say with assurance that well over 100 members of the CCAR are officiating at interfaith marriages without requiring conversion." His next step was to write to the rabbis in question, requesting permission to include their names on a "list of rabbis who officiate at intermarriages, with the clear understanding that this list may be given . . . to anyone else who needs it." The avowed purpose of all this was "[to] combat the defection of many of our people who are being lost to Judaism because of the spiritual insensibility of so many of our colleagues." The register is now available, though it includes fewer names than Eichhorn had hoped; apparently not every "intermarrying" rabbi, not even in an age where confession has become a way of life, is ready to proclaim himself to the world at large.

Undoubtedly, the list will have some utility, and Eichhorn's concern over "defections" is unquestionably sincere; but, as we have seen, it was never really difficult to find a rabbi to provide the particular service. The reason for the publication of the list therefore cuts deeper and clearly has to do with a bid for open acceptance by a significant segment of the Reform rabbinate who no longer want to be thought of as a species of rabbinical abortionists.

The most recent development in the continuing drama took place in Miami Beach last October, at the biennial convention of the Union of American Hebrew Congregations (UAHC), the congregational arm of Reform Judaism. Although it received no press attention, an entire session of the meeting was devoted to a discussion of whether or not Reform should reverse the stand against performing intermarriages adopted by the CCAR in 1909.

Presenting the case for the "traditionalists" was Rabbi Joseph Klein of Worcester, Massachusetts. Rabbi Klein began by saying that while he was a *Reform* rabbi, and thus under no obligation to observe all the minutiae of Jewish law, when it came to performing marriages he was a *rabbi*, charged with the responsibility for maintaining the unity of the Jewish people. He was therefore obliged to follow the basic requirements of the "law of Moses and Israel," as the traditional wedding formula has it, which precludes marriage of a Jew and a non-Jew. "If I abrogate these laws and proceed to perform intermarriages," he asked the assembly, "in what way am I different from a minister or a civil official?" He went on to state that his attitudes had never created any difficulties with his congregants, neither with parents who sought his services when a child was about to intermarry nor with the young couple themselves. Perturbed though they might be at first, almost invariably they came around to an understanding of his point of view. Finally, rebutting the "defection" argument, Rabbi Klein denied that his particular practice drove young people away from Judaism; after all, in the majority of cases it was not the interfaith couple who were eager for his presence but the parents of the Jewish partner.

Representing the proponents of legitimation—among whom is UAHC President Rabbi Maurice Eisendrath—was Rabbi Abraham Klausner of Yonkers, New York. (His name, incidentally, is not to be found in the Eichhorn register, but that, as he indicated, is only because he is already performing more intermarriages than he can handle; publicity would only make matters worse.) Rabbi Klausner built his case essentially around the you-can't-serve-two-masters theme: Reform Judaism, he argued, was, to its detriment, looking to have it both ways. On the one hand, it espoused the ideals of liberalism and egalitarianism; on the other, it discouraged its rabbis from officiating at intermarriages. How, he wondered, could Reform balance its espousal of the American creed of equality for all with a policy of exclusion that maintained, in effect, that a Gentile was not maritally acceptable? The inconsistency—intellectually and morally reprehensible—must be rectified, and Reform Judaism must therefore not only adjust its logic but return to its original universalist inspiration. (As Rabbi Klausner put it: "Reform believes that from every tree you may eat.") In the matter at hand, the alternatives before Reform Judaism were clear: either to sink back into the ghetto—unthinkable prospect!—or to legitimate the rabbis' role at intermarriages.

As Rabbi Klausner developed his argument, it became evident that an important Reform strategy heretofore closely tied up with intermarriage

—conversion to Judaism of the Gentile partner—was also being subjected to serious reconsideration. Apparently the new school of "intermarrying" rabbis regards conversion as passé. The inference which Klausner left was that he does not bother to urge, or even discuss, conversion with the Gentile partner. The most that he would concede was that conversion had the advantage of introducing religious unity in the household—it would prevent children from being pulled in opposite directions during their formative years. If conversion had any significance, then, it was in the area of promoting better mental health rather than better religion.

In presenting his view of conversion, Klausner conceded that there is such a thing as "true" conversion, which is the result of only the most rigorous intellectual and emotional re-education; but this in his view has nothing to do with the conversions-for-marriage which Reform rabbis perform by the thousands each year. He arrived at the conclusion that the Reform movement, with its liberal policy toward conversion, has been practicing self-deception: in his view, the great majority of the marriages which Reform rabbis have performed between Jews and converted Gentiles are still intermarriages. If Reform Jews were really sincere about conversion, he suggested, they would set sharply higher standards. Klausner was of course aware that any such policy would drastically reduce the number of converts and this apparently was one of the things he was after. In fact, in his condemnation of Reform's liberalism Klausner sounded like nothing so much as the most rigid member of a right-wing Orthodox rabbinical court, as for example the Beth Din of London which is noted for making conversion an exceedingly difficult process. The reason for this irony is clear: if intermarriage is to be legitimated, then the value of the present-day conversion process must be downgraded; at the very least, it must be looked upon as an exercise in futility. Furthermore, if most conversions are a fake, then the rabbi who requires conversion is no better, morally speaking (indeed he is worse), than his colleague who just goes ahead and marries the couple.

But something even deeper was at issue. Conversion, after all, is based on the idea of the superiority of the converting religion. Many of the Classical Reformers had in fact believed in the superiority of Judaism and in the uniqueness of a Jewish mission. As already noted, even when they did not insist upon conversion they frequently attached conditions to the performance of an intermarriage—for example, that the Gentile partner agree that the children be reared as Jews. To Klausner this constituted sheer arrogance: in an ecumenical age, he asked, how dare a religion make such demands; what a tragic error it would be for Judaism to assert its superiority at a time when even Catholicism was in the process of moderating its own claims to religious preeminence and of seeking to accommodate itself to the modern world.

Rabbi Klausner concluded his presentation with the thought that the least Reform Judaism could do if it were to retain the goodwill and respect of its adherents and not degenerate into a fossil was to revoke all pronouncements discouraging the rabbinical performance of intermarriage. A resolution to that effect was promptly introduced from the floor and a lively discussion ensued, from which it became evident that the motion enjoyed wide support among those who were in attendance. Apparently taken aback by this unexpected development, the chairman announced that the session had been intended for educational purposes only and ruled the motion out of order.

There the issue rests, but not, it is safe to predict, for long. The implications for the Jewish future of such an accommodation to intermarriage are too momentous to remain a matter of mere "sectarian" interest, of concern only to Reform Jews or to individuals contemplating intermarriage. The Jewish community as a whole is soon bound to find itself embroiled in a bitter debate over what this new development portends for its survival as a distinctive group.

The Culturally Advantaged: A Study of Japanese-American Pupils

AUDREY JAMES SCHWARTZ

Americans of Japanese ancestry—who comprise only one-fourth of one percent of the population of the United States—rank higher than any other physically identifiable subgroup on positive attributes like education and income, and lowest on negative attributes like unemployment, crime, and delinquency. With particular reference to education, in California, the home of 34 percent of Japanese-Americans, both Japanese-American men and women rank first of all major racial and ethnic groups in amount of formal schooling. In Los Angeles County, the home of more than half of the state's Japanese-Americans, the median completed school year is 12.4 in contrast with a median of 12 for the total population.[1]

This record in education is qualitative as well as quantitative. As discussed more fully later, comparisons of objective test scores for Los

[1] California Department of Industrial Relations, *Californians of Japanese, Chinese, Filipino Ancestry* (San Francisco: Division of Fair Employment Practices, 1965), 26.

Angeles City public school pupils show that the performance of Japanese-Americans is considerably higher than that of other minority groups and, in general, higher than Anglos.[2] That academic achievement is high for Japanese-Americans in other parts of the country as well is suggested by data from the United States Office of Education.[3]

In short, the educational attainment of Japanese-Americans, both in quantity and quality, has been outstanding in recent years. This fact has stimulated a variety of explanations for their achievement centering largely on cultural values.

There is little consensus, however, on which cultural values—Japanese or American—are responsible for the achievement of contemporary Japanese-Americans. One recent attempt to account for the successful adaptation of Japanese-Americans credits acculturation to middle class American values:

> If, however, successful adaptation to the larger society consists mainly in acculturation, measured by the ability of a group to share and follow the values, goals, and expected behaviors of the majority, then the Japanese-American group has been very successful. Japanese-American values, skills, attitudes, and behavior apparently do not differ markedly from those of the average American. "Scratch a Japanese American and find a white Anglo-Saxon Protestant" is a generally accurate statement.[4]

A contrary view supports the centrality of traditional Japanese values to Japanese-American achievement:

> It is one of the major tenets of this report that while the overt behavior of the Nisei may, in many situations, be indistinguishable from the behav-

---

[2] Audrey James Schwartz, *Traditional Values and Contemporary Achievement of Japanese-American Pupils* (Los Angeles: Center for the Study of Evaluation, University of California, 1970), Table I.

[3] United States Office of Education, *Equality of Educational Opportunity* (Washington, D.C.: Government Printing Office, 1966), 20.

[4] Harry H. L. Kitano, *Japanese Americans: The Evolution of a Subculture* (Englewood Cliffs: Prentice-Hall, Inc., 1969), 3. The acquisition of some selected middle class values has been documented by empirical study. See Abe Arkoff, "Need Patterns in Two Generations of Japanese Americans in Hawaii," *Journal of Social Psychology*, 50 (August, 1959), 75–79; Charlotte Babcock and William Caudill, "Personal and Cultural Factors in the Treatment of a Nisei Man," in G. Seward (Ed.) *Clinical Studies in Cultural Conflict* (New York: The Ronald Press, 1958), 409–49; William Caudill and George A. DeVos, "Achievement, Culture, and Personality: The Case of the Japanese Americans," in B. E. Segal (Ed.) *Racial and Ethnic Relations* (New York: Thomas Crowell and Co., 1966), 77–89; Mamoru Iga, "The Japanese Social Structure and the Source of Mental Strains of Japanese Immigrants in the U.S.," Social Forces, 35 (March, 1957), 271–78.

ior of the white middle class, this arises in considerable part from a Japanese system of values and personality structure.[5]

These traditional values, it is generally agreed, include orientation toward the family unit in its nuclear and extended forms, subordination of the individual to the collectivity, sense of duty, reliance on order and hierarchy, respect for authority, and rational means to attain long-range goals.[6]

The inconsistency in these two conclusions arises from the differences that can be drawn between acculturation or the internalization of the values of an alien culture, on the one hand, and socialization or the learning of norms that are specific to a social situation, on the other. While values are closely related to social norms, they are not the same. Values are

> conceptions of desirable states of affairs that are utilized in selective conduct as criteria for preference or choice or as justifications for proposed or actual behavior . . . Norms are the more specific, concrete, situation-bound specifications; values are the criteria by which norms themselves may be and are judged.[7]

The first explanation of achievement holds that Japanese-Americans have internalized many of the values of the American middle class and that they, in fact, utilize the same criteria in evaluating action; the second explanation is more concerned with traditional Japanese values and with the acquisition by Japanese-Americans of the social knowledge to participate successfully in American institutions.

For Japanese-Americans the distinction between socialization to the norms of American institutions and acculturation to American middle class values is justified by the fact that early socialization—and thus socialization most resistant to change—usually takes place within structures that are parallel, rather than identical, to those of the middle class. As mem-

[5] William Caudill, "Japanese-American Personality and Acculturation," *Genetic Psychology Monographs*, 45 (February, 1942), 3–102.

[6] Ruth Benedict, *The Chrysanthemum and the Sword: Patterns of Japanese Culture* (Boston: Houghton Mifflin, 1946); Leonard Broom and John I. Kitsuse, *The Managed Casualty: The Japanese-American Family in World War II* (Berkeley: University of California Press, 1956); Caudill, *op. cit.*, fn. 5; George A. DeVos, "Achievement Orientation, Social Self-Identity, and Japanese Economic Growth," *Asian Survey* 5 (December, 1965), 575–89; Iga, *op. cit.*, fn. 4; Kitano, *op. cit.*, fn. 4; Talcott Parsons, "Population and Social Structure of Japan," in T. Parsons, *Essays in Sociological Theory* (New York: The Free Press, 1949), 275–97.

[7] Robin M. Williams, Jr. "Individual and Group Values," *The Annals of the American Academy of Political and Social Science*, 371 (May, 1967), 20–37.

bers of a distinct minority group, the socialization of young Japanese-American children is circumscribed by the ethnic community "which both protects and impedes the individuals within it."[8] Although ethnic socialization anticipates participation in the systems of the larger society by transmitting the minority group's perception of the operating norms of that society, it is unlikely that it can equally perceive and transmit the value criteria by which these norms are judged.

The empirical determination of the relative import of traditional Japanese values and values of the American middle class to the educational achievement of Japanese-American pupils requires knowledge of (a) the extent to which traditional values are currently held by pupils of Japanese-American ancestry, (b) the extent to which traditional values are similar to those of Anglo pupils, and (c) the relationships between individually held values and academic success for both Japanese-American and Anglo pupils.

The thesis of this article is that the success of Japanese-American public school pupils depends more on the value orientations that differentiate the two groups than upon the value orientations held in common. The acculturation that has taken place thus far does not adequately account for achievement. Value differences related to the orientation of the individual toward the social system persist; these value orientations—which more nearly approximate the values institutionized in the formal educational system than do those of middle class Americans—furnish the best explanation for the comparatively high achievement of Japanese-Americans.

What follows is a description of research findings addressed to these issues. First is a description of the research design including the Japanese-American sample and the variables of prime interest; second is a discussion of educational achievement in the Japanese-American community; next is a comparison of the value orientations of Japanese-American and Anglo pupils and the relationships of these orientations to academic achievement; and finally, a discussion of the findings.

RESEARCH DESIGN

Data for this analysis were obtained in 1966 from a survey of 2200 pupils enrolled in the 6th, 9th, and 12th grades of 23 Los Angeles City schools. A purposive, nonprobability sampling technique was used to select schools with varying racial, ethnic, and socioeconomic composition, and quota sampling of state-mandated courses (in which there was no "ability grouping") was used within each school. Subsampling within classrooms was not permitted. Of the obtained sample, 254 were classified by visual inspection

[8] Leonard Broom and John I. Kitsuse, "The Validation of Acculturation: A Condition to Ethnic Assimilation," *American Anthropologist*, 57 (February, 1955), 44–48.

and by surname identification as Japanese-American. All of these pupils
were enrolled in racially mixed schools.[9]

Information about family background, educational and occupational
aspirations, educational plans, and value orientations was obtained from
pupil responses to a printed questionnaire presented by research personnel
in regularly scheduled class periods. Official achievement records were
made available for 85 percent of the Japanese-American sample—those
whose parents sent their written approval to the school.

About half of the Japanese-American respondents were in the last year
of high school (12th grade) and the remainder were in the last year of
junior high (9th grade) and the last year of elementary school (6th grade).
Pupils from blue collar and white collar homes are evenly represented in
the secondary school sample, although there is overrepresentation of blue
collar elementary school pupils. In the interest of clarity, socioeconomic
controls for Japanese-American pupils have been abandoned as a comparison of pupils from blue and white collar homes on a number of variables including school performance, value orientations, the relationship
between value orientations and achievement, and parents' educational
level showed no large or significant differences.

As used here, the term "value orientation" refers to the various emotional
rather than rational outlooks of the pupils. This concept is sometimes referred to by terms like attitudes, beliefs, dispositions, and feelings—the
unifying characteristic is that each involves individual sentiments or affects
more than cognitive processes. This is not to say that the relationship between the two can be completely severed, but the distinction is useful for
analytic purposes. The value orientations treated here are those for which
theory and previous research suggest a relationship to school achievement.[10] The variables can be divided into four groups according to the
functions they are expected to perform in the attainment of academic
success:

1. *The Goals toward which the Individual Strives.* These include Occupational Aspirations, Educational Aspirations and Plans, Occupational Rewards

[9] The larger ethnic enclaves in Los Angeles had been destroyed by the evacuation of
Japanese in 1942, and subsequent relocation created smaller areas of ethnic concentration. Thus Japanese-American pupils usually attend integrated schools. However,
there are several predominantly Japanese-American elementary schools, one of which
is included in the sample. For details of the sampling design and description of the
schools sampled see Audrey James Schwartz, "Affectivity Orientations and Academic
Achievement of Mexican-American Youth," doctoral dissertation, UCLA (Ann Arbor:
University Microfilm, 1967) or Schwartz, *Comparative Values and Achievement of
Mexican-American and Anglo Pupils* (Los Angeles: Center for the Study of Evaluation, University of California, 1969).

[10] For a summary of literature relating value orientations to scholastic achievement see
Audrey James Schwartz, 1967, *op. cit.*, fn. 9.

(the importance placed on extrinsic rewards like power, prestige, and security in occupational choice), and Idealized School Goals (the ends the school ought to help the pupil attain regardless of whether it does or not).

2. *Activities Appropriate for Goal Attainment.* These variables include Instrumental Orientation (the utility of attending school now for future benefit), Expressive Orientation (the extent to which school attendance affords the pupil pleasure), and Formal School Compliance (the choices the pupil would make between conflicting universalistic school expectations and peer loyalties and his unquestioned acceptance of teacher authority).

3. *The Pupil's Perception of the Feasibility of Attaining His Goals.* These include Self-Esteem (the individual's evaluation of himself in general and in relation to others whom he knows), Faith in Human Nature (the pupil's attitude toward people regardless of his personal knowledge of them), and Future Orientation (belief that the individual can control his environment and thereby affect his own destiny).

4. *Mode and Intensity of Interpersonal Relations,* that is, whether the individual is inclined to take action without approval of others. These include Orientation toward Family Authority (legitimacy of parental control over pupil activity) and Independence from Peers (sensitivity of the pupil to opinions of his age-mates and their effect on his own action).[11]

EDUCATIONAL ACHIEVEMENT IN THE JAPANESE-AMERICAN COMMUNITY

From all accounts the Isei who came to the United States were relatively well educated for an immigrant population and had high regard for the instrumental value of education for themselves and for their children. Compared with other groups, the Japanese children started school at an earlier age and remained in school longer, and the devotion of their parents to the task of providing them with educational opportunities is largely credited for the relatively high occupational attainment of the Nisei.[12]

The Isei's appreciation for formal education extended beyond its instrumental value, however, and they established parochial schools with instruction in Japanese reading, writing, history, and the like to supplement public education. It was the purpose of these schools to socialize

[11] Value orientation variables for the secondary pupils were created by combining responses to the relevant questionnaire items into scales and indices. Scalogram procedures were used wherever possible. For two variables items were combined into indices rather than scales and the index score implies nothing about the ordering of items or the unidimensionality of the value. Variables for the elementary school pupils were created from responses to single items selected for their discriminatory power in the value orientations of secondary school pupils. Zero-order correlations among the value orientation variables are sufficiently low to insure statistical independence. For details see Audrey James Schwartz, *op cit.,* fn. 2.

[12] Dorothy Swaine Thomas, "The Japanese American," in J. B. Gittler (Ed.) *Understanding Minority Groups* (New York: John Wiley and Sons, 1956), 84–108.

American-born children (who were not sent to Japan for prolonged visits with relatives) to the culture of Japan and thereby ensure its survival in the United States. The language schools flourished until the evacuation of West Coast Japanese during the Second World War. Although only a small number of these schools exist today, many of their cultural transmission functions have been absorbed by other ethnically-oriented voluntary associations.

Emphasis on formal education continues to be characteristic of the Japanese-American community. Sixty percent of all the Japanese-American pupils surveyed in Los Angeles report that their parents have graduated from high school and that 30 percent of their fathers and 23 percent of their mothers have attended college. Of the 9th and 12th grade pupils, 77 percent state that "many" or "some" of their relatives or friends of their parents have had education beyond high school which implies close acquaintance with college educated persons. Moreover, most pupils have high educational aspirations for themselves: over 85 percent of the secondary school sample indicate that both they and their parents would like them to receive an education beyond high school and the number who expect to do so is almost as high. In addition, the Japanese-American pupils ascribe high educational aspirations to their friends: 95 percent of the 12th grade, 75 percent of the 9th grade, and 61 percent of the 6th grade report that "all" or "most" of their friends desire to continue their education after high school completion.[13]

The occupational aspirations of Japanese-American pupils are consistent with their educational aspirations and plans. More than 80 percent of the secondary school sample aspire to upper white collar jobs, that is, to jobs that usually require a minimum of four years of college, and only 6 percent aspire to blue collar jobs which call for considerably less schooling. Of further interest is their high ambition for social mobility. A comparison of the status of their own aspirations with that of their parents' occupational level indicates that 68 percent of the 9th grade and 58 percent of the 12th grade pupils would be upwardly mobile if they enter their preferred occupation. And equally important, less than 5 percent would be downwardly mobile. The excellent achievement record of Japanese-American pupils indicates that these high aspirations are realistic.

A COMPARISON OF VALUE ORIENTATIONS

The Japanese-American and the Anglo secondary school samples were contrasted on the value orientation variables and found to differ significantly on a number of them. In general, Japanese-American vis-à-vis Anglo pupils are more Expressive in their orientation toward school, are more

[13] The supporting tables with statistical tests of significance for these and other findings discussed in this paper can be seen in detail in Audrey James Schwartz, *op. cit.*, fn. 2.

*Value Orientations of Japanese-American and
Anglo Secondary School Pupils*

Value Orientation[1]		Ninth Grade		Twelfth Grade	
		Japanese	*Anglo*	*Japanese*	*Anglo*
Expressive Orientation	x score	3.88	3.70*	3.70	3.58
(Scalogram)	s.d.	.59	.77	.83	.90
	% high	84	69**	73	64**
Faith in Human Nature	x score	3.18	3.29	3.50	3.54
(Scalogram)	s.d.	.90	.86	.75	.71
	% high	45	52	64	65
Family Authority	x score	3.11	2.85	2.72	2.55
(Scalogram)	s.d.	1.23	1.37	1.19	1.37
	% high	45	36**	29	27
Formal School Compliance	x score	3.32	3.14	3.22	3.02*
(Scalogram)	s.d.	.78	.89	.95	.96
	% high	52	44	50	39**
Future Orientation	x score	2.86	3.05	3.25	3.43*
(Scalogram)	s.d.	.95	.98	.96	.87
	% high	27	40**	54	61
Idealized School Goals	x score	3.77	3.82	3.83	3.79
(index)	s.d.	.54	.45	.46	.45
	% high	86	86	84	82
Independence from Peers	x score	3.01	3.06	2.97	2.97
(Scalogram)	s.d.	1.11	1.10	1.30	1.28
	% high	30	35	33	32
Instrumental Orientation	x score	3.79	3.73	3.76	3.74
(Scalogram)	s.d.	.45	.49	.45	.48
	% high	86	84	86	82
Occupational Reward Values	x score	3.58	3.37	3.59	3.32*
(Scalogram)	s.d.	1.05	1.15	1.10	1.18
	% high	26	18**	21	19
Self-Esteem	x score	3.59	3.69	3.76	3.93
(index)	s.d.	1.66	1.60	1.59	1.50
	% high	53	52	56	61
Occupational Aspirations					
1. Lower blue collar					
2. Upper blue collar					
3. Lower white collar					
4. Intermediate white collar					
5. Upper white collar	x score	4.41	4.21*	4.46	4.16*
	s.d.	.90	.88	.91	.95
Base N		67	558	122	473

[1] This table is abridged from Audrey James Schwartz, *Traditional Values and Contemporary Achievement of Japanese-American Pupils* (Los Angeles: Center for the Study of Evaluation, University of California, 1970), Table 8.

* $p \leq .05$ for t value of mean differences between Japanese-American and Anglo scale scores.

** $p \leq .05$ t-test for difference in proportion of Japanese-American and Anglo pupils who score "high" on the value orientation.

favorable toward Formal School Compliance and Family Authority, and are less oriented toward the Future in that their sense of personal fate control is low. Nevertheless, they have higher Occupational Aspirations and place greater value on extrinsic occupational rewards.

The two groups are similar in their Idealized School Goals from school attendance and in their Instrumental Orientation toward school activities —both very high in comparison with other ethnic groups—and in their expressed Independence from Peers. The value orientation scores for 9th and 12th grade Japanese-American and Anglo pupils are presented in Table 1.[14] Although they are not presented here, it should be noted that the data from 6th grade pupils are consistent with the findings just discussed.

The Japanese-American and Anglo pupils also differ from one another in the relationship of these value orientations to their academic success as measured by standardized objective tests. Four of the orientations are statistically related to the reading or mathematics achievement of Japanese-Americans and six to similar achievement of Anglos, yet only one— high Faith in Human Nature—is related to achievement in each group.

Related to the achievement of Japanese-American pupils are high Faith in Human Nature (significant at 6th, 9th, and 12th grades), low Independence from Peers (significant at 9th and 12th grades), low Self-Esteem (significant at 9th grade), and low Instrumental Orientation (significant at 12th grade).

Important to the achievement of Anglo pupils are high Future Orientation (significant at 6th, 9th, and 12th grades), high Idealized School Goals (significant at 9th and 12th grades), high Faith in Human Nature, orientation toward Family Authority, and, unexpectedly, low orientation toward Formal School Compliance (all significant at 9th grade), and high Self Esteem (significant at 12th grade).

DISCUSSION

These findings support the hypothesis that the comparatively high achievement of Japanese-American pupils is related more to values that are traditional in Japanese culture than to the acquisition of dominant American values. Although Japanese-American and Anglo pupils are similar with respect to several value orientations, there is little to support the position that the values they hold in common derive from the American middle class. These commonalities, (a) an emphasis on present school attendance

---

[14] Since dominant American values are generally believed to be those of white collar Anglos, comparisons were also made between the total Japanese and the white collar Anglo sample. The results are the same as those for comparisons with the entire Anglo sample.

for future benefit and (b) a concern for peer group opinion, can logically be derived from the Japanese culture as well as the Anglo.

For example, formal education has customarily been held in high regard in Japan and the literacy rate of that country has been exceptional, even before the establishment of universal schooling in 1872.[15] Furthermore, we have already noted the instrumental orientation of the Isei and Nisei generations in their consumption of public education for the occupational mobility of themselves and their children and in their provision of parochial education for transmission of Japanese culture.

In like manner, sensitivity to peer group approval can be traced to Japanese values which stress "collectivity" over "self" orientations in social systems like the family, employment, and school.[16] The "adolescent society" is now an equally relevant system to Japanese-American youth and their mode of relating to it, like the family and the school, is characteristically one of dependence and subordination rather than individual action.

More telling in the case against acculturation as an explanation of achievement are the *differences* in orientations of Japanese-American and Anglo pupils. Perhaps most germane is the generally favorable view of Japanese-Americans toward hierarchical authority (evidenced by higher Formal School Compliance and Family Authority scores). This finding is consistent with observations of the subordinate-superordinate structure of traditional Japanese culture.[17]

The point to be made here is that Japanese-American pupils seem to reject the notion of individual autonomy. Not only are they oriented toward the "collectivity" and acceptance of its authority structure (which is lineal for the family and school and collateral for the peer social system), they, in comparison with Anglos, express little personal mastery over the future. Whereas Japanese-American pupils indicate exceedingly high educational and mobility aspirations and express significantly greater desire than Anglos for extrinsic rewards—all characteristic of minority groups that have entered the occupational structure at the bottom—their mode of ascent is one of group cooperation rather than individual pursuit. What is more, the presence or absence of the belief that individual action can modify a person's destiny has little relationship to the achievement of Japanese-Americans, in spite of the fact that it is significant and positive for the achievement of comparable Anglos, Mexican-Americans, and Negroes.[18]

Another value that distinguishes Japanese-American from Anglo pupils is their more Expressive orientation toward school: more of them "like

[15] Tatsumi Makino, "Some Notes on Literacy and Education in Japan," *The Sociological Review*, Monograph 10 (September, 1966), 83–93.
[16] Talcott Parsons, *op. cit.*, fn. 6, 281 ff.
[17] Ruth Benedict, *op. cit.*, fn. 6; Talcott Parsons, *op. cit.*, fn. 6.
[18] Audrey James Schwartz, *op. cit.*, fn. 9; unpublished data.

school" and more think of school "mainly as a place for having fun." The difference noted in affective involvement may be an example of a more encompassing difference between the two populations that has been noted by others[19] in which the orientation of the Japanese toward social systems is characterized as Gemeinschaft and that of middle class Americans as Gesellschaft.[20]

From a theoretical point of view, it can be argued that the Gemeinschaft orientation tends to inhibit interaction and socialization experiences outside of the primary group and thereby presents an obstacle to Japanese-Americans in actively neutral or Gesellschaft social systems. These data suggest, however, that such obstacles can be overcome with a favorable universalistic orientation toward people in general. The positive relationship between the Faith in Human Nature measure and the academic achievement of Japanese-Americans is a case in point. In other words, given a Gemeinschaft social orientation, ultimate achievement in an affectively neutral system depends upon a universalistic orientation such as Faith in Human Nature: Those who possess the highest degree of the value will achieve the greatest; those who possess the lowest degree will achieve the least.

This is not to say that strong group affiliation in itself is detrimental to achievement; that depends upon the values of the group. For Japanese-American pupils, most of whom perceive their peers with similarly high educational aspirations, dependence upon peer approval is related to scholastic attainment. For the Anglos in this study, however, strong peer affiliation has no significant effect.

Another orientation that is closely associated with dependence upon peers is the evaluation of one's self in comparison with others. Though there is little difference between the measured Self-Esteem of the two groups, its influence is positive for the achievement of Anglos and negative for the achievement of Japanese-Americans. The reason for this negative relationship is unclear. Perhaps reluctance to view one's self competitively with others strengthens the collectivity orientation which has been shown to contribute to achievement, or low Self-Esteem may also influence the strong drive for mobility noted above.

In Summary, Japanese-American pupils have certain advantages for

---

[19] William Caudill and H. A. Scarr, "Japanese Value Orientations and Culture Change," *Ethnology*, 1 (January, 1962), 53–91; Mamoru Iga, *op. cit.*, fn. 4; Forrest E. LaViolette, *Americans of Japanese Ancestry* (Toronto: Canadian Institute of International Affairs, 1946).

[20] These orientations, introduced by Tönnies in 1887, are similar to other commonly used concepts like Cooley's primary and secondary groups, Durkheim's mechanical and organic solidarity, McIver's communal and associational relations, and Redfield's folk-urban continuum. Ferdinand Tönnies, *Community and Society,* Trans. and Ed. Charles P. Loomis (East Lansing: Michigan State University Press, 1957).

success in the American public school that appear to be rooted in the Japanese culture: first, the traditional family, with its rigid system of obligations subordinating individual interests to those of the group, provides an environment within which children internalize family-defined achievement goals that emphasize educational success and subsequent occupational mobility and are socialized to legitimate means for attaining them; second, the structure of interpersonal relations within the family, which subordinates all members to the authority of the father, anticipates the lineal authority structure of the public school and facilitates the child's adaptation to its bureaucratic organization; and third, the "collectivity" rather than "self" orientation of the family is congruent with the strong peer group affiliation characteristic of contemporary "teen-age" culture which, for Japanese-Americans, is supportive of achievement. This confluence of family, school, and peer values fosters the scholastic attainment of Japanese-Americans, and the affective gratification they receive from school attendance, which further sustains their instrumental efforts, is illustrative of the harmony of their three most relevant social systems.

Anglo pupils, on the other hand, must cope with a disjunction between the goals they hold from school attendance and the means they believe are legitimate to attain them. Like Japanese-Americans they place high instrumental value upon education, but they agree less with the concept of hierarchical authority—a difference that can logically be traced to the greater collateral orientation of the American family. Anglo pupils are less accepting of formal school norms than are Japanese-American pupils who, it appears, have been taught an ideal model of school social interaction. Other investigators have observed the negative influence of Anglo peer groups on individual Anglo achievement.[21] In light of the findings with respect to the positive influence of Japanese-American peer groups on achievement and their favorable orientation toward Formal School Compliance it would seem that the conflict between youth and adults in the school, first brought to attention by Waller[22] does not apply to Japanese-American pupils.

[21] For example, James S. Coleman, *The Adolescent Society* (New York: The Free Press, 1961).
[22] Willard Waller, *The Sociology of Teaching* (New York: John Wiley and Sons, 1932).

Voluntary Segregation: A Study of New York Chinatown

D. Y. YUAN

The Chinese population in the United States has exhibited a tendency to concentrate in segregated communities within the large cities. San Francisco's Chinatown ranks first numerically, that of New York City is second, and that of Los Angeles third. There are no Chinatowns to be found in cities under 50,000 population, nor are there Chinatowns in states having fewer than 250 Chinese.[1] In light of these statements, we may well ask ourselves the questions: Why do the Chinese tend to concentrate in a segregated community within a large city, and to what degree is it voluntary or involuntary segregation? It is the purpose of this paper to answer these questions.

This paper presents findings concerning a study of New York's Chinatown[2] and investigates the degree to which a Chinatown represents voluntary or involuntary segregation. Tentatively, therefore, a scale of intensity between voluntary and involuntary segregation is presented.

THE SCALE OF SEGREGATION

Voluntary Segregation:	*(1) Strict voluntary*
	(2) Voluntary
	(3) Voluntary involving involuntary factor(s)
Involuntary Segregation:	*(4) Involuntary involving voluntary factor(s)*
	(5) Involuntary
	(6) Strict involuntary

According to this scale, there are three forms of voluntary segregation and three forms of involuntary segregation. Segregation is an old phenomenon in human history and is universal. Segregation does not always mean "racial segregation." It may appear "in the usual class lines of a democratic society, or the castes of a stratified society; . . . the emergency use of force, as in concentration camps and restricted zones

---

[1] See Rose Hum Lee, "The Decline of Chinatowns in the U.S.A.," *American Journal of Sociology*, LIV (March, 1949), 422–32.

[2] This study was conducted in New York City in 1959. A questionnaire was given to 75 respondents. This paper is based on D. Y. Yuan's "Voluntary Segregation: A Study of New York Chinatown" (unpublished Master's thesis, The City College of New York, 1959).

during war time. . . ."[3] The scale has been devised for all types of segregation and is not limited to race relations only. However, this study of New York's Chinatown emphasizes race relations.

Theoretically, is the suggested scale of segregation possible? Firstly, strict voluntary segregation is almost impossible in the field of race relations but is possible in other relationships. For example, one order of Catholic sisters voluntarily enters a segregated convent, prohibits contacts with the outer world and prays for the salvation of the entire world. The Catholic church does not force them to enter; it is their choice whether they do so or not.

Secondly, voluntary segregation is possible in race relations. Two examples are given below. One is that of the white people in the African colonies who voluntarily segregate themselves from the native population in order to preserve so-called white supremacy. E. E. Bergel calls this activity "self segregation."[4] Another example is given by Brewton Berry in his analysis of race relations, namely, the process of voluntary segregation which "is illustrated by the Mennonites, who have striven to isolate themselves from the general population in their determination to resist the forces of assimilation."[5]

Thirdly, there is voluntary segregation involving involuntary factors, of which the Chinese community in New York is a good example. This will be discussed later. Another example of this kind of segregation is the Jewish ghetto. The ghetto is a form of voluntary segregation in which there are also some involuntary factors.

Fourthly, involuntary segregation involving voluntary factors is also found in present-day race relations. Berry calls this a voluntary choice of (involuntary) segregation.[6] This can be illustrated by the segregated communities established voluntarily by Negroes in the South, where segregation is involuntary for them.[7] Frazier calls these communities "racial islands."[8]

Fifthly, there is involuntary segregation, which applies to Negroes in the United States. It is not their volition to be treated under the principles of the so-called separate but equal doctrine; they are involuntarily separated from whites through enforcement by the dominant group.[9]

Finally, there is strict involuntary segregation, which is not often

---

[3] "Segregation," *Dictionary of Sociology*, 1955 edition, p. 289.

[4] Egon Ernest Bergel, *Urban Sociology* (New York, 1955), p. 89.

[5] Brewton Berry, *Race and Ethnic Relations* (Boston, 1958), p. 274.

[6] The term "segregation" used in race relations in the Southern United States always implies "involuntary" segregation for the Negroes.

[7] Berry, *op. cit.*, pp. 297–98.

[8] Franklin Frazier, *The Negro in the United States* (Chicago, 1939), Chapter II.

[9] Charles F. Marden, *Minorities in American Society* (New York, 1952), Chap. 9.

seen today. One possible example would be slavery, for slaves are treated under separate and unequal principles.

After enumerating the possibilities of different kinds of segregation on the suggested scale, which indicates the degree of intensity from strict voluntary to strict involuntary segregation, we are ready to proceed with this study by suggesting to what degree New York's Chinatown is a voluntarily- or an involuntarily-formed community.

THE DEVELOPMENT OF CHINATOWN

Effort was made in the analysis to exclude mutually the voluntary and the involuntary choice (factors). The involuntary choice of the Chinese preceded the voluntary development of New York's Chinatown. The period of defensive insulation is a period between these two, the last period being gradual assimilation. In short, the stages of the development of Chinatown may be illustrated in the following chart. The hypothetical stages are based on the analysis.

HYPOTHETICAL STAGES OF THE DEVELOPMENT OF CHINATOWN

Involuntary choice (discrimination and prejudice toward the Chinese)	*Defensive insulation (need for mutual help)*	*Voluntary segregation*	*Gradual assimilation*
(1)	*(2)*	*(3)*	*(4)*

GENERALIZATIONS

The Chinese people were welcomed to the United States. The social relationship between the Chinese, representing a minority group, and the Americans, representing a dominant group, is derived from the social interactions between them. In general, social interaction under a favorable situation may lead to friendship, but under unfavorable situations may lead to conflict and hostility. At first, the Chinese laborers were welcomed because of the demands for cheap labor after the discovery of gold in California. A pattern of demands and response developed, and as a result laborers from Canton Province, China, came to the United States. A sociological analysis of the historical data suggests that in general, a minority group, such as the Chinese, is welcomed by a majority group, if the minority group meets the needs of the majority group at that particular time.

Why did the anti-Chinese attitudes develop? Changing environment causes the changing of attitudes, and when the whites moved into the mining industry and began to compete with the Chinese, great hostility and conflict emerged. Racial discrimination and prejudice toward the Chinese developed because of this conflict and hostility. The Chinese became the scapegoat in the economic competition. On the basis of such facts, a second generalization can be stated. The prejudice or discrimination of a majority group towards a racial minority, such as the Chinese, often emerges because of the conflicting values between them. These conflicting values may be political, economic, ecological, or racial factors.

After the rise of anti-Chinese sentiments on the West Coast, some people tried to prevent the exclusion of Chinese laborers. For example, a book was written by George F. Seward, United States Minister to China, in 1881, one year before the adoption of the Chinese Exclusion Act, in which the author said: "I found, in brief, that the Chinese have been of great service to the people of the Pacific Coast; . . . that the objections which have been advanced against them are in the main unwarranted; . . . the fears of large immigration . . . are unnecessary. . . ."[10] His efforts were in vain. There was little choice (involuntary) for the Chinese but to find some means to survive in such an alien environment. The solution to this problem was similar to the pattern of voluntary mass-return to Japan of the Japanese in the United States previous to World War II. Thus, defensive insulation was employed by the Chinese. The applicable principle here is that when a minority, such as the Chinese, has been discriminated against, it has no choice but to develop some means of defense. In general, it will develop the means voluntarily.

When the Irish miners began to flow into the West, great hostility grew against the Chinese because of the competition. The Chinese, as a minority group, could not compete with organized labor. The Immigration Commission Report of 1910 stated that "vocationally there has been a clear tendency on the part of the Chinese to withdraw from the competitive forms of labor and business and to enter less productive urban callings."[11] A comparison of the occupational distributions of the Chinese population between 1870 and 1920 indicates that the Chinese withdrew from competition with organized labor.[12] Table 1 below shows this trend. Examination of the following data together with the previous historical analysis suggests that when majority and minority groups are in conflict, in general, the minority tends to withdraw from the field of com-

[10] George F. Seward, *Chinese Immigration, in Its Social and Economic Aspects* (New York, 1881), p. vi.

[11] Eliot Grinnel Mears, *Resident Orientals on the American Pacific Coast* (Chicago, 1928), p. 197.

[12] David Te-Chao Cheng, *Acculturation of the Chinese in the United States, A Philadelphia Study* (China, The Fukien Christian University Press, 1948), p. 59.

TABLE 1

Selected Occupations for the Chinese in the United States, 1870–1920

Occupation	Year	Number of Chinese	Percentage Increase or Decrease
Miners and Laborers	1870	27,045	− 99.45
	1920	151	
Domestic service workers	1870	9,349	+280.00
	1920	26,440	
Traders and Dealers	1870	779	+960.00
	1920	7,477	

Source: David Te-Chao Cheng, *ibid.*, p. 59.

petition in the long run, and shifts to more or less non-competitive fields in order to survive.

Owing to the nature of the relationship which the first generation of a minority group establishes with the majority group, the adjustment of the Chinese has been primarily economic, and only secondarily, cultural.[13] The withdrawal from competition with organized labor has been one of the economic adjustments. This phenomenon has been generalized in the above proposition. The processes of "consciousness of kind" and "consciousness of difference," which operate among the Chinese people, were especially strong during the period of adjustment when anti-Chinese prejudice and discrimination were intensive. The Chinese became conscious of their own group-identification on the basis of either cultural or biological similarities. "On one basis or another, these groups [minority groups] are singled out by the society in which they reside and in varying degrees and proportions are subjected to economic exploitation, segregation, and discrimination."[14] Bierstedt points out that "it is the similarities that people recognize in one another that induce them to seek one another out and to form groups. . . ."[15] The strong prejudice against the Chinese strengthens the "we-feeling" among them. They realize that they must help each other in an alien country to which originally they did not belong. They must defend themselves against further rebuffs by the majority. Toynbee, in his analysis of the

[13] For the adjustment of the Chinese in the United States, special interviews of the Chinese may be obtained from *Orientals and Their Cultural Adjustment* (Fisk University, Nashville, Tenn., 1946).

[14] Charles Wagley and Marvin Harris, *Minorities in the New World* (New York, 1958), p. 17.

[15] Robert Bierstedt, *The Social Order* (New York, 1957) p. 434.

origin and growth of civilization, points out the importance of the pattern of challenge-response. The Chinese tend to develop voluntary segregation as their way of responding to the challenge of the environment.

This type of response suggests that because of the unfriendly situation—the prejudice towards them, the consciousness of kind, the "we-feeling," and the withdrawal from the field of competition—the Chinese people have need of mutual help. Several patterns of defense have been employed by them. As has been noted, they have shifted to noncompetitive business. This withdrawal may be viewed as a kind of self-defense against greater hostilities which might occur if further competition were to continue.

Furthermore, due to the shift in their business to restaurant, laundry, and gift shop ownership, the Chinese have become urbanized. These businesses can be supported by only the greater cities, so a Chinatown flourishes only where large cosmopolitan populations desire "something different."

Protest is another type of defense. After the passing of the Chinese Exclusion Act, directed against Chinese laborers in 1882, the Chinese government protested.[16] These protests were only a gesture because of the weakness of China at that time.

It is said that a minority group voluntarily isolates itself in order to avoid insults. The Chinese moved from rural to urban areas where there was great hostility towards them because of competition. Some Chinese moved to the East Coast because anti-Chinese prejudice was strong along the West Coast. There was a tendency to integrate the "we-group" and gradually to establish segregated communities among large urban centers in which they could hold interaction with the majority to a minimum, and thus avoid conflicts, hostilities and insults. Nowadays, however, it is difficult to trace these defensive patterns because the old prejudices and discrimination towards the Chinese are no longer strong enough to make them aware of the necessity for self-defense.

This analysis, then, confirms indirectly the proposition, "To run away from prejudice and/or discrimination shown by a majority group toward a minority group helps the formation of voluntary segregation."

The principle which emerges from this analysis is that a minority, such as the Chinese, who have experienced rebuffs from the majority, develop a kind of defensive insulation that protects them against further rebuff. There are several patterns of defensive means: withdrawal against further rebuff, relocation (urbanization or ruralization), protest, avoidance, and so on. These patterns can be traced only when the prejudices and discrimination towards a minority are strong enough.

[16] Mary Roberts Coolidge, *Chinese Immigration* (New York, 1909), especially chapter XVI.

TABLE 2

Illiteracy Rates for the Chinese in the United States
*According to the 1920 Population Census**

Sex	California			Oregon		
	Total No.	Illiterate		Total No.	Illiterate	
		No.	Percent		No.	Percent
Both Sexes	22,638	4,352	19.2	2,484	774	31.2
Males	20,437	3,590	17.6	2,273	704	31.0
Females	2,201	762	34.6	211	70	33.2

Source: Eliot Grinnel Mears, *Resident Orientals on the American Pacific Coast* (Chicago, 1928), p. 423.

* For population 21 years and over.

Regarding the development of voluntary segregation involving involuntary factors, the Chinese had no choice (involuntary factor) but to develop some kind of defensive means in order to survive in such an unfriendly situation as has been noted above. But there are other possible reasons contributing to the formation of Chinatown, which may be summarized as follows: (1) Relatives like to live together. Under an unfriendly and uncertain situation, relatives live together for mutual help. This is an indication that "a strong system of group solidarity—subordination of the individual to the family, for instance—protects and supports the individual in such a way that breakdown of this solidarity intensifies insecurity."[17] The large family system is preserved in a country of "individualism," because of the necessity of observing group solidarity. The members of the groups help each other in many ways.

(2) Foreign-born minorities have language difficulties. The early Chinese immigrants were uneducated laborers; in the new country they had language difficulties. It is assumed that relatives and friends assisted one another in "interpreting" for those who did not understand English well. Even in 1920, seventy years after the first mass immigration, the percentage of illiteracy for the Chinese was high on the West Coast. Table 2 shows the percentages of illiteracy among those age twenty-one and over. Therefore, language barriers did slow down the process of assimilation; on the other hand, it contributed to voluntary segregation.

(3) The preservation of the Chinese way of life is one of the important factors which might explain why the Chinese live together. Like the reasons outlined above, the desire of the Chinese to preserve their early

[17] Talcott Parsons, *Essays in Sociological Theory* (Glencoe, Ill., 1954), p. 285.

customs and folkways is related to their cultural background. The disposition of the Chinese to settle in segregated communities in an effort to
cherish different traditions and peculiar folkways in the seclusion and
security of their own communities is also true.

Therefore, this analysis suggests, generally speaking, that the stronger
the traditional culture, the greater the desire of the minority group to
live together voluntarily.

(4) When the Chinese laborers transferred from mining to domestic
service, they migrated to urban low-rent areas in the large cities and, year
after year, the segregation of the Chinese community developed. It should
be kept in mind that these laborers were uneducated, and the best chance
for them to meet the challenge of the environment was to perform domestic
services such as they probably had done in China.

"The first arrivals are the most important since they establish the standards of comparison with other races. An unfortunate feature arises when
the later comers are of a higher social class."[18] It was the Chinese laborers
who established the pattern of comparison. This pattern could be misleading, for the Chinese are often associated with hand laundries. There are
not so many hand laundries in a city in China, but, as a result of economic
competition, there is a large number of them in New York.

(5) Other possible factors in the formation of Chinatowns are the
Buddhist religion, a strong Chinese nationalism, and racial discrimination
against the Chinese.[19]

Group tensions are another factor in voluntary segregation. As in other
immigrant minorities in the accommodation stage, the Chinese developed
a segregated community within a large city. "The two extreme solutions
for eliminating a given group conflict are (a) complete isolation, *e.g.*,
geographic exclusion and (b) complete assimilation."[20] The first part of
this theory is partly accepted by the majority in their policy-making towards the Chinese: "Let us exclude the Chinese laborers because with
their cheap labor they may lower our living standards." However, this did
not solve the problem of the Chinese laborers already in the United States.
Therefore, when the Chinese tended to form Chinatowns, the majority
groups tolerated the situation because they did not favor complete assimilation at that time. The voluntary segregation of the Chinese, who confined
themselves to the Chinese community, was a means to abate conflicts and

---

[18] Mears, *op. cit.*, p. 334.

[19] Assuming that "voluntary segregation involving involuntary factors" is the kind of
segregation which applies to Chinatown, we need to find the most important reasons
that would explain why the Chinese live together in Chinatown. A series of seven
possible reasons was given and respondents were asked to rank them by importance.
The most important reasons are listed above.

[20] Robin Williams, *Reduction of Intergroup Tension* (New York, 1945), p. 46.

hostilities. It has been found that "sustained interaction between majority and minority is essential if the lines of communication and understanding necessary for an effective intergroup relations program are to be established."[21] Thus, voluntary segregation is a temporary "safety zone" between group conflicts and tensions. In other words, there is a positive relationship between the decrease in competitive interaction and group conflicts. This analysis, together with the others given above, suggests that a decrease in the frequency of interaction between the members of a majority group and a minority group, if not by force, in general will increase the degree of voluntary segregation and thus decrease group conflict and tensions.

A revised Bogardus Social Distance Scale was used to measure the social distances between the Chinese and four other minorities, namely, Jew, Italian, Puerto Rican, and Negro. It was found, in general, that the present-day Chinese students show the greatest amount of prejudice. The first-generation immigrants show the least prejudice; and in between there is the second generation. MacIver and Page pointed out that group prejudice is learned. The Chinese students have a wider range of social interaction and contacts with the majority than the first generation. They are quick to absorb the "American prejudice" toward other minorities. The first-generation Chinese, who confine themselves to a segregated community, understand less because of fewer contacts with outside groups, and fewer contacts with majority members from whom they could learn "American prejudice." The second generation expresses moderate group prejudice between the other two groups because they are at the "marginal stage." The analyses of the social distance test and the range of social interactions suggest that the more frequently a member of a minority group interacts with members of the majority group, the stronger his prejudice towards other minorities is apt to be.[22]

The first generation, the second generation, and the present-day students were asked to rate the degree of acceptance of the Chinese by the majority group in six areas, namely, work, school, politics, housing, public affairs, and social activities. The results reveal that the Chinese are accepted in school and are not accepted in politics. They are accepted partially in work and in housing, and are less accepted in public affairs and social activities. If the Chinese were fully accepted by the majority, there would be no need for them to develop a voluntarily segregated community in which

---

[21] John P. Dean and Alex Rosen, *A Manual of Intergroup Relations* (Chicago, 1955), p. 7.

[22] This proposition is based on the assumption that group prejudice is learned. Some sociologists like William I. Thomas argue that race prejudice is organic and instinctive. For details see William I. Thomas, "The Psychology of Race Prejudice," *The American Journal of Sociology*, IX (March, 1904), 611.

their socio-emotional needs are met. This analysis suggests that the higher the legal, political, economic, and social barriers against assimilation, the more the minority group consolidates its advantages.

Nowadays, the prejudice and discrimination against the Chinese are not as strong as they were, and there is no necessity, therefore, for the Chinese to practice defensive insulation and voluntary segregation. It is interesting to note that in the great metropolitan area of New York, the Chinese population is about twenty-five thousand in addition to the eight thousand in and around New York's Chinatown. In other words, the great majority of the Chinese are living outside Chinatown, scattered all over the metropolitan area. They have not isolated themselves in order to avoid further rebuffs because they are accepted almost anywhere they choose. But New York's Chinatown still exists, and about eight thousand people voluntarily live there. This may be explained by the "institutionalization" of the voluntary segregation of Chinatown. The norms of the community sanction the leaving of people who do not want to stay. The original functions of voluntary segregation had been for defensive purposes; now, the main functions have been shifted to business purposes. The changing functions are possible because the norms of the community only push the deviant function to the existing degree of obedience. In other words, the changing function is a moving equilibrium. Even though the younger generations tend to move out, Chinatown will continue to exist as a "symbol" of voluntary segregation because it will become a commercial district in which not too many Chinese will remain as residents. With the change in its original function, New York's Chinatown tends to become a commercial district, or a "symbol" of voluntary segregation in place of the previous "defensive purpose."

Voluntary segregation does not curtail assimilation but delays the process to some extent. Since the situation for the Chinese has improved in the United States, and the younger generations are more or less "Americanized," the process of assimilation is quicker than it was. On the other hand, the more the tensions between the two nations lessen, the more the tensions between the Chinese living in America and Americans tend to decrease. And a decrease of tensions facilitates assimilation. In the social attitudes test, the results show that Chinese favor better intergroup relations, which relations also facilitate the acceptance of assimilation. The previous analysis indicates that Chinatowns will decline as the younger generations tend to move out. This is a good indication that the assimilation process is taking place. Therefore, in general, one can conclude that voluntary segregation of the Chinese does not curtail assimilation, but does delay the process to some extent.

Gradual assimilation is taking place, but complete assimilation is impossible until the resistance to intermarriage by both the majority and minority groups is removed. If the "color line" is crossed by interracial marriages, unequal treatment of a minority cannot be enforced. There are many ways to advocate intermarriage if improved race relations are desired. For example, Lee points out:

> A decision of the California Supreme Court has affected the assimilation process within the last two years (1948–1950). The law forbidding intermarriage in the state is declared non-enforceable, and the increase in mixed marriages is marked. Los Angeles alone reported almost a hundred cases within six months after the decision was publicized.[23]

There is no segregation in Hawaii because intermarriage is accepted and regarded as an "honor." Originally, "the king [in Hawaii] secured the services of a number of white men. . . . These men . . . were given positions of honor and were given native women of chiefly rank to be their wives . . . their half-blood children by the Hawaiians were accorded high rank."[24] But we should not over-emphasize the correlation between intermarriage and desegregation because there is also a positive correlation between the decrease of prejudice and desegregation. For example, in French Martinique, segregation of color is not visible today because there is little or no prejudice.[25] Therefore, it can be suggested that the norm of a group disapproving interracial marriage indirectly contributes to voluntary segregation of that group. On the other hand, where the interracial marriage is accepted, voluntary segregation is difficult to maintain.

A FINAL NOTE

This analysis suggests, in general, that the segregated community of the Chinese in New York is one kind or form of voluntary segregation on the devised scale, namely, the "voluntary segregation involving involuntary factor(s)." Theoretically, voluntary segregation is distinct from involuntary segregation. In practice, however, it is difficult to tell one from the other, as seen in the case of the Chinese. It is interesting to note that Leo Kuper also had difficulty in differentiating between voluntary segregation and compulsory (involuntary) segregation in his case study of Durban, South Africa.[26] The suggested scale of segregation, further breaking down the component parts of both kinds of segregation, is aimed at solving the difficulties.

Race relations are no longer a domestic problem which can be solved at national leisure. During the last few years, the United Nations Educational, Scientific and Cultural Organization has done a series of projects to

---

[23] Rose Hum Lee, "A Century of Chinese-American Relationships," *Phylon*, XI (Third Quarter, 1950), 240–45.

[24] Edward B. Reuter (ed.), *Race and Culture Contacts* (New York, 1934), p. 151.

[25] Wagley and Harris, *op. cit.*, pp. 108–09.

[26] Leo Kuper, *Durban, A Study in Racial Ecology* (New York, 1958).

study "international tensions and the techniques for their relief."[27] The suggested scale of segregation might help to discover different approaches to solve different kinds or forms of segregation in our present-day "international" race relations. Any conclusions or generalizations formulated in this paper, nevertheless, are, and should be, tentative. The author can only express the hope that his study of what has already been done, though incomplete, may stimulate others to make further scientific inquiry into Chinese-American relations, which is one aspect of "international" race relations.

[27] Otto Klineberg, *Tensions Affecting International Understanding* (New York, 1950), p. vii.

3.

Institutional Perspectives: Effects of Racism on Black Americans

A. SOCIOLOGICAL PERSPECTIVES ON THE BLACK FAMILY

The concepts of the family and socialization are important to persons who are familiar with the issues surrounding the efforts of governmental and private organizations to improve the living conditions of poor people in America. This is true especially for those concerned with eliminating racial differences in income, housing, health care, and educational and occupational attainment. When there are systematic inequalities involving a particular group in a society which have persisted for a long period of time, and there is a vigorous demand for the elimination of these inequities, we are faced with the question of why the inequity exists. One way of approaching the problem is to ask the following questions: "What is to account for America's failure to assimilate the Negro minority as it has absorbed other ethnic groups? Do the major stumbling blocks lie within the Negro or the white community?"[1]

The family life and life styles of Black Americans have been identified as the principal source of the "tangle of pathology" that now serves to perpetuate the cycle of poverty and deprivation. In 1965, a major controversy erupted following the publication of *The Negro Family: The Case for National Action* (The Moynihan Report). The "deterioration of

[1] These questions were posed by Sidney Wilhelm in his book *Who Needs the Negro?* (Cambridge, Mass.: Schenkman Publishing Co., 1970). While these questions are relevant for the discussion which follows and for understanding the context in which the controversy over the Moynihan Report developed, the reader should not assume that assimilation is a goal that is universally accepted by Black Americans. Most blacks agree, however, that inequalities in income, housing, education, employment, health care, and political opportunities should be eliminated.

the fabric of Negro society" was attributed to the "deterioration of the Negro family" by the authors of this report. The report placed great emphasis on the negative consequences of family instability, especially the absence of the father from many ghetto homes. The absence of fathers and the uncertain employment status of those who remain in the home leads to an "unhealthy" family situation which is described as "matriarchal."

As Yinger has pointed out in his article in Section One, this report was criticized because it emphasized socialization to a deviant sub-culture rather than emphasizing the pathological social system within which the family is forced to exist. The report implied that individuals and families must change their life styles in order to improve the conditions of ghetto life (and, implicitly, to gain acceptance by whites). Some critics argued that changes in living conditions—better jobs, better housing, better schools—would eliminate the stresses which result in family patterns that the dominant society labels deviant. Other critics have questioned the validity of the assumption that the American middle-class family with its emphasis upon the nuclear unit is the most effective adaptation to the stresses of urban life. Adaptations of extended family patterns may have greater utility in the ghetto.

The articles in this section were selected because they reflect some of the recent concerns of scholars interested in developing a broader understanding of black family life. The first article in this section by Poussaint and Atkinson deals directly with the issue of socialization for achievement in the black community. What does the system of segregation and discrimination do to the self-images of black children? These authors argue that the impact of racism is devastating and that the black child's self-image will be impaired as long as America remains a racist society. The potentially positive influences of the Black Power movement are not discussed by these authors at any length, although they do allude to decentralization of schools and the organization of black political power as significant steps toward black control of black institutions. The revolution in black attitudes is expressed more clearly in Cedric Clark's article and in some of the other selections in Section Three B.

The second article in this section deals directly with the question of the "Black Matriarchy." Robert Staples argues that the black matriarchy proposition is fallacious and represents a myth imposed by white society. He suggests that the myth has been functional for the white ruling class because it promotes divisiveness in the black community, and it also provides a rationalization for discrimination. By attributing the blame for black poverty to the personal or familial "disorganization" of blacks themselves, the society avoids the responsibility for improving living conditions for black people. The policy implications of the "matriarchy" theory lead to programs which would limit family size rather than to programs which would eliminate job and housing discrimination.

Some scholars may feel that Staples' article is too polemical to be given serious consideration as a scholarly critique of a long established sociological theory. The editor has, therefore, included another article which criticizes traditional studies of the black family. In "Jobs and the Negro Family: A Reappraisal," Harwood and Hodge question the basic assumption upon which the matriarchy theory is based. These authors review evidence from numerous sources and conclude that, "all the evidence we have for past periods offers no significant support for the assumption that Negro women ever were advantaged [compared to black men] in the search for jobs." They suggest that the black woman's handicaps in the job market may be more significantly related to the family patterns of urban blacks than the problems encountered by black men. It is clear, therefore, that the alleged economic basis for female dominance in black families is not supported by the evidence. This article provides empirical support for Staples' claim that the black matriarchy is a sociological myth. Whether or not one accepts the proposition that black family life is "unstable" or "disorganized," it is clear that new studies based on a reconceptualization of the problem are sorely needed.

The studies by Hannerz and Young are examples of recent approaches to the study of black family life. These authors have used anthropological techniques to develop an understanding of aspects of family life from the contexts within which they develop. The streetcorner male is the focus of "The Roots of Black Manhood," by Ulf Hannerz. The article addresses itself to the process by which young boys are socialized into the ghetto male role. The article by Young is a study of family life in a Southern community which attempts to show the functional relevance of black family organization and socialization patterns as they relate to the social situation in which the people live and work. Both articles emphasize the importance of customs and informal socialization in the development of adult sex-roles and family styles.

The sixth article in this section is concerned with two somewhat neglected groups, the black middle and working classes. Sociologists sometimes manage to give the impression that nearly all black families are poor and unstable. Students of race relations should be aware that within every group there is diversity, and that in spite of discriminatory barriers some members of even the most oppressed groups have achieved middle-class educational and occupational status. The article describes some of the differences in life styles of blue-collar workers and white-collar workers. The most important difference from the viewpoint of political activists is found in the area of political participation. The white-collar group reports a much higher level of participation in electoral politics and in demonstrations. On the other hand, blue-collar workers report greater hostility to whites. The blue-collar workers described here seem to be very similar to Hamilton's "Silent Black Majority" (see Section Three B).

If one accepts the matriarchy theory, it would seem logical to predict that black women would be more active than black men (or at least as active) in the struggle for equal rights. The final selection in this chapter is a report of a study conducted on a southern college campus which investigated sex differences in civil rights activities and attitudes toward the concept of "Black Power," and the violence in Detroit and Newark during 1967. The paper reviews some of the recent literature on the matriarchy hypothesis, some literature on sex differences (among whites) in political participation, and a study of black racial and political attitudes. A basic question implied in this study is whether sociologists can make more accurate predictions about black college students by using the literature on sex differences in political participation than we can by assuming that black females are "dominant" and, therefore, cannot be expected to differ from black males in level of political participation. The results of the study indicate that in the political arena, black males are more active than black females, thereby suggesting that sex is a better predictor in this instance than race. The fact that males are also more active among whites does not mean that this is a situation to be desired. It does imply that sexism has a negative impact on both black and white female opportunities and role definitions.

The selections included in this section suggest that it is incorrect to conceptualize the black family as a matriarchy. These articles also provide evidence in support of the hypothesis that it is inadequate to view the black family as simply a variant of the white American family. Cultural differences cannot be equated with cultural inferiority or with deviant behavior. The legitimacy of cultural differences in family patterns is rarely questioned when European or Asian ethnic minorities are considered. Today other groups (American Indians, Chicanos, Puerto Ricans, and blacks) are also demanding that their cultures be equally respected if America is to be considered a viable pluralistic society. While these articles deal only with blacks, the issues are equally pertinent to other racial groups.

Black Youth and Motivation

ALVIN POUSSAINT and CAROLYN ATKINSON

The Civil Rights movement of the 1960's in America spawned a new and vibrant generation of young black people. The degree of their commitment and determination came as a surprise for most white Americans, who, if they thought of blacks to any extent, considered them to be a rather docile, acquiescent people. As the events of the early 60's moved on with inexorable force, another, still younger generation of blacks stood on the periphery watching and waiting their turn. Their intense coming-of-age has brought still more surprise and puzzlement not only to white Americans, but to some Negroes. So busy have many been in "handling" or "coping with" the complex behavior of these young blacks, that relatively little has been done in terms of examining the basis for this behavior. This paper represents an attempt to pause in the on-going melee for an exploration of some of the factors of particular relevance to the motivation of Afro-American youth. Our analysis will focus on some of the "problem areas" so of necessity will not detail the many strengths and positive features of the black socio-cultural environment. Of primary interest in our discussion will be the areas of internal motivation: the individual's self-concept; certain of his patterned needs; and the external motivators: the rewards offered by society for satisfactory performance in any of its institutional areas.

Of obvious importance to the functioning of any individual is his concept or vision of himself. And like it or not, this concept is inevitably a part of how others see him, how others tell him he should be seen. According to Mead,[1] Cooley,[2] and others,[3] the self arises through the individual's interaction with and reaction to other members of society: his peers, parents, teachers and other institutional representatives. Through identification and as a necessary means of effective communication, the child learns to assume the roles and attitudes of others with whom he interacts. These assumed attitudes condition not only how he responds to others, but how he behaves towards himself. The collective

[1] George H. Mead, *Mind, Self, and Society* (Chicago: University of Chicago Press, 1934), Part III.
[2] Charles H. Cooley, *Human Nature and the Social Order* (Glencoe, Ill.: Free Press, 1956), passim.
[3] *Sociological Quarterly* (entire issue), Vol. 7, No. 3, Summer, 1966.

attitudes of the others, the community or "generalized other" as Mead calls them, gives the individual his unity of self. The individual's self is shaped, developed and controlled by his anticipating and assuming the attitudes and definitions of others (the community) toward him. To the extent that the individual is a member of this community, its attitudes are his, its values are his, and its norms are his. His image of himself is structured in these terms. Each self, then, though having its unique characteristics of personality, is also an individual reflection of the social process.[4] This idea can be seen more succinctly illustrated in Cooley's suggestion of the self as a looking-glass, a looking-glass mirroring the three principal components of one's self-concept: "the imagination of our appearance to the other person; the imagination of his judgment of that appearance; and some sort of self-feeling, such as pride or mortification."[5]

For the black youth in white American society, the generalized other whose attitudes he assumes and the looking-glass into which he gazes both reflect the same judgment: he is inferior because he is black. His self-image, developed in the lowest stratum of a color caste system, is shaped, defined, and evaluated by a generalized other which is racist or warped by racists. His self-concept naturally becomes a negatively esteemed one, nurtured through contact with such institutionalized symbols of caste inferiority as segregated schools, neighborhoods, and jobs and more indirect negative indicators such as the reactions of his own family who have been socialized to believe that they are sub-standard human beings. Gradually becoming aware of the meaning of his black skin, the Negro child comes to see himself as an object of scorn and disparagement, unworthy of love and affection. The looking-glass of white society reflects the supposed undesirability of the black youth's physical appearance: black skin and wooly hair, as opposed to the valued models of white skin and straight hair. In order to gain the esteem of the generalized other, it becomes clear to him that he must approximate this white appearance as closely as possible. He learns to despise himself and to reject those like himself. From the moment of this realization, his personality and style of interaction with his environment become molded and shaped in a warped, self-hating, and self-denigrating way. He learns that existence for him in this society demands a strict adherence to the limitations of his sub-standard state. He comes to understand that to challenge the definition the others have given of him will destroy him. It is impressed upon him that the incompetent, acquiescent and irresponsible Negro survives in American society, while the competent, aggressive

---

[4] Mead, *op. cit.*
[5] Cooley, *op. cit.*, p. 184.

black is systematically suppressed. The looking-glass of the black youth's self reflects a shattered and defeated image.

Several attempts have been made to determine how this shattered self-concept affects the black child's ability to function in society, his ability to achieve, to succeed or "make good," particularly in the area of education. Though the conclusions of these varied attempts have differed on occasion, there has been general agreement as to the reality of the black child's incomplete self-image.[6,7,8] One notable exception to this agreement, however, is the Coleman Report, a 1966 study by the United States Office of Education on the "Equality of Educational Opportunity."[9] This report maintains that the black child's self-concept has not been exceptionally damaged, and is in fact virtually no different from that of a white child. The report did, however, note that the white child is consistently able to achieve on a higher level than that of his black counterpart. The Coleman Study, therefore, concluded that self-concept has little to do with an individual's ability to achieve.[10] Other studies tend to disagree with these findings.

Another variation on this theme of the black child's self-concept is seen in a 1968 report on "Academic Motivation and Equal Educational Opportunity" done by Irwin Katz. Katz found that black children tended to have exaggeratedly high aspirations, so high, in fact, that they were realistically impossible to live up to. As a result, these children were able to achieve very little:

> Conceivably, their (low achieving Negro boys') standards were so stringent and rigid as to be utterly dysfunctional. They seem to have internalized a most effective mechanism for self-discouragement. In a sense, they had been socialized to self-impose failure.[11]

[6] Poussaint, A. F., "The Dynamics of Racial Conflict," *Lowell Lecture Series,* sponsored by Tufts-New England Medical Center, April 16, 1968.

[7] Joan Gordon, *The Poor of Harlem: Social Functioning in the Underclass,* Report to the Welfare Administration, Washington, D.C., July 31, 1965, pp. 115 and 161 and Irwin Katz, "Academic Motivation and Equal Educational Opportunity," *Harvard Educational Review,* Vol. 38, Winter, 1968, pp. 56–65.

[8] While we recognize the limitations of many measures of self-concept and that self-concept is often defined by how it is measured, an exploration of these considerations within the scope of this paper is clearly impossible. Therefore for the purpose of our presentation here, we are taking the measures of self-concept at face-value.

[9] James S. Coleman *et al., Equality of Educational Opportunity* (U.S. Office of Education, Government Printing Office: Washington, D.C., 1966), p. 281.

[10] *Ibid.,* p. 320.

[11] Katz, *op. cit.,* p. 60.

Katz presents evidence which indicates that the anticipation of failure or harsh judgment by adults produces anxiety in the child, and that in black children, this level of anxiety is highest in low achievers who have a high standard of self-evaluation.[12] Accordingly, a black child with an unrealistically elevated self-concept often tends to become so anxious concerning his possible failure to meet that self-concept that he does in fact fail consistently.

On the other hand, Deutsch's work has shown that Negro children had significantly more negative self-images than did white children.[13] He maintains that, among the influences converging on the black urban child,

> . . . is his sensing that the larger society views him as inferior and *expects* inferior performance from him as evidenced by the general denial to him of realistic vertical mobility possibilities. Under these conditions, it is understandable that the Negro child would tend strongly to question his own competencies and in so questioning would be acting largely as others expect him to act, an example of what Merton has called the "self-fulfilling prophecy"—the very expectation itself is a cause of its fulfillment.[14]

Similarly, Coombs and Davies offer the important proposition that:

> In the context of the school world, a student who is defined as a "poor student" (by significant others and thereby by self) comes to conceive of himself as such and gears his behavior accordingly, that is, the social expectation is realized. However, if he is led to believe by means of the social "looking-glass" that he is capable and able to achieve well, he does. To maintain his status and self-esteem becomes the incentive for further effort which subsequently involves him more in the reward system of the school.[15]

These views have been confirmed in such studies as that of Davidson and Greenberg.[16] In their examination of children from Central Harlem, these authors found that the lower the level of self-esteem, the lower the level of achievement; while consequently, higher levels of self-appraisal

---

[12] *Ibid.*, pp. 61–62.

[13] Martin Deutsch, "Minority Groups and Class Status as Related to Social and Personality Factors in Scholastic Achievement," in Martin Deutsch and Associates, *The Disadvantaged Child* (New York: Basic Books, Inc., 1967), p. 106.

[14] *Ibid.*, p. 107.

[15] R. H. Coombs and V. Davies, "Self-Conception and the Relationship between High School and College Scholastic Achievement," *Sociology and Social Research,* Vol. 50, July, 1966, pp. 468–469.

[16] Helen H. Davidson and Judith W. Greenberg, *Traits of School Achievers from a Deprived Background* (New York: City College of the City University of New York, May 1967), pp. 133, 134.

and ego strength—feelings of self-competence—were associated with higher levels of achievement. For example, high achievers were more able to give their own ideas and to express basic needs, suggesting that a stronger self-concept is associated with a greater willingness to risk self-expression, an obvious prerequisite for achievement.

Certainly these various studies cannot be considered as ultimately nor unanimously conclusive. However, it is important to note that none of these reports has found any evidence of high achievement resulting from a low self-concept. Obviously the black child with such a low self-concept competes at a disadvantage with white youth in the struggle to achieve in this society.

The question then arises as to why black youth bother to involve themselves at all in this struggle. If their negative self-image handicaps them so greatly in achieving, why not simply abdicate and in fact adhere to society's definition of them as sub-standard? An attempted response to this question moves us into another area, that of patterned needs.

In the course of the socialization process, the individual acquires needs which motivate behavior and generate emotions. Three such needs concern us here: the need for achievement, the need for self-assertion or aggression, and the need for approval.

Among the attitudes of the generalized other which the individual in this society internalizes are the norms and values of the wider community, including, of course, the major tenets of the Protestant Ethic-American creed, i.e., with hard work and effort the individual can achieve success, and the individual's worth is defined by his ability to achieve that success. The individual who internalizes these values is motivated to act consistently with them, as his self-esteem is heightened or maintained through behaving in a manner approved by the community. Thus, the need for achievement develops in both white and black Americans. Consequently, the black youth's participation in the struggle for success is at least in part an attempt to satisfy his own needs.

This need to achieve may be very high as illustrated in the findings of Coleman[17] and Katz[18] who note the exceptionally high aspirations of Negro youth with regard to schooling and occupational choice. In addition, Katz[19] and Gordon[20] indicate that the aspirations and demands for academic achievement of the parents of these youth are also often exceptionally high. All of these sources agree, however, that the achievement of these youth is far from commensurate with either their own

---

[17] Coleman, *op. cit.*, pp. 278–280.
[18] Katz, *op. cit.*, p. 64.
[19] *Ibid.*, pp. 63–65.
[20] Gordon, *op. cit.*, p. 115.

aspirations or those of their parents.[21] Thus, the problem does not seem to be, as some have suggested, one of insufficiently high levels of aspiration, but rather one of realizing these aspirations through productive behavior.[22] Gordon[23] and Katz[24] suggest that this discrepancy persists because the educational and occupational values and goals of white society have been internalized by black youth, but for one reason or another, the behavior patterns necessary for their successful attainment have not been similarly learned. Katz puts it succinctly:

> Apparently the typical Negro mother tries to socialize her child for scholastic achievement by laying down verbal rules and regulations about classroom (behavior), coupled with punishment for detected transgressions. But she does not do enough to guide and encourage her child's efforts at verbal-symbolic mastery. Therefore, the child learns only to verbalize standards of academic interest and attainment. These standards then provide the cognitive basis for negative self-evaluations . . . The low achieving Negro student learns to use expressions of interest and ambition as a verbal substitute for behaviors he is unable to enact . . . By emphasizing the discrepancy between the real and ideal performance, anxiety is raised in actual achievement situations.[25]

Thus, the black child's negative self-concept is further complicated by his internalization of white society's high-level goals, and the need to achieve them, without a true comprehension of how effectively to do so.

Further examination of the values of the Protestant Ethic leads to the conclusion that they imply that assertion of self and aggression is an expected and admired form of behavior. Through the socialization process, the individual internalizes those attitudes which reinforce his basic need to assert himself or express himself aggressively. Thus, random and possibly destructive aggression is channeled into a legitimate and rewarded avenue of achievement.[26]

What happens to the black child's need for aggression and self-assertion? What has been the nature of his socialization with respect to expressing aggression? Since slavery days and, to some extent, through the present, the Negro most rewarded by whites has been the "Uncle Tom," the exemplar of the black man who was docile and non-assertive,

---

[21] Coleman, *op. cit.*, p. 281; Katz, *op. cit.*, p. 63; Gordon, *op. cit.*, pp. 155, 160–161.

[22] David P. Ausubel and Pearl Ausubel, "Ego Development Among Segregated Negro Children," in A. Harry Passow, ed., *Education in Depressed Areas* (New York: Teachers College Press, 1963), p. 135.

[23] Gordon, *op. cit.*, pp. 115, 161.

[24] Katz, *op. cit.*, p. 63.

[25] *Ibid.*, p. 64.

[26] Davidson and Greenberg, *op. cit.*, p. 58.

who bowed and scraped for the white boss and denied his aggressive feelings for his oppressor. In order to retain the most menial of jobs and keep from starving, black people quickly learned that passivity was a necessary survival technique. To be an "uppity nigger" was considered by racists one of the gravest violations of racial etiquette. Vestiges of this attitude remain to the present day, certainly in the South, but also in the North: blacks who are too "outspoken" about racial injustices often lose their jobs or are not promoted to higher positions because they are considered "unreasonable" or "too sensitive." It is significant that the civil rights movement had to adopt passive-resistance and non-violence in order to win acceptance by white America. Thus, the black child is socialized to the lesson taught by his parents, other blacks, and white society: don't be aggressive, don't be assertive. Such lessons do not, however, destroy the need for aggression and self-assertion.

One asserts oneself for self-expression, for achievement of one's goals, and for control of one's environment. Thus, an individual's success in satisfying his need for self-assertion is to some degree determined by his sense of control of his environment. Coleman found that of three attitudes measured, sense of control over environment showed the strongest relationship to achievement.[27] He further discovered that blacks have a much lower sense of control over their environment than do whites,[28] but that this sense of control increased as the proportion of whites with whom they went to school increased.[29] These findings indicate that for blacks, a realistic inability for meaningful self-assertion is a greater inhibitor of ability to achieve than is any other variable. These findings also suggest, however, that when blacks are interacting in a school situation which approximates the world in which they must cope, i.e., one with whites, their sense of control and achievement increases. Our emphasis here is not that black students' being in the presence of white students increases their sense of control and level of achievement, but that their being in a proximate real world suggests to them that they can cope in any situation, not just one in which they are interacting with others who, like themselves, have been defined as inferior.

Coleman's findings are supported by those of Davidson and Greenberg: high achievers were more able to exercise control and to cope more effectively with feelings of hostility and anxiety generated by the environment than were low achievers.[30] Deutsch points out that black male children for whom aggressive behavior has always been more threatening (compared with black girls) have lower levels of achievement on a num-

[27] Coleman, *op. cit.*, p. 319.
[28] *Ibid.*, p. 289.
[29] *Ibid.*, pp. 323–324.
[30] Davidson and Greenberg, *op. cit.*, p. 54.

ber of variables than do black girls.[31] It is not surprising then that black people, objectively less able to control their environment than can whites, may react in abdicating control by deciding not to assert themselves. The reasons for this are clear. First, the anxiety that accompanies growth and change through self-assertion is avoided if a new failure is not risked and thus, a try is not made. Second, the steady state of failure through nonachievement rather than through unsuccessful trial is a pattern which many blacks have come to know and expect. They feel psychologically comfortable with the more familiar.

However, this effort by black people to deny their need for control and self-assertion inevitably takes its toll. Frustration of efforts to control the environment are likely to lead to anger, rage and other expressions of aggression.[32] This aggression can be dealt with in a variety of ways. It can be suppressed, leading one to act on the basis of a substitute and opposing emotional attitude, i.e., compliance or docility. It can be channeled through legitimate activities—dancing, sports, or through an identification with the oppressor and a consequent striving to be like him. Aggression can also be turned inward and expressed in psychosomatic illness, drug addiction, or the attacking of those like oneself (other blacks) whom one hates as much as oneself. Or aggression can be directed toward those who generate the anger and rage—the oppressors, those whom the individual defines as thwarting this inclination to self-assertion. This final form of aggression can be either destructive or constructive: dropping out of school or becoming delinquent are examples of the former case, while participation in black social action movements is an example of the latter instance. This latter form of aggressive behavior amongst black people is increasing in extent. The old passivity is fading and being replaced by a drive to undo powerlessness, helplessness and dependency under American racism. The process is a difficult one for those black people who manage to make the attempt. For their aggressive drive, so long suppressed by the ruling power structure, is exercised to the inevitable detriment of still another exigency: their need for approval.

With the development of the self and through the process of identification, the individual's need for approval develops and grows as does his need to avoid disapproval.[33] As we have stated earlier, the Protestant Ethic of American society approves behavior which follows the achievement motive and expresses the need for self-assertion. An individual's behavior in accordance with this ethic is often tied to a need for approval. On the other hand, for blacks in American society, the reverse

31 Deutsch, *op. cit.*, p. 108.
32 Alvin F. Poussaint, "A Negro Psychiatrist Explains the Negro Psyche," *New York Times Magazine*, August 20, 1967, pp. 58–80.
33 Davidson and Greenberg, *op. cit.*, p. 61.

is often the case, i.e., behavior which is neither achievement-oriented nor self-assertive is often approved by both blacks and whites (for different reasons), and thus, the need for approval may be met through behavior unrelated to either achievement or self-assertion.

Katz's study maintains that in lower-class black homes, children do not learn realistic (middle class) standards of self-appraisal and therefore do not develop (as do middle class children) the capacity for gaining "satisfaction through self-approval of successful performance."[34] Accordingly, Katz suggests that achievement should be motivated and rewarded by approval not from the home, but from fellow students and teachers.[35] The extent to which black children are responsive to approval for achievement in middle class terms is, however, problematic. Some evidence suggests that lower class black children are motivated to gain approval through physical characteristics and prowess rather than through intellectual achievement as are middle class white and black children.[36] Further, needs for approval, not often met in black children through the established institutional channels, may be met by others outside of these legitimate institutional areas. For instance, delinquent sub-cultures support and encourage the behavior of their members. As a result, such members are not often sensitive to the informal sanctions imposed by non-members of this sub-society.[37] If an individual's needs are not met by others to whose sanctions he is expected to be responsive, he will be less likely to fear their sanctions for non-performance and will seek to have his needs met by others to whose rewards of approval he will then be responsive.[38] Thus, for black youth no less than others, how the need for approval motivates behavior depends in large part upon how it is satisfied or rewarded.

The rewards which the institutions of this society offer to those whose behavior meets their approval or is "successful" consist of money, prestige, power, respect, acclamation, and love, with increasing amounts of each of these being extended for increasingly "successful" behavior. The individual is socialized to know that these will be his if he performs according to expectations. Hence, these rewards act as external motivators of behavior. Blacks have learned of the existence of these rewards. They have also learned, however, that behavior for which whites reap these rewards does not result in the same consequences for them. In the

---

[34] Katz, *op. cit.*, p. 57.

[35] *Ibid.*

[36] Edmund W. Gordon and Doxey A. Wilkerson, *Compensatory Education for the Disadvantaged* (New York: College Entrance Examination Board, 1966), p. 18.

[37] Claude Brown, *Manchild in the Promised Land* (New York: Macmillan Company, 1965), passim.

[38] Talcott Parsons, *The Social System* (Glencoe, Ill.: The Free Press, 1951), Ch. 7.

various institutional areas of society, blacks are often rewarded differen-
tially from whites for the same behavior—if they are rewarded at all.
How then can such a highly capricious system motivate their behavior?

That blacks orient some aspects of their behavior to society's reward
system is evidenced by the fact that many studies have shown that lower
class blacks, as opposed to middle class whites and blacks, have a utilitarian attitude toward education, viewing it primarily in terms of its market
value.[39] The system provides no assurance, however, that once they
obtain the proper education for a job, that they will in fact be allowed
to get that job. This inability to trust society to confer rewards consistently no doubt makes it difficult for blacks to be socialized to behave
in terms of anticipating future reward for present activity. Thus it is that
Deutsch found that young black children are unwilling to persist in
attempting to solve difficult problems. They respond to such situations
with a "who cares" attitude.[40] Similarly, another study showed that when
a tangible reward was offered for successful work on a test, the motivation of the deprived youngsters increased considerably.[41] In a New York
program, young men who had been working primarily as clerks and
porters were motivated to join a tutorial program for admission to a
construction trade union apprenticeship program when they were
promised that successful completion of the program (passing the union's
examination) would definitely result in their being hired immediately at
a salary often double what they were able to command previously.[42]

However, motivation to achieve certain rewards may have different
consequences for behavior. As Merton explained, when the goals of
society are internalized without a corresponding internalization of normative means for achieving these goals, what often results is the resort to
illegitimate (deviant) means to achieve the socially valued goals.[43]

Just as a child unable to satisfy his need for approval through legitimate
channels may turn to delinquent sub-cultures for support and encouragement, so too might such a child, unable to gain society's rewards by
legitimate means, turn to illegitimate methods in order to attain them.
Such forms of behavior as numbers running, dope pushing, and prostitution effectively serve to net the rewards of society, while circumventing
the institutional channels for achievement of societal rewards. That
Negro children early learn that such behavior is rewarded is suggested
by Gordon's study in which young (9–13) Central Harlem boys were

[39] Gordon and Wilkerson, *op. cit.*, p. 18.
[40] Deutsch, *op. cit.*, p. 102.
[41] Elizabeth Douvan, "Social Status and Success Striving," cited in Frank Riessman,
The Culturally Deprived Child (New York: Harper and Row, 1962), p. 53.
[42] Personal Communication (C.A.)
[43] Robert K. Merton, *Social Theory and Social Structure* (Glencoe, Ill.: The Free
Press, 1957), Ch. 4.

asked if they knew people who had become rich, and if so, how they thought they had managed to do so. Of those who responded affirmatively, a majority felt that they had become rich through illegitimate means or luck.[44]

Consequently, for many black youth, external rewards are weak motivators of behavior, as they are discriminatorily and inconsistently given. The more immediate and direct the reward is, the stronger a motivator it is likely to be.

It would appear from this analysis that the standards and rewards of white American society simply do not work effectively to motivate productive behavior in young blacks. Clearly there is urgent need for a fundamental restructuring of the system. First, with respect to self-concept, all institutional segments of society must begin to function in a non-racist manner. To the extent that the self is shaped with reference to a generalized other, to that extent will the black child's image be impaired as long as America remains racist. The growth of black consciousness and pride have had salutary consequences for the black's self-image. But this alone is not sufficient. The operation of self-image as a motivator for behavior is like a self-fulfilling prophecy: blacks are continuously told and some believe that they are inferior and will fail. Therefore, they fail. For the black child to be motivated to achieve in school, the school must negate everything that the society affirms: it must tell the child that he can succeed—and he will.[45]

The relationship between self-concept and achievement is not clearcut, but it appears to be a weaker motivator of behavior than the motive to self-assertion and aggression. More attention should be given to examining this dimension of personality as a motivator of the black youth's behavior than to continuing inquiries into his self-image. It has been noted that the black youth's sense of control of his environment increases as the proportion of whites in his school increases. It is imperative to keep in mind, however, that participation in all-or-predominantly-black structures need not be self-destructive if the black youth chooses rather than is forced to participate in them. For if he chooses, he is asserting control over his environment. Those structural changes being made in American society in the direction of blacks having the opportunity to be more aggressively in control of their environment must be continued and expanded. The plans to decentralize New York City schools, to develop black business, and to organize and channel black political power are significant steps in this direction.

Most of the data indicate that black youth and their parents have high

[44] Gordon, *op. cit.*, p. 164.
[45] Kenneth B. Clark, *Dark Ghetto* (New York: Harper and Row, 1965), pp. 139–148.

educational and occupational aspirations, which are not carried through
to achievement levels. The reward systems of American society are often
irrelevant to the lives and aspirations of most black youth. Approval is
rewarded primarily for forms of behavior in which the black youth has
managed to achieve little proficiency, making him less likely to make the
effort. Something is obviously wrong with any school system which
permits so much young potential to be wasted simply because it cannot
be developed within the confines of traditional methods. New frameworks must be developed which will enable the educational aspirations
of black youth to correspond to their interests and proficiencies. With the
establishment of a pattern of consistent reward, there is every possibility
that intellectual endeavors would have immediate relevance to their
lives.

Certainly these suggested changes are sweeping, but so too have been
the dangerous effects of the maintenance of the old systems. The time for
being surprised at the behavior of black youth has passed. The time for
lengthy, nonproductive attempts at understanding them has too, in its
turn, come to an end. The time remaining must be effectively used in
action to bring about these and similar changes. America cannot afford
to wait for the next generation.

The Myth of the Black Matriarchy

ROBERT STAPLES

In dealing with the question of the role of the black woman in the black
struggle one must ultimately encounter the assertion that the black community is organized along matriarchal lines, that the domineering black
female has been placed in a superordinate position in the family by the
historical vicissitudes of slavery, and that her ascendency to power has resulted in the psychological castration of the black male and produced a
host of other negative results that include low educational achievement,
personality disorders, juvenile delinquency, etc. One of the solutions to
the "Negro" question we hear is that black males divest themselves of this
female control of black society and reorganize it along patriarchal lines
which will eventually solve the problem created by black female dominance.

And one can easily understand how the typical black female would
react when told that the problem of black liberation lies on her shoulders,
that by renouncing her control over the black male, their other common

problems such as inadequate education, chronic unemployment and other pathologies will dissipate into a dim memory.

The myth of a black matriarchy is a cruel hoax.

It is adding insult to injury to black liberation. For the black female, her objective reality is a society where she is economically exploited because she is both female and black; she must face the inevitable situation of a shortage of black males because they have been taken out of circulation by America's neo-colonialist wars, railroaded into prisons, or killed off early by the effects of ghetto living conditions. To label her a matriarch is a classical example of what Malcolm X called making the victim the criminal.[1]

To explode this myth of a black female matriarchy, one must understand the historical role of the black woman and the development of that role as it was influenced by the political and economic organization of American society. Like most myths, the one of a black matriarchy contains some elements of truth. Black women have not been passive objects who were satisfied with watching their menfolk make history. If they had been contented to accept the passive role ascribed to the female gender, then the travail of the past four centuries might have found the black race just as extinct as the dinosaur. It is a poor tribute to their historical deeds to characterize them as "sapphires," an opprobrious term that belies their real contribution to the black struggle.

Referring to black women as matriarchs is not only in contradistinction to the empirical reality of their status but also is replete with historical and semantic inaccuracies. It was in the study by J. J. Bachofen[2] that the term matriarchy was first employed. He was attempting to present a case for the high position of women in ancient society. His conclusion was that since free sexual relations had prevailed during that time and the fathers of the children were unknown, that this gave women their leading status in the period he called "mother-right."

A matriarchy is a society in which some, if not all, of the legal powers relating to the ordering and governing of the family-power over property, over inheritance, over marriage, over-the-house—are lodged in women rather than men.[3] If one accepts this formal definition, the consensus of most historians is that "men reign dominant in all societies; no matriarchy (*i.e.*, a society ruled by women) is known to exist."[4]

From a historical perspective, the black woman has always occupied a highly esteemed place in black culture. The African woman who first reached the shores of the American continent was already part and

---

[1] George Breitman, *Malcolm X Speaks* (New York: Merit Publishers, 1965).

[2] J. J. Bachofen, *Das Mutterrecht* (Stuttgart, 1861).

[3] Margaret Mead, *Male and Female* (New York: William Morrow and Company, 1949), p. 301.

[4] William Goode, *The Family* (Englewood Cliffs: Prentice-Hall, 1964), p. 14.

parcel of the fabric of history. She was descended from women who had birthed some of the great militarists of antiquity and from whose number had come some of the most famous queens to sit upon the thrones of ancient Egypt and Ethiopia. Her exploits and beauty were remembered by Semitic writers and fused into Greek mythology.[5]

Despite her important historical role, there is little doubt about the respective authority patterns in the black family of the pre-slave period of African civilization. There, the family organization was patriarchal in character and was a stable and secure institution. E. Franklin Frazier described the African patriarchal family this way:

> His wife and children gathered around him, and served him with as much respect as the best drilled domestics serve their masters; and if it was a fete day or Sunday, his sons-in-law and daughters did not fail to be present, and bring him some small gifts. They formed a circle about him, and conversed with him while he was eating. When he had finished, his pipe was brought to him, and then he bade them eat. They paid him their reverences, and passed into another room, where they all ate together with their mother.[6]

The ordeal of slavery wrought many changes in the family life of Afro-Americans, including the male and female roles. Family life of the African model was an impossibility when the slave's existence had to be devoted primarily to the cultivation and manufacture of tobacco and cotton. The buying and selling of slaves involved the splitting up of families, while the maintenance of discipline on the plantation prevented the husband and father from protecting his wife and children against his white masters and other more favored slaves. The financial value set on slave children and the rewards given to successful motherhood in cash, kind, and promotion from field slave to house slave gave an especially high status to the mother, a status which the father could only enjoy if placed in a position akin to that of a stud animal, this leading to a breaking of family ties and the degradation of family life still further.

Under the conditions of slavery, the American black father was forcefully deprived of the responsibilities and privileges of fatherhood. The black family's desire to remain together was subordinated to the economic interests of the slave-owning class. Only the mother-child bond continually resisted the disruptive effect of economic interests that dictated the sale of fathers away from their families. Not only did the practice of selling away fathers leave the black mother as the prime authority in the household but whenever the black male was present he was not allowed to play the normal masculine role in American culture. Davie reports that:

[5] John Hope Franklin, *From Slavery to Freedom* (New York: Random House, 1947).
[6] E. Franklin Frazier, *The Negro Family in the United States* (Chicago: University of Chicago Press, 1939), p. 7.

In the plantation domestic establishment, the woman's role was more important than that of her husband. The cabin was hers and rations of corn and salt pork were issued to her. She cooked the meals, tended the vegetable patch, and often raised chickens to supplement the rations. If there was a surplus to sell, the money was hers. She made the clothes and reared the children. If the family received any special favors it was generally through her efforts.[7]

Just as in the society at large, power relationships in the family are aligned along economic lines. The power base of the patriarchal family is, in large part, based on the economic dependence of the female member. In the black slave family, the black woman was independent of the black male for support and assumed a type of leadership in her family life not found in the patriarchal family. At the same time, white society continued to deny black males the opportunity to obtain the economic wherewithal to assume leadership in the family constellation.

The reasons for this suppression of the black male are found in both the economic imperatives of slavery and the sexual value system of white America. In the early period of colonial America, the white family was strongly patriarchal and many of the income and property rights enjoyed by women and children were those 'given' to them by the husband or father. White women had primarily a chattel status, particularly in the Southern part of the country. They were expected to remain chaste until marriage while white southern males were permitted, or often encouraged, to sow their wild oats before, during and after marriage.[8]

A double standard of sexual behavior allowing premarital sex for men while denying it to women, always poses the problem of what females will provide the source of sexual gratification for the bachelor males. There is adequate historical evidence that black slave women were forced into various sexual associations with white males because of their captive status. That physical compulsion was necessary to secure compliance on the part of black women is documented by Frazier, in relating this young man's story:

> Approximately a century and a quarter ago, a group of slaves were picking cotton on a plantation near where Troy, Alabama, is now located. Among them was a Negro woman, who despite her position, carried herself like a queen and was tall and stately. The overseer (who was the plantation owner's son) sent her to the house on some errand. It was necessary to pass through a wooded pasture to reach the house and the

[7] Maurice Davie, *Negroes in American Society* (New York: McGraw-Hill, 1949), p. 207.

[8] Arthur W. Calhoun, *A Social History of the American Family* (New York: Barnes and Noble, 1919).

overseer intercepted her in the woods and forced her to put her head between the rails in an old stake and rider fence, and there in that position my great-great-grandfather was conceived.[9]

Thus, the double-standard of premarital sexual behavior allowed the Southern white woman to remain "pure" and the bodies of the captive female slaves became the objects of their ruler's sexual passion. Consequently, black males had to be suppressed to prevent them from daring to defend the black woman's honor. For those black males who would not accept their suppression passively, the consequences were severe. As one person reports the story of his father's defense of his mother:

> His right ear had been cut off close to his head, and he had received a hundred lashes on his back. He had beaten the overseer for a brutal assault on my mother, and this was his punishment. Furious at such treatment, my father became a different man, and was so morose, disobedient, and intractable, that Mr. N. decided to sell him. He accordingly parted with him, not long after, to his son, who lived in Alabama; and neither mother nor I ever heard from him again.[10]

During the period of slavery, the physical resistance of black males to the rape of their women was met with all the brutal punishment white society could muster. That they were not totally successful in their efforts to crush the black man is evidenced in the heroic deeds of Denmark Vesey, Nat Turner, Frederick Douglass, David Walker and others. The acts of these black males are sometimes played down in favor of the efforts of Harriet Tubman, Sojourner Truth and other black females in securing the slave's freedom. Such favoritism can be expected of a racist society bent on perpetuating a myth of a black female matriarchy, with males pictured as ineffective husbands and fathers who are mere caricatures of real men. The literary castration of the black male is illustrated by the best selling novel, *The Confessions of Nat Turner*,[11] which generated much heat and little light, in terms of understanding one of the most important black revolutionists of his time.

The cultural stereotype of the domineering black woman belies the existence of the masses of black women who constituted a defenseless group against the onslaught of white racism in its most virulent sexual and economic manifestations. That black women are still involuntarily subjected to the white male's lust is reflected in the revelations of a white employer to John Howard Griffin, as reported in his book, *Black Like Me*:

> He told me how all of the white men in the region crave colored girls. He said he hired a lot of them both for housework and in his business. 'And

9 E. F. Frazier, *op. cit.*, p. 53.
10 *Ibid.*, p. 48.
11 William Styron, *The Confessions of Nat Turner* (New York: Random House, 1967).

I guarantee you, I've had it in every one of them before they ever get on the payroll.'

'Surely some refuse,' I suggested cautiously.

'Not if they want to eat—or feed their kids,' he snorted. 'If they don't put out, they don't get the job.'[12]

Black women have frequently been slandered by the cultural folklore that the only free people in the South were the white man and the black woman. While there have been a few black women who have gained material rewards and status through the dispensation of their sexual favors to white men, the massive indictment of all black women for the acts of a few only creates unnecessary intra-group antagonisms and impedes the struggle for black self-determination.

Many proponents of the black matriarchy philosophy assert that the black female gained ascendency in black society through her economic support of the family. Although the unemployment rate of black males is disproportionately higher than that of white males, only a very small minority of black families with both parents present are dependent on the mother for their maintenance. It is a rather curious use of logic to assume that black females, who in 1960 earned an annual wage of $2,372 a year as compared to the annual wage of $3,410 for white women and $3,789 for black men,[13] have an economic advantage over any group in this society.

However, what semblance of black female dominance that is found in our society can be traced to the persistent rate of high unemployment among black males which prevents them from becoming the major economic support of their family. The economic causes of female dominance are manifest. For instance, the percentage of black women in the labor market declines as the percentage of black males employed in manufacturing and mechanical industries is increasing. The effect of higher black male employment is the male's added responsibility for his family's support; the authority of the wife declines and that of the husband increases.

Many black men have not been permitted to become the kings of their castles. If black women wanted to work, there was always employment for them—even during depressions. Sometimes it was even a higher kind of work than that available to black men. Historically, black males have suffered from irregularity of employment more than any other segment of the American proletariat. Thus, they have been placed in a weak economic position which prevents them from becoming steady providers for their families. Any inordinate power that black women possess, they owe to white America's racist employment barriers. The net effect of this phe-

[12] John Howard Griffin, *Black Like Me* (New York: Signet, 1963).
[13] *United States Census of Population Report,* 1960.

nomena is, in reality, not black female dominance but greater economic deprivation for families deprived of the father's income.

The myth of a black matriarchy was strengthened by the Moynihan Report released in 1965.[14] Moynihan's central thesis was that the black family was crumbling and that a major part of the blame lay with the black matriarchy extant in the black community. Some of the evidence cited would lack credibility to all but a group bent on making the victim responsible for the crimes of the criminal. Such sources of proof as the higher educational level of black females vis-à-vis black males conveniently overlook the alternative possibility—that many black males are forced to terminate their formal education early in order to help support their family. Instead, they cite the wholly unsupported statement by a "Negro" expert that, "Historically, in the matriarchal society, mothers made sure that if one of their children had a chance for higher education the daughter was the one to pursue it."[15] In a society where men are expected to have a greater amount of education and earn a higher income, it is difficult to imagine black women celebrating the fact that over 60 percent of the college degrees awarded American blacks are received by women. The end result of this disparity, according to one study, is that almost 50 percent of black female college graduates are married to men employed at a lower socioeconomic level than their wives.[16]

Moreover, according to Moynihan and his cohorts, the black matriarchy is responsible for the low educational achievement of black males. In marshalling this arsenal of evidence, Moynihan was apparently unable to find any likelihood that the racist educational system, with its concomitant racist teachers, bore any responsibility for the failure of black males to reach acceptable educational levels by white standards. In the criminalization of the victim, countervailing evidence is dismissed out of hand. The fact that black schools are more likely to be housed in inadequate buildings, with inferior facilities, staffed by inexperienced and racist teachers and over-crowded,[17] only confuses the issue, especially when there is a matriarchal structure that is more handily blamed.

According to the "experts" on the black family, the black male is harshly exploited by the black matriarchy. Many black mothers, they report, express an open preference for girls.[18] This charge is confirmed by

14 *The Negro Family: The Case for National Action* (United States Department of Labor, 1965).

15 Whitney Young, *To Be Equal* (New York: McGraw-Hill, 1964), p. 25.

16 Jean Noble, *The Negro Woman College Graduate* (New York: Columbia University Press, 1956), p. 64.

17 *Equality of Educational Opportunity* (United States Department of Health, Education and Welfare, Office of Education, 1966).

18 Thomas F. Pettigrew, *A Profile of the Negro American* (Princeton, New Jersey: D. Van Nostrand, 1964), p. 16.

a white psychologist, described by a major magazine as devoid of any racism, who states that black males have an inordinate hatred for their mothers.[19] Although there are research studies that reveal no sex-role preference on the part of black mothers,[20] it appears that the practitioners of white social science have not been content with pitting husband against wife but also wish to turn sons against mothers, brothers against sisters. The evidence for these assumptions is not only flimsy, but in some cases also non-existent. If the research is similar to other psychological studies, they have probably used a sample of ten blacks who, on the verge of a psychotic breakup, wandered into their mental clinic.

These charges of black men hating their mothers must be very puzzling to the black mothers aware of them. They would be puzzled because they realize that if a preference is shown for any sex-role in the black family, it would more likely be expressed in favor of the male child. The problems of raising a black male child in a racist society have been great. Many black mothers out of fear—real or fancied—repressed the aggressive tendencies of their sons in order to save them from the white man's chopping block. For to act as a man in a society which feared his masculinity, the black male was subject to the force of brutal white retaliation. The black mother had to constantly live with the realization that her son might be killed for exercising the prerogatives of manhood. For those black mothers who exorcised their son's aggressive drives out of concern for their safety, hatred seems to be an inappropriate, and most improbable, response.

In addition to the host of pathologies putatively generated by the black matriarchy, the familiar theory of a relationship between fatherless homes and juvenile delinquency is brought up again. While there is nothing inherently wrong with a woman heading a family, the problem arises when she tries to compete in a society which promotes, expects and rewards male leadership. Consequently, she is unable to bring to her family the share of the social and economic rewards received by father-headed households. It is this very factor that probably accounts for any discernible correlation between mother-headed households and juvenile delinquency. The children in a fatherless home are frequently relegated to the lowest living standards in our society. The problems facing husbandless women with children are compounded by the inequities in American society based on sex role ascriptions.

It is impossible to state that the black woman is just like the women of other races. Her history is different from that of the prototypical white

[19] The particular psychologist in question, Herbert Hendin, was quoted in *Newsweek*, November 17, 1966, pp. 119–120.
[20] Robert Bell, *The One-Parent Mother in the Negro Lower Class*, Unpublished paper presented to the Eastern Sociological Society, 1965.

a result, the father's power is reduced in these areas, and he is relegated to enacting the "feminine" role of handyman.[25] This observation has prompted one person to suggest that exhorting black slum dwellers to emulate the presumably more stable white middle-class, restore father to his rightful place, and build a more durable family life will subsequently expose them to the threat of the suburban matriarchy.[26]

Any profound analysis of the black matriarchy proposition should reveal its fallacious underpinnings. Recognition of this fact raises the crucial question as to why white society continues to impose this myth on the consciousness of black people. This writer submits that it has been functional for the white ruling class, through its ideological apparatus, to create internal antagonisms in the black community between black men and black women to divide them and to ward off effective attacks on the external system of white racism. It is a mere manifestation of the divide-and-conquer strategy, used by most ruling classes through the annals of man, to continue the exploitation of an oppressed group.

In the colonial period of Algeria, the same situation existed wherein the colonists attempted to use the female population to continue their colonial rule. Fanon reports that the colonial administration devised a political doctrine for destroying the structure of Algerian society. By encouraging Algerian women to break the bonds of male domination in their society—setting male against female—the colonists hoped to dilute the Algerian capacity for resistance. According to Fanon, it was:

> . . . the woman who was given the historic mission of shaking up the Algerian man. Converting the woman, winning her over to the foreign values, wrenching her free from her status, was at the same time achieving a real power over the man and attaining a practical, effective means of destructing Algerian culture.[27]

In contemporary America, a female liberation movement is beginning to gain impetus.[28] This movement is presently dominated by white women seeking to break out of the centuries-old bondage imposed upon them by the male chauvinists of the ruling class. Whether black women should participate in such a movement is questionable. Hatred of a social curse which is part and parcel of an exploitative society that discriminates not only against blacks but also women should not be confused with

[25] Ernest W. Burgess and Harvey J. Locke, *The Family* (New York: American Book Co., 1960), p. 112.

[26] Eric Josephson, "The Matriarchy: Myth and Reality," *The Family Coordinator* (1969), pp. 18, 268–276.

[27] Frantz Fanon, *A Dying Colonialism*, tr. by Haakon Chevalier (New York: Grove Press, 1967), p. 39.

[28] See Evelyn Reed, *Problems of Women's Liberation* (New York: Merit Publishers, 1969) for one white radical's approach to the matriarchal origin of society question.

vidual has in a situation where there is a conflict of interests. It is here where the black male achieves the upper level of the power dimension.

Whenever a black man and black woman find themselves in objective and irremediable conflict, the best solution is to find another mate. The objective reality of black women is that black men are scarcer than hen's teeth. For a variety of reasons, there is an extremely low sex ratio in the black community, especially during the marriageable years—18 to 45 years.[23] This means that black women must compete for a relatively scarce commodity when they look forward to marriage. They are buyers in a seller's market. Black women, like all women, have their affectional and sexual needs. Many a black male's shortcomings must be tolerated for the sake of affection and companionship. In a sense, many black women have to take love on male terms.

The low sex ratio hardly allows black women to exercise any meaningful control over black men. In fact, as one black woman states:

> As long as she is confined to an area in which she must compete fiercely for a mate, she remains the object of sexual exploitation and the victim of all the social evils which such exploitation involves.
>
> In the Negro population, the excess of girls is greatest in the fifteen-to-forty-four age group which covers the college years and the age when most marriages occur . . . the explosive social implications of an excess of more than half a million Negro girls and women over fourteen years of age are obvious. . . . How much of the tensions and conflicts traditionally associated with the matriarchal framework of Negro society are in reality due to this imbalance and the pressures it generates?[24]

Another index of the matriarchy is simply the percentage of female-headed households in the black community. The Moynihan theory of the black matriarchy derives from his findings that 25 percent of all black families have a female head. This "proof" of a matriarchal family structure brings up many interesting questions, not excluding the important one: over whom do these women have control? Logically, the only power they have is to face a super-exploitation by the system of white racism that bi-parental black families do not encounter to the same degree.

The matriarchal myth is not always applied to only black families. A number of social scientists claim that suburban white families are matriarchal. They point out that the commuting father's disappearance during the day leaves the mother in charge of the home and children. As

[23] In New York City, for instance, there are only 75 black men for every 100 black women in about this same age range.

[24] Pauli Murray, *The Negro Woman in the Quest for Equality*, paper presented at Leadership Conference, National Council of Negro Women (Washington, D.C., November, 1963), pp 11–12, 12–13.

woman and her present-day behavioral patterns have evolved out of her historical experiences. In general, she is more aggressive and independent than white women. There are studies that show that black females are more non-conforming than white females as early as age ten. The reason for her greater self-reliance is that it has been a necessary trait in order for her and her children to survive in a racist and hostile society. Moreover, the society has permitted her more self-assertion than the white female.

Among male chauvinists, aggressiveness per se may be considered an undesirable trait in women and should be restricted to the male species. But this is all part of the age-old myth about the inherent nature of woman as a passive creature. More often than not, it has served as a subterfuge for the exploitation of women for the psychological and material gain of the male species. Black women lose nothing by their greater tenacity. That tenacity has, historically, been a source of strength in the black community. While white women have entered the history books for making flags and engaging in social work, black women have participated in the total black liberation struggle.

While recognizing these differences, the question before us now is how much power do black women really have and how is it exercised? Power is commonly defined as the ability to dominate men, to compel their action even against their wishes.[21]

The black woman has often been characterized as a more powerful figure in the family because she participates more in making decisions about what kind of car to buy, where to go on a vacation, etc.[22] In certain cases, she is the only one to make major decisions. A closer inspection of her decision-making powers often reveals that she does not make decisions counter to her husband's wishes, but renders them because he fails to do so. The reason he defers to her in certain decisions is simply because she is better equipped to make them. Usually, she has more formal education than her mate and in matters relating to the white society, she knows her way around better. She is more familiar with the machinations of white bureaucracies since contacts with the white world have been more available to black women than to black men.

Making decisions that black men cannot, or will not, make is a poor measure of the power a black woman has in the family. The chances are good that no decisions are made which he actively opposes. The power of black women is much like American democracy—it is more apparent than real. Power alignments are frequently based on the alternatives an indi-

21 Henry P. Fairchild, *Dictionary of Sociology and Related Sciences* (Totowa, New Jersey: Littlefield, Adams and Co., 1965), p. 227.
22 Robert Blood and Donald Wolfe, *Husbands and Wives* (Glencoe, Illinois: The Free Press, 1960).

hatred of men. The adversary is not one sex or the other—it is the racist, capitalist system which needs, breeds and preys upon oppressions of all types.

Any movement that augments the sex-role antagonisms extant in the black community will only sow the seed of disunity and hinder the liberation struggle. Whether black women will participate in a female liberation movement is, of course, up to them. One, however, must be cognizant of the need to avoid a diffusion of energy devoted to the liberation struggle lest it dilute the over-all effectiveness of the movement. Black women cannot be free *qua* women until all blacks attain their liberation.

The role of the black woman in the black liberation struggle is an important one and cannot be forgotten. From her womb have come the revolutionary warriors of our time.[29] The revolutionary vanguard has a male leadership but the black woman has stepped beside her man engaged in struggle and given him her total faith and commitment. She has thrust herself into the life or death struggle to destroy the last vestige of racism and exploitation in the American social structure. In the process of continuing her life-long fight against racist oppression, the myth of her matriarchal nature will soon join the death agony of America's racist empire. Until that time arrives, the black woman should be revered and celebrated—not only for her historical deeds in the building of African civilization, in the struggle to maintain the black peoples of America as a viable entity—but for her contemporary role in enabling black people to forge ahead in their efforts to achieve a black nationhood.

[29] It is interesting to note that, despite unfounded rumors about the emasculation of the black male, the thrust of the black liberation struggle has been provided almost exclusively by a black male leadership. In selecting leaders of black organizations, black females inevitably defer to some competent black male, an act which shows how much they really prefer the dominating position they supposedly have in black society.

Jobs and the Negro Family: A Reappraisal

EDWIN HARWOOD AND CLAIRE C. HODGE

Louise Meriwether's recent novel, *Daddy Was a Number Runner,* deals with an adolescent Negro girl in Harlem at the depth of the Depression. Although the young heroine manages to fend off a variety of local predators—mostly whites who make sexual advances—she proves powerless to prevent the disintegration of her family, a process that becomes the dramatic anchor in the book's plot. When her father stumbles hard against New York's job-scarce labor market, her mother starts work as a domestic for a suburban housewife, at first for a few half-days a week, but, towards the end of the novel, on almost a full-time basis. She knows it wounds Dad's pride, but the children must eat. What little Dad does manage to earn, by running numbers slips for the racketeers, he squanders on bets. The conclusion is foregone. Bitter at his wife's taking relief and going to work as a domestic, he fades from the home and becomes "a street-corner man."

None will deny that tragedies of this kind occurred. None will deny that economic recessions have posed serious problems for Negro city dwellers all along. Yet Meriwether's tale of woe relies heavily on a prevalent—and largely erroneous—stereotype of the Negro's economic condition. This is to the effect that, relative to their menfolk, Negro women have enjoyed an advantage in the urban labor market, and that in this their situation has differed sharply from that of working-class whites. Recent fantasies about "internal colonialism" have sharpened this stereotype to the point where it is sometimes said that the black man has been kept down in order to keep him in line, and that black women have been allowed a freer economic adjustment as a part of this same strategy. These and other such notions have helped fuel the animosities of black militants during the past decade. What better justification could there be for the rage of angry young men if, as Richard Rubenstein claims in his thinly-veiled apology for black violence, *Rebels in Eden,* "young [Negro] men have been degraded by this lack of control over their lives—by their inability to get or keep jobs and the need to send their women out to clean Goldberg's floor."

This stereotype is so familiar, and so widely-accepted, that it is hard to believe it could be false. Yet false is what available evidence shows it to be. Today, even in the poorest urban neighborhoods, Negro men enjoy a clear economic superiority over Negro women, as the findings of the United States Bureau of Labor Statistics' 1968–9 Urban Employment Survey demonstrated. Moreover, and more surprising, all the evidence we have for past periods offers no significant support for the assumption that Negro women ever were advantaged in the search for jobs.

Since 1890, when separate tabulations for whites and Negroes first became available, every decennial census has revealed Negro men to have enjoyed a markedly greater diversification of jobs than Negro women. In the urban or nonagricultural labor force, this difference is particularly striking. While Negro men could be found in substantial numbers in jobs in every major industry, Negro women were concentrated in just a handful of the several hundred occupational classifications. As late as 1930, of 1.3 million Negro women in nonagricultural jobs, over one million (or roughly 85 percent) were in domestic and personal service occupations. Over half were "laundresses not in laundries" and servants in private households. Of the Negro men outside agriculture, by contrast, less than 25 percent (425,000 of over 2 million) were to be found in the domestic and personal service classification. When, after studying Harlem's working population at the turn of the century, George Edmund Haynes concluded that Negroes would, when given the opportunity, expand their job horizons, he could only have been referring to Negro men. For his statistics showed that over half of the men had moved into jobs in firms and businesses, whereas 90 percent of all Negro female workers in his canvass were still confined to domestic and personal service jobs.

Taking economic dominance in its most literal sense, we might ask who held the supervisory and managerial jobs available to Negro workers then. Men did. With the exception of restaurants and boarding and lodging houses, Negro females in supervisory positions are rarely to be found at all in 1930. Second, and most contrary to popular belief, Negro men outnumbered women by heavy margins in white-collar clerical occupations (as did white men in relation to white women a generation ago). In 1930, Negro men in clerical occupations numbered almost 30,000 compared with 11,000 Negro women. In the single category, "Clerks" (except "clerks" in stores) the census located over 20,000 Negro males but only 5,000 Negro females in that year. In sum, *the historical pattern of occupational and earnings differences between the sexes reveals a striking similarity between whites and blacks, and not the reversal of roles or, as one writer phrased it, the "unnatural superiority" of women* that so many scholars have allowed themselves to believe without a careful review of the facts.

When it is argued that higher proportions of Negro women than men hold white-collar jobs today, it is forgotten that the same holds true of female whites in relation to men—simply because our economy employs more cashiers, "girl fridays," and telephone operators than it does lawyers, physicians, and corporation executives. Women moved into these more numerous white-collar occupations as men took better-paying jobs in other sectors of the economy, including blue-collar jobs. It is *not* true, as is often assumed, that female white-collar workers, black or white, earn more than male blue-collar workers. In 1969, annual earnings for Negro men in white-collar, blue-collar, and service (excluding private household) occupations were higher on average than earnings for Negro women in clerical and sales jobs. In the top bracket of the earnings scale, Negro female professional workers rank third, following Negro male professionals and managerial workers. However, these women, who are predominantly elementary and secondary school teachers, nurses, or medical and health technicians, are only 10 percent of all employed Negro women; they earn on average a mere $17 more per year than Negro male craftsmen and foremen. Twice as many Negro women are still to be found in the lowest paying of all job classifications, private household work.

Thus, the facts simply do not support the notion that the Negro man had a rougher go in the urban labor market than the Negro woman. On the contrary, his economic problems shrivel by comparison with hers. If she had to work, she found a limited range of jobs to choose from, most of them in private households, which paid the lowest wages. In New York City 70 years ago, more than half (53 percent) of the Negro women in service work earned less than five dollars a week, whereas only 28 percent of Negro male service workers had earnings that low. Elevator operator, butler, fireman, houseman, even "usefulman," paid better than "general housework, chambermaid, and laundress."

The argument for the Negro female's advantaged labor market position fails precisely where one might expect it to be strongest—in times of economic depression. Consider the facts turned up by the Division of Social Research of the Works Progress Administration (WPA). A thorough study of urban workers on relief in 79 major cities in the early 1930's was published in the two-volume study, *Urban Workers on Relief*. We learn:

1) The single occupational group that had the heaviest representation among relief applicants was "servants." Women, and particularly Negro women, were disproportionately represented in the unskilled service jobs included in that category. Among Negro women, a large majority were general houseworkers and laundresses.

2) Negro women on relief were twice as apt to be employed at the time of the study as Negro men on relief—but they enjoyed no special economic advantage because of that fact. The WPA researchers point out that the women earned less than men (17 cents an hour against the male's 25 cents an hour). And because she worked fewer than half the median hours her working male counterpart obtained in a week (17 hours for her; 35 for him), her median *weekly* earnings ($2.80) were less than half of what he earned ($6.30).

To argue that Negro women had the edge in the Depression labor market simply because at any given time she was more apt to get some job in unskilled service work is to rest the argument for her superiority on a shallow and incomplete statistic. In any case white men faced the same situation in relation to white females. Negro men may very well have been unemployed for longer stretches, but *when they did get jobs they worked more hours per week and earned substantially more money, such that in the aggregate they may very well have been doing much better by far than Negro women.* What proponents of the "dominant-female" view have never established is crucial: Did the female domestic work more days during the course of a given *year* in and out of depressions? The fact that in a given week she could often locate some job does not prove that she had more work over a longer span. Did she receive anywhere near the annual earnings received by a male laborer? According to Charles S. Johnson, research director for the National Urban League, women domestics in Waterbury, Connecticut were averaging three dollars a day in 1923 in work "that could rarely be secured for more than four days a week." Wages for Negro men averaged $4.38 per day; men in skilled manual jobs earned as much as five dollars and six dollars per day.

3) What the WPA researchers chose to emphasize in their study is even more significant in view of the strenuous attempt scholars have made to stress the differences in the adjustments of blacks and whites to a recession. The WPA study emphasized that *both* Negro and white males were unemployed for longer stretches than their female counterparts because *both* white and Negro men had a more diverse occupational distribution. This meant that, though they enjoyed the higher earnings that jobs in industrial and commercial firms paid in good times, they would suffer longer stretches of unemployment during a recession. It is reasonable to think that the casual service employment which women willingly took was not an acceptable alternative to either the white or black male worker, in any case. Reports issued by the United States Employment Service during the Depression years showed that a large proportion of the job placements in household work were for very short periods, often only for a given day, which supports the WPA's finding that most women obtained casual laboring jobs characterized by high turnover. Household workers in Wisconsin, for example, were so poorly paid that the state set a minimum weekly wage of $6 for a 50 hour week if board alone was furnished. We have no comparable data on the conditions of employment and pay in service jobs available to men, but we can be reasonably sure that the male janitor or porter, for example, would have been guaranteed a job of longer duration at higher pay.

The irony here is that the facts gathered by the WPA research team require something on the order of an about-face in our thinking. If Negro men had made even *further* advances in occupations and earnings, and hence in expectations as well, beyond what they had already achieved, then they would have experienced *longer* stretches of unemployment. They would have been more reluctant to take casual low-paying jobs. *Their problem of finding an acceptable job would have approached in severity that of white males who held the record for unbroken spells of unemployment!*

Clearly, it was because most reform-minded scholars wanted to do the Negro good, not ill, that they were led consistently to emphasize the *differences* between white and black Americans in their performances in the labor market. Only thus could special remedial action urged on the Negro's behalf have a plausible basis. Moreover, the troublesome issue of Negro marital instability had to be explained. If this could be linked to an economic plight not shared by white Americans, then it followed that most scholars would first seek out and then emphasize some critical difference observed in the adjustment of blacks and whites to the labor market.

It is important to keep two facts in mind: First, that an economic explanation was not logically compulsory for understanding family instability. E. Franklin Frazier's early monograph, *The Negro Family in Chicago*, hardly mentions employment handicaps—let alone handicaps peculiar to the Negro—in accounting for the disintegration of families in the slum. If Frazier later changed his mind, it was most probably because others were changing theirs, and his professors at the University of Chicago no longer insisted that the adjustment of Negro migrants—whom Frazier called peasants—fit the same model they had used earlier to explain the adjustment of European peasants who had come to Chicago from Poland and southern Italy. (Then, family disintegration was attributed to the clash between a secular urban and a traditional agrarian ethos.)

Secondly, even granting that the antecedent of an aberrant social pattern might be an aberrant economic pattern, was there one and only one important and critical difference between whites and blacks in their relation to the occupational order? Was it not possible that some other difference had been overlooked that might explain the instability of Negro marriages just as well?

If it is hard to imagine that the working Negro woman could resent her husband, or he her, on the basis of the jobs, wages, and the amount of work she could command in relation to him, then we must turn to another clue in trying to answer the riddle of the urban North's peculiar institution —the matriarchal Negro family. For clearly it was the woman who faced near insurmountable obstacles in getting jobs beyond the level of unskilled domestic work, and this heavy concentration of Negro women in domestic service suggests an intriguing alternative explanation. She had not just a second job, but a job in a second *household*, with a second family. How this competition between obligations to two households could tear at the fabric of her own family's solidarity we can just imagine—not alone in the burden of doing double duty with long hours spent away from her own home, but also in the continual awareness of the differences in living standards, the competition of dual loyalties and possibly of dual affections.

If the status of the employing household mattered to the domestic, how might this have affected her perception of the conditions in her own? Negro women at service in Carlisle, Pennsylvania, a contributor to *Gunton's Magazine* (January, 1896) observed, "will only serve in a Negro family when hard pressed for money, and then for a few days only." If, as the writer suggests, the domestic was accustomed to taking home foodstuffs from her employer's table, such considerations of status would make sense. Might it also, along with all the other invidious comparisons to be made, condition her to think less highly of the breadwinner in her own family? Or, taking the problem from the other end: Did her husband find her efforts at home less than satisfactory because she had to do so much for the other household? It is hard, perhaps impossible, to arrive at clear-cut answers to these questions. We can only hypothesize that if Negro women had had access to a broader range of jobs beyond household work fewer complications would have entered into the picture.

It is instructive that white female houseworkers, including the many European immigrant women who took domestic jobs, seem to have solved the dual-household problem by staying single for as long as they worked, and then quitting domestic service upon marriage. Doubtless the strong sentiments of Catholicism about the requirements of normal family life insured this outcome in the case of the Irish, for example, who had a tradition of delaying marriage until economic conditions permitted. The available evidence on this point is sketchy, but a 1925 study of working women in four cities revealed that domestics in Passaic, New Jersey, who were overwhelmingly native or foreign-born whites, were much more apt to be single at the time of the canvass than were domestics in Jacksonville, Florida, who were overwhelmingly black. Whereas almost half (45 percent) of Jacksonville domestics were either married or married but separated, only a quarter (24 percent) of Passaic's domestics were thus classified. Mary V. Robinson's report to the Women's Bureau in the United States Department of Labor a year earlier established two facts from a survey of applicants for domestic work in Baltimore: Negro women were clearly reluctant to take jobs that required living in. Only 36 percent of the black women stated a willingness to do so, whereas 80 percent of white females were prepared to live in. Mary Robinson related this fact to another—namely, the significantly higher proportion of Negro women compared with white females who remained in domestic service after marriage—and she came to a judgment about the difficulties of carrying the work of two households that should not surprise us:

[Matrimony] usually means added responsibilities which tend to demand more time than many women in domestic service are able to find for such important private matters, especially if they are compelled to live in the home of employers or to have the usual hours of labor expected in domestic service. When women live in the homes of their employers, they rarely have opportunity to go to their own homes more than once or twice a week, and can have little private life with their families. . . .

At the turn of the century, a researcher assigned to canvass Sandy Springs, Maryland, reported to the United States Department of Labor that he found a tragic division between the Negro woman's "real family" and her "economic family" (the employing household) that her heavy concentration in domestic work had caused. Noting the heavy turnover of domestic workers and how better wages in the bigger cities north lured girls away, he concluded that "the future of the Negro race would seem to be more in danger from a certain general looseness of the younger generations of women than from lawlessness of the younger generations of men."

Certainly more research is needed to settle this historical issue. Again returning to the 1930 Census we find industrial cities in which a very low proportion of Negro women are holding jobs—Flint, Gary and Youngstown, for example. Perhaps domestic work was harder to find in small industrial cities than in the large northern cities having a wealthier citizenry. Were marriages correspondingly more stable in cities where, regardless of the women's interest in or need of work, jobs for domestics simply did not exist in the number needed? We do not know.

Accepting this alternative view of the Negro family problem does not require that we refuse to consider the Negro male's hardships, or their effect on his role in the family. Certainly if his rents had been lower and his wages higher, fewer of his women would have found it necessary to seek out domestic jobs. And it is quite proper to think that family stress would be closely associated with cyclical business fluctuations that affected the man's employment, as Daniel P. Moynihan showed in his 1965 report, *The Negro Family: The Case for National Action.* But we still need to know why Negroes, of all groups, were disproportionately affected in their family life by bad times that in their season hit *every* working-class group, and hit much harder in times past than now. This requires looking for that combination of unique historical experiences peculiar to many Negro Americans. The "peculiar institution" of the south, slavery, was very probably the most important factor in the emergence of the peculiar institution of the urban north, the female-headed family. But if an economic cause is to be sought in addition, we suggest that it may have been the Negro woman's handicaps in the labor market, not the man's.

Roots of Black Manhood:
Sex, Socialization and Culture in the
Ghettos of American Cities

ULF HANNERZ

Some 5.7 million people were simply not counted in the 1960 census, and most of them, it now appears, were Negro men living in northern cities. This statistical oversight, if that is what it was, is not unique to the government's census takers. Ever since the beginnings of the scholarly study of black people in the Americas, there has been an interesting fascination with the differences between the family life of Negroes and that of their white counterparts, the chief difference being seen as the dominant, not to say dominating, role of women in black families.

From E. Franklin Frazier's pioneering 1932 study of *The Negro Family in Chicago* through Melville Herskovits' *The Myth of the Negro Past* in 1941 to the so-called Moynihan Report of 1965, social scientists have been repeatedly rediscovering, analyzing and worrying over the crucial role of the mother (or grandmother) in the family structure of blacks in the New World. Herskovits saw the centrality of the mother as an African vestige, typical of the polygynous marriage in which every woman, with her off-spring, formed a separate unit. Frazier is generally regarded as the first to ascribe to the institution of slavery itself the strongest influence in undermining the stability of marriage, an influence that was later rein-forced when blacks encountered what Frazier perceived as the peculiarly urban evils of anonymity, disorganization and the lack of social support and controls. Moynihan, like Frazier, sees the matriarchal family as being practically without strengths, at least in the context of the larger American society, but his Report emphasizes the ways in which employer discrimina-tion and, more recently, welfare policies have contributed to the breaking up (or foreclosure) of the male-dominated family unit among blacks.

In all of these studies, however, the black *man*—as son, lover, husband, father, grandfather—is a distant and shadowy figure "out there some-where" . . . if only because his major characteristic as far as the household is concerned is his marginality or absence.

I do not mean to suggest that the black man is undiscovered territory. Obviously he is not. His popular image was fixed for one (long) era in *Uncle Tom's Cabin* and prophetically fashioned for our own time in Norman Mailer's essay "The White Negro." Here is Mailer's Hipster, modeled on the Negro: "Sharing a collective disbelief in the words of men who had too much money and controlled too many things, they knew almost as powerful a disbelief in the socially monolithic ideas of the

single mate, the solid family and the respectable love life." And here is
Mailer's black man:

> Knowing in the cells of his existence that life was war, nothing but war,
> the Negro (all exceptions admitted) could rarely afford the sophisticated
> inhibitions of civilization, and so he kept for his survival the art of the
> primitive, he lived in the enormous present, he subsisted for his Saturday
> night kicks, relinquishing the pleasures of the mind for the more obliga-
> tory pleasures of the body, and in his music he gave voice to the charac-
> ter and quality of his existence, to his rage and the infinite variations of
> joy, lust, languor, growl, cramp, pinch, scream and despair of his orgasm.

Certainly there is poetic exaggeration in Mailer's description, and perhaps a conscious effort to mythicize his subject; and certainly too there is
a great deal of stereotyping in the general public's imagery of the people
of the black ghetto. But hardly anyone acquainted with life in the ghetto
can fail to see that Mailer's portrait captures much of the reality as well.
Lee Rainwater's sketch of the "expressive life-style" of the black male
shows a trained social scientist's analysis that is remarkably similar to
Mailer's. And undoubtedly there *is* a sizable segment of the black male
population that is strongly concerned with sex, drinking, sharp clothes
and "trouble"; and among these men one finds many of those who are
only marginally involved with married life. Of course, ghetto life styles
are heterogeneous, and there are many men who live according to "mainstream" values; but it is to the ones who do not that we should turn our
attention if we want to understand what kinds of masculinity go with the
female-dominated family.

This essay is an attempt to outline the social processes within the ghetto
communities of the northern United States whereby the identity of streetcorner males is established and maintained. To set the stage and state the
issues involved in this essay, I'd like to look at the views of two other observers of the ghetto male. One is Charles Keil, whose *Urban Blues* (1966)
is a study of the bluesman as a "culture hero." According to Keil, the
urban blues singer, with his emphasis on sexuality, "trouble" and flashy
clothes, manifests a cultural model of maleness that is highly valued by
ghetto dwellers and relatively independent of the mainstream cultural
tradition. Keil criticizes a number of authors who, without cavilling at this
description of the male role, tend to see it as rooted in the individual's
anxiety about his masculinity. This, Keil finds, is unacceptably ethnocentric:

> Any sound analysis of Negro masculinity should first deal with the state-
> ments and responses of Negro women, the conscious motives of the men

themselves and the Negro cultural tradition. Applied in this setting, psychological theory may then be able to provide important new insights in place of basic and unfortunate distortions.

Keil, then, comes out clearly for a cultural interpretation of the male role we are interested in here. But Elliot Liebow in *Tally's Corner* (1967), a study resulting from the author's participation in a research project that definitely considered ghetto life more in terms of social problems than as a culture, reaches conclusions which, in some of their most succinct formulations, quite clearly contradict Keil's:

> Similarities between the lower-class Negro father and son . . . do not result from "cultural transmission" but from the fact that the son goes out and independently experiences the same failures, in the same areas, and for much the same reasons as his father.

Thus father and son are "independently produced look-alikes." With this goes the view that the emphasis on sexual ability, drinking and so forth is a set of compensatory self-deceptions which can only unsuccessfully veil the streetcorner male's awareness of his failure.

Keil and Liebow, as reviewed here, may be taken as representatives of two significantly different opinions on why black people in the ghettos, and in particular the males, behave differently than other Americans. One emphasizes a cultural determinism internal to the ghetto, the other an economic determinism in the relationship between the ghetto and the wider society. It is easy to see how the two views relate to one's perspective on the determinants of the domestic structure of ghetto dwellers. And it is also easy to see how these perspectives have considerable bearing on public policy, especially if it is believed that the ghetto family structure somehow prevents full participation by its members in the larger American society and economy. If it is held, for example, that broad social and economic factors, and particularly poverty, make ghetto families the way they are—and this seems to be the majority opinion among social scientists concerned with this area—then public policy should concentrate on mitigating or removing those elements that distort the lives of black people. But if the style of life in the ghetto is culturally determined and more or less independent of other "outside" factors, then public policy will have to take a different course, or drop the problem altogether *qua* problem.

Admittedly, the present opportunity structure places serious obstacles in the way of many ghetto dwellers, making a mainstream life-style difficult to accomplish. And if research is to influence public policy, it is particularly important to point to the wider structural influences that *can* be changed in order to give equal opportunity to ghetto dwellers.

Yet some of the studies emphasizing such macrostructural determinants have resulted in somewhat crude conceptualizations that are hardly warranted by the facts and which in the light of anthropological theory appear very oversimplified.

First of all, let us dispose of some of the apparent opposition between the two points of view represented by Keil and Liebow. There is not necessarily any direct conflict between ecological-economic and cultural explanations; the tendency to create such a conflict in much of the current literature on poverty involves a false dichotomy. In anthropology, it is a commonplace that culture is usually both inherited and influenced by the community's relationship to its environment. Economic determinism and cultural determinism can go hand in hand in a stable environment. Since the ecological niche of ghetto dwellers has long remained relatively unchanged, there seems to be no reason why their adaptation should not have become in some ways cultural. It is possible, of course, that the first stage in the evolution of the specifically ghetto life-style consisted of a multiplicity of identical but largely independent adaptations from the existing cultural background—mainstream or otherwise—to the given opportunity structure, as Liebow suggests. But the second stage of adaptation—by the following generations—involves a perception of the first-stage adaptation as a normal condition, a state of affairs which from then on can be expected. What was at first independent adaptation becomes transformed into a ghetto heritage of assumptions about the nature of man and society.

Yet Liebow implies that father and son are independently produced as streetcorner men, and that transmission of a ghetto-specific culture has a negligible influence. To those adhering to that belief, strong evidence in its favor is seen in the fact that ghetto dwellers—both men and women—often express conventional sentiments about sex and other matters. Most ghetto dwellers would certainly agree, at times at least, that education is a good thing, that gambling and drinking are bad, if not sinful, and that a man and a woman should be true to each other. Finding such opinions, and heeding Keil's admonition to listen to the statements and responses of the black people themselves, one may be led to doubt that there is much of a specific ghetto culture. But then, after having observed behavior among these same people that often and clearly contradicts their stated values, one has to ask two questions: Is there any reason to believe that ghetto-specific behavior is cultural? And, if it *is* cultural, what is the nature of the coexistence of mainstream culture and ghetto-specific culture in the black ghetto?

To answer the first question, one might look at the kinds of communications that are passed around in the ghetto relating to notions of maleness. One set of relationships in which such communications occur frequently is the family; another is the male peer group.

DEFICIENT MASCULINITY?

Much has been made of the notion that young boys in the ghetto, growing up in matrifocal households, are somehow deficient in or uncertain about their masculinity, because their fathers are absent or peripheral in household affairs. It is said that they lack the role models necessary for learning male behavior; there is a lack of the kind of information about the nature of masculinity which a father would transmit unintentionally merely by going about his life at home. The boys therefore supposedly experience a great deal of sex-role anxiety as a result of this cultural vacuum. It is possible that such a view contains more than a grain of truth in the case of some quite isolated female-headed households. Generally speaking, however, there may be less to it than meets the eye. First of all, a female-headed household without an adult male in residence but where young children are growing up—and where, therefore, it is likely that the mother is still rather young—is seldom one where adult males are totally absent. More or less steady boyfriends (sometimes including the separated father) go in and out. Even if these men do not assume a central household role, the boys can obviously use them as source material for the identification of male behavior. To be sure, the model is not a conventional middle-class one, but it still shows what males are like.

Furthermore, men are not the only ones who teach boys about masculinity. Although role-modeling is probably essential, other social processes can contribute to identity formation. Mothers, grandmothers, aunts and sisters who have observed men at close range have formed expectations about the typical behavior of men which they express and which influence the boys in the household. The boys will come to share in the women's imagery of men, and often they will find that men who are not regarded as good household partners (that is, "good" in the conventional sense) are still held to be attractive company. Thus the view is easily imparted that the hard men, good talkers, clothes-horses and all, are not altogether unsuccessful as men. The women also act more directly toward the boys in these terms—they have expectations of what men will do, and whether they wish the boys to live up (or down) to the expectations, they instruct them in the model. Boys are advised not to "mess with" girls, but at the same time it is emphasized that messing around is the natural thing they will otherwise go out and do—and when the boys start their early adventures with the other sex, the older women may scold them but at the same time point out, not without satisfaction, that "boys will be boys." This kind of maternal (or at least adult female) instruction of young males is obviously a kind of altercasting, or more exactly, socialization to an alter role—that is, women cast boys in the role complementary to their own according to their experience of man-woman relationships. One single mother of three boys and two girls put it this way:

> You know, you just got to act a little bit tougher with boys than with girls, 'cause they just ain't the same. Girls do what you tell them to do and don't get into no trouble, but you just can't be sure about the boys. I mean, you think they're OK and next thing you find out they're playing hookey and drinking wine and maybe stealing things from cars and what not. There's just something bad about boys here, you know. But what can you say when many of them are just like their daddies? That's the man in them coming out. You can't really fight it, you know that's the way it is. They know, too, But you just got to be tougher.

This is in some ways an antagonistic socialization, but it is built upon an expectation that it would be unnatural for men not to turn out to be in some ways bad—that is fighters, drinkers, lady killers and so forth. There is one thing worse than a no-good man—the sissy, who is his opposite. A boy who seems weak is often reprimanded and ridiculed not only by his peers but also by adults, including his mother and older sisters. The combination of role-modeling by peripheral fathers or temporary boyfriends with altercasting by adult women certainly provides for a measure of male role socialization within the family.

And yet, when I said that the view of the lack of models in the family was too narrow, I was not referring to the observers' lack of insight into many matrifocal ghetto families as much as I was to the emphasis they placed on the family as *the* information storage unit of a community's culture. I believe it is an ethnocentrism on the part of middle-class commentators to take it for granted that if information about sex roles is not transmitted from father to son within the family, it is not transmitted from generation to generation at all. In American sociology, no less than in the popular mind, there is what Ray Birdwhistell has termed a "sentimental model" of family life, according to which the family is an inward-turning isolated unit, meeting most of the needs of its members, and certainly their needs for sociability and affection. The "sentimental model" is hardly ever realistic even as far as middle-class American families are concerned, and it has even less relevance for black ghetto life. Ghetto children live and learn out on the streets just about as much as within the confines of the home. Even if mothers, aunts and sisters do not have streetcorner men as partners, there is an ample supply of them on the front stoop or down at the corner. Many of these men have such a regular attendance record as to become quite familiar to children and are frequently very friendly with them. Again, therefore, there is no lack of adult men to show a young boy what men are like. It seems rather unlikely that one can deny all role-modeling effect of these men on their young neighbors. They may be missing in the United States census records, but they are not missing in the ghetto community.

Much of the information gained about sex roles outside the family comes not from adult to child, however, but from persons in the same age-grade or only slightly higher. The idea of culture being stored in lower age-grades must be taken seriously. Many ghetto children start participating in the peer groups of the neighborhood at an early age, often under the watchful eye of an elder brother or sister. In this way they are initiated into the culture of the peer group by interacting with children—predominantly of the same sex—who are only a little older than they are. And in the peer-group culture of the boys, the male sex role is a fairly constant topic of concern. Some observers have felt that this is another consequence of the alleged sex role anxiety of ghetto boys. This may be true, of course, at least in that it may have had an important part in the development of male peer-group life as a dominant element of ghetto social structure. Today, however, such a simple psychosocial explanation will not do. Most ghetto boys can hardly avoid associating with other boys, and once they are in the group, they are efficiently socialized into a high degree of concern with their sex role. Much of the joking, the verbal contests and the more or less obscene songs among small ghetto boys, serve to alienate them from dependence on mother figures and train them to the exploitative, somewhat antagonistic attitude toward women which is typical of streetcorner men.

"MOTHER!"

This is not to say that the cultural messages are always very neat and clear-cut. In the case of the kind of insult contest called "playing the dozens," "sounding" or (in Washington, D. C.) "joning," a form of ritualized interaction which is particularly common among boys in the early teens, the communication is highly ambiguous. When one boy says something unfavorable about another's mother, the other boy is expected either to answer in kind or to fight in defense of his honor (on which apparently that of his mother reflects). But the lasting impression is that there is something wrong about mothers—they are not as good as they ought to be ("Anybody can get pussy from your mother"), they take over male items of behavior and by implication too much of the male role ("Your mother smokes a pipe"). If standing up for one's family is the manifest expected consequence of "the dozens," then a latent function is a strengthening of the belief that ghetto women are not what they ought to be. The other point of significance is that the criteria of judgment about what a good woman should be like are apparently like those of the larger society. She should not be promiscuous, and she should stick to the mainstream female role and not be too dominant.

The boys, then, are learning and strengthening a cultural ambivalence involving contradictions between ideal and reality in female behavior. I will return to a discussion of such cultural ambivalence later. But the point remains that even this game involves continuous learning and strengthening of a cultural definition of what women are like that is in some ways complementary to the definition of what men are like. And much of the songs, the talk and the action—fighting, sneaking away with girls into a park or an alley or drinking out of half-empty wine bottles stolen from or given away by adult men—are quite clearly preparations for the streetcorner male role. If boys and men show anxiety about their masculinity, one may suspect that this is induced as much by existing cultural standards as by the alleged nonexistence of models.

This socialization within the male peer group is a continuing process; the talk that goes on, continuously or intermittently, at the street corner or on the front steps may deal occasionally with a football game or a human-interest story from the afternoon newspaper, but more often there are tales from personal experience about adventures of drinking (often involving the police), about women won and lost, about feminine fickleness and the masculine guile (which sometimes triumphs over it), about clothing, or there may simply be comments on the women passing down the street. "Hi ugly . . . don't try to swing what you ain't got."

This sociability among the men seems to be a culture-building process. Shared definitions of reality are created out of the selected experiences of the participants. Women are nagging and hypocritical; you can't expect a union with one of them to last forever. Men are dogs; they have to run after many women. There is something about being a man and drinking liquor; booze makes hair grow on your chest. The regularity with which the same topics appear in conversation indicates that they have been established as the expected and appropriate subjects in this situation, to the exclusion of other topics.

> Mack asked me did I screw his daughter, so I asked: "I don't know, what's her name?" And then when I heard that gal was his daughter all right, I says, "Well, Mack, I didn't really have to take it, 'cause it was given to me." I thought Mack sounded like his daughter was some goddam white gal. But Mack says, "Well, I just wanted to hear it from you." Of course, I didn't know that was Mack's gal, 'cause she was married and had a kid, and so she had a different name. But then you know the day after when I was out there a car drove by, and somebody called my name from it, you know, "hi darling," and that was her right there. So the fellow I was with says, "Watch out, Buddy will shoot your ass off." Buddy, that's her husband. So I says, "Yeah, but he got to find me first!"

Let me tell you fellows, I've been arrested for drunkenness more than two hundred times over the last few years, and I've used every name in the book. I remember once I told them I was Jasper Gonzales, and then I forgot what I had told them, you know. So I was sitting there waiting, and they came in and called "Jasper Gonzales," and nobody answered. I had forgotten that's what I said, and to tell you the truth, I didn't know how to spell it. So anyway, nobody answered, and there they were calling "Jasper Gonzales. Jasper Gonzales!" So I thought that must be me, so I answered. But they had been calling a lot of times before that. So the judge said, "Mr. Gonzales, are you of Spanish descent?" And I said, "Yes, your honor, I came to this country thirty-four years ago." And of course I was only thirty-five, but you see I had this beard then, and I looked pretty bad, dirty and everything, you know, so I looked like sixty. And so he said, "We don't have a record on you. This is the first time you have been arrested?" So I said, "Yes, your honor, nothing like this happened to me before. But my wife was sick, and then I lost my job you know, and I felt kind of bad. But it's the first time I ever got drunk." So he said, "Well, Mr. Gonzales, I'll let you go, 'cause you are not like the rest of them here. But let this be a warning to you." So I said, "Yes, your honor." And then I went out, and so I said to myself, "I'll have to celebrate this." So I went across the street from the court, and you know there are four liquor stores there, and I got a pint of wine and next thing I was drunk as a pig.

Were you here that time a couple of weeks ago when these three chicks from North Carolina were up here visiting Miss Gladys? They were really gorgeous, about 30–35. So Charlie says why don't we step by the house and he and Jimmy and Deekay can go out and buy them a drink. So they say they have to go and see this cousin first, but then they'll be back. But then Brenda (Charlie's wife) comes back before they do, and so these girls walk back and forth in front of the house, and Charlie can't do a thing about it, except hope they won't knock on his door. And then Jimmy and Deekay come and pick them up, and Fats is also there, and the three of them go off with these chicks, and there is Charlie looking through his window, and there is Brenda looking at them too, and asking Charlie does he know who the chicks are.

Groups of one's friends give some stability and social sanction to the meanings that streetcorner men attach to their experiences—meanings that may themselves have been learned in the same or preceding peer groups. They, probably more than families, are information storage units for the ghetto-specific male role. At the same time, they are self-perpetuating because they provide the most satisfactory contexts for legitimizing the realities involved. In other words, they suggest a program for maleness, but they also offer a haven of understanding for those who follow that program and are criticized for it or feel doubts about it. For of course all streetcorner males are more or less constantly exposed to the definitions and values of the mainstream cultural apparatus, and so some cultural ambivalence can hardly be avoided. Thus, if a man is a dog for running after women—as he is often said to be among ghetto dwellers—he wants to talk about it with other dogs who appreciate that this is a fact of life. If it is natural for men to drink, let it happen among other people who understand the nature of masculinity. In this way the group maintains constructions of reality, and life according to this reality maintains the group.

It is hard to avoid the conclusion, then, that there is a cultural element involved in the sex roles of streetcorner males, because expectations about sex are manifestly shared and transmitted rather than individually evolved. (If the latter had been the case, of course, it would have been less accurate to speak of these as roles, since roles are by definition cultural.) This takes us to the second question stated above, about the coexistence of conventional and ghetto-specific cultures. Streetcorner men certainly are aware of the male ideal of mainstream America—providing well for one's family, remaining faithful to one's spouse, staying out of trouble, etc.—and now and then every one of them states it as his own ideal. What we find here, then, may be seen as a bicultural situation. Mainstream culture and ghetto-specific culture provide different models for living, models familiar to everyone in the ghetto. Actual behavior may lean more toward one model or more toward the other, or it may be some kind of mixture, at one point or over time. The ghetto-specific culture, including the streetcorner male role, is adapted to the situation and the experience of the ghetto dweller; it tends to involve relatively little idealization but offers shared expectations concerning self, others and the environment. The mainstream culture, from the ghetto dweller's point of view, often involves idealization, but there is less real expectation that life will actually follow the paths suggested by those ideals. This is not to say that the ghetto-specific culture offers no values of its own at all, or that nothing of mainstream culture ever appears realistic in the ghetto; but in those areas of life where the two cultures exist side by side as alternative guides to action (for naturally, the ghetto-specific culture, as distinct from mainstream culture, is not a "complete" culture covering all areas of life), the ghetto-specific culture is often taken to forecast what one can actually expect from life, while the mainstream norms are held up as perhaps ultimately more valid but less attainable under the given situational constraints. "Sure it would be good to have a good job and a good home and your kids in college and all that, but you got to be yourself and do what you know." Of course, this often makes the ghetto-specific cultural expectations into self-fulfilling prophecies, as ghetto dwellers try to attain what they believe they can attain; but, to be sure, self-fulfilling prophecies and realistic assessments may well coincide.

On the whole, one may say that both mainstream culture and ghetto-specific culture are transmitted within many ghetto families. I have noted how socialization into the ghetto male role within the household is largely an informal process, in which young boys may pick up bits and pieces of information about masculinity from the women in the house as well as from males who may make their entrances and exits. On the other hand, when adult women—usually mothers or grandmothers—really "tell the boys how to behave," they often try to instill in them mainstream, not to say puritanical, norms—drinking is bad, sex is dirty and so forth. The male peer groups, as we have seen, are the strongholds of streetcorner maleness, although there are times when men cuss each other out for being "no good." Finally, of course, mainstream culture is transmitted in contacts with the outside world, such as in school or through the mass media. It should be added, though, that the latter may be used selectively to strengthen some elements of the streetcorner male role; ghetto men are drawn to Westerns, war movies and crime stories both in the movie house and on their TV sets.

Yet, even if the nature of men's allegiance to the two cultures makes it reasonably possible to adhere, after a fashion, to both at the same time, the bicultural situation of streetcorner males involves some ambivalence. The rejection of mainstream culture as a guide to action rather than only a lofty ideal is usually less than complete. Of course, acting according to one or the other of the two cultures to a great extent involves bowing to the demands of the social context, and so a man whose concerns in the peer-group milieu are drinking and philandering will try to be "good" in the company of his mother or his wife and children, even if a complete switch is hard to bring about. There are also peer groups, of course, that are more mainstream-oriented than others, although even the members of these groups are affected by streetcorner definitions of maleness. To some extent, then, the varying allegiance of different peer groups to the two cultures is largely a difference of degree, as the following statement by a young man implies.

> Those fellows down at the corner there just keep drinking and drinking. You know, I think it's pretty natural for a man to drink, but they don't try to do nothing about it, they just drink every hour of the day, every day of the week. My crowd, we drink during the weekend, but we can be on our jobs again when Monday comes.

However, although where one is or who one is with does bring some order into this picture of bicultural ambivalence, it is still one of less than perfect stability. The drift between contexts is itself not something to which men are committed by demands somehow inherent in the social structure. Ghetto men may spend more time with the family, or more time with the peer group, and the extent to which they choose one or the other, and make a concomitant cultural selection, still appears to depend much on personal attachment to roles, and to changes in them. The social alignments of a few men may illustrate this. One man, Norman Hawkins, a construction laborer, spends practically all his leisure time at home with his family, only occasionally joining in the streetcorner conversations and behavior of the peer group to which his neighbor, Harry Jones, belongs. Harry Jones, also a construction worker, is also married and has a family but stays on the periphery of household life, although he lives with his wife and children. Some of the other men in the group are unmarried or separated and so seldom play the "family man" role which Harry Jones takes on now and then. Harry's younger brother Carl, also with a family, used to participate intensively in peer group life until his drinking led to a serious ailment, and after he recuperated from this he started spending much less time with his male friends and more with his family. Bee Jay, a middle-aged bachelor who was raised by his grandmother, had a job at the post office and had little to do with street life until she died. Since then, he has become deeply involved with a tough, hard-drinking group and now suffers from chronic health problems connected with his alcoholism. Thus we can see how the life careers of some ghetto men take them through many and partly unpredictable shifts and drifts between mainstream and ghetto-specific cultures, while others remain quite stable in one allegiance or another.

TWO CULTURES

The sociocultural situation in the black ghetto is clearly complicated. The community shows a great heterogeneity of life-styles; individuals become committed in some degree to different ways of being by the impersonally-enforced structural arrangements to which they are subjected, but unpredictable contingencies have an influence, and their personal attachments to life-styles also vary. The socioeconomic conditions impose limits on the kinds of life ghetto dwellers may have, but these kinds of life are culturally transmitted and shared as many individuals in the present, and many in the past, live or have lived under the same premises. When the latter is the case, it is hardly possible to invent new adaptations again and again, as men are always observing each other and interacting with each other. The implication of some of Frazier's writings, that ghetto dwellers create their way of life in a cultural limbo —an idea which has had more modern expressions—appears as unacceptable in this case as in any other situation where people live together, and in particular where generations live together. The behavior of the streetcorner male is a natural pattern of masculinity with which ghetto dwellers grow up and which to some extent they grow into. To see it only as a complex of unsuccessful attempts at hiding failures by self-deception seems, for many of the men involved, to be too much psychologizing and too little sociology. But this does not mean that the attachment to the ghetto-specific culture is very strong among its bearers.

The question whether streetcorner males have mainstream culture or a specific ghetto culture, then, is best answered by saying that they have both, in different ways. There can be little doubt that this is the understanding most in line with that contemporary trend in anthropological thought which emphasizes the sharing of cultural imagery, of expectations and definitions of reality, as the medium whereby individuals in a community interact. It is noteworthy that many of the commentators who have been most skeptical of the idea of a ghetto-specific culture, or more generally a "culture of poverty," have been those who have taken a more narrow view of culture as a set of values about which an older generation consciously instructs the younger ones in the community.

Obviously, the answer to whether there is a ghetto-specific culture or not will depend to some extent on what we shall mean by culture. Perhaps this is too important a question to be affected by a mere terminological quibble, and perhaps social policy, in some areas, may well proceed unaffected by the questions raised by a ghetto-specific culture. On the other hand, in an anthropological study of community life, the wider view of cultural sharing and transmission which has been used here will have to play a part in our picture of the ghetto, including that of what ghetto males are like.

Family and Childhood in a Southern Negro Community

VIRGINIA HEYER YOUNG

Current interpretations of American Negro personality formation have been hampered by lack of field data and by faulty conceptualization. Personality formation has been studied through interviews with children and adolescents, through interviews with adults concerning childrearing practices, and through psychoanalytic interpolation from persons in therapy (Davis and Dollard 1940; Davis and Havighurst 1946; Kardiner and Ovesey 1951). Field observations of childhood, however, have never been

undertaken, and there has never been a check on what mothers say they
did and what is recalled from childhood. Furthermore, the applicability
of psychoanalytic interpretations to American Negro life has been assumed with a minimum of knowledge about prevailing styles of interpersonal behavior and the way these might modify the psychoanalytic
scheme of cause and effect. An additional interpretative problem arises
from the fact that the Negro family has been widely analyzed with a
strong bias toward White American family values, its functionality being
judged by the degree to which it exemplifies white forms. American
Negro life styles generally have been seen as impoverished versions
of White American culture, impoverished by dependency and dehumanization under slavery and impoverished by lack of access to many of the
rewards of American culture. Herskovitz' (1941) demonstration of the
retention of African forms especially in the areas of interpersonal behavior and deep levels of communication was ignored to a surprising
degree by anthropologists and sociologists who have interpreted American Negro life. Many intellectual currents and habits have contributed
to this bias, not the least of which is the common emphasis on institutions
at the expense of interpersonal behavior. In this case we are witnessing
a people wrongly pigeonholed who are protesting and declaring they
have a culture of their own. That there are distinctive American Negro
cultural styles of interpersonal behavior was one conclusion of a field
study of Negro childhood conducted in a Georgia town during the
summers of 1961, 1962, and 1966. Negro family organization also was
found to be so different from the current stereotypes about it that the
literature on the subject was reviewed to see a resolution of the apparent
contradiction. These two subjects are the substance of this paper.

Georgiatown is a county seat of under ten thousand population, approximately twenty percent to twenty-five percent Negro.[1] Milling of
cotton products and light manufacturing provide most of the jobs in
the town, and farming has dwindled to minor importance in the county
(U. S. Department of Labor 1965). The 1960 Census shows forty percent
of the Negro men in the county labor force employed as nonfarm
laborers, twenty-six percent as operatives and twelve percent as service
workers. Among Negro women in the labor force sixty-six percent are
employed as private household workers and sixteen percent as other
service workers. There is little Negro-owned business and no Negro
upper class. One Negro doctor and the teachers of the centralized Negro
elementary school and high school are the only professional persons.

[1] Census on the racial proportions of the population give approximately sixteen percent nonwhite in the county and nineteen percent in Georgiatown. Several Negro
hamlets are situated just beyond the town limits and their occupants are employed in
the town. These persons, counted by the Census as county residents, are actually towns-
people socioeconomically and are so counted in the estimate here.

In settlement pattern and social habits Georgiatown Negroes resemble the people of Kent described by Hylan Lewis (1955).

The method of this study was to observe and record in detail the behavior of parents and children in their own houses and yards. Conversations were used to establish rapport and to obtain information, but the primary aim was always to avoid disrupting the natural social situation as much as possible. Visits lasted as long as they could be comfortably prolonged, sometimes only thirty minutes, usually an hour and a half, often three hours. Almost all families were visited at least twice, and most were observed four or more times. The subjects of closest study were the members of thirty-four households. Twelve additional households were known less well but well enough to yield information on some subjects. Forty-two children under the age of three and sixteen children between the ages of three and six were observed. Older brothers and sisters between six and fourteen numbered twenty-eight. Four of the closely studied households and one of the less closely studied were middle class, the heads of four out of these five being schoolteachers. The other forty-one households were lower class, the heads of family being employed at unskilled or semiskilled jobs or unemployed. Class designation is on the basis of prestige of occupation, a small difference in standard of living, and observed deference-superiority behavior. The main bias in the sample is toward families with young children since this was the family composition sought.

These subjects lived in the three Negro sections of town and in one rural hamlet adjoining the town. Housing ranged from brick two-story row houses with five rooms in a public housing project to the more usual two- or three-room frame house with porch that is typical of this section of the country. As in the town of Kent, all rooms but the kitchen usually serve as bedrooms. Television sets are common but few comforts or decorations enhance these houses. A county clinic in Georgiatown is used widely for children's medical care, and all births of the children in this study had taken place in the county hospital, also located in town.

FAMILY ORGANIZATION

Central to all interpretations of Negro personality has been the contention that the Negro man plays a relatively insignificant role in family life in the lower class. It was therefore surprising to find the large majority of Georgiatown Negro families in this study had husbands present and supporting them. Among forty-one lower-class families, men are the main providers or coequal providers with their wives in thirty-eight of the households, as Table 1 shows. The basis for selection of families to be studied, the presence of young children, would tend to

TABLE 1

Sources of Household Support

Household support type	Lower class	Middle class
Husband's employment sole support	20	1
Husband's pension sole support	3	0
Husband main support, wife contributes much less	2	0
Husband and wife contribute about equal amounts	13	4
Husband present, wife contributes more than husband	0	0
Female-headed household, no male provider	3	0
Total	41	5

give an under-representation of complete families in this community because marriages of older couples are the most stable.

Not only do Georgiatown Negro men support their families, but their earning ability far exceeds women's as is demonstrated by U. S. Census figures for 1950 and 1960 (Table 2). Women earn approximately forty percent of what men earn in Georgia cities and towns despite a slight tendency between 1949 and 1959 for Negro women's incomes to increase in relation to Negro men's incomes. Georgiatown County in 1959 con-

TABLE 2

*Medium Income of Nonwhite Persons with Income**

	1949			1959		
	Male median income	*Female median income*	*Fe Med Inc as % of M Med Inc*	*Male median income*	*Female median income*	*Fe Med Inc as % of M Med Inc*
U.S.A.†	$1571	$672	42.8	$2254	$905	40.1
Georgia	919	389	42.3	1489	660	44.3
G'tn County	‡	‡	‡	1780	647	36.3
Ga. Urban	1259	477	37.9	1947	785	40.3
Ga. Rural NF§	855	322	37.8	1153	478	41.5
Ga. Rural F	459	288	62.7	770	368	47.4

* Source: U. S. Census of Population, 1950, Vol. II, Pt. 11, table 88, p. 343; Vol. II, Pt. 1, table 139, p. 302; U. S. Census of Population, 1960, Vol. I, Pt. 12, table 67, p. 209, and table 88, p. 351; Vol. I, Pt. 1, table 218, p. 578.

† 1949 U.S.A. figures are for all nonwhite; 1959 U.S.A. figures are for Negroes.

‡ Not available for 1949.

§ Georgiatown is classified as a Rural Non-Farm place in both Censuses.

forms to the 1949 income ratios for cities and towns, perhaps reflecting conservatism in wage scales or the fact that the county was a depressed area at the time (being so classified by the U. S. Department of Labor). That Georgia Negroes are in this respect typical of Negroes in the nation is also seen in Table 2. Wages in industry, which employs many more men than women, far exceeded wages for domestic work, the main occupation for women. While industrial wages are not matched in other forms of male employment, they have had the effect of raising men's wages in general. Yard work, for instance, offers a higher wage for men than domestic work does for women. There have been periods when jobs for men have been scarcer than domestic work for women and some male employment is seasonal and subject to lay-offs, but in general men are at present, and have been in the recent past, able to provide for their families better than their wives and have the prestige that goes with better-paying jobs. Since Georgiatown County was in economic depression during this study, the favorable income of Negro men compared to Negro women cannot be laid to prosperity, a relationship some observers have conjectured. One cornerstone of the prevailing interpretation of the lower-class Negro family as female-headed is a supposed advantage of Negro women over Negro men in wage earning (Davie 1949:207; Powdermaker 1939:145; Kardiner and Ovesey 1951:54), but such an advantage has never been found to be substantiated by factual data. Lewis (1955:121) estimates Kent Negro women's annual incomes to be about half of Negro men's incomes. Table 2 shows the fallacy of assuming women's superior earning power in the recent period.

Other evidence for an important male role in Georgiatown families is abundant. Rural family traditions are still close to the people of the town since many are of the first generation to have left the countryside. In informants' reminiscences of rural life there is frequently a strict authoritarian father who supervised the whole family in their farm chores, punished the children, read aloud from the Bible daily, and said he could spell better than the schoolteacher. Some men in the community today are spoken of in a similar vein, as hardworking and authoritarian. In family behavior, men are usually accorded or assume authority in the house. Women act as though their husbands had authority, and children are respectful of them. Women observed in casual behavior with their husbands and with male visitors are deferent. Especially indicative of the important familial role of men in Georgiatown is the fact that the grandmothers who supervise large households of children, grandchildren, and great grandchildren all have husbands supporting them.

Since men head a large proportion of households it is not surprising that illegitimate and orphaned children are often cared for in the households of male kinsmen—the paternal grandfather, a paternal uncle, a maternal uncle, and a maternal great uncle in cases known. Responsibility for a son's illegitimate children as well as a daughter's may be assumed by older stable couples. In one case an illegitimate child's mother regularly visited the child where he lived in his father's parents' household with the father absent. Care of children while their mothers work is extended by older women and men to a son's children as well as daughter's children. Thus family ties through men and emotional attachments of men to their kinsmen are socially important in this town, as well as mother-daughter ties.

At the same time there are many illegitimate births, multiple sequential marriages, and frequent dissolution of marriage; practices the prevailing literature on the American Negro associates with family breakdown and the female-headed family.

These apparent incongruities point up the confused state of analysis of American Negro culture and especially of the lower-class family. The widespread construct that interprets the lower-class Negro family as disorganized and dysfunctional, represented in the work of E. Franklin Frazier and Daniel P. Moynihan and dominating the social work and sociological perspectives in this field, has been called into question by several writers (Lewis 1960; Bernard 1966; Valentine 1968). Valentine has demonstrated many of the sources of misconception and bias in their analyses and has pointed out that statistical data showing high frequencies of female-headed families fail to show the whole pattern of the Negro family for the very reason that it does not take into consideration the external stimulation for male absence provided by the welfare system. As Valentine points out, the female-headed family is viewed as a broken family, as a product of failure to achieve a norm. The norm is explicitly assumed to be the nuclear family of a generalized American culture: "On the institutional side, the family structure of the lower-class Negro is the same as the white. However, in the actual process of living, the vicissitudes of the lower-class family are greater and its stability much less" (Kardiner and Ovesey 1951:307). The validity of a generalized American white family pattern is itself open to question, but what concerns us here is the assumption that there is no distinctive American Negro family system. That assumption rests on the explicit rejection of Herskovitz' thesis of the retention of African cultural elements by New World Negroes and the denial that there could be significant independent social and cultural development of Negroes in this country.

New constructs and new data are needed. M. G. Smith's analysis of family organization in five Negro communities in the West Indies (1962) establishes a model for the family system of the New World Negro culture area, showing basic patterning and variant forms and placing the female-headed family in perspective in the systematic whole. The functionality of Negro family types in the United States, including those headed by women, has been advocated before but this point has been forgotten in the popular despair over the Negro's lack of a middle-class style family. Johnson (1934a, 1934b, 1941) and Powdermaker (1939) point out that Negro families, whether headed by males or females, provide secure groups for child raising and that marriage patterns accommodate the accepted styles of interpersonal behavior between men and women. Johnson's analysis of egalitarian values and behavior patterns of men and women in mating customs is especially relevant to the attempt in this paper to define the distinctive aspects of the Negro family (Johnson 1934a:29ff). Johnson's sample of 612 households in rural Alabama contained two-thirds complete nuclear families, yet high rates of illegitimacy and marital breakup. The pattern is similar to Georgiatown's and suggests that the variable of male or female head of house does not necessarily alter the occurrence of illegitimacy and the customs of marriage. Even Frazier (1939) must be credited with describing functional systems in the matriarchal family and in the male-headed tenant farm family, all useful data in spite of the shortcomings of his general analysis.

In Georgiatown the Negro family is functional and systematic. The potential for social dysfunction in the high illegitimacy rate and frequent marital dissolutions is compensated for by other parts of the system, so that as a whole the patterns of family organization are functional. Indeed, illegitimacy and separation are necessary concomitants of the emotional underpinning of the system. Illegitimate births are especially common before the first marriage. Of forty-four women who gave life histories, at least twenty-one had one or more children before marriage. The unwed mother almost never forms a separate household, but remains with her own childhood family, sometimes working and relying on her family for help in child care. Having children out of wedlock is not approved, even though it is so common. The father is almost always known, but opinion is likely to weigh less heavily against the boy than against the girl, and the girl is almost always said to be the instigator of the union. She is criticized within her family and by others for a time, but she bears the shame rather lightly, showing typical independence of public opinion. Her mother may demonstrate scorn for her or may accept the embarrassment lightly.

The child probably does not suffer from its illegitimacy. Its mother shows the immense pride in her baby that is typical of all births in this community. The baby has the mother's surname and her household dotes over it. One proud authoritarian man took his daughter's new-born illegitimate son to show the mother of the baby's father, who was himself working in the North, and said, "I have a real pretty baby here and I'm going to name him after your boy so he'll grow up to be as smart as your boy." The grandmother, who related the story, was embarrassed, as she was expected to be, but the grandfather was doing more than embarrassing her: he was showing his own intention to care for the child. By the time this story was told the boy had become the paternal grandmother's indulged favorite and a frequent visitor to the maternal grandfather. Sometimes the father of the illegitimate baby helps support it and, as it grows, sends for it to visit him. The child usually has two or even three households where he has a berth—the paternal and maternal relatives who helped raise him and his own mother's house after she marries. The first two are most likely to be secure homes. In his own mother's home the potentiality of a hostile relationship with the stepfather seemed little developed, and the useful role that oldest children play in households provides them with a means of creating a secure position for themselves.

The first child is the most fondled and most stimulated and often becomes the most self-confident and capable of all the children in a family, whether or not he is illegitimate as many first children are. Because illegitimacy is common and because there is little derogation of the child born out of wedlock, these children themselves seem relatively undisturbed by their status. The children know their real father's name and where he lives. Overt signs of anxiety about being deserted by their father were occasionally seen, but there is also a casual acceptance of the multiplicity of fathers that characterizes most families. Children explain about themselves, "We're halves," meaning half-siblings. They can be heard comparing their relatives and are quick to deny a half-sibling's claim to a cousin who is really only theirs. Although many Georgiatown children do not have their own father's care, they usually have the example of a male provider in the home and a man filling an authoritative role in the home. The grandfather often fills the affectional role that the father deserts.

In Georgiatown illegitimacy does not endanger the child, nor does it force the mother into a disadvantageous social position or reduce her prospects for forming a stable marriage. The inconsequentialness of illegitimacy to both mother and child was observed by Johnson (1934b:214–215) in rural Alabama in the 1920's, and by Powdermaker (1939:204–206) in Mississippi, and the pattern in this manufacturing town in the 1960's is essentially the same.

Georgiatown Negro family life is relatively secure despite the instability of some of its phases. Although many families achieve stability well after childrearing is underway, the grandparental families usually serve as secure social units for children until their mothers make a stable marriage. Childbearing usually begins in the middle or late teens, and most women have achieved a relatively stable marriage by their midtwenties. The sequence is essentially the same as Smith (1962) found in the two more stable family systems in his sample, from extra-residential mating to consensual union to marriage, with the exception that consensual union is not acknowledged openly, and in Georgiatown it would be more accurate to speak of a sequence of extraresidential mating, unstable marriage, and stable marriage. In many families the mother is thus the permanent figure. Her children may have a series of fathers as she first has children out of wedlock and then may have one or more marriages. The family is centered on her in this sense, but not in the sense that she provides the main support for the family or is a stronger authority than the man who supports her and her children.

Marriage and family in Negro society differ culturally and structurally from their counterparts in other American groups. Marriage is thought of as a relationship concerning only the couple, and neither the community nor individual families attempt to regulate marriage beyond a qualified adherence to an ethic of obligations between mating couples. Adolescents are free to engage in sexual behavior, but marriage as an acceptance of enduring obligations and as an economic arrangement comes about with more maturity and primarily as a matter of choice and with a minimum of social pressure. In the family, husband and wife both contribute economically, both have authority, both can take the initiative to bring about separation, and both may find separation advantageous. Although many marriages dissolve, remarriage is usual, and middle-aged persons not living in a married state are uncommon. In contrast to the two-generation white nuclear family, the Negro family maintains strong ties over three or four generations. It is not organized as a multigenerational household, but the grandparental tie on either side is easily and often invoked in a variety of arrangements. These multigenerational ties lend stability to the system by protecting unmarried mothers and children born outside of marriage.

Children usually remain with their mother while she may have a series of unions; this makes the ties between mother and child strong and culturally significant. The Negro man, however, has a role in the system. His absence from the household of his own children and his periodic moves to different households, at least while he is young, is not a measure of psychic inadequacy. It is his role in a functional system, the values of which, judging from Liebow's and C. S. Johnson's material, are free response to emotions and true and continuing compatibility between man and woman.

Negro marriage and family practices provide social and psychological security for childbearing and child training; they embody cultural values and serve human needs. As such they deserve to be recognized as functionally integral parts of an American Negro culture. To interpret these practices as deteriorated forms of a general American culture introduces an ethnocentric bias and obscures some of the values and inner workings of Negro society.

CHILDHOOD

Within the Negro family, this loose yet structured group, this group geared to emotional compatibility of egalitarian spouses, what are interpersonal relations like? Davis and Dollard (1940), Davis and Havighurst (1946), Kardiner and Ovesey (1951), Rohrer and Edmonson (1960), and Liebow (1967) almost alone among social scientists have explored the question. Liebow's participant observation is unique, and the results are invaluable. The other studies, however, use the clinical interview to reconstruct the reality of life experiences. Clinical interviews can not elicit a factual, properly weighted, or complete account of experience, especially when recalled from distant childhood. They give data about the subject's current thought processes, but not about his environment or his behavior, either current or past, except in a gross way. If, furthermore, the subject grew up in a family tradition fundamentally different from that to which the theoretical system of the clinician applies, what are the chances of constructing an accurate picture through this method? Half of Kardiner and Ovesey's subjects, furthermore, were in psychotherapy, making dubious their typicality. Rohrer and Edmonson's work presents welcome new typologies but lacks the perspective of observational study and child-training data.

The clinical method, heavily buttressed with psychoanalytic deductions from incorrect stereotypes of the Negro family, has produced a picture of distressed human relations. "The mother is ill-tempered, imposes severe and rigid disciplines, demands immediate obedience, and offers only sporadic affection. . . . Mothers in this group [Negro lower class] are often loveless tyrants. Coldness, scoldings, and frequent beatings are the rule" (Kardiner and Ovesey 1951:65). "Fathers are either seclusive, taciturn, violent, punitive, and without interest in the children or they are submissive to the mother" (Kardiner and Ovesey 1951:66). "Sibling attitudes in the lower class show that animosity and hatred are the rule, with complete severence of relations" (Kardiner and Ovesey 1951:67). "Lower class Negro children grow up to be fighters, cutters, and shooters and they are reinforced in this behavior by their parents" (Davis and Dollard 1940:270). "Early controls upon the child's use of his erogenous zones are equally effective in all classes [white and Negro] and . . . the rigors of this training give rise to the same kind of personality strain [in all classes]" (Davis and Dollard 1940:270).

Interpersonal relations within the Negro family were considered the product of psychological maladjustment resulting from white society's definition of the Negro as a lesser human being and its systematic deprivation of his wants. Racial discrimination was thought to determine fundamentally the character of relationships between Negro parents and children and husbands and wives. The Negro was assumed to have no life style of his own and to make no adjustments to society except the destructive ones based on his agreement with whites' judgments of him. Certainly some individuals' life experience would match the construct. But where a historically and culturally distinct social group is studied, cultural differences should be assumed and the direct applicability of personality theory derived from another culture should not. It was in this context of knowledge that the present observational study of childhood was undertaken; it will be seen that the generalizations about Negro parent-child relationships that derive from clinical studies were not found in this field situation and that other types of experience not derivable from psychoanalytic theory were found to exist and to be significant.

In their relations with their young children the Negroes of Georgiatown find perhaps the greatest pleasures of their lives. Everyone with the slightest claim to do so holds and plays with the baby. The unmarried mother of fifteen displays her baby as proudly as does the veteran child-bearer sitting on her porch and giving orders to her flock of offspring. The baby finds that its environment is almost wholly human. Cribs, baby carriages, and highchairs are almost never seen. The baby is held and carried most of the time, and when it is laid down it is seldom without company.[2]

Being held is an active relationship between holder and baby, a highly personal experience. Most mothers hold babies with relaxed posture, usually cradling the baby on one arm or in the lap. As she cradles him the mother's free hand wipes, pets, pokes, investigates, and her eyes explore the baby's face and body. Newborn and very young babies are often laid in the groove between the legs as the mother sits, with the baby's feet toward the mother. In either position mother and baby look into each other's faces and the mother's hands caress the baby. She talks to it, expressing in her manner pride and amusement and enjoyment in it. When not being held young babies are laid on a bed, usually lying on their backs, and children and adults lean over the young baby and talk to it. Babies old enough to turn over and pull themselves along are laid on a folded blanket on the floor, where the little children are likely to join them, leaning over or on top of them and testing the baby's responses. Seldom is a baby seen held against the shoulder and looking behind the mother,

[2] The behavioral forms discussed in this section were as fully exhibited among middle-class as among lower-class families. The class differences in general were not very great in this town and would not be expected to affect these fundamental styles of interpersonal behavior, except as different expectations of achievement did in some ways affect child training.

and seldom does the mother hold it while doing chores. These more impersonal ways of holding a baby, where the mother's main attention is directed at something other than the baby, are not characteristic. In the mother's care there is typically a higher degree of personal involvement.

This highly personal, highly active relationship between mother and baby takes place in a crowded household. Household composition varies widely, but one aspect of the human environment is almost certain, a full and crowded house. The baby experiences many different types of people of all ages, all of whom hold the baby and play with it. The father and male relatives play with it as readily as the women and children, and although they are not home much of the time, they enjoy babies and are competent in handling them.

Patterns of sleep are distinctive. The interest in playing with babies not uncommonly interferes with the infant's own inclination to sleep. Naps are characteristically short and irregular, since they are taken in the midst of the many disturbances of normal household activities, and usually are ended by the household commotion or by a person seeking the napper to play with. Long periods of sleep at night are usually established very early. The infant sleeps next to the mother in the mother's and father's bed, or sometimes with either parent alone. The mother may have both the infant and the knee-baby sleeping in her bed with her, but if there are older children the knee-baby is more likely to join them in their bed. The environment does not respond to the baby's own periodicity of rest and activity, tending to prevent establishment of natural rhythms in this area. Sleep does, however, reinforce the usual state of physical closeness.

Infant feeding habits vary widely, but certain attitudes about eating and about the giving and receiving of food run through the variations in behavior. Some mothers breast feed a few weeks or months and then wean to a bottle. Most use a bottle entirely, while some use the breast and bottle concurrently, depending on convenience and privacy. Whether the baby is fed by breast or bottle the periods of eating are typically brief and the milk is offered frequently. When the baby shows discomfort the mother almost invariably offers the bottle. She typically says: "I know you not hungry. You hungry? You just ate a while ago." But she offers the bottle. The feeding is casually interrupted at any signs of decreased demand from the baby and as casually begun again at any interval. The rhythm of eating is like the rhythm of napping, short periods of each activity and frequent repetition. The environment is ever ready to interrupt and ever ready to offer gratification. This rhythm is very different from the disciplined long spans of attention cultivated in middle-class childrearing and expected in schools.

Mothers speak as though weaning occurred abruptly, but toddlers keep their bottles until three in the face of strong parental resistance and teasing. The mother may stop the bottle and the father accede to the baby's demand to have it, and the mother casually accepts the situation. One sees a mother repeatedly refuse the bottle to a demanding knee-baby, even while going to the kitchen to prepare it. It is not fixed habits of eating and feeding with which one is impressed, but rather that mothers and children act on whim and willfully in these matters. The wide variation in practice and in feelings about different practices gives much leeway for idiosyncratic behavior, in fact requires it. The behavioral constant is will on both mother's and child's part. Neighbors' practices and neighbors' opinions are not thought to have any bearing on what any individual mother does. She sees herself as acting on sudden personal decisions. Being decisive and abrupt is admired and is one aspect of these people's strong sense of individualism.

Related also to decisiveness is the emphasis on giving and demanding food. The mother does not speak of infant feeding and weaning in terms of the infant's needs but of her own giving of food. She deemphasizes two objective aspects of eating, nourishment and routineness, and emphasizes two other aspects of eating, the giving and the receiving. The mother gives the satisfaction of eating and the child demands and receives it. It is the giving and the receiving, the demanding and the choosing to satisfy the demand—that is, the interpersonal exchange aspects of eating—that seem most important. Need, nourishment, succoring, routine—all possible aspects of eating and emphasized in white culture—are not usual concepts.

Family food habits also represent food as a voluntary gift from the parents. The hour of eating is not routinized within families, nor are there habitual meal times within the community. Meals are geared to the hours of work of the father and mother, which are irregular and varied since men work different shifts and domestic work keeps women away at conventional meal times. It is typical for a family to have two cooked meals a day, one in the morning or midday and the other at evening. The mother cooks at her convenience, not at a routine time, neither routinely for her family nor in coordination with the community. Between these times pick-up meals are gotten by each child for himself and eaten while walking around. During the day the mother may bring out sweet snacks or send children to a nearby store with money to buy a soft drink or popsicle. Mothers enjoy these treats and give them with largess. Occasionally the family will have to wait for its first meal of the day until the father wakes up after bringing his pay home the night before from a late shift job. When he wakes up he walks to town to buy food, then all wait while the mother cooks it. In this situation the parents' roles as providers are abundantly clear. Eating is less a matter of routine than of individualistic voluntary giving and receiving.

Babies who are held so much of the time urinate and have their bowel movements while being held, and these actions are responded to immediately and directly. The action and response may be clearly associated in the baby's mind from a very early age. The diaper is usually changed quickly and quietly as soon as it is soiled or wet. If the mother's clothes get wet she usually shows her annoyance with a jerk and a long, pentrating scolding look into the baby's eyes. A five-month-old baby was told reproachfully: "You should have gotten down to pee-pee." The quick wiping away of the urine and feces is a forerunner of bladder and bowel training usually begun and quickly accomplished between nine and fifteen months. Some mothers wait until twenty or twenty-two months to begin it, showing the idiosyncratic tendency seen in the widely varied feeding habits. The highly personal conditions for care of these functions in early infancy may make the mother's expectations for control later an easier transition than for infants whose functions have occurred typically alone. The mother's intrusion in the functioning of bladder and bowel has been established from birth. In contrast, among middle-class white Americans the mother begins to interfere with the infant's bladder and bowel release only after many months of paying no attention to these functions. The greater continuity in the Negro mother's behavior undoubtedly eases the effects of early and stringent toilet training, which is commonly reported for American Negroes (Davis and Dollard 1940; Davis and Havighurst 1946) and which is the practice of many but not all mothers in this group.

Cleanliness, as distinguished from control of sphincters, is emphasized not only in the immediate wiping away of urine and feces, but also in the wiping of the mouth. The young baby's regurgitated milk is quickly wiped away and clothing soiled in this way is changed. A teething baby's mouth is wiped whenever drooling is noticed. Wiping is both a measure of cleanliness and also a tactile experience similar to the caressing with fingers that is so commonly done while holding the baby. The tactile experiences of the bath are similar. The baby is laid on the mother's lap and wiped with a cloth that is wetted and lathered in a small basin of water; it is then wiped again with the cloth rinsed clean of soap. The baby is never stood or seated in the basin. Young babies are sponged in this manner twice a day and this form of bath is usual throughout early childhood. The rubbing with a damp cloth is analogous to the caressing hand. The communication of a sense of care and attention through the skin is maximized while there is no opportunity for water play and the exploration of its properties.

The most usual kind of play with babies revolves around pretending the baby is aggressive. The young baby's reflexive extensions of its arms and legs are called hitting and kicking and its explorations with its lips are called biting. It is a great joke and everyone enjoys it. The mother will duck the flying two-month-old fist and say: "She sure is mad at me." Two babies will be propped beside each other and their wavering lunges and grasps and leaning on one another are laughingly called fighting.

The playful accusations of biting are the most usual form of the game.

The mother brings the baby to her face and caresses its face lightly with her lips or forehead, and when the baby tries to suck or feel with its mouth the mother jerks it away in mock anger saying, "Don't you bite me." She brings the baby to her face again and repeats the thrust and accusation. She laughs admiringly while accusing it over and over. This episode is played with boy and girl babies, fathers play it with babies, and older nurse-girls play it with their charges, although not with as much pleasure as the adults. It is one of the most specifically stylized and most often observed forms of behavior with babies. In contrast to this game, babies' attempts to suck on the mother's fingers or other exposed areas of skin bring reactions of strong disgust. She jerks her hand away and reprimands with a harsh tone and angry look. This type of spontaneous oral incorporative behavior brings an angry reaction, whereas teasing the baby to the point of, but not the fulfillment of, similar mouth activity is a pleasurable game. There is only sporadic interference with young babies sucking and chewing their own fingers.

As babies gain control of the extensor muscles, the playful accusations of kicking and hitting are no longer made, but the interpretation of lip explorations as biting begins before babies have teeth and reaches a peak at about eight to ten months. By fifteen months, or by the time the baby walks well, the face-to-face play is no longer seen, but the child of that age is regularly told not to bite the new baby or the borrowed baby who is held up for it to kiss. By this time lip explorations seem to have ceased, and when urged to kiss a young baby a child in his second year is very cautious, hardly touching its lips to the baby and keeping its arms stiffly at its sides. The linkage of kissing and biting, of love and aggression, is understood by the fifteen-month-old baby but not mastered as a form of play. It is mastered by six, the earliest age at which children play the game almost like adults. Infantile oral pleasures are frustrated and replaced by structured parental demonstrativeness.

Frustrations for infants in this culture arise from less vital experiences than the satisfaction of hunger and the provision of attentive care. Frustration is undoubtedly experienced from interference with oral pleasures, from disruption of the natural rhythms of sleep, and from the frequently stringent restrictions on bowel and bladder movements. Rich compensation is offered for these frustrations, all of it interpersonal. The mother frustrates the lip explorations and at the same time rewards them with playfulness and admiration. The mother who toilet trains early requires difficult control and yet her frequent physical contact and accustomed attentiveness, which enable her to get compliance, are themselves satisfactions. The aggression that is generated is admired and tolerated to a great extent, and yet the mother even as she is encouraging and admiring aggressiveness indicates that she is regulating its expression. There is a complex interplay of permissiveness and regulation, of indul-

gence and frustration, and all are carried out with a deep level of interpersonal involvement.

When the infant is accused of biting, the young children who surround
it learn that the baby is an individual capable of bold initiative. The
baby is attributed these characteristics in many other ways also. There
is much talk about babies' meanness. Mothers and nurse-children will
sigh about how mean a baby was who would not nap, while they are
greatly enjoying holding and displaying the mean baby. A four-month-old
baby who held tight to a glass of water after drinking was told, "Uh-uh,
stop trying to fight. You's a mean little old girl." The mother was admiring the baby's assertiveness and attesting to the highly developed
character assumed in babies.

The individuality of the baby is stressed through questioning the baby
about its wants, especially its hunger, and through interpreting its random
or directed movements as expressions of wants: he wants to get some-
where; he wants a certain person. As Old American Whites might say
"Hello," over and over again, a frequent remark to a baby is: "What you
want? What you want?" The focusing on wants is an important expression of these peoples' life experience. An infant's wants are well satisfied,
whereas later life is full of unsatisfied wants. The new baby is usually
the best dressed member of the family. Little girls and adolescent girls
long for pretty clothes but go without. Small items such as baby brushes,
plastic bags for carrying bottles and plastic baby toys are sometimes
seen and are conspicuous because of the general lack of paraphernalia
and gadgets in this culture. Older children fondle the baby's booties
admiringly or defiantly use the baby's hair brush, or plead to play with
the baby bag. Having these things enhances the baby's high status.

Babies are taught to be responsive orally. The baby held up before
the mother's or father's face is teased about biting for a while, and then
is likely to be urged to imitate the parent's sounds. One hears five-
month-old babies spontaneously imitating single sounds of their parents,
and often babies show precociousness that tends to be lost in later
childhood when the stimulus falls off. Babies will be distracted by calling
their attention to a person, seldom an object: "Look yonder, who's coming?" "What you want? Jean? You want Jean to come?" Before they can
talk babies are said to know the name of a favorite visitor. Parents will
say the name of the favorite over and over to bring a smile to the baby's
face.

In contrast to this great stimulation of the baby's responsiveness to
people, its explorations of the inanimate environment are limited. Few
objects are given to babies or allowed them when they do get hold of
them. Plastic toys are almost the only objects ever seen in the hands of a
prewalker, and their use seems to result from shopping in supermarkets.
Babies' reachings to feel objects or surfaces are often redirected to feel-

ing the holder's face, or the game of rubbing faces is begun as a substitute. Sometimes the reaching is turned into a teasing game in which the baby is said to want to bite what it reaches for, and is teasingly brought up to and away from it. Such a degree of inhibition of exploration is possible only because there are always eyes on the baby and idle hands to take away the forbidden objects and then distract the frustrated baby. The personal is thus often substituted for the impersonal.

Babies are kept from crawling on the floor by holding them and passing them along from one holder to another. Walkers are the one piece of baby gadgetry that is rather commonly seen. The baby who is not safe on a bed and not adequately restricted on a pallet is likely to be put in a walker. He gets little chance to explore since he is usually chaperoned by older children who push him in the walker. It serves more as a restrictive seat than a device for learning to walk. Babies learn to stand on people's laps. They are jumped generously when they want to flex and stiffen their leg muscles. They are stood momentarily on the floor between the mother's or father's legs and jumped. But they are seldom allowed to stand alone, sink down on the floor or pull themselves up. All their standing is done on a lap. Babies are observed to walk at ten months, and claims were recorded of walking at nine months, while those learning to walk after twelve months seem relatively few. The baby who is ready to walk is stood on the floor; in the midst of great excitement it lunges and steps to waiting arms and is stood up when it falls either to try again or to be put in the lap.

The baby on the verge of the great change that walking and toilet training bring, the one-year-old, has been held almost all the waking hours of his first year, has been fed often and allowed to refuse food whenever inclined, has slept close to his parents and has been treated as a willful assertive individual. His natural rhythms of sleep and perhaps also hunger have not been perceived and have been interrupted, probably a very common enculturation experience. His desire to explore his nonhuman environment has been frustrated and human contact substituted. His own tactile expressions both oral and manual have been severely restricted, yet he has been constantly handled. He is taught to be passive in tactile experiences. He is urged to precocious speech development and walking, becomes accustomed to a high level of stimulation and is encouraged to avow an aggressiveness beyond what is probably natural in his situation. He should be a secure baby with confident expectations of gratification, self-assertive, and accustomed to close and continuous human contacts. The restrictions placed on him in tactile exploration and the systematic removal of objects from his range have certainly made him much more a stranger to his material environment than to his human one.

Walking brings an enormous change in the scope of experience of any baby, and especially the baby who has not had much chance to crawl. For people in this community the accomplishments of walking and toilet training, which come at about the same time, signify the transition to different expectations of the baby. His mother now requires him to use a pot or the outdoors for his excretion. Beyond this requirement he has free rein in his behavior, but he is expected to cause his mother no trouble. She punishes him by switching, starting with a light switch but using it frequently and with seriousness, although often with playfulness. The new behavioral expectations bring about a change in attitude toward the one-year-old child. One can speak of the one-year-old as the knee-baby, as the Georgiatown people do, the ambulatory child who leaves the mother and returns to her, who stands at her knee whether there is a new baby in her lap or not.

When there is a new baby, jealousy is usual, sometimes accompanied by psychosomatic symptoms, but it is usually short-lived. The knee-baby's aggressive feelings toward the lap-baby are acknowledged and aggressive expressions toward it tolerated to some extent. The knee-baby can hit or pinch the unwanted infant in his mother's lap and run off with little scolding or punishment. After a month or two the knee-baby's anxiety over the younger child becomes more concerned with the continuance of the mother's attention than with jealousy of the infant. He shares the lap with the new born, or has it to himself while the newborn sleeps, but he is not treated as an infant in the lap. It is made clear to him what his role is. He is urged to mother the baby as everyone else in the household does. The infant is held out to him and he is asked, "You want the baby?" He looks hostile or puzzled. He is urged to kiss the baby and, if he does so, does it stiffly and frowning. The infant is held up to the knee-baby to dance with him, and joggled in time to music as though held in the knee-baby's arms. I have seen this with knee-babies as young as fifteen months. The eighteen-month-old acts the same when urged to take or kiss the infant. But by twenty to twenty-four months both girls and boys enjoy this game with a baby. The child who is said not to like his sibling is nevertheless offered the baby to kiss and hold. For the child who has no younger sibling, neighbors or relatives or nurse-girls offer their babies. Learning to mother the baby is an important lesson in this culture.

Children in their second year, the knee-babies, seem typically secure. Their close relationship with their mothers continues, but their world expands to include the children's gang, a group of children primarily from the family, sometimes from the neighborhood, ranging in age from the fifteen-month-olds through a nurse-girl or boy of at least six. Usually children up to ten or twelve are included. The youngest child is the toy of all children who are six or older and who can claim the right to carry it. It is the center of attention of the gang, the favorite, never the interferer, for the gang has little to do but look after the young ones. Some children in their second year who have a baby sibling have transferred their main attachments to a substitute mother, to the father if he is home in the daytime, or to the grandmother if she is present, or even to a child nurse who is sufficiently reliable and devoted.

But the strong sense of security of the child in his second year is observed most interestingly in his relations with his mother. She sits, passively enjoying his assertiveness, playing the fetching games that his new-found independence of walking has led him to, and waging contests over innumerable issues, whether he will kiss or pinch the lap baby, whether he will be allowed to go off with someone, whether he will obey his mother's command or not. Mother and child smile slyly as they challenge each other. If the issue must be settled or if she wants to assert her authority, she does so with threat or use of a switch. She asks the little aggressor to bring her a switch and sits flicking it while he provokes her, to her enjoyment, as long as she wants him to. Children watch their mother's face to see whether they must cringe in fear and obey when she gets the switch or whether they can make a new challenge on top of a switching. The knee-baby is the one most likely to be allowed to make a new challenge. The contests between mother and knee-baby are staged for enjoyment and as demonstrations of the toddler's stalwart individualism. The mother is continuing the encouragement of aggression and the control of its expression as she and the father so regularly did in the baby's first year. An occasional mother is overbearing in this play and her knee-baby is unplayful. These mothers wield their authority more strictly than most and rigidly control their baby's responses to them. The result is usually a sullen child.

The first two or three years of life would seem to lay the groundwork for a healthy and resilient self-image. The two-year-old acts out the aggressiveness and assertiveness that are natural for his age and that were stimulated during his first year. It is an age of great self-confidence, mastery over all persons in the environment, and lavish admiration. Interpersonal activity continues to predominate in contrast to the manipulation of objects and the exploration of the environment, and a strong preference for this range of activity seems to have been established already, since restrictions on explorations are no longer seen. This preference continues all through childhood without further restrictions on use of natural materials. The typical two-year-old, the admired, assertive and playful knee-baby, seems to be doing well in terms of developing his potential and adjusting to his environment. But at the end of the knee-baby stage comes a marked change in experience, an almost complete cessation of the close relationship with the mother and father and a shift in orientation to the children's gang.

A change in the mother-child relationship comes when the knee-baby is pushed out of that lordly position by a growing younger sibling, and is expected to transfer his dependence to the gang of older children in the family and to the oldest child in it who is in charge of the gang. This transition to the gang takes place at about three. If the displaced knee-baby is the oldest in the family he becomes attached to a neighboring family group of older children. Only one child at a time is involved with the parents in the typical knee-baby relationship. The youngest child in a family or a set of children often retains the teasing relationship with its parents typical for the knee-baby, which seems to indicate that the third-position child is not thought to outgrow the relationship, but that a younger child is preferred if available. With this exception parents no longer play with children after the knee-baby position. The stimulation that was so intense ends almost entirely. The separation from the mother at this time seems to be taken well in stride except by those displaced very young and by some who show an unusually strong and exclusive dependence on their mother. The gang's forays away from home and the easy-going authority of the nurse-child seem to be attractions that substitute for the old closeness to the mother. Some children seem to prefer the nurse-child to their mothers even while still knee-babies. These are the children of the overly aggressive mothers who so dominate the contests that the knee-babies become unresponsive and sullen. The very independent and assertive child manages best while the insecure child is truly lost, hanging on to the nurse-child or mother, but no one's favorite. He is no longer the toy of the gang because like the parents the gang prefers the knee-baby to play with. Most children seem to manage well by acquiring solemnity and stolidity and quietly following the gang. Others retain the playful and assertive personalities that are typical of the knee-baby, but aggressiveness seems well controlled at this age. The three-year-old is sometimes intimidated by the toddler. He is told, "You have hands don't you?" but he seldom fights back effectively and seldom is reprimanded for aggressiveness. Once the baby's aggressiveness was fully managed by the parent, both encouraged and restricted. The older gang members keep up constant pressure for cooperative behavior, and the young ones show remarkably little aggressiveness.

The most apparent loss at this time due to the abrupt ending of parental stimulation is not seen in the form of anxiety, but in loss of precociousness of speech development. Often speech becomes an indistinct children's patois in contrast to the clear enunciation used by the knee-baby with his parents. Children speak less to adults and get along adequately with "Yes'm" and "No'm." Exploration of the environment seems to have been thoroughly inhibited by this age. Children become subsumed in the small community of the family-based gang.

The core of any gang is the children of one family. Single children or several young children of neighbors may also be regular parts of the gang. Nurse-children who are friends sometimes bring their gangs together but for both nurse-child and younger gang members the family orientation of the gang overrides friendship with age mates. The gang is essentially a child-tending group and the oldest child is fully occupied with the responsibility. There is little other activity to attract the nurse-child away and he or she seems content to manage the gang. Boys from about nine years leave the mixed-sex gang if they themselves are not the nurse-child. They range farther from home than the gangs with young children, playing games of athletic skill and keeping their promises to their mothers or older sisters to be back at a certain hour. The gang with young children sits and gossips, runs, climbs, swings, lines up for inspection, teases. Sitting in a circle of chairs, it passes a joke around the group, each one repeating the punch line in much the same way as a group of women tells a joke. Occasionally an imaginary family game will be seen, but most of the play uses only the real relationships of the children. There are almost no toys, almost no use of natural materials, no "projects" such as the middle-class child, whether in the sandbox or supplied with paper and crayons or dress-ups, is usually involved in. Equipment such as swings and slides are used where available, chairs are lined up for the gossip circle, but simple equipment, such as ropes, poles, sticks, balls, and stones, is almost never seen in use. Junebugs are an exception, the one part of the natural environment that is used, creatures, significantly, not objects. They are tied by one leg to fly from a string and raced on the ground. For the most part children are the playthings and the players. The youngest is the center of attention. He is carried and kissed and shepherded and talked to lovingly, and his words and acts are discussed with great interest. Children sit close to one another, rub bare feet with each other, tease, tell stories and jokes. There are few displays of proficiency of the kind learned at school and little use of school as a play model.

Aggression, punishment, and acceptance of authority in Georgiatown childhood diverge markedly from what has been reported before. Fighting is not encouraged as Davis and Dollard's interviewees said it was (1940:270–271). Possibly this is a case in which interviews bring out bragging, or perhaps, since parents' advice to children over three or four was so infrequent in the course of observations, directives to "Fight it out" in Georgiatown may have been given and missed. In the children's gangs, however, quarrels are infrequent and children seldom resort to blows. Word battles and glaring matches take their place. A child may be threatened with exclusion and make counter claims of his right to play. An older child may hit a younger, who usually sulks without hitting back, but this is unusual. No bullies were seen and no wrestling matches. Play was mild and even-tempered. One blow and the other children would take the victim home.

In visiting for a few hours at a time one seldom sees punishments, although occasionally the resounding cracks of prolonged spanking and the steady crying of a child are heard from a neighboring house and the remark is made, "Hear her beating on that girl!" Sometimes a mother reports somberly that she had to "beat on him," for some misdeed and the child sulks on the edges of the household activity. Adolescent boys and girls are also whipped by their mothers. Punishments, however, do not seem to be extreme or more frequent than in middle-class American society. The mother unquestionably has authority over her children but she also cultivates a degree of defiance in them. Even after the games of defiance in knee-babyhood are over, mothers indicate to their children that they will be allowed to get away with things. In so doing they are actually asserting their ultimate authority, like the mother who likes to see her infant bite and fight and likes to scold him for it, but the children are also being taught playful defiance. Children defy their mothers on many small issues, and they watch her closely to see if they will be allowed to get away with it. The behavior is similar to the mother's games with the knee-baby except that the mother is not playful. She quietly watches or looks impassive to indicate that she is allowing whatever small liberties are being taken. Aggression in childhood situations is not an adequate analogy for aggression in adulthood, and childhood experience as observed in this relatively secure community does not show the origins of the aggressiveness found in much adult Negro behavior. These findings do not alter the common perception that the sheer amount of Negro aggression is more directly related to race relations than to other aspects of their experience. The mother's admiring and encouraging attitude toward limited expressions of aggression and defiance may become a prototype for children's expectations of this kind of attitude from other authorities.

The position of nurse-child is held by the oldest in the family, boy or girl. He or she is responsible for all the other children, tends the food the mother may have left cooking before going to work, or makes the sandwiches, serves lunch to the children, diapers the baby and knee-baby if they are left in his charge, fixes bottles for them, puts them in bed for naps. The nurse-children are bossy but gentle and protective and easy-going. The heightened attention that nurse-girl or boy, as first baby, got prepares him for his responsible position. Their competence demonstrates that illegitimate birth, the lot of so many first babies, and that of many nurse-children observed, does not hamper development.

A girl retains this responsibility as a teenager and until she leaves the household. Boys at thirteen or fourteen are expected to desert their regular responsibilities and go off with age-mates although at home they display deep attachments for the younger children. None of the younger children, even if only a year younger than the nurse-child, has major responsibilities and they tend not to show the managerial personality of the oldest child. They are given tasks by the mother, however, and take over some of the care of the younger children because it is privileged activity, and all children have been exhorted from the first appearance of their own younger sibling to mother the younger child. The training that the one-year-old gets in kissing and holding the newborn is his training for all of childhood. A young child may be demanding of an older child, yet turns to a younger one and mothers it, gives in to it, and protects it. Gestures of love for young children are commonplaces in this culture, from the fourteen-year-old boy who rides home on his bicycle and buries his face against the stomach of the baby in his cousin's lap, to the twenty-two-month-old boy, hungry and distressed because his mother is leaving, diverted to pleasurably kiss his three-month-old half-sister in his aunt's lap.

Since mothering is proper behavior for boys as well as girls and for fathers as well as mothers, the question is raised of the behavioral differences between the sexes. In knee-babyhood boys are expected to be assertive, playful, and "bad," while girls are expected to be assertive, playful, coy, and cooperative. The slight but significant difference is as great a contrast as is made at any time in childhood between boys' and girls' expected behavior. The very common, admiring adjective "bad" is used only through knee-babyhood. After that boys are neither bragged on as bad nor are they unruly. Little boys in the family gang have the same activities as the girls and no patterned differences of behavior are seen. Differences between the sexes are marked only in specifically sex-related behavior, just as coyness in baby girls and greater assertiveness in boys are the main differences in babyhood. Girls are encouraged to dance. A baby boy may be a partner, but young boys are never asked to show off in this way. A coy little girl of four climbed into a visiting young man's lap and wriggled and flirted. "I can get me a big 'un," he said. Children are not considered asexual. Children are knowledgeable about birth, menstruation, and sex at an early age. There is a sense of strong continuity between childhood and adulthood. This seems to reinforce in children their sexual identity even though that identity has few indicators other than dress in the organization of children's activity before the age of nine or ten when boys may be expected to leave the young children's gang. In adulthood sex roles are also similar in authority at home, in supporting the family, in styles of child care, and in initiative in forming and breaking up a marriage. Contrasting behavior, however, is also characteristic as has been described in the deferent, yielding, and flirtatious behavior of women and the assertive behavior of men.

The adolescent girls remain in charge of the younger children, but they now manage their broods with subdued and resigned manner. This behavior characteristic of girls in their early teens is one of the most striking and consistent patterns. They stay at home and watch television and read fiction magazines and often show a deep attachment for a baby. If there is no baby or young child in their family they attach themselves to a relative's household to care for the baby. They seem to have only weak ties with girl friends, seem to withdraw solemnly and await the beginning of a love affair that comes to so many in the few years after fourteen. The adolescent girls' feelings of resignation seem to foreshadow the whole course of the adulthood they are about to enter, which will lack material security and material pleasures, lack any attainment of status, but will soon bring their first love affair and the pride and pleasure and heavy responsibility of children. It is as though the irony of their culture is suddenly perceived. The most valued experience in life, parenthood, and perhaps also sex, will foreclose the paths to achievement in American society, education and freedom from emotional entanglement, and with the loss of opportunity to achieve any more of the televised dream that a Southern town offers Negroes. The Negro boy and girl, with their safe and satisfying childhood devoted to care of young children and spent in warm human contacts, and with the threatening and unrewarding world of unskilled work and poverty in prospect, seek their own emotional fulfillment as they have been taught to do.

One theme that keeps recurring in the behavior observed is best reviewed after many appearances. It is a polarity of individuality and interrelatedness. The baby is treated as though willful and assertive beyond his natural inclination and able beyond his natural abilities. He is highly stimulated and admired for his assertiveness, and his acceptance of authority is expected to be defiant. Individualistic behavior is seen also in neighborhood relations. It is striking how separate each family remains from its neighbors, how uncommon the favors exchanged, how independent each family feels of the opinions of others. All of women's work is done inside the houses or in the private backyards, each woman working alone. Shared gardens or communal work of any kind is not undertaken. Only children gather in groups outdoors, playing with neighbor children but seldom involving their mothers in their play or quarrels. Women go to neighbors' houses on brief errands, but are not likely to spend an idle hour. The occasional caller is received on the front porch or in the living-room if there is no porch, and the visitors sit and talk awhile and never were seen offered food. Interchange of services or hospitality or dependence on these things is at a minimum. Much of religious behavior also is highly individualistic. In social organization there are no strongly organized groups to overshadow the individualistic style of behavior in the loosely structured small groups. The girl and boy in adolescence are remarkably free of any community restraint on premarital relations even though there is general disapproval and criticism of license. Strong individuality,[3] however, is paired with strong interpersonal connectedness, not absorption in a group or acceptance of group identity as higher than individual identity, but merely relatedness as distinguished from the isolation that characterizes individualism in the Western tradition. Human contacts are the whole substance of life for the infant. He learns early to be disinterested in the natural environment and entirely occupied by his human one. When the knee-baby is abruptly expected to merge into the quiet and cooperative children's gang and get along with little attention from his parents, individualistic stimulation lessens but the succoring, playful human environment continues.

There is a quality of mutuality in family relations, often heard in remarks that pass between mothers and children, "I'm tired," the three-year-old girl complains. "I'm tired too," her mother responds. "I want some ice cream," the eight-year-old says wistfully as the ice cream truck passes. "I want some too," is the mother's way of saying no. This echoing of words and tone of voice is a common speech pattern. One does not see mothers and children clash and contend. The minimal amount of verbal exchange that has been remarked in lower-class families is in this group connected with abundant communication in other forms. These Georgiatown people are often seen to look deeply into each other's eyes, not speaking but seeming to communicate fully. Parents use this means to impress a point on a child. The observation has been made that Negroes avoid meeting the eyes of whites, and this has been interpreted as a gesture of nonequality. It may also, or instead, be a gesture of uncommunicativeness in view of the extensive communication through looking into the eyes within their own group. The mother's idle caressing of the baby and children sitting in a circle rubbing bare feet are other forms of nonverbal communication. The communication of news in this community is rapid and thorough despite the fact that it is physically scattered and has no central organization of any kind. A mother's communication of directions in household tasks uses few words, and tasks for which she has to give instructions are broken down into small units with brief directions for each short task following on completion of the previous one.[4] The children seem thoroughly familiar with the directions. They respond immediately even when they seem to be napping when an order comes. The rhythm of children's household chores repeats the periodicity of early eating and napping: immediate response to the request, whether for food, to stop napping and play, or to do a task, and brief intervals of the sought activity. Routinized or planned activity with long-range objectives in either house-

---

[3] Hylan Lewis notes that "individuality and idiosyncrasies of character flourish" (1967: 169) and also "despite the overall conformity a striking fact about Kent Negro society is the manner in which everyone tends to be a 'character'" (1955:322ff).

[4] The mother's way of directing household chores is similar to the call and response in music (see Lomax 1967).

hold chores or gang activities is minimal. Personal interaction again emerges as the central element in behavior. The combination of interpersonal responsiveness and strong individuality in all this behavior is suggestive for the present day when the modes of individualistic disciplined achievement have been found of limited adaptability in modern society and where inability to relate genuinely to other persons has been found a common personality malformation.

Negro childhood and family represent a distinctive complex both institutionally and behaviorally. They exhibit organization, values, and behavioral styles that differ from the white cultural tradition. The indulgence of the baby, the constant human environment, linking of aggression and love, the simultaneous encouragement and control of aggressiveness, the early entry into the children's gang and the devotion of childhood to baby-tending and to the cooperative group of brothers and sisters, all are distinctive forms of behavior that, taken as a whole, represent an integrated cultural pattern. The Negro family should be analyzed as part of the social structure of Negro communities, but little analytic work has been done on American Negro social structure. What has been done suggests an unorganized network of loose social groupings with a high level of communication and a low level of authority and coercion. The Negro family is an internally consistent system that fits with this hypothesized social structure. Individual independence in sexual behavior and marriage, comparability of role of husband and wife, and the strengthening of the nuclear family by unpatterned use of the grandparental ties are consistent with such a social structure. Furthermore, the family functions well within a stable community, providing security for children and adjusting well to the high level of emotional expressiveness that is nurtured. We speak therefore of American Negro culture as an entity expressing itself in child-rearing and family forms, and we assume it can be described in other aspects of Negro life, especially small group structure. American white culture may dominate in the areas of life where Negroes participate in American institutions and many items of general American culture are used throughout Negro life, but in small groups and to some extent in any all-Negro group the organizational and behavioral styles of American Negro culture would be expected to be manifest.

Negro family styles are different enough from the white that psychoanalytic interpretations of modal personality would have to be modified for use in this culture. It is a task beyond the scope of this paper, but some relevant considerations emerging from this work may be summarized: early toilet training and the encouragement of autonomy are pursued together; love and aggression and control of aggression are linked in an unusual way; a mother with much authority is also indulgent and erotically provoking; the father's proper role vis-à-vis the baby is quite similar to the mother's indulgence and erotic stimulation.

It also appears from this study of childhood that certain cultural styles are as significant as the parent-child drama, namely the elaboration of interpersonal contacts and the elimination of experience with the object world, the ever-present polarity of individuality and absorption in interpersonal and group experience, the cultivation of will and volition, even a valuing of arbitrariness, and also the playfulness of so many relationships. Cultural styles such as these as well as the institutional structure of American Negro society are the milieu for Negro personality formation.

REFERENCES

Bernard, Jessie. 1966. *Marriage and Family among Negroes*. Englewood Cliffs: Prentice-Hall.

Davie, Maurice R. 1949. *Negroes in American Society*. New York: McGraw-Hill.

Davis, Allison, and John Dollard. 1940. *Children of Bondage*. American Council on Education. New York: Harper and Row (Torchbook edition).

Davis, Allison, and Robert J. Havighurst. 1946. *Social Class and Color Differences in Child-rearing*. American Sociological Review 2:698–710.

Frazier, E. Franklin. 1939. *The Negro Family in the United States*. Chicago: University of Chicago Press.

Herskovitz, Melville J. 1941. *The Myth of the Negro Past*. New York: Harper.

Johnson, Charles S. 1934a. *Shadow of the Plantation*. Chicago: University of Chicago Press.

————. 1934b. "Negro Personality Changes in a Southern Community," in *Race and Culture Contacts*. E. B. Reuter, ed. New York: McGraw-Hill.

Kardiner, Abram, and Lionel Ovesey. 1951. *The Mark of Oppression*. New York: World.

Lewis, Hylan. 1955. *Blackways of Kent*. Chapel Hill: University of North Carolina Press.

————. 1960. "The Changing Negro Family," in *The Nation's Children*. Eli Ginsberg, ed. White House Conference on Children and Youth. New York: Columbia University Press.

————. 1967. "Culture, Class and Family Life Among Low-income Urban Negroes," in *Employment, Race, and Poverty*. Arthur M. Ross and Herbert Hill, eds. New York: Harcourt, Brace, Jovanovich.

Liebow, Elliot. 1967. *Tally's Corner*. Boston: Little, Brown.

Lomax, Alan. 1967. "The Homogeneity of African-New World Negro Musical Style." Paper presented at the 66th Annual Meeting of the American Anthropological Association, Washington, November 30–December 6.

Moynihan, Daniel P. 1965. "The Negro Family: the Case for National Action." Washington: U.S. Department of Labor, Office of Policy Planning and Research.

Powdermaker, Hortense. 1939. *After Freedom.* New York: Viking Press.

Rohrer, John H., and Munro S. Edmonson. 1960. *The Eighth Generation.* New York: Harper.

Smith, M. G. 1962. *West Indian Family Structure.* Seattle: University of Washington Press.

U.S. Department of Labor. 1965. *Labor Market Report.* Washington: U.S. Government Printing Office.

Valentine, Charles A. 1968. *Culture and Poverty.* Chicago: University of Chicago Press.

Some Neglected Aspects of Negro Class Comparisons

SIDNEY KRONUS

The Negro middle class has long been an analytic category used by students of race relations. However, the defining criteria used to identify this class have been varied and even loose at times. E. Franklin Frazier, the best known student of the Negro middle class, defined it very broadly. When he spoke of the occupational base of the black bourgeoisie, he discussed a range from physicians and lawyers, through officials and clerks, down to and including craftsmen and mail carriers.[1] In terms of family income, Frazier used the 1949 figure for the North and West of $2,500 per year as a minimum and stated that the majority of the black bourgeoisie earned between $3,000 and $4,000 per year.[2] Frazier's definition thus covered both blue-collar and white-collar workers.

Drake and Cayton did not define middle-class status in socioeconomic terms; rather, they based their definition on life style and standard of living. In discussing the middle-class style of life, they stated:

> . . . neither occupation nor income is, in the final analysis, the decisive measuring rod. Rather, the middle class is marked off from the lower class by a pattern of behavior expressed in stable family and associational relationships, in great concern for "front" and "respectability" and in a drive for "getting ahead." All this finds an objective measure in standard of living—the way people spend their money, and in public behavior.[3]

[1] E. Franklin Frazier, *Black Bourgeoisie* (New York, 1957), p. 47.

[2] *Ibid.,* p. 43.

[3] St. Claire Drake and Horace Cayton, *Black Metropolis* (New York, 1945), pp. 661–62.

Gunnar Myrdal in *An American Dilemma* also used the criteria of striving and general standards of behavior rather than delineating occupational and income requirements for middle-class status.[4] Finally, Nathan Hare felt that socioeconomic position was not germane to an analysis of the Black Anglo-Saxons.[5]

Clearly, the earlier treatments have not found it useful to make the socioeconomic differentiations within higher groups conventional in analyzing whites. Perhaps this was appropriate in an earlier era, when the Negro socioeconomic order was much more homogeneous. In any case, a contrary position shall be taken here, suggesting that given any of the criteria of earlier writers which shall be developed, the blue-collar, stably employed Negroes are sufficiently different from the white-collar so that combining the two in one category masks some very important distinctions. Blue-collar Negroes should be viewed as a distinct entity, not middle class and also not lower class, a term which shall be reserved for the unemployed or sporadically employed, poverty-stricken, unstable bottom stratum of the Negro population. The label *working class* is much better suited for the blue-collar Negroes than is *middle class*.

The case for this class distinction rests on a number of theoretical bases. Max Weber, in his discussion of the determinants of class-situation, suggested three criteria based on market situation.

> We may speak of a "class" when (1) a number of people have in common a specific causal component of their life chances, in so far as (2) this component is represented exclusively by economic interests in the possession of goods and opportunities for income, and (3) is represented under the conditions of the commodity or labor markets.[6]

These determinants are somewhat in line with Frazier's definition, but, beyond these, one can add the additional criteria of classes as collectivities of "people who have a sense of solidarity by virtue of sharing common values and who have acquired an attendant sense of moral obligations to fulfill role-expectations."[7] This sense of values and role expectations reflects the positions of Myrdal and Drake and Cayton. The

[4] Gunnar Myrdal, *An American Dilemma* (New York, 1944), p. 704.

[5] Nathan Hare, *The Black Anglo-Saxons* (New York, 1965), *passim.*, but especially p. 15.

[6] Max Weber, *Essays in Sociology*, trans. with an introduction by Hans H. Gerth and C. Wright Mills (New York, 1958), p. 181. Although Weber makes clear distinctions between class and status, it is extremely difficult to operate empirically and even theoretically without enmeshing the two. The reason, of course, is that education is a very powerful determinant of market position and tastes and values. Therefore, class and status really are combined in this paper and called class. This is surely not incompatible given that both concepts rest upon the common base of education.

[7] Robert K. Merton, *Social Theory and Social Structure* (New York, 1957), p. 299.

combination of these criteria with a third, namely, class consciousness—a
term which shall be taken only in the singular sense of class identification
and not the rigorous sense in which Ossowski uses it[8]—gives a more comprehensive definition than has been used in the past. Using this definition, it shall be shown that there are major differences between the
white-collar and blue-collar groups in the Negro community.

These differences are based upon the factors of social change which
have been operating in the Negro community during recent years. Beginning during the Second World War and continuing through to the present
time, Negroes, especially those outside of the South, have made substantial gains toward the condition of equality as compared to the pre-war
situation of Negroes.[9] Previous restrictions in housing, education, and
employment have been lifted through legal channels. As a result, Negroes are more able to differentiate among themselves than they were
two or three decades ago. The differentiation has proceeded to such an
extent in white America that many writers feel class lines are blurring.[10]
Although there may be some blurring of class lines in the Negro community, one may expect to find meaningful differences between the
blue-collar and the white-collar segments of it. This proposition shall be
investigated for the six areas of socioeconomic status, family life, religion, consumption patterns, political participation and interracial feelings.

[8] Stanislaw Ossowski, "Different Concepts of Social Class," in *Class, Status, and
Power*, ed. Reinhard Bendix and S. M. Lipset (New York, 1966), p. 92.

[9] This is not to say that Negroes have advanced greatly in relation to whites in the
areas of education, occupation, and income. Indeed, compared to whites, gains by
Negroes have been at best minimal. See Peter M. Blau and Otis Dudley Duncan, *The
American Occupational Structure* (New York, 1967), pp. 207–83.

[10] The effects of industrialization on class distinction in white America first brought
to the attention of social scientists by Harold Lasswell in *Politics: Who Gets What,
When, How* (Cleveland, 1936), p. 17:

> The lesser middle class is composed of those who exercise skills which are re-
> quired by modest money returns. Hence the class comprises small farmers,
> small businessmen, low salaried professional people, skilled workers and crafts-
> men. The manual workers are those who have acquired little skill; they are the
> true proletariat. The line between plutocracy, lesser bourgeoisie, and proletariat
> is a matter of acrimonious debate in practical politics, and of great uncertainty
> among scientists.

Recently, Harold Wilensky and Charles Lebeaux have taken a similar position in
Industrial Society and Social Welfare (New York, 1965), pp. xxvi-xxvii, where they
state:

> The lines between the upper-working class and the lower-middle class—between
> the mass of foremen, craftsmen, and high-paid operatives, on the one hand, and
> the mass of clerks, salesmen, small entrepreneurs, managers with a few subor-
> dinates, semi-professionals, semi-technical people, on the other—these lines are
> blurring.

METHOD

The sample was designed to approximate an area probability sample stratified by occupation. It consists of 60 Negro males employed in white-collar positions and 20 Negro males employed in blue-collar occupations. The respondents were chosen from the Chatham community area of Chicago.[11] The information presented below was collected by three Negro females using an extensive interview schedule, one taking approximately three hours to administer.

The white-collar group consisted of 17 professionals, 7 semi-professionals (5 public school teachers and 2 social workers), 5 proprietors, 13 managers and supervisors, and 18 clerical and sales personnel. Their ages ranged from 21 to 61 years, with a median of 42 years. The blue-collar group was comprised of 8 skilled, 6 semi-skilled, and 6 unskilled workers who had been stably employed for at least three years prior to the interview.[12] Their ages ranged from 21 to 62 years, with a median age of 39 years. All of the respondents were heads of households and were either married at the time of the interview or had previously been married.

RESULTS

Class Identification

The first clue to the differences between these groups is given by their class identifications. As the data in Table 1 show, the blue-collar

[11] The following sampling procedure was utilized. The area was bisected into two units, the southernmost containing practically all of the single family dwelling units and the northernmost half containing most of the apartment buildings. A listing was made of the dwellings by house number. Then the sample was drawn from these households; half from the north and half from the south. The interviews were screened as they came in; and if it became apparent that too many old or young persons were being interviewed, or too many clerks and not enough professionals, then the interviewers were instructed to pass up individuals with those characteristics. The interviewers were also instructed to discontinue interviews with manually employed respondents who had not been stably employed for at least three years.

[12] It is obvious that with a large proportion of skilled workers in the blue-collar group and the large proportion of professionals in the white-collar group that the sample is not representative of the occupational structure in the Negro community. Nor is it quite representative of the residential community. The reason for these departures is that a larger original study focused on a comparison of three occupational groups: professionals and proprietors, bureaucratically employed white-collar workers, and blue-collar workers. Although these factors restrict the generalizability of the findings in this paper, the absence of internal differentiation among the white-collar group due to occupational differences in the more detailed study (see Sidney Kronus, "The Negro Middle Class: An Empirical Analysis," unpublished Ph.D. dissertation, Department of Sociology, University of Chicago, 1967), allows the inference that differences found in comparing the white and blue-collar groups are valid.

workers overwhelmingly identify with the working class and do not perceive themselves as bourgeois. The majority of the white-collar group identify themselves as middle class, but a significant proportion (almost two-fifths) also perceive themselves as working class. Therefore, there is a blurring of class lines seen by the actors themselves, but the identifications for each group as a whole are clearly different. It is interesting to note that two individuals, one from each group, identify themselves as upper class. One, a physician with a personal income of over $20,000 per year, and of Haitian parentage, can quite rightly be considered upper class, but the other is a machine operator who earns $7,000 per year, lives in his own house, but does not own an automobile or any other consumption item which would give him feelings of grandeur.

Socioeconomic Status

These groups are occupationally different, whether they are classed as white-collar, blue-collar, or non-manual. In terms of income they also differ considerably. The median personal income of the white-collar group is approximately $9,000 per year as compared to only $6,000 for the blue-collar group. In terms of family income the gap is even wider, with the white-collar workers earning a median income of approximately $15,000 per year as compared to only $9,000 for the manual workers.[13]

Educational attainment differs significantly between these groups also. Of the white-collar group, almost two thirds hold college degrees; of the blue-collar workers, only one person, or 5 percent, can claim a college degree, and two fifths have not been graduated from high school. Since wives can influence the life style of a family as much as husbands, educational backgrounds of the wives were investigated, and again the difference between groups is apparent. Over half of the white-collar wives have been graduated from college, and an additional 35 percent have had some college experience. For the blue-collar group, approximately one third of the wives have had some college training, but only one has received a degree.

In conclusion, it can be said that the blue-collar workers have considerably less education, and earn much less income than the white-collar

---

[13] Since knowledge of central tendency is meaningless without some measure of dispersion, the interquartile ranges of these means are offered.

Income by Occupation

	Personal		Total Family	
	White-Collar	Blue-Collar	White-Collar	Blue-Collar
Median	$ 9,000	$ 6,000	$15,000	$ 9,000
P 75	$12,000	$ 7,500	$19,000	$12,000
P 25	$ 8,000	$ 5,500	$12,000	$ 6,500

TABLE 1

Percentage Distribution of Class Identification by Occupation

	White-Collar	Blue-Collar
	Percentage	Percentage
Upper Class	2	5
Middle Class*	55	22
Working Class*	38	75
Lower Class	—	—
Would not class himself	5	—
TOTAL	100	100
N =	(60)	(20)

* $X^2 = 6.7$, 2 d.f. $p < .05$, comparing just middle-class and lower-class identification.

workers. Thus in terms of their market-determined class situation, these groups fit the classic pattern of clear distinctions.

Family Patterns

One area of social life in which the blue-collar workers correspond most closely to the white-collar group is that of family patterns. Both groups report about the same proportion of marital dissolution (25 percent) and they show similar patterns of fertility, with three fourths of both having two children or less. Their color preferences for females are also similar. Two fifths of each group married females of the same color shade as themselves, and two fifths married lighter-colored females. Only one fifth of each group married women of a darker shade than themselves, indicating that the preference for lighter-colored females is prevalent in both the white-collar and the blue-collar strata.

Religion

Earlier descriptions of the Negro community indicate that religion is practiced differently by the lower class and the middle class. To the lower class, religion is a very expressive and emotion-laden activity, characterized by individuals "flailing their arms about, crying, running up and down the aisles, yelling *Amen* and *Hallelujah*."[14] For the middle class it is more staid; instead of stirring emotions, the quality of the classic religious music and the sober message given by the minister give the congregation a very orderly and subdued appearance. The fundamentalist expressive behavior is attributable to Baptist affiliation especially, but also to Methodist.[15] Looking at the religious affiliations of these

[14] Drake and Cayton, *op. cit.*, p. 621.
[15] *Ibid.*, p. 612.

TABLE 2

Percentage Distribution of Religious Affiliation by Occupation

	White-Collar	Blue-Collar
	Percentage	Percentage
Catholic	18	5
Methodist	13	10
Episcopalian	7	5
Baptist*	13	45
Congregationalist	5	5
Presbyterian	7	10
Protestant, no denomination	8	—
Muslim	2	—
Jehovah's Witness	—	5
No affiliation	27	15
Total	100	100
N =	(60)	(20)

* $X^2 = 9.0$, 3 d.f. $p < .05$ comparing Baptist vs. other vs. no affiliation.

groups (Table 2) shows that the blue-collar group more closely fits the lower-class description.

These data show that more blue-collar workers belong to the Baptist Church (lower status) and fewer are Catholic (higher status). It is interesting that one of the white-collar workers claims Muslim affiliation, which is usually associated with the lower class.[16] However, this person cannot be considered a "good Muslim" as he drinks alcoholic beverages and attends parties, both of which are taboo behavior for the Black Muslims.

Overall, the blue-collar group does not have the status in religious affiliation that would characterize it as middle class, yet some element of "middle-classness" is present. Approximately one fifth of the white-collar group had changed their religion and the majority of these religious changes were from Baptist to some higher status religion. This is also the case for the blue-collar group. The 20 percent who changed their religion changed from Baptist to a higher status religion. The reasons for the changes were the same as those given for the white-collar group, namely, the religion of the wife. The male married up in status and changed to the higher status religion of the wife. In one case, the change was prompted by another middle-class aspiration, that of providing a good education for their children. A forty-nine-year-old pullman porter changed his religion from Baptist to Catholic because of the "cooperation of pa-

16 E. U. Essien-Udom, *Black Nationalism* (Chicago, 1962), pp. 201–12; and C. Eric Lincoln, *The Black Muslims in America* (Boston, 1961), pp. 48–49.

rochial teachers and school officials that you can't receive as a Negro from the public school." (Case No. 77)

In general, however, the blue-collar segment does not resemble the middle-class in religious affiliation. In addition to the differences in types of affiliation, there is also a difference in the percentages reporting no religion. If one interprets the lack of religious affiliation as a rational secularizing trait, then the white-collar group must be considered slightly more secular, with over one fourth reporting no religion as compared to 15 percent of the blue-collar group.

Consumption Patterns

Since many students of race relations and class structure define middle-class status in terms of standard and style of living, consumption behavior is a critical comparison to make in order to classify blue-collar workers as middle class. The expectation is that although there may be many similarities between white- and blue-collar workers in this area, there should be major differences that stem from the differing educational backgrounds of these groups.

Considering the financial management aspect of consumption behavior, the blue-collar group in fact presents an element of middle-class striving. A close comparison of the credit purchasing and saving patterns of the two groups showed no appreciable differences. Also the blue-collar group's consumption of mass media in newspaper reading, radio listening, and television viewing was similar to that of the white-collar group. However, educational differences, it could be argued, are mirrored in the differing magazine reading habits of these two groups. (See Table 3)

It is apparent that the blue-collar group reads fewer magazines than the white-collar group, as two fifths of them read none as compared to only 5 percent of the white-collar group. In addition to the difference in frequency, there are also important differences by type. Four out of five persons in the white-collar category read news magazines regularly in contrast to only two out of five in the blue-collar group. Also, almost one third of the white-collar workers read technical and professional journals compared to only one person doing so in the blue-collar group.

The differences in educational background also influence differential participation in the cultural activities of these groups. These data (Table 4) show that in no area does the blue-collar group compare favorably with the white, except perhaps in the attendance of jazz concerts.

The two major expensive items of consumption, housing and transportation, were investigated but no meaningful differences were found between the groups in terms of size of dwelling unit or in number and type of automobile(s). However, the very fact that there were no differences implies that the blue-collar workers must be spending a greater proportion of their incomes for these items than the white, given the mean fam-

TABLE 3

*Percentage Distribution of Types of Magazines Read Regularly by Occupation**

	White-Collar	Blue-Collar
	Percentage	Percentage
None**	5	40
Sports	3	15
News	80	40
Family	17	25
Male (white)	25	10
Negro (*Ebony, Jet*, etc.)	63	55
Technical and Professional	32	5
N = ...	(60)	(20)

* Percentages add up to more than 100 because of multiple response.

** $X^2 = 7.1$, 2 d.f. $p < .05$ comparing None vs. Some.

ily income gap of $6,000 per year between these groups. Therefore, it can be concluded that blue-collar Negroes consume a greater part of their spendable income on major material items than do middle-class Negroes. This leads to the conclusion that either the manual workers experience greater indebtedness than the non-manual or that consumer expenditures in other areas differ between these groups.

Finally, these groups responded similarly on the specific item of drinking behavior and for leisure time activities in general. It appears that the blue-collar group is slightly less "respectable" than the white, as 35 percent of them report engaging in the activities of nightclubbing, partying, and playing cards once a week or more as compared to one fourth of the white-collar men.

TABLE 4

*Percentage Distribution of Participation in Cultural Activities (More Than Once or Twice Per Year) by Occupation**

	White-Collar	Blue-Collar
	Percentage	Percentage
Classical Music Concerts	45	10
Jazz Concerts	60	50
Theaters	83	35
Lectures	52	40
Museums	73	45
Reading Books	88	45
N = ...	(60)	(20)

* Percentages add up to more than 100 because of multiple response.

TABLE 5

Percentage Distribution of Party Affiliation by Occupation

	White-Collar	Blue-Collar
	Percentage	Percentage
None	5	—
Democratic*	47	85
Republican	3	5
Independent	45	10
Total	100	100
	(60)	(20)

* $X^2 = 7.8$ d.f. p $<$ .50 comparing Democratic vs. other.

In sum, although there is a good deal of similarity between these groups in terms of consumption behavior, differences are evident, largely due to the lower educational and income levels of the blue-collar workers.

Political Attitudes and Participation

The primary emphasis of this section will be on the degree of acquiescence to the Democratic political organization evidenced by the blue-collar group. James Q. Wilson's study of Negro politics in Chicago indicates that middle-class Negroes express a great deal of independence from the Chicago Democratic political organization.[17] They tend to vote independently, split their tickets, and support machine-opposing candidates for public office. In contrast, the Negro lower class is almost completely controlled and dominated by the Democratic political interests, as evidenced by large voter turnouts and a greater degree of straight-ticket Democratic voting.

The data on party affiliation (See Table 5) reveal that the blue-collar group is much more closely allied with the Democratic party than are the white-collar workers, with 85 percent claiming Democratic affiliation in contrast with less than half of the white-collar group. In terms of interest in politics and voting, both groups appear to take their citizenship seriously, for over 90 percent of each group reported that they voted in the 1964 elections and more than 80 percent of each group professed high interest in the 1964 campaigns.[18] Although their professed interest and voting turnout is similar, from the differences in affiliation very different voting patterns would have been expected. (See Table 6)

It is apparent that the majority of the blue-collar workers have suc-

[17] James Q. Wilson, *Negro Politics* (New York, 1960), p. 67.
[18] *Ibid.*, pp. 21–77.

TABLE 6

*Percentage Distribution of Voting Preferences in the 1964
Elections by Occupation*

	White-Collar	Blue-Collar
	Percentage	Percentage
Straight ticket, Democratic*	23	65
Straight ticket, Republican	—	—
Split ticket, mostly Democratic	60	15
Split ticket, mostly Republican	—	5
Independent	12	5
Did not vote	5	10
Total	100	100
N = ...	(60)	(20)

* $X^2 = 10.6$, 2 d.f. $p < .05$ comparing straight ticket Democratic with other.

cumbed to the Democratic party's influence, as almost two thirds of them voted the straight Democratic party ticket and only one person voted strictly independent. In contrast, almost three fourths of the white-collar workers voted on a split ticket, independent basis. Therefore in terms of voting behavior it must be concluded that the blue-collar group resembles lower-class Negroes more than middle-class Negroes in Chicago.

Finally in the realm of political action, one can include participation in civic and political voluntary organizations as indicative of political interest and sophistication. Here, also, the blue-collar workers do not resemble the white-collar group. Fully four fifths, or 80 percent, of the blue-collar group do not belong to or attend any voluntary organizations as compared to only 22 percent of the white. And, of the four individuals that hold memberships in organizations, all hold them in social and religious organizations, not in civic or political clubs. In contrast, over 40 percent of the white-collar group belong to and attend civic and political organizations regularly.

Perhaps more significant is the fact that in the crucial area of civil rights, one half of the blue-collar group do not participate in any way. Even more striking is the finding that of the ten people who have done something, nine have limited their involvement to monetary contributions only. The lone active participant was active in Cleveland before moving to Chicago and has not resumed any sort of active participation since his move. This minimal involvement in civil rights by the blue-collar group stands in striking contrast to the high level of support for civil rights given by the white-collar respondents. Fully three fourths of the white-collar group have contributed to the movement; one third with financial donations and fully 40 percent with physical activity—marching,

	White-Collar	Blue-Collar
	Percentage	Percentage
None	22	30
Yes, toward particular whites*	27	5
Yes, toward whites in general	51	65
Total	100	100
N = ...	(60)	(20)

* $X^2 = 3.9$, 2 d.f. $p < .05$ comparing particular vs. general hostility.

demonstrating, and picketing. From these comparisons, it is evident that the blue-collar group comes off a poor second best in the realms of politics and civil rights.

Interracial Attitudes

The studies that have investigated the interracial attitudes of Negroes, or attitudes of Negroes toward whites by social class, are consistent in that they show that lower-class Negroes possess stronger anti-white feelings than middle-class Negroes.[19] This study found no differences in both groups' desires to work for or with, and live with whites. Yet, this does not mean that they feel the same about whites, as there are other aspects of the issue to be considered. In order to gain greater depth of response in this area, the respondents were asked if they ever felt hostility toward particular whites or whites in general. (See Table 7)

These data show that as a whole the blue-collar group feels slightly more hostile toward whites than does the white-collar group; but even more interesting is that their hostility is more of a general nature, focusing on whites as a group rather than on any specific persons. For the white-collar group, specific hostility was felt most toward co-workers and secondly toward whites in sales and service positions. Since the apparent difference between these groups is qualitative, specific versus general hostility, the explanation could lie in the amount and intensity of interracial contact between these groups. One possible hypothesis would be that those who have had contact with specific whites would be more prone to hold hostility toward a particular individual while those with less interpersonal contact would possess generalized feelings of anti-

[19] Robin Williams, *Strangers Next Door* (Englewood Cliffs, 1964), p. 260; Frank B. Westie and D. H. Howard, "Social Status Differentials and the Race Attitudes of Negroes," *American Sociological Review*, XIX (January, 1954), 584–91; and T. C. Cothran, "Negro Conceptions of White People," *American Journal of Sociology*, LVI (March, 1951), 458–67.

white hostility. Table 8 presents information concerning the interracial contact of these groups.

The comparison of interracial contact in Table 8 shows striking differences between these groups. The only area where interracial contact is frequent for both groups is that of the work setting. In all other comparisons, the white-collar workers have significantly more contact with whites than do the blue. Therefore, the contention is supported that the

TABLE 8

*Percentage Distribution of Interracial Contacts in the Home, at Place of Work, at Parties, in Voluntary Organizations and While in School, by Occupation**

	White-Collar	Blue-Collar
	Percentage	Percentage
Contact in the Home		
None	38	75
Some**	62	25
Total	100	100
N =	(60)	(20)
Contact at place of work		
None	2	—
Some	98	100
Total	100	100
N =	(60)	(20)
Contact at parties		
None	17	70
Some	83	30
Total	100	100
N =	(60)	(20)
Contact in Voluntary Organizations		
None	38	95
Some	59	5
No information	3	—
Total	100	100
N =	(60)	(20)
Contact while in school		
None	22	65
Some	78	35
Total	100	100
N =	(60)	(20)

* All chi square values $p < .05$, 2 d.f. except in comparison of contact at place of work where $X^2 = $ n.s.

** "Some" contact is defined as occurring at least once per month.

group with the higher interpersonal contact, namely the white-collar workers, hold stronger specific anti-white feelings, and the blue-collar group, who have only minimal contact outside the sphere of work, feel the greatest amount of generalized anti-white hostility.

The significant question of whether the type of hostility, general or specific, has any impact on the desirability of more contact with whites can be asked. From the data it is fairly clear that it does not, as three fourths of each group do not want more contact. The remainder of each group (25%) want to increase social contact with whites to create greater understanding between the races.

Finally, the realm of discrimination by whites, both objective and perceived, was investigated to see if any differences existed between these groups. This effort proved fruitless, for objective descriptions of instances of discrimination were reported by all of the respondents regardless of occupation. Perceived discrimination, as measured by a graded scale from very little to a great deal, also revealed no differences between these groups.

To delineate completely the configurations affecting anti-white feelings among Negroes is a difficult task, but from these modest efforts, it can be concluded that in the area of interracial sentiments, the blue-collar workers feel more hostile toward whites in general than the white-collar group. This feeling stems from fewer interracial contacts where specific targets of hostility are available.

DISCUSSION

In this paper an attempt has been made to draw a comparison between white-collar Negroes and stably employed blue-collar Negroes to see if the blue-collar segment is truly part of the Negro middle class or is a separate entity. In the strictest sense of occupational, educational, and income lines of demarcation, the blue-collar group falls far below the white-collar group. As a consequence of these differences, there are major disparities between these groups in certain areas such as cultural style of life, although not in the consumption of durable goods. The family patterns of the two groups are similar; but their religious behavior is quite different, with the blue-collar group resembling the lower class. Differences in political life and interracial sentiments are easily traceable to less education, lack of sophistication, and less integration with the white community rather than to any intrinsic ideological position. In short, there are meaningful differences between blue-collar and white-collar Negroes. Therefore, on the basis of such differences, it is proposed that the blue-collar, stably employed stratum of the Negro community should be conceptualized as a distinct analytical social category located between the middle and lower classes.

Although this group would be analytically separate from the middle class, they are much closer to the middle class than to the lower class in the areas of market situation, shared value orientations, and class identification. One has but to compare these data with the lucid descriptions of the lower class given by Drake and Cayton, Moynihan, and Caplovitz[20] to see that just the fact of their stable employment sets the blue-collar workers far apart from lower-class Negroes, with their insecure economic position, lack of primary group ties, large family patterns, and an almost total loss of the many rewards and gratifications that American society has to offer.

[20] Drake and Cayton, *op. cit.*, pp. 563–658; Daniel Patrick Moynihan, *The Negro Family: The Case for National Action* (Washington, March, 1965); David Caplovitz, *The Poor Pay More* (New York: The Free Press of Glencoe, 1963).

Sex Differences in Attitudes Toward Black Consciousness and Integration Among Southern Black College Students

EDGAR G. EPPS

This paper is concerned with the extent to which black males and females differ in their acceptance of the ideology of black consciousness and their desire for integration with whites. Students of political attitudes (Levitt 1967; Robinson, *et al.* 1968) have usually found that compared to men, women in America are less interested in politics, but tend to be more moralistic, more conservative and less militaristic. If this same pattern exists among Black Americans, we would hypothesize that black male college students are more favorably inclined toward ideas like "Black Power," militancy and separatism than black female college students. On the other hand, we would expect black females to be more inclined than males to accept the more "conservative" non-militant integrationist ideology.

One author (Lasch 1969: 166) has suggested that the Black Power movement is likely to appeal more to the black male than to the black female because it represents a way for the male to rebel against the female-dominated family. Another argument is based on the notion that the caste system has favored the black female over the black male in everything from sexual opportunities to job opportunities (Dollard 1957). Since the system has (allegedly) taken a greater toll on the black male's self-image and self-respect, he is expected to be more involved in the assertive movement to enhance his black identity.

Other studies emphasize differences in the attitudes and value orientations of black and white females. "The image of Negro women invoked by sociologists and community practitioners is most often that of 'matriarch'" (Noble 1966). It is argued that the pressures of the social system have resulted in a sex-role identity pattern in which black women are more dominant and aggressive than white women. It has also been observed that the motivations and aspirations expressed by black women follow a different pattern from those expressed by white women (Lott and Lott 1963; Weston and Mednick 1969). Such comparisons usually conclude that black women's attitudes and values are more "masculine" (liberated) than those of white women. Hypotheses based on this line of argument would lead us to expect few differences in the political attitudes of male and female black college students.

Recently, several authors have seriously questioned the existence of the matriarchy (Hyman and Reed 1969), the scholarship which led to its acceptance in the literature (Billingsley 1968), and its utility as a predictor variable (Rosen 1969). They argue that there is insufficient evidence to warrant the widespread acceptance of the matriarchal concept. The assumption one would draw from these authors is that black women in America are less different from their white counterparts than has been commonly assumed. If there is a matriarchy in America, it is an *American* characteristic rather than a black characteristic. Following this line of reasoning, we would hypothesize that black women should be less militant and more conservative than their men.

One recent study (McCord and Howard 1969) has compared the attitudes of black males and females on several relevant questions. Generally, males and females in Watts and Houston are in agreement about the main problems facing black people, the speed of integration, and the means that should be used to fight the white establishment. The one area of disagreement in these samples was that males more often approved of the use of violence. On the basis of these results, it seemed most appropriate to hypothesize that the college men and women in this sample would respond in a manner similar to the urban adults in McCord's study. Our research hypothesis, therefore, is as follows: *There are no significant differences in the responses of male and female students attending a southern black college to questions concerning racial strategies with the exception of those involving the use of violence.*

METHODOLOGY

The data for this paper were collected as part of the 1968 Tuskegee Area Study. The sample consisted of randomly selected students of Tuskegee

Institute. From the list of all students enrolled as of the first semester, 1967, every fifth name was taken. This gave a total of 600 names. Of this 600, 145 students could not be located. In a large number of cases, these were people who had dropped out of school by the start of the second semester when interviewing began. A smaller number could not be contacted because they had moved from the address given in the student directory; 45 other students were not interviewed. Of these 3 refused. The other 42 either were not contacted or could not work out a time with the interviewer. All told, 410 students of the original 600 were interviewed. Females and freshmen are over-represented in the sample as compared to their proportions in Tuskegee's total enrollment.

The interviewing was done by a class of 40 Tuskegee students. The instrument used was an interview schedule consisting of over 100 questions designed to obtain data on students' social background, and attitudes toward Tuskegee Institute, political issues, and black consciousness. As part of a larger study (Friedman, *et al.* 1970), responses to questions on integration and black consciousness were used to construct an integration scale and a black consciousness scale. Scale scores were not constructed for persons with missing data on any item. Thus, of the 410 students in our sample, scores for both scales were obtained for 398 students: 163 males and 235 females.

The Attitude toward Integration Scale was constructed from four items: (1) What percent of the Tuskegee Institute student body should be white? (2) Have you ever taken part in civil rights activities? (3) Which organization, NAACP, SCLC or SNCC most closely represents your position on civil rights? (4) Should people of our race work for nationalism or integration? The integration scale scores ranged from 0–6. Persons with scale scores 0–4 (54 percent) were categorized as being Low on the Integration Scale. Those with scale scores of 5–6 (46 percent) were classified as being High on Integration.

The Black Consciousness Scale was constructed from five items: (1) Which country do you consider your ancestors to be from? (2) How do you rate Stokely Carmichael as a leader? (3) Would you wear an Afro? (4) Has Black Power helped or hurt black people? (5) How do you feel about being called black (Negro, colored, etc.)? The Black Consciousness Scale Scores ranged from −1 to 7. Persons with scores of −1 to 3 (49 percent) were categorized as being Low on Black Consciousness; those with scores of 4–7 (51 percent) were classified as being High on Black Consciousness.

Assuming theoretical independence of Orientation toward Integration and Black Consciousness, a typology was constructed using the High-Low categorizations on each scale. The typology utilized four categories of racial orientation: (1) Assimilationist; (2) Cultural Pluralist; (3) Tradi-

Typology Based on Black Consciousness and Favorableness to Integration

Black Consciousness	Favorableness to Integration	
	High	*Low*
Low	Assimilationist (1)	Traditional Separatist (3)
High	Cultural Pluralist (2)	Nationalistic Separatist (4)

tional Separatist; (4) Nationalistic Separatist. Table 1 illustrates the typology.

In this conceptualization, *Assimilationists* are viewed as those Black Americans who want to submerge their African heritage and become merged into a color-blind, melting pot society. *Cultural Pluralists* are described as individuals who want to be integrally involved in the basic institutions of American society (economic, political, etc.) while maintaining their unique group identity. Like DuBois, they wish to make it possible for a man to be both a black man and an American. *Nationalistic Separatists* want to celebrate their blackness while opting out of the white society; they agree with Malcolm X that when one pours cream into coffee one makes it weak. Their goal is physical separation of the races and black control of black institutions. The final category, given the label *Traditional Separatists,* is reserved for those persons in the black population who are eager neither to advertise their blackness nor to compete with whites; they do not participate emotionally or literally in either the black awareness or the civil rights movements. They are willing to accept the *status quo* without overt resistance. In accord with the major hypothesis, it is expected that females will be more *assimilationist* in their orientations and that males will be more *nationalistic.*

Males and females were also compared on the individual items in the two scales and on other relevant items. The examination of differences and similarities on individual items helps to provide a more complete understanding of the relationship of sex to racial attitudes in this sample. Chi square was used as the test of significance in all comparisons.

RESULTS

Typology

The results by sex for black consciousness, orientation toward integration, and the typology are given in Table 2. As expected, males are signifi-

TABLE 2

Comparisons of Males and Females on Attitude Toward Integration, Black Consciousness and Typology

	Males	Females
A. Black Consciousness Scale	(N = 163)	(N = 235)
High	66	38
Low	34	62
Total	100%	100%
$\chi^2 = 29.44$, P < .001		
B. Integration Scale		
High	54	54
Low	46	46
Total	100%	100%
C. Black Consciousness—Integration Typology		
Assimilationist	23	38
Cultural Pluralist	31	16
Traditional Separatist	12	23
Nationalistic Separatist	34	22
Total	100%	100%
$\chi^2 = 29.62$, P < .001		

cantly more likely than females to have high black consciousness scores. Sixty-six percent of the males are high scorers on the Black Consciousness Scale as compared to only 38 percent of the females. The results also indicate, however, that males and females do not differ on orientation to integration. The typology further illustrates the difference between the sexes. It shows that males are most often nationalistic separatists or cultural pluralists while females are most likely to be assimilationists. If we assume that these categories are rank ordered in terms of racial aggressiveness, the results support our overall hypothesis that all males are more likely to support strategies that involve violence.

Orientation to Integration

Male and female responses to individual questions pertaining to favorableness toward integration were also examined. Students were asked: "What percent of Tuskegee Institute students should be white?" Males and females differed very little in their responses to this question. Females were a little more likely to endorse a high percent of white students, but the difference was not significant. Males and females also did not differ when asked whether black people should be working for integration or for black nationalism. More than three-fourths of both sexes selected integration. There were, however, significant differences on two questions. One of these asked if the student had ever taken part in civil rights activities. Males were more likely to say they had been involved in such activities

(P $<$ .001). The other item which yielded a significant sex difference asked respondents "Which organization most closely represents your position on civil rights?" In choosing between the NAACP, SCLC, and SNCC, females were more likely to choose the NAACP (although a majority of both sexes chose this organization). Males were over-represented among the respondents who selected SNCC. The response pattern which resulted from this analysis indicates that males are more likely than females to act aggressively (take part in civil rights activities) and to endorse the organization with the most aggressive civil rights stance.

Black Consciousness

Significant differences between males and females were found on responses to three of the five Black Consciousness items. Two of these items are related to the respondent's attitude toward violence. Students were asked to rate Stokely Carmichael (a leader whose name is associated with a willingness to accept violent strategies) as a leader. Males were significantly more likely than females to give Carmichael a rating of "good." Females were more likely to consider him a poor or harmful leader. The Black Power ideology is also associated with willingness to accept violent strategies. Again males were more likely than females to say that use of the phrase Black Power has helped black people. A majority of both sexes said that Black Power had helped, but the proportion selecting this response was significantly larger for males.

Two items in this scale are more concerned with acceptance of the African heritage than with the aggressiveness of civil rights strategies. On one of these, male responses differed considerably from those of females. Males were much more likely to say they would wear the Afro hair style than females. This is understandable because the new hair style requires a greater break with tradition for females than for males.

Endorsement of Violence

When students were asked "Do you believe in non-violence?" females, as expected, were more likely to say yes to this statement (80 percent as compared to 61 percent). We also asked respondents if they thought the riots in Newark and Detroit had helped or hurt the black cause. Sixty-six percent of male students as compared to 49 percent of female students said that the riots had helped. Another indirect item asked students to select either Stokely Carmichael, Martin Luther King or someone else as their most admired leader. The majority of students of both sexes chose Dr. King, but the difference in proportion selecting him was statistically significant (54 percent of males; 74 percent of females). Students did not differ on the last violence related question. When asked if they thought

Negroes should fight in Viet Nam, slightly more than half of the students of both sexes said no.

DISCUSSION

The results of this study support the results of other research (Lessing 1969; McCord and Howard 1969) which indicate that black males are more likely than black females to endorse violent strategies. These results should not be surprising given the general knowledge that males are more likely to be involved in violent activities (from sports to crime). The results are interesting only in the context of the continuing debate concerning sex-role relations in the black community.

Noble (1966) has pointed out that a number of black women have played important leadership roles in the civil rights movement. The names of Mrs. Rosa Parks, Mrs. Daisy Bates, and Mrs. Gloria Richardson are well known to students of the civil rights movement. Many others could be named. For the most part, however, the national leaders of the movement have been males (King, Carmichael, Wilkins, etc.). It is very significant that the women who played the most active roles in the civil rights movement came to prominence during a period when the focus was on *non-violence*. When the focus changed (in 1965) to a more aggressive stance of striking out at the perceived oppressor, the leadership role of women in the civil rights movement began to decline.

When these data are considered in conjunction with the research of Hyman and Reed (1969), the whole question of the alleged dominant role of women in the black community must be seriously questioned. It is also interesting to note how little empirical support there is for the commonly accepted folklore that black women are more successful occupationally and educationally than black men. While more black females than males have completed high school and (until recently) college, males are much more likely to hold advanced degrees and high level professional occupations (Noble 1966: 534). The fact that 75 percent of non-white poor families are headed by females leaves no doubt about the relative income of black males and females. The conclusion that must be drawn from all of this is that the status of black males is superior to that of black females especially when they have the same level of educational attainment. Another conclusion that may be drawn is that the same types of generalizations that are made when comparing the political participation of white American males and females would generally hold true for comparisons involving Black American males and females. One example of this is the fact that 74 percent of the males in this study say they are very interested in civil rights as compared to 49 percent of the females.

The implications for the civil rights movement that may be drawn from this study suggest that males will continue to play a dominant role in the movement. The role of women in the movement will probably fluctuate in direct relation to the importance of aggressive confrontation in the ideology of the black revolution.

Finally, a word of caution. The data reported in this study were collected early in 1968. Since that time, there has been a strong shift in the ideology of the black revolution. There is little doubt that a much smaller proportion of Tuskegee Institute students would endorse integration today (1971) than was true three years ago. It is also fairly obvious that a much larger proportion of the students would rate militant leaders favorably today. With this in mind, there is also a distinct possibility that male and female attitudes toward racial violence may be more in conjunction today than they were at the time these data were collected.

REFERENCES

Billingsley, Andrew. 1968. *Black Families in White America*. Englewood Cliffs: Prentice-Hall.

Dollard, John. 1957. *Caste and Class in a Southern Town*. Garden City: Doubleday Anchor.

Friedman, Neil, Agatha White, and Edgar G. Epps. 1971. "Attitudes of Southern Black College Students Toward Black Consciousness and Integration." *Afro-American Studies* 1(January):191–202.

Hyman, Herbert H., and John S. Reed. 1969. " 'Black Matriarchy' Reconsidered: Evidence from Secondary Analysis of Sample Surveys." *Public Opinion Quarterly* 33(Fall): 346–354.

Lasch, Christopher. 1969. *The Agony of the American Left*. New York: Random House.

Lessing, Elise E., and Susan W. Zagorin. 1969. "Some Demographic, Value and Personality Correlates of Endorsement of Negro Militancy by Negro and White Youth." Proceedings, 77th Annual Convention, American Psychological Association: 295–296.

Levitt, Morris. 1967. "The Political Role of American Women." *Journal of Human Relations* 15(First Quarter): 23–35.

Lott, A. J., and Bernice E. Lott. 1963. *Negro and White Youth: A Psychological Study of a Border-State Community*. New York: Holt, Rinehart and Winston.

McCord, William, and John Howard. 1969. "Negro Opinions." Pp. 78–104 in William McCord, John Howard, Bernard Friedberg, and Edwin Harwood (eds.), *Life Styles in the Black Ghetto*. New York: W. W. Norton.

Noble, Jeanne L. 1966. "The American Negro Woman." Pp. 522–547 in John P. Davis (ed.), *The American Negro Reference Book*. Englewood Cliffs: Prentice-Hall.

Robinson, John P., Jerrold G. Rusk and Kendra B. Head. 1968. *Measures of Political Attitudes*. Ann Arbor: Survey Research Center.

Rosen, Lawrence. 1969. "Matriarchy and Lower Class Negro Male Delinquency." *Social Problems* 17(Fall): 175–189.

Weston, Peter J., and Martha T. Mednick. 1970. "Race, Social Class and the Motive to Avoid Success in Women," *Journal of Cross-Cultural Psychology* 1(September):284–291.

3.

Institutional Perspectives: Effects of Racism on Black Americans

B. PERSPECTIVES ON THE POLITICAL PROCESS AND BLACK AMERICANS

The last section of this book brings together a set of articles which focus on the political aspects of the Black Revolution. The word political is used in the sense of struggle for power rather than in the sense of electoral politics. Therefore, the book virtually ignores the gains made by blacks in recent elections and focuses on the ideological aspects of the black struggle for political power instead of including articles which would provide an accounting of the electoral victories. The article on Newark, however, provides a vivid illustration of the problems associated with black political control in large cities.

The concept of colonialism has gained favor as an analytic tool considered to be useful in explaining the condition of the black man in America. Traditionally used to describe relations between European nations and the "dependencies" over which they maintained political and economic control, this concept is now being used to analyze relations between the ghetto and the white power structure. Robert Blauner discusses the potential utility of this concept noting the similarities and differences between the true colonial situation and "ghetto colonialism."

Charles Hamilton, an early advocate of Black Power, describes "The Silent Black Majority" which is not intensely caught up in the ideological aspects of Black Power. But as Stokely Carmichael stated in a speech to a college audience in 1968, "every Negro is a potential black man." At present, however, Hamilton sees working class blacks as hard-working sympathizers, but only occasional participants in the revolutionary aspects of the struggle for liberation. The article by Andrew Hacker paints a dismal picture of the potential for peaceful race relations within the immediate future. Hacker argues that whites will not provide the resources needed to improve social conditions in the ghetto. (He assumes that blacks cannot develop their own resources.) Black discontent, based on the contrast between black and white life styles, will lead to violent conflict, guerrilla warfare, and possibly massive repression.

Hacker sees little reason to assume that white youth will be appreciably less racist than their parents. One way of interpreting this conclusion (which does not agree with opinion poll results in which youth give less prejudiced responses than adults) is that youth will express a belief in equality but as they mature they, like their parents, will attempt to maintain neighborhood segregation and protect their educational and occupational privileges. Another way of expressing the same pessimism is to argue that even if the professed liberalism is honest, the institutions of our society will still operate in such a manner as to encourage discrimination and segregation. In other words, racial practices change when institutions change. Significant institutional change takes place only as a result of conflict between groups competing for economic and political power. Since blacks are not likely to stop pressing for improvements in their power position and whites are not likely to give up power without a struggle, future conflict seems inevitable.

One response to the intransigence of white dominated social institutions is voluntary withdrawal from many aspects of competition. Yuan, in his article in Section Two, referred to this strategy as defensive insulation.

Barbara A. Sizemore presents a comprehensive analysis of separatism, particularly black separatism, as it relates to gaining full participation in American society. She draws parallels between the black minority and other excluded groups—the early immigrant groups, the Irish Catholics, the Amish. She also analyzes the Black Muslim movement within the context of separatism.

Rejecting the "supply and demand" paradigm that permits the inclusion of *individuals* in the mainstream of American life, Mrs. Sizemore presents a five-stage power-inclusion model which is designed to promote social mobility for excluded minority *groups*. What is missing from this analysis is an acknowledgement of the possibility that both individual and group mobility strategies can operate simultaneously and that perhaps the two in combination will be more effective than either strategy alone.

A recurrent theme that permeates the rhetoric of the Black Revolution is the notion that white scholars cannot provide a perspective on race relations that accurately reflects the experiences of blacks. Therefore, black scholars have organized separate professional associations and developed their own journals to provide opportunities for black intellectuals to communicate with each other and develop new (Black) perspectives on the racial situation in America and throughout the world.

One of the most insightful works on black psychology is the essay prepared for this volume by Cedric Clark. His treatment of concepts such as *recognition, respect,* and *legitimacy* is an outstanding example of

the creative thinking which can be brought to bear on a psychological
question where a scholar uses his racial identity in developing his conceptualization of a theoretical paradigm.

Clark presents a cogent argument in support of his contention that
blacks are de-legitimated in America through the denial of recognition
and respect. Only when the activities of blacks are perceived (by whites)
as related to the goals or interests of whites (either positively or negatively) are the activities of Black Americans taken fully into account. As
Clark suggests, the new Black Awareness involves the re-assessment as
well as the redefinition of black behavior. These changes in self-definition
often conflict with white values and white assessments of black behavior,
goals, and values. Thus, there is now an element of "unpredictability" in
race relations (Black Americans no longer know their place). This unpredictability should be a strong force pressing for change in the institutions which have for centuries supported black subordination.

Another frequently expressed concern of black people is that there is a
need for black representation at the policy level. Important decisions
which may have drastic consequences for blacks are usually made without
their knowledge or consent. The article by Stafford and Ladner explores
the relationship between urban planning and racism.

While blacks in cities are becoming geographically more isolated from
whites than ever before, there has been a proliferation of programs designed to change the conditions of ghetto life. Urban renewal and model
cities are two such programs which involve the relatively new discipline
of urban planning. Planners rarely design their programs in such a way
that blacks benefit from them. Institutional supports for the status quo
operate to maintain present patterns of segregated housing, improve
transportation for white commuters, and remove blacks from properties
desired by whites. Today, these programs are increasingly meeting resistance from the black community as awareness of the need for power
through cultural and political unity increases. These authors argue that
urban intervention programs are designed to foster individual social
mobility but that such programs are doomed to failure because they fail
to take into account the necessity for institutional change. The demand
for "black control of black institutions" is increasingly heard in urban
areas as political awareness increases among Black Americans.

The problem of institutional change cannot be solved by control of local
institutions alone. The frustrations of big city mayors illustrate the extent
to which local problems are inextricably connected with larger institutional
structures. Local economic problems are bound to state, national, and international economic operations. Local educational problems are related to
state and federal educational problems. The list could be compiled at
length, but these examples should be sufficient to establish the point that
local control is not enough.

The problems associated with attempting to improve the conditions of black people through black control of local political institutions are described in the article on Mayor Gibson of Newark. Similar problems face blacks in other cities as they attempt to attain equity through the political process.

During the 1970's, blacks will gain political control of other cities and increase their influence in rural areas of the South where they still maintain numerical majorities. Other minorities will also strengthen their political positions as they become increasingly mobilized. The challenge to social scientists, and to policy-makers, is to help the people in these areas mobilize their resources so that they can provide better living conditions for their constituents at the same time they are developing a sense of group identity and group pride. The present trend suggests that minority groups will insist on self-determination with respect to programs, and minority control of institutions serving minority communities. Social scientists can be most helpful by cooperating with minority leaders as they work with their own people through programs based on group cohesion, shared cultural patterns, and group pride, to develop sufficient economic and political power to demand dignity and respect within American society.

Internal Colonialism and Ghetto Revolt

ROBERT BLAUNER

It is becoming almost fashionable to analyze American racial conflict today in terms of the colonial analogy. I shall argue in this paper that the utility of this perspective depends upon a distinction between colonization as a process and colonialism as a social, economic, and political system. It is the experience of colonization that Afro-Americans share with many of the nonwhite people of the world. But this subjugation has taken place in a societal context that differs in important respects from the situation of "classical colonialism." In the body of this essay I shall look at some major developments in black protest—the urban riots, cultural nationalism, and the movement for ghetto control—as collective responses to colonized status. Viewing our domestic situation as a special form of colonization outside a context of a colonial system will help explain some of the dilemmas and ambiguities within these movements.

The present crisis in American life has brought about changes in social perspectives and the questioning of long accepted frameworks. Intellectuals and social scientists have been forced by the pressure of events to look at old definitions of the character of our society, the role of racism, and the workings of basic institutions. The depth and volatility of contemporary racial conflict challenge sociologists in particular to question the adequacy of theoretical models by which we have explained American race relations in the past.

For a long time the distinctiveness of the Negro situation among the ethnic minorities was placed in terms of color, and the systematic discrimination that follows from our deep-seated racial prejudices. This was sometimes called the caste theory, and while provocative, it missed essential and dynamic features of American race relations. In the past ten years there has been a tendency to view Afro-Americans as another ethnic group not basically different in experience from previous ethnics and whose "immigration" condition in the North would in time follow their upward course. The inadequacy of this model is now clear—even the Kerner Report devotes a chapter to criticizing this analogy. A more recent (though hardly new) approach views the essence of racial subordination in economic class terms: black people as an underclass are to a degree specially exploited and to a degree economically dispensable in an automating society. Important as are economic factors, the power of race and racism in America cannot be sufficiently explained through class analysis. Into this theory vacuum steps the model of internal colonialism. Problematic and imprecise as it is, it gives hope of becoming a framework that can integrate the insights of caste and racism, ethnicity, culture, and economic exploitation into an overall conceptual scheme. At the same time, the danger of the colonial model is the imposition of an artificial analogy which might keep us from facing up to the fact (to quote Harold Cruse) that "the American black and white social phenomenon is a uniquely new world thing."[1]

During the late 1950's, identification with African nations and other colonial or formerly colonized peoples grew in importance among black militants.[2] As a result the U.S. was increasingly seen as a colonial power and the concept of domestic colonialism was introduced into the political analysis and rhetoric of militant nationalists. During the same period black social theorists began developing this frame of reference for explaining American realities. As early as 1962, Cruse characterized race relations in this country as "domestic colonialism."[3] Three years later in *Dark Ghetto*, Kenneth Clark demonstrated how the political, economic, and social structure of Harlem was essentially that of a colony.[4] Finally in 1967, a full-blown elaboration of "internal colonialism" provided the theoretical framework for Carmichael and Hamilton's widely read *Black Power*.[5] The following year the colonial analogy gained currency and new "respectability" when Senator McCarthy habitually referred to Black Americans as a colonized people during his campaign. While the rhetoric of internal colonialism was catching on, other social scientists began to raise questions about its appropriateness as a scheme of analysis.

The colonial analysis has been rejected as obscurantist and misleading by scholars who point to the significant differences in history and social-political conditions between our domestic patterns and what took place in Africa and India. Colonialism traditionally refers to the establishment of domination over a geographically external political unit, most often inhabited by people of a different race and culture, where this domination is political and economic, and the colony exists subordinated to and dependent upon the mother country. Typically the colonizers exploit the land,

[1] Harold Cruse, *Rebellion or Revolution* (New York: 1968), p. 214.

[2] Nationalism, including an orientation toward Africa, is no new development. It has been a constant tendency within Afro-American politics. See Cruse, *ibid*, esp. chaps. 5–7.

[3] This was six years before the publication of *The Crisis of the Negro Intellectual*, (New York: Morrow, 1968), which brought Cruse into prominence. Thus the 1962 article was not widely read until its reprinting in Cruse's essays, *Rebellion or Revolution, op. cit.*

[4] Kenneth Clark, *Dark Ghetto* (New York: Harper and Row, 1965). Clark's analysis first appeared a year earlier in *Youth in the Ghetto* (New York: Haryou Associates, 1964).

[5] Stokely Carmichael and Charles Hamilton, *Black Power* (New York: Random House, 1967).

the raw materials, the labor, and other resources of the colonized nation; in addition a formal recognition is given to the difference in power, autonomy, and political status, and various agencies are set up to maintain this subordination. Seemingly the analogy must be stretched beyond usefulness if the American version is to be forced into this model. For here we are talking about group relations within a society; the mother country —colony separation in geography is absent. Though whites certainly colonized the territory of the original Americans, internal colonization of Afro-Americans did not involve the settlement of whites in any land that was unequivocally black. And unlike the colonial situation, there has been no formal recognition of differing power since slavery was abolished outside the South. Classic colonialism involved the control and exploitation of the majority of a nation by a minority of outsiders. Whereas in America the people who are oppressed were themselves originally outsiders and are a numerical minority.

This conventional critique of "internal colonialism" is useful in pointing to the differences between our domestic patterns and the overseas situation. But in its bold attack it tends to lose sight of common experiences that have been historically shared by the most subjugated racial minorities in America and nonwhite peoples in some other parts of the world. For understanding the most dramatic recent developments on the race scene, this common core element—which I shall call colonization—may be more important than the undeniable divergences between the two contexts.

The common features ultimately relate to the fact that the classical colonialism of the imperialist era and American racism developed out of the same historical situation and reflected a common world economic and power stratification. The slave trade for the most part preceded the imperialist partition and economic exploitation of Africa, and in fact may have been a necessary prerequisite for colonial conquest—since it helped deplete and pacify Africa, undermining the resistance to direct occupation. Slavery contributed one of the basic raw materials for the textile industry which provided much of the capital for the West's industrial development and need for economic expansionism. The essential condition for both American slavery and European colonialism was the power domination and the technological superiority of the Western world in its relation to peoples of non-Western and nonwhite origins. This objective supremacy in technology and military power buttressed the West's sense of cultural superiority, laying the basis for racist ideologies that were elaborated to justify control and exploitation of nonwhite people. Thus because classical colonialism and America's internal version developed out of a similar balance of technological, cultural, and power relations, a common *process* of social oppression characterized the racial patterns in the two contexts—despite the variation in political and social structure.

There appear to be four basic components of the colonization complex.

The first refers to how the racial group enters into the dominant society (whether colonial power or not). Colonization begins with a forced, involuntary entry. Second, there is an impact on the culture and social organization of the colonized people which is more than just a result of such "natural" processes as contact and acculturation. The colonizing power carries out a policy which constrains, transforms, or destroys indigenous values, orientations, and ways of life. Third, colonization involves a relationship by which members of the colonized group tend to be administered by representatives of the dominant power. There is an experience of being managed and manipulated by outsiders in terms of ethnic status.

A final fundament of colonization is racism. Racism is a principle of social domination by which a group seen as inferior or different in terms of alleged biological characteristics is exploited, controlled, and oppressed socially and psychically by a superordinate group. Except for the marginal case of Japanese imperialism, the major examples of colonialism have involved the subjugation of nonwhite Asian, African, and Latin American peoples by white European powers. Thus racism has generally accompanied colonialism. Race prejudice can exist without colonization—the experience of Asian-American minorities is a case in point—but racism as a system of domination is part of the complex of colonization.

The concept of colonization stresses the enormous fatefulness of the historical factor, namely the manner in which a minority group becomes a part of the dominant society.[6] The crucial difference between the colonized Americans and their ethnic immigrant minorities is that the latter have always been able to operate fairly competitively within that relatively open section of the social and economic order because these groups came voluntarily in search of a better life, because their movements in society were not administratively controlled, and because they transformed their culture at their own pace—giving up ethnic values and institutions when it was seen as a desirable exchange for improvements in social position.

In present-day America, a major device of black colonization is the powerless ghetto. As Kenneth Clark describes the situation:

> Ghettoes are the consequence of the imposition of external power and the institutionalization of powerlessness. In this respect, they are in fact social, political, educational, and above all—economic colonies. Those confined within the ghetto walls are subject peoples. They are victims of the greed, cruelty, insensitivity, guilt and fear of their masters. . . .
>
> The community can best be described in terms of the analogy of a powerless colony. Its political leadership is divided, and all but one or two of its political leaders are shortsighted and dependent upon the larger

[6] As Eldridge Cleaver reminds us, "Black people are a stolen people held in a colonial status on stolen land, and any analysis which does not acknowledge the colonial status of black people cannot hope to deal with the real problem." "The Land Question," *Ramparts*, 6 (May, 1968), p. 51.

political power structure. Its social agencies are financially precarious and dependent upon sources of support outside the community. Its churches are isolated or dependent. Its economy is dominated by small businesses which are largely owned by absentee owners, and its tenements and other real property are also owned by absentee landlords.

Under a system of centralization, Harlem's schools are controlled by forces outside of the community. Programs and policies are supervised and determined by individuals who do not live in the community . . .[7]

Of course many ethnic groups in America have lived in ghettoes. What make the black ghettoes an expression of colonized status are three special features. First, the ethnic ghettoes arose more from voluntary choice, both in the sense of the choice to immigrate to America and the decision to live among one's fellow ethnics. Second, the immigrant ghettoes tended to be a one and two generation phenomenon; they were actually way-stations in the process of acculturation and assimilation. When they continue to persist as in the case of San Francisco's Chinatown, it is because they are big business for the ethnics themselves and there is a new stream of immigrants. The black ghetto on the other hand has been a more permanent phenomenon, although some individuals do escape it. But most relevant is the third point. European ethnic groups like the Poles, Italians, and Jews generally only experienced a brief period, often less than a generation, during which their residential buildings, commercial stores, and other enterprises were owned by outsiders. The Chinese and Japanese faced handicaps of color prejudice that were almost as strong as the blacks faced, but very soon gained control of their internal communities, because their traditional and ethnic culture and social organization had not been destroyed by slavery and internal colonization. But Afro-Americans are distinct in the extent to which their segregated communities have remained controlled economically, politically, and administratively from the outside. One indicator of this difference is the estimate that the "income of Chinese-Americans from Chinese-owned businesses is in proportion to their numbers 45 times as great as the income of Negroes from Negro owned businesses."[8] But what is true of business is also true for the other social institutions that operate within the ghetto. The educators, policemen, social workers, politicians, and others who administer the affairs of ghetto residents are typically whites who live outside the black community. Thus the ghetto plays a strategic role as the focus for the administration by outsiders which is also essential to the structure of overseas colonialism.[9]

[7] *Youth in the Ghetto, op. cit.*, pp. 10–11; 79–80.

[8] N. Glazer and D. P. Moynihan, *Beyond the Melting Pot* (Cambridge, Mass.: M.I.T., 1963), p. 37.

[9] "When we speak of Negro social disabilities under capitalism, . . . we refer to the fact that he does not own anything—*even what is ownable in his own community.*

The colonial status of the Negro community goes beyond the issue of ownership and decision-making within black neighborhoods. The Afro-American population in most cities has very little influence on the power structure and institutions of the larger metropolis, despite the fact that in numerical terms, blacks tend to be the most sizeable of the various interest groups. A recent analysis of policy-making in Chicago estimates that "Negroes really hold less than 1 percent of the effective power in the Chicago metropolitan area. [Negroes are 20 percent of Cook County's population.] Realistically the power structure of Chicago is hardly less white than that of Mississippi."[10]

Colonization outside of a traditional colonial structure has its own special conditions. The group culture and social structure of the colonized in America is less developed; it is also less autonomous. In addition, the colonized are a numerical minority, and furthermore they are ghettoized more totally and are more dispersed than people under classic colonialism. Though these realities affect the magnitude and direction of response, it is my basic thesis that the most important expressions of protest in the black community during the recent years reflect the colonized status of Afro-America. Riots, programs of separation, politics of community control, the black revolutionary movements, and cultural nationalism each represent a different strategy of attack on domestic colonialism in America. Let us now examine some of these movements.

RIOT OR REVOLT?

The so-called riots are being increasingly recognized as a preliminary if primitive form of mass rebellion against a colonial status. There is still a tendency to absorb their meaning within the conventional scope of as-similation-integration politics: some commentators stress the material

Thus to fight for black liberation *is to fight for his right to own.* The Negro is politically compromised today because he owns nothing. He has little voice in the affairs of state because he owns nothing. The fundamental reason why the Negro bourgeois-democratic revolution has been aborted is because American capitalism has prevented the development of a black class of capitalist owners of institutions and economic tools. To take one crucial example, Negro radicals today are severely hampered in their tasks of educating the black masses on political issues because Negroes do not own any of the necessary means of propaganda and communication. The Negro owns no printing presses, he has no stake in the networks of the means of communication. Inside his own communities he does not own the house he lives in, the property he lives on, nor the wholesale and retail sources from which he buys his commodities. He does not own the edifices in which he enjoys culture and entertainment or in which he socializes. In capitalist society, an individual or group that does not own anything is powerless." H. Cruse, "Behind the Black Power Slogan," in Cruse, *Rebellion or Revolution, op. cit.,* pp. 238–39.

[10] Harold M. Baron, "Black Powerlessness in Chicago," *Trans-action,* 6 (Nov., 1968), pp. 27–33.

motives involved in looting as a sign that the rioters want to join America's middle-class affluence just like everyone else. That motives are mixed and often unconscious, that black people want good furniture and television sets like whites is beside the point. The guiding impulse in most major outbreaks has not been integration with American society, but an attempt to stake out a sphere of control by moving against that society and destroying the symbols of its oppression.

In my critique of the McCone report I observed that the rioters were asserting a claim to territoriality, an unorganized and rather inchoate attempt to gain control over their community or "turf."[11] In succeeding disorders also the thrust of the action has been the attempts to clear out an alien presence, white men and officials, rather than a drive to kill whites as in a conventional race riot. The main attacks have been directed at property of white business men and at the police who operate in the black community "like an army of occupation" protecting the interests of outside exploiters and maintaining the domination over the ghetto by the central metropolitan power structure.[12] The Kerner Report misleads when it attempts to explain riots in terms of integration: "What the rioters appear to be seeking was fuller participation in the social order and the material benefits enjoyed by the majority of American citizens. Rather than rejecting the American system, they were anxious to obtain a place for themselves in it."[13] More accurately, the revolts pointed to alienation from this system on the part of many poor and also not-so-poor blacks. The sacredness of private property, that unconsciously accepted bulwark of our social arrangements, was rejected; people who looted apparently without guilt generally remarked that they were taking things that "really belonged" to them anyway.[14] Obviously the society's bases of legitimacy and authority have been attacked. Law and order has long been viewed as the white man's law and order by Afro-Americans; but now this perspective characteristic of a colonized people is out in the open. And the Kerner Report's own data question how well ghetto rebels are buying the system:

[11] R. Blauner, "Whitewash Over Watts," *op. cit.*

[12] "The police function to support and enforce the interests of the dominant political, social, and economic interests of the town" is a statement made by a former police scholar and official, according to A. Neiderhoffer, *Behind the Shield* (New York: Doubleday, 1967) as cited by Gary T. Marx, "Civil Disorder and the Agents of Control," *Journal of Social Issues,* forthcoming.

[13] Report of the National Advisory Commission on Civil Disorders (N.Y.: Bantam, March, 1968), p. 7.

[14] This kind of attitude has a long history among American Negroes. During slavery, blacks used the same rationalization to justify stealing from their masters. Appropriating things from the master was viewed as *"taking* part of his property for the benefit of another part; whereas *stealing* referred to appropriating something from another slave, an offense that was not condoned." Kenneth Stampp, *The Peculiar Institution* (Vintage, 1956), p. 127.

In Newark only 33 percent of self-reported rioters said they thought this country was worth fighting for in the event of a major war; in the Detroit sample the figure was 55 percent.[15]

One of the most significant consequences of the process of colonization is a weakening of the colonized's individual and collective will to resist his oppression. It has been easier to contain and control black ghettoes because communal bonds and group solidarity have been weakened through divisions among leadership, failures of organization, and a general disspiritment that accompanies social oppression. The riots are a signal that the will to resist has broken the mold of accommodation. In some cities as in Watts they also represented nascent movements toward community identity. In several riot-torn ghettoes the outbursts have stimulated new organizations and movements. If it is true that the riot phenomenon of 1964–68 has passed its peak, its historical import may be more for the "internal" organizing momentum generated than for any profound "external" response of the larger society facing up to underlying causes.

Despite the appeal of Frantz Fanon to young black revolutionaries, America is not Algeria. It is difficult to foresee how riots in our cities can play a role equivalent to rioting in the colonial situation as an integral phase in a movement for national liberation. In 1968 some militant groups (for example, the Black Panther Party in Oakland) had concluded that ghetto riots were self-defeating of the lives and interests of black people in the present balance of organization and gunpower, though they had served a role to stimulate both black consciousness and white awareness of the depths of racial crisis. Such militants have been influential in "cooling" their communities during periods of high riot potential. Theoretically oriented black radicals see riots as spontaneous mass behavior which must be replaced by a revolutionary organization and consciousness. But despite the differences in objective conditions, the violence of the 1960's seems to serve the same psychic function, assertions of dignity and manhood for young blacks in urban ghettoes, as it did for the colonized of North Africa described by Fanon and Memmi.[16]

CULTURAL NATIONALISM

Cultural conflict is generic to the colonial relation because colonization involves the domination of Western technological values over the more communal cultures of non-Western peoples. Colonialism played havoc with the national integrity of the peoples it brought under its sway. Of course, all traditional cultures are threatened by industrialism, the city, and

---

[15] Report of the National Advisory Commission on Civil Disorders, *op. cit.*, p. 178.
[16] Frantz Fanon, *Wretched of the Earth* (New York: Grove, 1963); Albert Memmi, *The Colonizer and the Colonized* (Boston: Beacon, 1967).

modernization in communication, transportation, health, and education. What is special are the political and administrative decisions of colonizers in managing and controlling colonized peoples. The boundaries of African colonies, for example, were drawn to suit the political conveniences of the European nations without regard to the social organization and cultures of African tribes and kingdoms. Thus Nigeria as blocked out by the British included the Yorubas and the Ibos, whose civil war today is a residuum of the colonialist's disrespect for the integrity of indigenous cultures.

The most total destruction of culture in the colonization process took place not in traditional colonialism but in America. As Frazier stressed, the integral cultures of the diverse African peoples who furnished the slave trade were destroyed because slaves from different tribes, kingdoms, and linguistic groups were purposely separated to maximize domination and control. Thus language, religion, and national loyalties were lost in North America much more completely than in the Caribbean and Brazil where slavery developed somewhat differently. Thus on this key point America's internal colonization has been more total and extreme than situations of classic colonialism. For the British in India and the European powers in Africa were not able—as outnumbered minorities—to destroy the national and tribal cultures of the colonized. Recall that American slavery lasted 250 years and its racist aftermath another 100. Colonial dependency in the case of British Kenya and French Algeria lasted only 77 and 125 years respectively. In the wake of this more drastic uprooting and destruction of culture and social organization, much more powerful agencies of social, political, and psychological domination developed in the American case.

> Colonial control of many peoples inhabiting the colonies was more a goal than a fact, and at Independence there were undoubtedly fairly large numbers of Africans who had never seen a colonial administrator. The gradual process of extension of control from the administrative center on the African coast contrasts sharply with the total uprooting involved in the slave trade and the totalitarian aspects of slavery in the United States. Whether or not Elkins is correct in treating slavery as a total institution, it undoubtedly had a far more radical and pervasive impact on American slaves than did colonialism on the vast majority of Africans.[17]

Yet a similar cultural process unfolds in both contexts of colonialism. To the extent that they are involved in the larger society and economy, the colonized are caught up in a conflict between two cultures. Fanon has described how the assimilation-oriented schools of Martinique taught him to reject his own culture and blackness in favor of Westernized, French, and

[17] Robert Wood, "Colonialism in Africa and America: Some Conceptual Considerations," December, 1967, unpublished paper.

white values.[18] Both the colonized elites under traditional colonialism and perhaps the majority of Afro-Americans today experience a parallel split in identity, cultural loyalty, and political orientation.[19]

The colonizers use their culture to socialize the colonized elites (intellectuals, politicians, and middle class) into an identification with the colonial system. Because Western culture has the prestige, the power, and the key to open the limited opportunity that a minority of the colonized may achieve, the first reaction seems to be an acceptance of the dominant values. Call it brainwashing as the Black Muslims put it; call it identifying with the aggressor if you prefer Freudian terminology; call it a natural response to the hope and belief that integration and democratization can really take place if you favor a more commonsense explanation, this initial acceptance in time crumbles on the realities of racism and colonialism. The colonized, seeing that his success within colonialism is at the expense of his group and his own inner identity, moves radically toward a rejection of the Western culture and develops a nationalist outlook that celebrates his people and their traditions. As Memmi describes it:

> Assimilation being abandoned, the colonized's liberation must be carried out through a recovery of self and of autonomous dignity. Attempts at imitating the colonizer required self-denial; the colonizer's rejection is the indispensible prelude to self-discovery. That accusing and annihilating image must be shaken off; oppression must be attacked boldly since it is impossible to go around it. After having been rejected for so long by the colonizer, the day has come when it is the colonized who must refuse the colonizer.[20]

Memmi's book, *The Colonizer and the Colonized,* is based on his experience as a Tunisian Jew in a marginal position between the French and the colonized Arab majority. The uncanny parallels between the North African situation he describes and the course of black-white relations in our society is the best impressionist argument I know for the thesis that we have a colonized group and a colonizing system in America. His discussion of why even the most radical French anti-colonialist cannot participate in the struggle of the colonized is directly applicable to the situation of the white liberal and radical vis-à-vis the black movement. His portrait of the colonized is as good an analysis of the psychology behind Black Power and black nationalism as anything that has been written in the U.S. Consider for example:

[18] F. Fanon, *Black Skins, White Masks* (New York: Grove, 1967).
[19] Harold Cruse has described how these two themes of integration with the larger society and identification with ethnic nationality have struggled within the political and cultural movements of Negro Americans. *The Crisis of the Negro Intellectual, op. cit.*
[20] Memmi, *op. cit.,* p. 128.

Considered *en bloc* as *them, they,* or *those,* different from every point of view, homogeneous in a radical heterogeneity, the colonized reacts by rejecting all the colonizers *en bloc.* The distinction between deed and intent has no great significance in the colonial situation. In the eyes of the colonized, all Europeans in the colonies are de facto colonizers, and whether they want to be or not, they are colonizers in some ways. By their privileged economic position, by belonging to the political system of oppression, or by participating in an effectively negative complex toward the colonized, they are colonizers. . . . They are supporters or at least unconscious accomplices of that great collective aggression of Europe.[21]

The same passion which made him admire and absorb Europe shall make him assert his differences; since those differences, after all, are within him and correctly constitute his true self.[22]

The important thing now is to rebuild his people, whatever be their authentic nature; to reforge their unity, communicate with it, and to feel that they belong.[23]

Cultural revitalization movements play a key role in anti-colonial movements. They follow an inner necessity and logic of their own that comes from the consequences of colonialism on groups and personal identities; they are also essential to provide the solidarity which the political or military phase of the anti-colonial revolution requires. In the U.S. an Afro-American culture has been developing since slavery out of the ingredients of African world-views, the experience of bondage, Southern values and customs, migration and the Northern lower-class ghettoes, and most importantly, the political history of the black population in its struggle against racism.[24] That Afro-Americans are moving toward cultural nationalism in a period when ethnic loyalties tend to be weak (and perhaps on the decline) in this country is another confirmation of the unique colonized position of the black group. (A similar nationalism seems to be growing among American Indians and Mexican-Americans.)

THE MOVEMENT FOR GHETTO CONTROL

The call for Black Power unites a number of varied movements and tendencies.[25] Though no clear-cut program has yet emerged, the most

21 *Ibid.,* p. 130.
22 *Ibid.,* p. 132.
23 *Ibid.,* p. 134.
24 In another essay, I argue against the standard sociological position that denies the existence of an ethnic Afro-American culture and I expand on the above themes. The concept of "Soul" is astonishingly parallel in content to the mystique of "Negritude" in Africa; the Pan-African culture movement has its parallel in the burgeoning black culture mood in Afro-American communities. See "Black Culture: Myth or Reality" in Peter Rose, editor, *Americans From Africa* (Atherton, 1969).
25 Scholars and social commentators, black and white alike, disagree in interpreting the

important emphasis seems to be the movement for control of the ghetto. Black leaders and organizations are increasingly concerned with owning and controlling those institutions that exist within or impinge upon their community. The colonial model provides a key to the understanding of this movement, and indeed ghetto control advocates have increasingly invoked the language of colonialism in pressing for local home rule. The framework of anti-colonialism explains why the struggle for poor people's or community control of poverty programs has been more central in many cities than the content of these programs and why it has been crucial to exclude whites from leadership positions in black organizations.

The key institutions that anti-colonialists want to take over or control are business, social services, schools, and the police. Though many spokesmen have advocated the exclusion of white landlords and small businessmen from the ghetto, this program has evidently not struck fire with the black population and little concrete movement toward economic expropriation has yet developed. Welfare recipients have organized in many cities to protect their rights and gain a greater voice in the decisions that affect them, but whole communities have not yet been able to mount direct action against welfare colonialism. Thus schools and the police seem now to be the burning issues of ghetto control politics.

During the past few years there has been a dramatic shift from educational integration as the primary goal to that of community control of the schools. Afro-Americans are demanding their own school boards, with the power to hire and fire principals and teachers and to construct a curriculum which would be relevant to the special needs and culture style of ghetto youth. Especially active in high schools and colleges have been black students, whose protests have centered on the incorporation of Black Power and black culture into the educational system. Consider how similar is the spirit behind these developments to the attitude of the colonized North African toward European education:

> He will prefer a long period of educational mistakes to the continuance of the colonizer's school organization. He will choose institutional disorder in order to destroy the institutions built by the colonizer as soon as possible. There we will see, indeed a reactive drive of profound protest. He will no longer owe anything to the colonizer and will have definitely broken with him.[26]

contemporary Black Power movement. The issues concern whether this is a new development in black protest or an old tendency revised; whether the movement is radical, revolutionary, reformist, or conservative; and whether this orientation is unique to Afro-Americans or essentially a black parallel to other ethnic group strategies for collective mobility. For an interesting discussion of Black Power as a modernized version of Booker T. Washington's separatism and economism, see Harold Cruse, *Rebellion or Revolution, op. cit.*, pp. 193–258.

[26] Memmi, *op. cit.*, pp. 137–138.

Protest and institutional disorder over the issue of school control came to a head in 1968 in New York City. The procrastination in the Albany State legislature, the several crippling strikes called by the teachers union, and the almost frenzied response of Jewish organizations makes it clear that decolonization of education faces the resistance of powerful vested interests.[27] The situation is too dynamic at present to assess probable future results. However, it can be safely predicted that some form of school decentralization will be institutionalized in New York, and the movement for community control of education will spread to more cities.

This movement reflects some of the problems and ambiguities that stem from the situation of colonization outside an immediate colonial context. The Afro-American community is not parallel in structure to the communities of colonized nations under traditional colonialism. The significant difference here is the lack of fully developed indigenous institutions besides the church. Outside of some areas of the South there is really no black economy, and most Afro-Americans are inevitably caught up in the larger society's structure of occupations, education, and mass communication. Thus the ethnic nationalist orientation which reflects the reality of colonization exists alongside an integrationst orientation which corresponds to the reality that the institutions of the larger society are much more developed than those of the incipient nation.[28] As would be expected the movement for school control reflects both tendencies. The militant leaders who spearhead such local movements may be primarily motivated by the desire to gain control over the community's institutions —they are anti-colonialists first and foremost. Many parents who support them may share this goal also, but the majority are probably more concerned about creating a new education that will enable their children to "make it" in the society and the economy as a whole—they know that the present school system fails ghetto children and does not prepare them for participation in American life.

There is a growing recognition that the police are the most crucial institution maintaining the colonized status of Black Americans. And of all establishment institutions, police departments probably include the highest proportion of individual racists. This is no accident since central to the workings of racism (an essential component of colonization) are attacks on the humanity and dignity of the subject group. Through their normal

[27] For the New York school conflict see Jason Epstein, "The Politics of School Decentralization," *New York Review of Books*, June 6, 1968, pp. 26–32; and "The New York City School Revolt," *ibid.*, 11, no. 6, pp. 37–41.

[28] This dual split in the politics and psyche of the Black American was poetically described by Du Bois in his *Souls of Black Folk*, and more recently has been insightfully analyzed by Harold Cruse in *The Crisis of the Negro Intellectual, op. cit.* Cruse has also characterized the problem of the black community as that of underdevelopment.

routines the police constrict Afro-Americans to black neighborhoods by harassing and questioning them when found outside the ghetto; they break up groups of youth congregating on corners or in cars without any provocation; and they continue to use offensive and racist language no matter how many intergroup understanding seminars have been built into the police academy. They also shoot to kill ghetto residents for alleged crimes such as car thefts and running from police officers.[29]

Police are key agents in the power equation as well as the drama of dehumanization. In the final analysis they do the dirty work for the larger system by restricting the striking back of black rebels to skirmishes inside the ghetto, thus deflecting energies and attacks from the communities and institutions of the larger power structure. In a historical review, Gary Marx notes that since the French revolution, police and other authorities have killed large numbers of demonstrators and rioters; the rebellious "rabble" rarely destroys human life. The same pattern has been repeated in America's recent revolts.[30] Journalistic accounts appearing in the press recently suggest that police see themselves as defending the interests of white people against a tide of black insurgence; furthermore the majority of whites appear to view "blue power" in this light. There is probably no other opinion on which the races are as far apart today as they are on the question of attitudes toward the police.

In many cases set off by a confrontation between a policeman and a black citizen, the ghetto uprisings have dramatized the role of law enforcement and the issue of police brutality. In their aftermath, movements have arisen to contain police activity. One of the first was the Com-

---

[29] A recent survey of police finds "that in the predominantly Negro areas of several large cities, many of the police perceive the residents as basically hostile, especially the youth and adolescents. A lack of public support—from citizens, from courts, and from laws—is the policeman's major complaint. But some of the public criticism can be traced to the activities in which he engages day by day, and perhaps to the tone in which he enforces the 'law' in the Negro neighborhoods. Most frequently he is 'called upon' to intervene in domestic quarrels and break up loitering groups. He stops and frisks two or three times as many people as are carrying dangerous weapons or are actual criminals, and almost half of these don't wish to cooperate with the policeman's efforts." Peter Rossi *et al.*, "Between Black and White—The Faces of American Institutions and the Ghetto," in Supplemental Studies for the National Advisory Commission on Civil Disorders, July 1968, p. 114.

[30] "In the Gordon Riots of 1780 demonstrators destroyed property and freed prisoners, but did not seem to kill anyone, while authorities killed several hundred rioters and hung an additional 25. In the Rebellion Riots of the French Revolution, though several hundred rioters were killed, they killed no one. Up to the end of the Summer of 1967, this pattern had clearly been repeated, as police, not rioters, were responsible for most of the more than 100 deaths that have occurred. Similarly, in a related context, the more than 100 civil rights murders of recent years have been matched by almost no murders of racist whites." G. Marx, "Civil Disorders and the Agents of Social Control," *op. cit.*

munity Alert Patrol in Los Angeles, a method of policing the police in order to keep them honest and constrain their violations of personal dignity. This was the first tactic of the Black Panther Party which originated in Oakland, perhaps the most significant group to challenge the police role in maintaining the ghetto as a colony. The Panthers' later policy of openly carrying guns (a legally protected right) and their intention of defending themselves against police aggression has brought on a series of confrontations with the Oakland police department. All indications are that the authorities intend to destroy the Panthers by shooting, framing up, or legally harassing their leadership—diverting the group's energies away from its primary purpose of self-defense and organization of the black community to that of legal defense and gaining support in the white community.

There are three major approaches to "police colonialism" that correspond to reformist and revolutionary readings of the situation. The most elementary and also superficial sees colonialism in the fact that ghettoes are overwhelmingly patrolled by white rather than by black officers. The proposal—supported today by many police departments—to increase the number of blacks on local forces to something like their distribution in the city would then make it possible to reduce the use of white cops in the ghetto. This reform should be supported, for a variety of obvious reasons, but it does not get to the heart of the police role as agents of colonization.

The Kerner Report documents the fact that in some cases black policemen can be as brutal as their white counterparts. The Report does not tell us who polices the ghetto, but they have compiled the proportion of Negroes on the forces of the major cities. In some cities the disparity is so striking that white police inevitably dominate ghetto patrols. (In Oakland 31 percent of the population and only 4 percent of the police are black; in Detroit the figures are 39 percent and 5 percent; and in New Orleans 41 and 4.) In other cities, however, the proportion of black cops is approaching the distribution in the city: Philadelphia 29 percent and 20 percent; Chicago 27 percent and 17 percent.[31] These figures also suggest that both the extent and the pattern of colonization may vary from one city to another. It would be useful to study how black communities differ in degree of control over internal institutions as well as in economic and political power in the metropolitan area.

A second demand which gets more to the issue is that police should

---

[31] Report of the National Advisory Commission on Civil Disorders, *op. cit.*, p. 321. That black officers nevertheless would make a difference is suggested by data from one of the supplemental studies to the Kerner Report. They found Negro policemen working in the ghettoes considerably more sympathetic to the community and its social problems than their white counterparts. Peter Rossi *et al.*, "Between Black and White —The Faces of American Institutions in the Ghetto," *op. cit.*, chap. 6.

live in the communities they patrol. The idea here is that black cops who lived in the ghetto would have to be accountable to the community; if they came on like white cops then "the brothers would take care of business" and make their lives miserable. The third or maximalist position is based on the premise that the police play no positive role in the ghettoes. It calls for the withdrawal of metropolitan officers from black communities and the substitution of an autonomous indigenous force that would maintain order without oppressing the population. The precise relationship between such an independent police, the city and county law enforcement agencies, a ghetto governing body that would supervise and finance it, and especially the law itself is yet unclear. It is unlikely that we will soon face these problems directly as they have arisen in the case of New York's schools. Of all the programs of decolonization, police autonomy will be most resisted. It gets to the heart of how the state functions to control and contain the black community through delegating the legitimate use of violence to police authority.

The various "Black Power" programs that are aimed at gaining control of individual ghettoes—buying up property and businesses, running the schools through community boards, taking over anti-poverty programs and other social agencies, diminishing the arbitrary power of the police —can serve to revitalize the institutions of the ghetto and build up an economic, professional, and political power base. These programs seem limited; we do not know at present if they are enough in themselves to end colonized status.[32] But they are certainly a necessary first step.

THE ROLE OF WHITES

What makes the Kerner Report a less-than-radical document is its superficial treatment of racism and its reluctance to confront the colonized relationship between black people and the larger society. The Report emphasizes the attitudes and feelings that make up white racism, rather than the system of privilege and control which is the heart of the matter.[33] With all its discussion of the ghetto and its problems, it never faces the question of the stake that white Americans have in racism and ghettoization.

This is not a simple question, but this paper should not end with the impression that police are the major villains. All white Americans gain

[32] Eldridge Cleaver has called this first stage of the anti-colonial movement *community* liberation in contrast to a more long-range goal of *national* liberation. E. Cleaver, "Community Imperialism," Black Panther Party newspaper, 2 (May 18, 1968).

[33] For a discussion of this failure to deal with racism, see Gary T. Marx, "Report of the National Commission: The Analysis of Disorder or Disorderly Analysis," 1968, unpublished paper.

some privileges and advantage from the colonization of black communities.[34] The majority of whites also lose something from this oppression and division in society. Serious research should be directed to the ways in which white individuals and institutions are tied into the ghetto. In closing let me suggest some possible parameters.

1. It is my guess that only a small minority of whites make a direct economic profit from ghetto colonization. This is hopeful in that the ouster of white businessmen may become politically feasible. Much more significant, however, are the private and corporate interests in the land and residential property of the black community; their holdings and influence on urban decision-making must be exposed and combated.

2. A much larger minority have occupational and professional interests in the present arrangements. The Kerner Commission reports that 1.3 million nonwhite men would have to be upgraded occupationally in order to make the black job distribution roughly similar to the white. They advocate this without mentioning that 1.3 million specially privileged white workers would lose in the bargain.[35] In addition there are those professionals who carry out what Lee Rainwater has called the "dirty work" of administering the lives of the ghetto poor: the social workers, the school teachers, the urban development people, and of course the police.[36] The social problems of the black community will ultimately be solved only by people and organizations from that community; thus the emphasis within these professions must shift toward training such a cadre of minority personnel. Social scientists who teach and study problems of race and poverty likewise have an obligation to replace themselves by bringing into the graduate schools and college faculties men of color who will become the future experts in these areas. For cultural and intellectual imperialism is as real as welfare colonialism, though it is currently screened behind such unassailable shibboleths as universalism and the objectivity of scientific inquiry.

3. Without downgrading the vested interests of profit and profession, the real nitty-gritty elements of the white stake are political power and bureaucratic security. Whereas few whites have much understanding of the realities of race relations and ghetto life, I think most give tacit or at least subconscious support for the containment and control of the black population. Whereas most whites have extremely distorted images of Black Power, many—if not most—would still be frightened by actual

---

[34] Such a statement is easier to assert than to document but I am attempting the latter in a forthcoming book tentatively titled *White Racism, Black Culture*, to be published by Little, Brown, 1970.

[35] Report of the National Advisory Commission on Civil Disorders, *op. cit.*, pp. 253-256.

[36] Lee Rainwater, "The Revolt of the Dirty-Workers," *Trans-action*, 5 (Nov., 1967), pp. 2, 64.

black political power. Racial groups and identities are real in American life; white Americans sense they are on top, and they fear possible reprisals or disruptions were power to be more equalized. There seems to be a paranoid fear in the white psyche of black dominance; the belief that black autonomy would mean unbridled license is so ingrained that such reasonable outcomes as black political majorities and independent black police forces will be bitterly resisted.

On this level the major mass bulwark of colonization is the administrative need for bureaucratic security so that the middle classes can go about their life and business in peace and quiet. The black militant movement is a threat to the orderly procedures by which bureaucracies and suburbs manage their existence, and I think today there are more people who feel a stake in conventional procedures than there are those who gain directly from racism. For in their fight for institutional control, the colonized will not play by the white rules of the game. These administrative rules have kept them down and out of the system; therefore they have no necessary intention of running institutions in the image of the white middle class.

The liberal, humanist value that violence is the worst sin cannot be defended today if one is committed squarely against racism and for self-determination. For some violence is almost inevitable in the decolonization process; unfortunately racism in America has been so effective that the greatest power Afro-Americans (and perhaps also Mexican-Americans) wield today is the power to disrupt. If we are going to swing with these revolutionary times and at least respond positively to the anti-colonial movement, we will have to learn to live with conflict, confrontation, constant change, and what may be real or apparent chaos and disorder.

A positive response from the white majority needs to be in two major directions at the same time. First, community liberation movements should be supported in every way by pulling out white instruments of direct control and exploitation and substituting technical assistance to the community when this is asked for. But it is not enough to relate affirmatively to the nationalist movement for ghetto control without at the same time radically opening doors for full participation in the institutions of the mainstream. Otherwise the liberal and radical position is little different than the traditional segregationist. Freedom in the special conditions of American colonization means that the colonized must have the choice between participation in the larger society and in their own independent structures.

The Silent Black Majority

CHARLES V. HAMILTON

There are a lot of Black Americans who have never been in jail, never been on dope, never participated in a riot or even a civil-rights demonstration, are not on welfare—and they are not members of the so-called black bourgeoisie or black middle class. This may sound strange to some people who have become accustomed in the last few years to a racial discussion that has tended to divide the black community into categories representing either the tormented soul of an Eldridge Cleaver, the manchild of a Claude Brown, or the attaché case of an upwardly mobile black man newly appointed to the New York Stock Exchange.

"The traditional civil-rights movement was largely beneficial to the black middle class," James Farmer recently said, "but there are masses of black people on the lower rungs who cannot afford to eat in Howard Johnson's or take advantage of the new opportunities opening up." This is true, and it has conjured up visions of a slowly but steadily growing black middle class on the one hand, and a trapped, oppressed and frequently unemployed black under class on the other. This, too, is a true division, but an incomplete one.

The facts are that there are millions of Black Americans who go to work every day, pay their taxes, root for the home team, worry about the high cost of living, shop for bargains, and go over the children's homework just like millions of other Americans. The problem with even saying this, however, is that immediately it will be grabbed up by different kinds of polemicists to prove a particular political point.

Some will say, "See there, that proves that black people want the same things as whites, and they want to work within the system to get them."

One will hear, "Those people are becoming radicalized, and they are on the move. They know they are victims of capitalist oppression, and they have come close to the point where they will not take it any more."

Daniel Patrick Moynihan called them the "silent black majority," not members of the middle class, but of the working class, who have the same aspirations for themselves and their children as millions of the silent white majority.

Simplistic conclusions are tempting when discussing Black Americans, precisely because many of us want so badly *simply* to understand (and therefore *simply* to deal with) the racial problems in this country.

One popular route to simplicity is to compile figures and take a head count. Thus, an earlier sentence in this article said ". . . there are millions of Black Americans. . . ." How many? How do their numbers compare with those on welfare or in the latest demonstration? How many follow the teachings of Martin Luther King Jr. as opposed to the call of the Black Panthers? How many favor integration over separatism? And we find support for one view or another in the statistical answers.

We can learn only so much from a poll "among a nationwide cross section of 1,255 blacks," recently conducted by one public opinion company. Some observers would suggest that a better barometer is the election results in two Chicago Congressional districts where black voters recently went substantially for the "moderate," Daley-supported black candidates against "militant," independent black candidates. In a democratic, electoral system, the argument goes, what better way to measure mass moods and meanings than at the ballot boxes?

After a point, aggregate data became overwhelming, and one can make out of them virtually anything one wants. In addition, it is a reasonable argument that improved conditions for an aggregate group of black people in, say, Harlem might mean nothing to blacks in Bedford-Stuyvesant, not to mention larger geographical breakdowns, and not to mention various different age groups in a particular city. Some examples of the enormity of the numbers process can be found in a recent report from the Bureau of Labor Statistics of the U.S. Department of Labor:

The number of employed persons of Negro and other races rose 1.5 million in the nine-year period from 1960 to 1969—increasing 21 percent compared with 18 percent for whites.

The unemployment rate for Negro and other races in 1968 and the first 11 months of 1969, was the lowest since the Korean war, but still about double the white rate.

The unemployment rate for married men of Negro and other races has been declining more rapidly than that of white married men. However, the rate of the former group is about twice that of the latter.

In 1969 there were a million more workers of Negro and other races employed in white-collar, craftsmen, or operative occupations than in laborer or service jobs. Employment of persons of Negro and other races in these occupations increased 67 percent between 1960 and 1968, compared with 22 percent for whites.

In the period 1960 to 1969, the percent of workers of Negro and other races in the highly skilled, well-paying jobs increased much more sharply than the percent of white workers in these jobs.

The proportion of young men and women having at least a high-school education is greater today than it was at the beginning of the decade. Among Negro men 25 to 29 years old in 1969, about 60 percent had completed four years of high school or some college. In 1960 the comparable figure was 36 percent.

Negroes have made substantial gains since 1960 in completing college.

By 1969, about 7 percent of all Negroes 25 to 34 years old had completed college compared with about 16 percent of all whites in this age group.

Negro group enrollment rose 85 percent between 1964 and 1968. The increase was much greater for colleges not predominantly Negro than for Negro colleges.

One-half of Negro female heads of families are separated or divorced as compared with about one-third of white female heads. The percent of Negro female heads separated from their husbands is three times as great as that for whites. However, the percent divorced is greater among white female heads of families than among Negro heads.

Although the ratio of illegitimate births to all live births is higher for Negro and other races than for whites—29 percent for the former as compared with a 5 percent for the latter—the relative increase since 1950 has been much greater for whites than for Negro and other races.

For the country as a whole, the average income of Negro husband-wife families was 72 percent of the white average in 1968 and in the North and West it was 85 percent of the white average. This represents a marked change from the situation a decade ago when the income gap between young Negro families and white families outside the South was 25 percent and where there was little variation in this gap by age. The clear implication of these figures is that the incomes of young Negro couples in the Northern and Western States are responding favorably to the efforts that have been made in recent years to improve their education, training and job opportunities.

And on and on it goes, 96 pages of statistical data. Take your pick and proceed to make whatever point you want to make: that the country is on a steady road of improvement of conditions for black people; that, in comparison with whites, the blacks are not only not improving in many significant areas, but retrogressing; that the "peaceful" route to change is possible; that only out of violence and crises will even the slightest improvement come.

This is not to suggest that figures are not useful, but only to say that in some matters they have been overrated and have very limited value.

Frankly, there is no ironclad, scientific way to measure the mood of large numbers of people—black or white. But we continue, nonetheless, to try to get a reading. One way, not unknown to some observers, and one used here is to spend considerable time living among, working with and talking to people. It is possible to get a sense, a feeling of things in the barber shops, the beauty parlors, in shopping centers, on lunch hours, coffee breaks, in living rooms.

These are the black people who drive buses, work in the post office, on an assembly line, in stores and factories, in gas stations, as shipping clerks. They are not doctors, lawyers, middle-level executives or college professors. They are not featured on television, and they have not "made it" in the upper middle-class, strivers' sense of the term.

Some of them might be "going back to school" by taking an English or math or typing course at a community college—or talking about doing so "next semester." Why? "To better myself." "I never had the chance earlier." (Which may or may not be exactly true.) "I didn't realize the value of an education, like I try to tell these young people today." (Which is probably more likely true.)

They do not attend church as often as they feel they should, but they rationalize by saying, "It isn't necessary to be a good Christian to be always sitting up in church every Sunday morning where you find some of the biggest hypocrites." But they send their children to Sunday school.

Their homes are beginning to include more African art objects, but they are not in the least concerned about any movement of "Back to Africa." They see Africa increasingly as a place of their heritage and nothing to be ashamed of as in an earlier time. More and more, the wish is expressed to be able to visit the continent "someday."

They are not nearly as dogmatic on race issues as the popular literature and many of their spokesmen would have one believe. They are supporters of "Black Power" and "integration" at the same time, and the apparent paradox does not bother them in the least. This is understandable after discussion. By "Black Power" they mean, "we've got to learn to stick together like the Jews and stand up for our rights." By "integration" they mean overcoming racial discrimination.

They are not intimately familiar with the debate between the Black Panthers and the black cultural nationalists over Marxism. And if asked if they believe in "working with whites," their first reaction is to understand this to refer to "on the job," not "in the movement."

In many ways this group reacts to the Black Panthers in much the way it reacted to the Black Muslims and to other highly visible black organizations with a reputation for "militancy." That is, these organizations represent many of the feelings but not the sense of feasibility of masses of blacks. To the extent that the Panthers speak and act "boldly" their courage and forthrightness are admired. Their breakfast programs are applauded and are seen as "worthwhile"; their goal of revolution is seen as "unrealistic" and "idealistic." Their bravado is unimpressive and is viewed as "mind-blowing," intended largely for whites—especially the guilty and self-conscious ones.

Standing in line last December to view the apartment on the West Side of Chicago where two Panthers were killed in a police raid, one black man said, "I don't agree with what all these kids say, but you don't treat a dog like this, let alone a human. Man this is some terrible stuff." He walked away shaking his head, and one got the impression that the Panthers had gained a stronger sympathizer, if not an active recruit.

If this is a "silent black majority," it is not to be confused with the connotations of the "silent white majority." The latter has implications of conservatism on racial and economic matters, of supporting the Administration's policies in Vietnam, of supporting "our police," of "being fed up to here" with the "riots" and campus disturbances.

The blacks do not want a period of "benign neglect," however the phrase is applied. They believe the Vietnam policy is wrong ("We should get out of there and leave those people alone, and use that money back here where it can do some good"). The police are not pigs, but neither are they seen as dedicated protectors of the black community. These people are as concerned about "crime in the streets" as any middle-class person, and they want effective measures taken to combat it. But they want police protection, not police persecution, and because they believe that the incidence of the latter is greater than the former, they believe the present law-enforcement systems must be viewed suspiciously, rather than optimistically.

The protesting black students "have a point, and they just aren't going to take what some of us took." At the same time, a college education is seen as clearly the single most important factor to advancement. (A black cab driver picked me up at Columbia University one afternoon and began that fascinatingly peculiar New York City experience of negotiating the traffic into midtown. The conversation—essentially on the faults of "people"—ended with his peering through the rear-view mirror and saying: "But the answer for us is where I picked you up. Our people get that education and that's it, brother. No two ways about it.")

They disagree totally with the white radical youth culture and its use of drugs, because "I've seen what that stuff has done to our people." "Man, how in the hell are you going to fight The Man if you're nodding and scratching all day, leaning up against some damn car." They also believe that "the system" is heavily involved in the drug traffic, from the policeman on the street to the authorities downtown to the Mafia.

What is not usually understood by some white radicals is that the black culture is not a permissive culture. The cult of individualism, in the sense of "do your own thing," is subordinated to a communal characteristic much more dominant in the black culture. Thus, the scene at Woodstock in the summer of 1969 was not appealing to many blacks who are far more tuned in to day-to-day struggle than to the essentially middle-class youth culture of "freedom high."

The point is that the Abbie Hoffmans and the Jerry Rubins are, in fact, irrelevant to most of the blacks who see the white radical thrust as just one more "trip" black people cannot afford to take—precisely because black people must always come home to a fundamentally different reality!

They believe it is better to work than to be on welfare, but they do not believe that most welfare recipients are freeloaders. Some came from a welfare background, and many still have friends and acquaintances who are recipients. They condemn fathers who desert their children, and, interestingly, are generally unsympathetic to the position that economic conditions forced the father out of the home. This latter view is equally prevalent among men and women.

On the one hand, they are quite concerned about the exploitation and depressed conditions in their black neighborhoods, and on the other, they resent the constant picture painted of "the ghetto" as a "den of thieves and whores and addicts." As one man in his mid-30's, who works in a factory (he makes $7,400 a year) said: "From the way it sounds to hear them tell it, all of us who live over here are on dope and cut each other every night. There are some hard-working people here and we care about this community like other folks care about theirs." This attitude is a mixture of resentment at being stereotyped, and a feeling that outside forces control things to keep ghetto conditions the way they are.

What is the attitude toward local community politics and organizations? In one sense, "The only way we're going to get anything is to organize and keep the pressure on." But this usually means someone else has to do it. "I'm not a leader, myself," one shipping clerk said, "but I'm a good backer-upper." Then, you talk to a local leader trying to get a turnout to a meeting to protest police brutality or bad schools, and you get another story: "People around here are apathetic. They don't believe they can win." Large numbers of people admired Martin Luther King Jr. and Malcolm X "for the way they stood up," but there was a strong tendency to be suspicious of the motives of many local (as opposed to national) leaders.

The likelihood is great that they are going out in the evening to a second job (or looking for one) instead of to the local P.T.A. meeting, or they will stay home in front of the television resting up from "10 hours on the slave, Jim." They know it is good "for people to be involved in what's going on, and I will as soon as I put a few things together," but not this week or this month—or this year. Comes a big rally, however, at the church, with a national figure, they will make it and probably agree strongly with the mass sentiment.

Many of these people are not bursting with wild hope either for themselves or for their children, but they do believe that if they "keep meeting The Man," they can pay off some of the bills and put the kids through college. And things will be better for the children, because "they gotta be. We're not going to keep being denied time after time." There are no dreams of someday owning the company, but there are dreams—of having a little cushion in the bank, of being able to afford a trip one summer. And goals get defined in these limited, realistic ways. Occasionally, a parent will tell you that a child is certain to be a doctor or a lawyer and will "make it." And you are back to a discussion of education again. There is no naïveté about the absence of discrimination, "but with that good education it's a cinch they won't have it as tough as I did."

They are neither "Uncle Toms" nor "militants," and one does not get much discussion from them on the subject. These are categories that are applied to and by the public spokesmen, and in different settings one can get different points of view from the same person. For example, in a barber shop one Saturday morning, a man in his late 20's, who worked in the local auto factory, engaged in a vehement argument with others over a boycott of classes and picketing of the local college by some black college students.

This man supported the students unequivocally, maintaining that the only way to get what they felt they deserved was to "lean on that white man until he knows you mean business." He admired the courage of the students and announced that if he were in college, "I'd be right there with them." He tried to get his adversaries in the barber shop to understand the students in the same way that they understood and agreed with Martin Luther King. To him, he argued, there was no difference between a Southern white sheriff and a Northern, polite racial bigot. (He knew, incidentally, that invoking King's name would win points in the argument.)

That same evening, I took this man with me to a meeting called by the same black student organization. The purpose of the meeting was "to reach the black community and explain to them our movement." My friend was basically sympathetic with the tactics and the goals (more black faculty and students, a black studies program). But throughout the meeting (there were about six students and 30 black adults present), he kept reminding the students that their main function was "to get an education." He hoped they did not want the school closed down, because "nobody wins in that situation."

My impression was that the students were generally disappointed with his less than wholehearted endorsement, and they saw him as a non-supporter "when the deal goes down." (They had hoped to get black-community support for a seizure of a campus building, if it came to that.)

Later, I tried to discuss his two different positions with my friend, and he just shrugged, and drank his beer. We sat for a long time in silence, and I recalled to myself the words of W. E. B. Du Bois written in "The Souls of Black Folk" in 1903:

> . . . One ever feels his twoness,—an American, a Negro; two souls, two
> thoughts, two unreconciled strivings; two warring ideals in one dark
> body, whose dogged strength alone keeps it from being torn asunder.

The history of the American Negro is the history of this strife—this
longing to attain self-conscious manhood, to merge his double self into a
better and truer self. In this merging he wishes neither of the older selves
to be lost. He would not Africanize America, for America has too much
to teach the world and Africa. He would not bleach his Negro soul in a
flood of white Americanism, for he knows that Negro blood has a message for the world. He simply wishes to make it possible for a man to
be both a Negro and an American, without being cursed and spit upon
by his fellows, without having the doors of Opportunity closed roughly
in his face.

These are some of the characteristics of America's "silent black majority," to the extent that there is one. There are many similarities with
masses of white Americans, but the dissimilarities are important. Unlike
his white counterpart, the American black is angry about racial conditions and wants to see more done *now* at all levels to end discrimination.
He is a patriot in the tax-paying, law-abiding, "this is my country too,"
sense, but not in the sense of "my country, right or wrong, my country."
He believes that this country is basically racist, but he does not dwell
on this, because it could immobilize him. It could mean that he would
not even try to get that extra part-time job to make ends meet, because
he would not believe he would get it. In fact, at times the discussion of
racial problems irritates him, because he sees it as leading to a frustrating
conclusion. He might even see this article as just one more piece "on the
subject" written for white people "who really are going to do just so
much."
He is not at this point going to throw bombs, and he knows it, so there
is no reason for him to engage in rhetoric advocating it. He is intensely
pragmatic and unideological. He is not a believer in the "boot-strap" theory of advancement, but every time you see him, he is tugging at his
shoes—going to meet The Man. He knows the blatant truth of the "last-
hired, first-fired" maxim, and he is willing to attest to the injustice of this.
But not too long, because it never occurred to him that this society, basically, was built on justice in the first place as far as the black man is
concerned.
Well, if he is so suspicious, so distrustful, what is to prevent him from
joining his brothers and sisters in the street who believe that a more
violent path is necessary? What happens when he loses his job and has to
scramble for another, knowing the racial odds? What happens when the
bills get one too many or when a white taxi driver flicks on his "off-duty"
sign when approaching him once too often? What happens when a Black

Panther is shot and he knows that his own good credit rating is good at Macy's, but has no value to the policeman who sees a *black* man when he sees him?

I do not know, and prediction is risky. In the fifties, how many saw the ferment and turmoil of the sixties? It is dangerous to conclude too much, precisely because we know so little about what moves people to social action. America's "silent black majority" might be one catalyzing event away from explosion, or it might have almost infinite capacity to endure pain and suffering and indignities.

In all candor, America has this group going for it now, and wisdom (if not will) would argue for viable policies to enlarge the group and to give it more political and economic power. But this has to do, also, with where America's "silent white majority" is, and the readings we get from that side are not too encouraging. All we know, with reasonable assurance, is that no tomorrow is precisely like the day before, and predictions—in this delicate area of social dynamism and human emotion—are something one makes with respectful caution.

Civil War

ANDREW HACKER

During the nineteen-thirties in New York City, the black-white boundary ran along Morningside Avenue. My family lived on 123d Street, just on the west—the white—side of that frontier. East of Morningside, one was in Harlem. Yet, only whites crossed this line. Apart from some domestic servants and an occasional delivery boy, entire days might go by without a black face appearing in adjacent white neighborhoods. On the other hand, those of us who were white never regarded Morningside Avenue as a barrier. We felt entirely free to wander into Harlem at any hour of the day or night, feeling secure that we would be neither accosted nor attacked. These were Depression years, and Harlem was by all odds the poorest of the city. It could well have been dangerous territiory for any white trespasser. Nevertheless, it was entirely safe.

The reason, of course, was that the blacks knew their place. Not only did they avoid white territory; they also realized that they must not approach whites who happened to stroll through their slum. Fear of the police obviously helped maintain this submission, for in those days Harlem's station houses were even less attentive to due processes of law than they are now.

A far more effective control, however, lay in the tacit understanding that members of America's subordinate races simply did not touch or threaten their betters. This is by no means to suggest that Black Americans were happy with their condition. Their mood was rather one of resignation; any impulse to protest fell victim to the presence of white domination within the black consciousness.

Before World War II, America's black population constituted neither a threat nor a problem for the white nation. The black minority subsisted under effective control in the rural South and also in the Northern slums, where intimidation and oppression were usually implicit but nonetheless real. Moreover, little attention was paid to the condition of Black Americans.

It was assumed, for example, that a docile pool of black labor would always be available for the arduous and unskilled services required by white society. No thoughts were raised concerning where housemaids or porters went or what they did after their working hours. Black America remained unobtrusive, apparently uncomplaining, and virtually invisible to white eyes.

These were placid years for white Americans. No serious civil-rights movement or organized protests arose to upset white sensibilities. No talk of Black Power was heard, and only the barest whispers of equalitarian aspirations could be detected. Aware of the totality of their thralldom, Black Americans simply saw no prospect for improving their bleak experience of life. They knew that they were marginal members of the nation, and realized that white America looked upon them as an awkward appendage, not quite human in major respects, and to be consigned to the end of the queue when scarce commodities were apportioned.

The most significant change for the black man has been not in his condition relative to white America, but rather in his perception of himself. Black Americans now feel entitled to more from the society that surrounds them. This transformation began during World War II, when, for the first time, Black Americans were actually courted by the white society. A labor shortage in private industry forced employers to offer jobs to workers who would previously have been excluded from consideration. Even the most exploited of domestic servants discovered that they, too, could exact better wages and working conditions. A human being's discovery that he is needed and wanted can be a catalyzing experience, forging a new conception of his own identity and accelerating the desire for even greater recognition. Once a society has told men and women that it cannot function without their participation, they will not willingly revert to less favorable conceptions of themselves when the crisis has passed.

Thus, the notions of civil rights and racial integration, the ideas of social equality and Black Power, had their origins in the wartime years. A new black mind was forged by events that had been neither planned nor anticipated. For even so brief a sojourn in the sun as the wartime years afforded was sufficient to introduce Black Americans to incomes, occupations and expectations that had hitherto been the exclusive preserve of whites.

The protests of the postwar generation signified an end to an acceptance of the half-slave, half-free status that had persisted for almost a century following the Civil War. Now blacks mounted new responses to displays of injustice. Now the white nation encountered arrogance and anger for which it was not prepared.

The unintended effect of World War II was thus to destroy the controls that had given race relations a placid appearance. Just as the war transformed the white population, instilling in average people new aspirations, so Black Americans found reason to believe that their history could take a new turn. Blacks showed themselves willing to jeopardize their lives and livelihoods as never before. The risks of arrest and imprisonment and bodily harm are now accepted, as is even the eventuality of death.

But if the psychology of black America has been altered, the material reality of black life has changed only at the margin. By all comparative measures, the nation's black citizens still find themselves confined to the status they knew a generation ago in terms of the jobs they manage to obtain, the quality of education their children receive, the habitations in which they must live and their overall level of health and well-being. Such amelioration as has occurred has been part of the general escalation in the living standard of the entire society. Today's blacks may be better off than were those of a generation ago, but the test is whether the gap between the races shows signs of diminishing. So far, this has not occurred.

In other words, for all the social and material gains that some blacks have experienced, no white man has been supplanted in the process. Given the existence of many talented and imaginative blacks and many whites having only marginal abilities, any meaningful moves toward racial equality would necessarily entail the demotion of several million whites so that more capable blacks could take their places. The fact that such transpositions have not occurred has not gone unobserved by blacks.[1]

---

[1] To be sure, a disproportionate number of blacks have recently been appointed to judgeships, admitted to top-ranking colleges and given promotions in the armed services. And it must obviously follow that if such scarce positions are given to blacks, then some white candidates will be passed over. But there is no shortage of alternative rewards for the whites who are deprived of prizes due to the symbolic admission of a number of blacks. Certainly the white youth who finds that "his" place at Harvard has been taken by a black applicant need not look forward to a lifetime as an unskilled

Thus, by all significant indices, America's blacks remain clustered at the bottom of the nation's social structure. Moreover, for all the protests and the inflation of black expectations, time will bring little noteworthy progress toward a racial parity. Indeed, all signs now point to a hardening of racial lines, and there is reason to believe that the relative condition of blacks will actually worsen over the coming decades.

A candid analysis of the social character of America's black population compels such a forecast. It is certainly true that some hundreds of thousands of blacks have come to share incomes and occupations once open only to whites, but this fact diminishes in significance when set against the accelerating growth of a vast black underpopulation. Listing statistics on the numbers of blacks admitted to universities or given corporate white-collar jobs only deflects attention from those beyond the reach of education or employment. The critical figures are far more elementary; black birth rates and black patterns of migration give the real picture of the racial future.

For a child conceived tonight will be the adolescent of tomorrow and the adult of the day after. The tenant farmer currently subsisting in rural Mississippi will soon move to New Orleans and thence to Chicago. The growing bulk of black America consists not of a few hundred thousand who have attained middle-class status but rather of the millions of marginal men, women and children for whom white society has neither need nor sympathy. These Black Americans will make their presence felt, no matter what the opinion or reaction of white America turns out to be.

The Southern economy has declared that it no longer needs its black minority. Blacks have been deemed superfluous people for whom fewer and fewer productive jobs will be available each year. Not only have the mechanization of agriculture and the consolidation of farming rendered black labor redundant, but the large cities of the South hold out little promise of honorable employment for those forced off the land. The unwritten economic code of the region is clear: whatever new jobs may be created must first be offered to the white citizenry. The South has more than enough underemployed whites to take over the workbenches of new factories, the desks of new offices and the counters of new shopping centers. Blacks are invited into the labor force only when the pool of available whites is depleted. Better than anyone, the Southern black understands the rules of this game. He realizes he will have to bide his time at the tail end of the "Help Wanted" lines, and he has seen all too many of those signs taken down before his name was called. So he travels North.

laborer. He will have to settle for Cornell. There are enough honorable opportunities for whites of even middling talent so that the promotion of a few blacks to what were once white echelons does not result in any perceptible sacrifice for the white community.

Buses and trains have been pulling into Chicago, Detroit, Cleveland, Los Angeles, New York and Philadelphia every day and night for a generation, disgorging exiles from Alabama, Mississippi, Louisiana and South Carolina. Sometimes a father comes alone, to search for a job and a place to live, intending to send for his family later on. Not infrequently the arrival will be a weary mother with a brood of young children, coming to find the husband who had departed some months earlier and whose subsequent silence casts doubts on his future family role.

But the North, like the South, has no real need for this flood of strangers. Few meaningful jobs can be created for these migrants, and they must squeeze themselves into the already overcrowded tenements that white map-makers designate as their territory. But at least no one need suffer malnutrition in the North. Welfare departments provide subsistence for unemployable women and children, and in the interstices of urban life men can find the small pickings of odd jobs and petty crime. The real scarcity lies in steady and moderately remunerative employment for black men, and even those who manage to get and hold jobs for sustained periods find few prospects for advancement.

The conventional precept that intelligence and industry will be rewarded with promotion and affluence applies only to those born with white skins. Blacks realize that, no matter how hard they may work, they still will remain society's porters and janitors and dishwashers. If one requisite for promotion is the ability to make a favorable impression on others, the mere possession of a black exterior precludes being taken wholly seriously. Excluded from traditional rewards and incentives, millions of black men move out of the system. Given similar prospects for success, the same proportion of whites would end up on urban street corners.

The facts of ghetto life compound this condition. These enclaves are created and sustained not by their actual residents but by whites who live elsewhere. Simply by denying blacks freedom of housing, white America stakes out the residual areas where blacks may live. To be sure, a few blacks do manage to break out of these confines (and others claim that they could move, but remain in the ghetto by choice). However, the majority, and especially the new arrivals, must make homes in the slums. The ghetto's boundaries are always expanding as a few more blacks move into proximate streets, thereby accelerating the exodus of remaining whites. But every better-off black knows the difficulty of leapfrogging into white neighborhoods: the humiliations he will encounter in his search for a home in such off-limits territory, and the risks he and his family will endure if he tries to settle among inhospitable householders. For this reason alone much of the black middle class continues to live in the ghetto.

Department stores and restaurants, hospitals and universities, municipal offices and police stations, even airplanes and interstate highways are all white estates. Indeed, the entire country—apart from its ghettos—is white property where nonwhites know they have no license to tarry after they have completed the approved errands that brought them there.

The black ghetto may well be a community; indeed, it may warrant that designation far more than most white neighborhoods. Yet, for all the shared experience and camaraderie of its residents, the ghetto also exhibits a greater measure of anarchy than any other region of American society. Crime, violence and the sheer risk to life and limb are of epidemic proportions. (The odds that a resident wi'l suffer physical assault are 130 times greater in a black slum than in a white middle-class suburb.) The police provide protection at only minimal levels; danger lurks on the streets and in the tenements, for blacks have no compunctions about preying on their fellow blacks.[2] Quite clearly, the ghetto is no fit place to raise children. Any hope that parents may have of exerting influence over their children suffers defeat once their youngsters reach the streets. School-yards and sidewalks become recruiting grounds for gangs, and youthful friends as often as not lead one another into temptations that take a mortal toll before adolescence has ended. The street forms the focus of life, and exacts its price: heroin addiction, arrest and imprisonment, prostitution, or simply the lackluster life of semiliteracy and sporadic employment. Boys

[2] It is no paradox that black citizens complain about *both* the lack of police protection and the incidence of police brutality. Most crime is intraracial: that is to say, the majority of crimes committed by blacks are perpetrated against members of their own race. And this is the chief reason why the police show less concern when responding to calls in the ghetto. For the typical policeman cannot bring himself to believe that the criminal injuries suffered by blacks deserve the attention accorded to those inflicted on whites. This double standard results in inadequate police protection for the residents of black slums.

At the same time, police efforts to preserve order are based on shotgun methods and racial stereotypes. Hardly a black American of any class has not experienced discourtesy—or worse—at police hands. For most policemen make no attempt to distinguish between law-abiding blacks and those who may be presumptive criminals. Hence, all blacks are treated in the same way. All are regarded either as having committed a crime or as likely to be embarked on one. If the black demand is for more police protection—which means more police patrolling the ghetto—it is also for policemen who treat black citizens with some semblance of human respect.

The answer, however, is not simply recruiting more black policemen to urban forces and then assigning them to ghetto duty. For so long as black policemen depend for their promotions and preferment on white superiors, they will simply mirror the behavior of their white colleagues and supervisors. Indeed, it is a ghetto truism that black police can be even more vicious and vindictive toward members of their own race. The only "solution" would be to permit ghetto areas to recruit and control their own police forces, including choice of commanders and supervision of procedures. But there is little prospect of white city councils and state legislatures permitting such a move. Quite clearly, white lawmakers feel that black citizens lack the capacity for handling so critical a responsibility. (Let me add, finally, that the election of black mayors will not be much help. For mayors are remarkably powerless when it comes to controlling the police.)

have police records before their 15th birthday; girls become pregnant before turning 16. (This is not, of course, a "racial pathology"; white Americans of all classes engage in self-destructive behavior. But far fewer whites are raised in ghettos, and thus their chances of prison or pregnancy are lower.)

And in these pregnancies lies the future of black America. Half the black births in Northern cities occur out of wedlock, a figure unlikely to undergo substantial reduction during the next several decades. Moral censure, or even the threat of lessened welfare payments, will not alter the ghetto's sexual habits. For these progenitive adolescents live in a world where puritanical or even precautionary morality has little relevance. To expect such boys and girls to exhibit self-restraint or to adhere to a code created by an alien and uncaring society is self-deception. Those who preoccupy themselves with the immorality and irresponsibility found in slum society would do well to turn their attention to the new generations of youngsters being spawned in our ghettos this very moment. These infants will be adolescents 15 years hence, and potential criminals, terrorists and unemployed adults a decade thereafter. Having come into the world unwanted by their parents and unneeded by society, they stand only the slightest chance of knowing love or encouragement or even recognition of their humanity. In the process of creation right now are rioters and rapists, murderers and marauders, who will despoil society's landscape before this century has run its course.

This underpopulation dominates the black birth rate and by sheer power of numbers decelerates all efforts at racial amelioration. Prior to 1970 it was customary to refer to blacks as comprising one-tenth of the American nation. However, white America would be well advised to pay closer heed to the official statistics. Of the infants now being born, blacks account not for one in ten but closer to one in six. Black Americans will always be a minority; but as the white birth rate declines, that minority will start to approach 20 or perhaps 25 percent of the population.

The time has come for some unwelcome candor: to admit that white America does not want to deploy its resources toward redeeming the black citizenry. Any meaningful amelioration of black America's condition would require money and effort, personnel and priorities—indeed, moral and emotional commitments—that the white society simply will not muster. If the merest hope of survival were to be granted to millions of black children, they would have to have care and attention costing many times what even the most prosperous of suburbs give to their own sons and daughters. Such a mission of rehabilitation would call for a virtual army of nursery-school teachers, public health nurses, building inspectors, rat exterminators, probation officers, welfare workers and—not least important—policemen willing and able to render effective service in the black ghettos.

However, white America, which pays most of the country's taxes and elects all save a handful of its lawmakers, cannot be stirred beyond a conversational concern. Although the nation may seem preoccupied with racial vicissitudes, its principal output has been little more than a series of paper programs and endless conferences, commissions and committees. (Indeed, simply talking about "race" and "poverty" earns comfortable incomes for no small number of publishers, publicists and social scientists.) And while white America debates the wisdom of spending another billion dollars on yet another public project, the condition of the black under-population continues to worsen. The much publicized preschool centers, job-training agencies and birth-control clinics reach only a fraction of those in need of such assistance. And when we take into account the annual arrival of new infants and immigrants, the services which are available actually end up aiding an even smaller segment of our urban ghettos than they did the year before.

Those who write reports almost invariably conclude their remarks with the word "massive." They tell us that programs and appropriations must be "massive" if slums are to be rehabilitated, schools reformed and the employment system restructured. This is true, but America's racial situation has reached the point where deploying a major portion of the nation's resources would only just begin to alter prevailing imbalances. However, the only "massive" endeavor will be the continued use of that word. White taxpayers have no disposition to sacrifice their personal prosperity, especially to assist blacks—and no evidence can be produced to show that this attitude can or will be transformed by new information, exhortations, or appeals.

Black Americans realize this. Few have any illusions about white America's readiness to underwrite anything more than research and conferences. No one should be surprised at the more open displays of black resentment and rage. At the same time, it would be a mistake to attribute these stirrings to disillusionment over unfilled promises. It is certainly true that for almost two decades official pronouncements have appeared to hold out prospects for substantial amelioration. Supreme Court decisions, Presidential directives and acts of Congress have declared that school segregation, housing discrimination and poverty itself would be brought to an end. These pledges, impressive on paper, may well have raised some black expectations; their meager implementation certainly fueled black cynicism. But three centuries of experience have inured Black Americans to the failure of white promises, even those issued by the most authoritative of agencies.

Black discontent, therefore, does not arise from inadequate delivery on official assurances. Rather, its source lies in the contrasting conditions of life known by the two races. That contrast, so evident to blacks, is the chief wellspring of anger. And that mood would still be present even had Government been less grandiose in its commitments to racial reform.

Violence will mark relations between the races. Whites will live in increasing fear of depredations against their persons and property. And the grim overtones of race will exacerbate white fears, for being accosted by a black carries an added quotient of terror compared with robbery by a member of one's own race. The condition of the black population is such that the number entering its criminal class—particularly adolescents and young adults—rises each year. Consider the black infants born this morning: there is no reason to believe that the lives most of them will know in the next 16 years will deter them from committing acts of violence. No special prescience is needed to forecast the treatment they will receive from their birth through adolescence, so their subsequent behavior should hardly surprise us.

Moreover, black animosities now express themselves more openly, and each criminal act against a white yields not only its material dividend but also the pleasure of extracting some small revenge for centuries of racial wrongs. Even though black criminal violence is not part of any organized strategy, the fears aroused by such activity are as real as those stirred by purposive demonstrations.

The number of attempts to sabotage the mechanisms of government and society will grow. In addition to peaceful demonstrations such as marches and picketing, the country will be confronted by not-so-peaceful efforts at blocking traffic, impeding business and disrupting white America's normal routines. Millions of Black Americans have no incentive to identify with these institutions, and hence no compunctions about undermining their functioning. On occasion these disruptions will simply be mischievous; sending in false fire alarms, tying up telephone lines, closing off entrances to buildings, jamming roads at rush hours. However, the time will come when the malice will outweigh the mischief, often involving serious destruction: dynamiting of bridges and water mains, firing of buildings, assassination of public officials and private luminaries.

And of course there will be occasional rampages, for which the raw ingredients are always available. Start with a spring or summer day when cramped apartments force ghetto residents onto the streets, combine with a rumor of police brutality, add the thunderclap of a nearby store window shattering to the pavement. It requires no more than this to release energies pent up by a lifetime of frustration. However, these exercises in violence occur only within the confines of the slums, and most participants content themselves with a little looting. No sorties into white territory follow, if only because anyone who might attempt such an expedition knows he would be cut off, surrounded and decimated once he entered enemy ground. (White householders who arm themselves against a black invasion of their suburban homes underestimate black intelligence.) Ghetto rampages cannot be called "race riots," at least not in the traditional understanding of that term, for they do not involve physical confrontations between one race and another. They are, rather, excursions in community vandalism having at least some insurrectionary overtones, for the chief targets are alien-owned property inside the ghetto.

Not all violence involves assaults on persons or property. While human relationships can range from amiable to abrasive, most people become habituated to at least the appearance of civility. Therefore, when friction starts, those unprepared begin to find everyday life a more jarring experience. Until very recently white Americans could take it for granted that their relations with blacks would move according to form. Blacks wore the appropriate mask in the white man's presence, smiling or deferential as the occasion warranted. This demeanor was itself evidence that whites were in control. The capacity to exact an expected countenance is an impressive display of power.

But black eyes no longer smile so readily. More and more blacks glare straight back, their expressions reflecting insolence and contempt. This black gaze unsettles white sensibilities, undermining all traditional feelings of command. (To white liberals it is disturbing in a special way—individuals who profess sympathy for the black cause feel they should be exempted from such scornful glances.) The ways people look at, pass by, or brush against one another always imply their respective standings. The readiness of blacks to say—with their eyes, their dress, their intonations—that they will no longer wear their old masks is a gauntlet thrown at white faces. Given the accustomed conventions, it is an act of violence.

For all the erosion of black deference, expressions of black power are sporadic. The consciousness of more than 20 million people does not change overnight. Nevertheless, the emergence of black pride has been surprisingly sudden, and for this reason real mobilization may occur much sooner than current disorganization would suggest. But Black Americans have yet to mount the kind of rebellion typical of a people victimized by alien oppressors. It is noteworthy—at least with the close of the nineteen-sixties—how few acts of organized terror have been staged by blacks.

Only a dozen or so young, committed men and women in any slum of several hundred thousand are required for a series of symbolic acts. Why, for example, have no white policemen been found in ghetto alleys or tenement hallways, their throats slit ear to ear? (Of course, neighbors must be willing to shield the perpetrators, risking arrest, interrogation and imprisonment.) This sort of violence prevailed in Europe throughout the German occupation, in Palestine during the British mandate and in Algeria prior to the French withdrawal. But it has yet to happen in New York's Harlem and Bedford-Stuyvesant or Chicago's South and West

Sides. Moreover, blacks in the South have had endless opportunities to fire shots at white sheriffs patrolling rural roads. The failure of black America to produce even a score of men willing to display such resistance shows how strong are the controls which have held that race submissive for so long. Yet, given the contemporary ferment, the occurrence of symbolic terrorism becomes more and more likely. The very laws of chance—the emergence of 25 guerrilla warriors from among 25 million—hurtle in this direction.

White America's responses can easily be predicted. Unwilling to undergo either the emotional adjustments or material sacrifices necessary to correct racial inequalities, whites will adhere to less costly alternatives: retreat, resistance, repression.

Indeed, the white majority has already committed itself to a course whose effect, if not intention, will be to frustrate the most pressing of black aspirations. White wealth, white votes, plus the sheer preponderance of white numbers, will be used to preserve the style of life white Americans have won for themselves in recent decades. The white population has nothing to gain and everything to lose by any significant alteration of the lines now separating the races. For if a single word characterizes white attitudes, it is *fear*.

But how can a black minority, a small and impoverished segment of a huge society, arouse such anxiety in 180 million hearts and minds? The threat, of course, lies not so much in the power blacks can deploy as in the vulnerability of whites when faced with the prospect of black proximity. Material prosperity, heightened status, enhanced schooling, increased articulateness—none of these advantages have succeeded in dispelling white fears of the black presence. Indeed, the spread of affluence and education actually serves to exacerbate this disquiet. Individuals who have experienced recent elevations in status are the most easily frightened.

Nightmares of racial inundation alternate with prayerful daydreams of blacks voluntarily reverting to earlier roles. Why don't *they* remain in their own parts of town instead of trying to push into places where they are not wanted? Why can't *they* send their children to the schools in their own neighborhoods rather than unsettle the entire system with demands for altering traditional boundaries? Why don't *they* work their own way up the economic ladder instead of insisting upon preferential consideration? Why don't *they* teach their sons and daughters respect for law, order and authority? Underlying such meditations is the hope that they will cease their demands and return to a status and psychology less threatening to white sensibilities.

While these hopes linger in most white hearts, styles of expression differ. Conservatives air their views with little diffidence. Those professing a greater liberality must ponder such thoughts in silence, for commitments to equality are now accompanied by fears of violence. Hence, the liberal wants blacks to stay in their ghettos, with the hope that they will be happy there. The conservative also favors such sequestration, but does not really care whether the blacks are happy in the ghetto or anywhere else.

Hence, the end of all illusions that Black Americans may have harbored about an alliance with white liberalism. While liberals may extend verbal sympathy on appropriate occasions, they continue their exodus to the suburbs or the more secure portions of the city, they place their children in private schools and they ask fewer questions about the way the police guard them from presumptive criminals. Apart from rhetoric ("massive expenditures" for rehabilitation of the ghettos, "crash programs" of job training), little distinguishes the behavior of white liberals from that of their conservative neighbors. The latter express their obduracy and animosity with a candor that may be frightening, but at least has the virtue of frankness.

The scenario is all too familiar. A black couple enters a white neighborhood on a Sunday afternoon to inquire about purchasing a house or renting an apartment. This in itself is enough to arouse tremors, for such visitors are seen as heralds of an invasion. Every map of metropolitan America shows territory lost to the blacks: once one is let in, the rest will follow. Admit a black teacher or even a physician or engineer, and on his heels will arrive unwed mothers, drug addicts and adolescent gangs. To be sure, some white householders profess their desire to have a black family on their block and one or two well-scrubbed and well-mannered black youngsters in their own children's classrooms. Tokens of this sort can be redeemed at the bank of conscience with compounded interest. ("Well, we have one four doors down from us." "My daughter has one in her class.") Yet second thoughts often follow, for what begins as a magnanimous gesture can become an aperture through which a flood will rush. This is why the United States has no "integrated" neighborhoods to speak of, only "changing" ones.

Thus, the tide moves on, sometimes slowly but always inexorably. Areas once immaculately white turn speckled and then black. The rear guard eventually flees, abandoning homes and schools in rapid disarray. But fewer and fewer hiding places remain. Having retreated to the city's outer reaches or into the adjacent suburbs, resettled homeowners may discover specks beginning to blemish the terrain they thought would be secure.

Why this fear of black contagion? Part of the reason lies in attempts by white citizens to safeguard their modest material fortunes. A majority of Americans now own their own homes, or at least bear responsibility for discharging an unpaid mortgage. The graduation of so many to the rank of homeowner has been widely applauded, for it was thought that attainment of this status would enhance identity and personal independence. Yet the burdens of ownership can be emotional as well as financial: not only does a change in a neighborhood's racial composition threaten a lifetime's investment, but anxieties begin to take their toll well before the day of crisis actually arrives. Current preoccupations over status, economic loss and physical safety create and exacerbate racial antagonisms to a far greater degree than prevailed when people lacked so proprietary an interest in their homes.

The majority of Black Americans are poor. The poorest Americans are black, and even the most prosperous blacks are still poorer than great numbers of whites. If all 25 million Black Americans were to be ranked by their incomes, every single individual on that list would have less money than his white counterpart of parallel ranking. Thus, the black who stands 17,376,289th among the 25 million blacks has a lower income than the white man standing 128,584,539th among the 184 million whites.

The implications in these figures should be apparent. Racial integration of American neighborhoods would have to be class integration as well. If 50 blacks moved into any neighborhood now containing 370 whites, every one of these blacks would be poorer than at least some of the whites, and a majority of them would be poorer than any of their white neighbors.

Very few Americans want to live among individuals of a class lower than their own. The disappearance of traditional tokens of status has caused a person's residence to become a critical measure of his social standing. The casual question, "Where do you live?" seeks not only information about a person's tastes but also some approximation of his class ranking. Where you live signals not only what you can afford but also whether you are headed up, down or marking time. To reside in a successful neighborhood is a symbol of personal success; to remain in one that is failing conveys a less joyous message. Few of us wish to risk an unfavorable judgment. Those who live amid inferior classes jeopardize the image they present to employers and associates whose favor they may require.

The very presence of poor people—especially poor blacks—unsettles middle-class sensibilities. Were neighborhoods to contain a mixture of races and classes, middle-class individuals would find themselves living amid conditions they now manage to avoid. The poor reside in more crowded circumstances, often with several families inhabiting a single-family dwelling. (For this reason and because money is unavailable for other activities, they also spend more time on the sidewalks and street corners.) The poor have more fatherless families, more free-wheeling children, and seem less committed to civil proprieties. And the poorer an area, the greater the incidence of drunkenness, drug addiction and violence both on and off the streets. Personal property and bodily safety are more vulnerable to depredations in less prosperous settings, and police seem to feel that the poor deserve less protection or attention than do better-off citizens.

As blacks arrive in a district and whites depart, such territory becomes more susceptible to burglary and assault. Once even a few blacks begin to reside in an area, their faces become part of the local landscape and members of their race who are not residents find it easier to make criminal forays into that zone. Given this, middle-class Americans prefer to escape to neighborhoods that are clean and secure. Moreover, the middle class has become quite fastidious when confronted by violence: men who wear white collars and work at sedentary jobs have had little experience fighting, and for them the prospect of being mugged may be far more terrifying than for those who live and work in less prepossessing surroundings.

This condition of mind precludes any possibility of establishing interclass—and certainly interracial—neighborhoods. In the past, mixed neighborhoods were not totally unknown. In small towns and parts of large cities, private houses and tenements often stood side by side. But in those generations social controls were effective; the poor understood their place, and their presence held no threat to citizens of higher station. Such residential patterns were possible because each neighbor appreciated where he ranked in the community, and he was aware that certain behavior would be deemed presumptuous for one of his income. But with the erosion of these controls, interclass living has become too great a gamble for the classes that have most to lose by such integration.

And there are, of course, the children. A democracy's parents must fight to guarantee the success of their children just as the animals of the jungle struggle to protect their young.

Most offspring of a democracy arrive in the world with neither inherited wealth nor the promise of subsequent prosperity. If they are to pass the tests and secure the credentials that society requires of those who inhabit its upper reaches, then parental assistance is necessary in the formative years.

Hence, the attempts to bestow on the children the advantages they will need in the competitions to come. Anxious and often obsessive attention becomes focused on the right school, the right college, the right course of study, the right career. In the upper middle classes only an irresponsible handful fails to attend parents' meetings. They come not so much to check up on the school and its teachers—although that motive is often present—as to pledge their allegiance to an institution that promises to ensure their children's ascent to a more elevated status.

A democracy's children must be taught to avoid improper associations if they are to emerge as successful adults in a competitive society. But such an education can only be achieved in a good school in a good neighborhood—a white middle-class school in a white middle-class neighborhood.

Unless properly shielded from injurious influences, every boy and girl is a candidate for the nether world of failures. (For one's offspring to have failed, moreover, becomes a commentary on the parents' ability to carry out the enterprise of child-rearing.) Adults who have made modest progress toward new plateaus know from their own upbringing the consequences of misguided associations. They realize how slum environments and inferior schools can nullify a youngster's prospects. Hence, the frantic effort of white Americans to insulate their sons and daughters from the presence of subordinate classes. The fear is of contagion; the disease is failure.

Because of the separation of races and classes, a generation of white children has been raised overhearing endless discussions concerning the gap that divides black from white and poor from prosperous. Most of these children have been reared in white neighborhoods and attended white schools, facts that further instill in them the idea that races belong apart. Even if their parents refrain from lecturing them on the results of admitting blacks to their schools and neighborhoods, white boys and girls overhear enough to become convinced that such incursions would have baneful consequences. The racial attitudes of today's children—tomorrow's adults—become ingrained at an early age; outlooks implanted during these years may not be extirpated after the beginning of adulthood.

There is little reason, then, to believe that oncoming generations of white Americans will display more tolerance than did their parents. For all the espousals of human equality and racial brotherhood heard from adolescents and young adults, they will in time assume responsibilities that will preclude the fulfillment of these vows. They, like their elders before them, will become burdened with families, mortgages and careers. The comforts and pleasures of possessions will make them less than eager to undergo sacrifices for the sake of others, and anxieties over the advancement of their own offspring will send them to the safety of all-white suburbs. Given the opportunities they will grasp and the lives they will lead, it is impossible to see how tomorrow's adult generation will differ from today's. The proximity of contaminating races and classes would certainly threaten their status and security no less than it has their parents'. And the conversations their children will overhear may well be marked by bitterness and fear.

Of course, conditions can change. But change can take the direction of increasing tension, rising animosity and exacerbated conflict. Anyone who argues that tomorrow's Americans will act more salubriously in matters of race and class must show that the future will somehow exempt these individuals from the strains and anxieties that attend child-raising, career-building and competition for social success. If people are to be more relaxed about their surroundings and less preoccupied with their personal status and safety, then the structure and psychology of the nation will have to undergo deep-seated changes. Otherwise, the growth of racial amity will remain a wishful forecast rather than a reality.

The white retreat will be accompanied by efforts at resistance and repression. As criminal violence, riots and guerrilla activity become more frequent, white Americans will seek to maintain order by force. Police will be granted an even wider latitude in their enforcement procedures and will not have to answer for their methods. New centers of incarceration will be built, new weaponry invented and distributed to accommodate the assumption that every black man between the ages of 15 and 35 may be considered a presumptive criminal. No explanation will need to be given for detaining citizens of such race and age, for in the eyes of white society the statistical probabilities demonstrate that enough individuals in these categories will sooner or later run afoul of the law or jeopardize public order.

These assumptions will inflict unjust punishments on many innocent blacks simply because they are members of a group having an above-average record of criminal convictions. But the burden will be placed on each black man to prove his innocence of any wrongdoing—past, present, or future. And his consignment to jail, with or without much attention to the evidence, will be regarded as the removal of one more miscreant from society's streets.

And having concluded that official agencies can no longer guarantee protection, more and more citizens of both races will purchase guns. Women's purses, executives' attaché cases and automobiles' glove compartments will hold such weapons, as will the drawers of bedside tables in countless homes across the country. As more people own guns, the use of firearms will inevitably increase, accompanied by the plea of "self-defense." Judges and juries will find themselves under growing pressure to render verdicts of "justifiable homicide," particularly in cases where white householders take the lives of black intruders.

Whether construed as a state of siege or a condition of civil war, strains between the races will suffuse all aspects of the nation's life. The resentments harbored by Black Americans have yet to erupt in full expression; the generation of young blacks now emerging will mount demands that white America cannot possibly accommodate; and society's conventional instruments of amelioration will prove both inadequate and irrelevant as both races react in an atmosphere of tension and fright.

What scares and frustrates white Americans most, however, is their knowledge that racial arrangements are no longer under control. After 10 generations of submission, blacks now display anger and arrogance that white society can neither command nor understand. Thus, black behavior must be seen as an exercise of power—psychological and physical as well as political—which American society never anticipated. The riots, robberies and assaults, even the modes of dress and contemptuous stares with which blacks meet white glances, are all symbols of racial uprising. As much a mood as a movement, as much guerrilla war as partisan maneuvering, Black Power has already achieved its greatest victory: the demoralization of white society. The awareness that blacks can no longer be ruled by hitherto effective controls has undermined white self-confidence. Repression will surely follow. But the use of force will only be a frantic quest for protection and survival by a people whose morale has been shattered by the surfacing of an inequality that was always inherent in our society.

Separatism: A Reality Approach to Inclusion?

BARBARA A. SIZEMORE

In this chapter, the separatist movement will be discussed as a special form of power-oriented movement to win a position of advantage for a minority group and its members. Black Americans have been involved in the struggle for position in the social order since 1619, and the nature of this involvement has been given many names. Among these have been: pluralist, assimilationist, secessionist, and militant (Turner and Killian 1957). To be militant is to be aggressive and vigorously active; consequently, because of the constraints imposed by the caste system, any black struggle would be militant. Other names have been given to the goal of Black Americans: integration, inclusion, and separatism.

Separatism as a black movement was catapulted into prominence by the fiery oratory of Malcolm X. He used "black nationalism" and "separation" interchangeably but defined black nationalism to include non-separatists. In Malcolm X's final months, he sought to describe his philosophy more precisely and more completely than black nationalism alone (Breitman 1965).

Black nationalism has given impetus to the rise of black consciousness, black power, black heritage, and black pride. This new mood has been discussed widely in the journals and the newspapers. On the one side, many have fears that the separatists' militancy may lead to a greater polarization of the races; yet others feel that these beliefs deal constructively with the reality of separation.[1]

To develop an understanding of the relation between separatism and education, this chapter will: review the effects of integration and racism; study concepts related to group participation in American life; consider separatism as a possible route to participation; and indicate the implications for quality education.

INTEGRATION AND RACISM

The conclusions of the Kerner Report stress Black Power as a response to the frustrations, hopes, and expectancies provoked by the failure of the civil rights movement to deliver the promises of its judicial and legislative victories. This posture has been generally accepted and appears frequently in the literature.[2] The Kerner Report accuses separatists of retreating from a direct confrontation with American society on the issue of integration and of functioning as an accommodation to white racism.

But there are other ways to view the conclusions of the Kerner Report. First, confrontation, in a sense, implies the act of bringing together two ideas or cultures for examination or comparison. The black community—through separatism and its emphasis on political, social, economic, and cultural programs—has submitted the declared white Anglo-Saxon Protestant value system to rigorous examination and comparison with its actual accomplishments (Carmichael and Hamilton 1967). Second, the great demand for housing in the black communities of major metropolitan cities has forced black people to initiate desegregation. This is a direct confrontation with American society on the issue of integration. The white response has been separation or resegregation.

Cruse (1967) may offer some insight into the view that blacks are "functioning as an accommodation to white racism." He discusses the American group reality as a struggle for democracy among ethnic groups rather than between two races and describes the civil rights struggle as such a contention. Cruse argues that the three most apparent minorities in this "nation of nations" are white Anglo-Saxon Protestants, African-Americans, and Jewish-Americans. The Jewish people, strong allies in the fight for integration, reject integration for themselves. They cling tenaciously to the Jewish right to a separate cultural existence and fight fiercely for a special kind of nationalism called Zionism.

---

[1] For a full discussion of this rationale, see L. Wirth, "Types of Minority Movements," and R. Linton, "Nativistic Movements," in R. H. Turner and L. M. Killian, *Collective Behavior*.

[2] Martin Luther King, Jr., takes important notice of this and also offers a searching analysis of the white backlash in *Where Do We Go From Here: Chaos or Community?* (New York: Harper and Row, 1967), pp. 12, 18, 94, 117–118.

Moreover, Cruse says that ethnic groups in the United States constitute a "motley collection of refugees from Fatherland poverty who worship daily at the altar of white Anglo-Saxon Protestant superiority."[3] As a result of such collective worship, this has become a nation of minorities ruled by a minority of one. He charges the white Anglo-Saxon ideal with effectively dissuading, crippling, and smothering the development of democratic cultural pluralism in this country. Cruse questions the policy of integration through the imposition of this ideal which stigmatizes the cultures of other ethnic groups. This policy makes the choice of integration impossible. Considering this argument, one could say that any group which integrates on these terms would be "functioning as an accommodation to white superiority."

Handlin (1965) asserts that the civil rights movement has never made a clear choice between available alternatives, and herein may lie the test of the "white Anglo-Saxon ideal." Handlin gives two definitions of integration. One refers to the openness of society, to a condition in which every individual can make the maximum number of voluntary contacts with others without regard to qualifications of ancestry. If this alternative were effected, all barriers to association would be leveled except those based on ability, taste, and personal preference. The other definition refers to integration as racial balance, which means that individuals of each racial or ethnic group are randomly distributed throughout the society so that every realm of activity contains a representative cross-section of the population. The former definition indicates free choice to equals; the latter makes no such assumption. For Handlin, the only barriers left in his "open society" would be taste, ability, and personal preference. For Cruse's "ethnic pluralism," the remaining barrier is culture, based on one's personal taste and preference. Neither one of these positions precludes separatism.

Despite these views, most planning for integration has been based on the concept of racial balance with desegregation of black people as the first step.[4] This goal-decision is probably due to the lack of well-defined means for achieving integration as an open society. Therefore, the liberals, determined to correct segregation and armed with the decision of the Supreme Court, have chosen alternatives best suited to already defined goals and interests but which fail to correspond to the interests of the black masses. The differing goals and interests of middle class white liberals and Negroes have obscured the real issues and obstructed critical analysis. A closer look at the social arrangements would have revealed the patterns of white resegregation and raised a more relevant question:

[3] H. Cruse, *Crisis of the Negro Intellectual* (New York: William Morrow, 1967), p. 456.

[4] See the literature on the Evanston, Ill., school desegregation and G. Coffin, "Moving Toward Integration," *Illinois Education* (November, 1968).

How does one desegregate whites? This question might have led to a new set of definitions and alternatives.

As a result, many blacks have refused to support the concept of racial balance. They argue that eighty percent white and twenty percent black is also racial imbalance. They decry the assumption that a school is bad because it is predominantly black or poor. Carmichael and Hamilton declare this position:

> Clearly, "integration"—even if it would solve the educational problem—has not proved feasible. The alternative presented is usually the large-scale transfer of black children to schools in white neighborhoods. . . . Implicit is the idea that the closer you get to whiteness, the better you are.[5]

They propose a course of self-determination for better black definitions of social arrangements and more productive solutions for black people. In their proposal there is a rejection of belief in the "universal rightness of the white Anglo-Saxon ideal."

Myrdal (1962) explored this belief and the psychic resistance which it caused. His work indicated that the legitimate task of education is to correct the "crudely false but popular beliefs" concerning the blacks and their relation to the larger society by subjecting these beliefs to careful examination. This educational objective would have to be achieved in the face of psychic resistance mobilized by people who feel an urgent need to retain their biased beliefs in order to justify their way of life.

Moreover, this psychic resistance has crippled seriously whatever chances exist for a genuine open society. The flight to the suburbs curtails opportunities for open housing, open enrollment, busing, pairing, and transfer. As the core cities become blacker and blacker, the number of available voluntary contacts between the races decreases. Thus, it would seem that "psychic resistance" and the manifestation of racism are real problems with which the desegregation of blacks simply does not deal.

Consequently, to say that black power is a withdrawal policy of frustration and hopelessness seems to oversimplify a much more basic issue. Racism and its attendants—poor education, poverty, and unemployment—create a situation unable to sustain life. Black people, then, must find a way to survive. The black man searches for this way—by a careful study of his history, an agonizing analysis of the data from empirical studies, a critical examination of circulating myths, and an ongoing evaluation of the great welfare programs. More than ever, he attempts to create his own definitions and develop his own concepts.

[5] S. Carmichael and C. V. Hamilton, *Black Power* (New York: Random House, 1967), p. 157.

CONCEPTS RELATED TO GROUP PARTICIPATION

The concept of identity appears frequently in the literature of the black separatist movement. Elijah Muhammad (1965) discusses it within the framework of "Original Man." He urges his followers to "Know thyself, love yourself, understand self, help self, get knowledge to benefit self and use knowledge of yourself." He also deals with what the so-called Negro must do for himself.

Essien-Udom subtitled his report on the Muslim community "A Search for an Identity in America":

> The tragedy of the Negro in America is that he has rejected his origins— the essentially human meaning implicit in the heritage of slavery, prolonged suffering, and social rejection. By rejecting his unique group experience and favoring assimilation and even biological amalgamation, he thus denies himself the creative possibilities inherent in it and in his folk culture. This "dilemma" is fundamental: it severely limits his ability to evolve a new identity or a meaningful synthesis, capable of endowing his life with meaning and purpose.[6]

Erikson (1968) develops the concept more fully and arrives at three different identities: personal, ego, and group. Personal identity is the perception of the continuity of one's existence in time and space and the perception of the fact that others recognize one's sameness and continuity. Ego identity concerns the quality of that existence or the awareness of the fact that there is a selfsameness and continuity to the ego. Group identity is the group's basic way of organizing experience, which is transmitted through child training to the foundation of the ego.

Erikson argues that man has survived as a species by being divided into pseudospecies:

> First each horde or tribe, class and nation, but then also every religious association has become *the* human species, considering all the others a freakish and gratuitous invention of some irrelevant deity. To reinforce the illusion of being chosen, every tribe recognizes a creation of its own, a mythology and later a history: thus was loyalty, to a particular ecology and morality secured.[7]

Therefore, the development of the pseudospecies becomes a program of group cohesion and group solidarity to protect the group from other

[6] E. U. Essien-Udom, *Black Nationalism* (Chicago: University of Chicago Press, 1962). Reproduced by permission.

[7] E. H. Erikson, *Identity, Youth and Crisis* (New York: W. W. Norton, 1968), p. 41. Reproduced by permission.

pseudospecies. Concomitant to such cohesion is the rejection of others, which Erikson explains as negative identity. The negative identity of other pseudospecies is "perversely based on all those identifications and roles which are most undesirable" and "dictated by the necessity of finding and defending a niche of one's own."[8]

So it becomes necessary for the well-defined pseudospecies to project its negative identities toward the other tribes. Erikson says that for this reason the pseudospecies is one of the more sinister aspects of group identity, for "this projection in conjunction with their territoriality gave men the reason to slaughter one another." He questions whether or not:

> . . . identity, can be said to be a good thing in human evolution since it has vastly overburdened the system of mortal divisions with the need of reaffirming for each pseudospecies its own superiority.[9]

Notwithstanding this universal position and all-human ethic, such divisions do exist in American group reality so that one group's identity is relative to another's. The desire for emancipation from a more dominant group identity may be the central dynamic in groups of stigmatized individuals.

Stigma is a useful concept in understanding the dynamics of negative identity. Moreover, various kinds of racial discrimination are devised on this assumption:

> We construct a stigma-theory, and ideology to explain his inferiority [the minority member] and account for the danger he represents, sometimes rationalizing an animosity based on other differences, such as those of social class.[10]

For Goffman, personal identity is the means available to differentiate an individual from all others by a single, continuous record of intertwined and entangled social and biographical facts. Social and personal identity are part of other persons' definitions regarding the individual while ego identity is a subjective reflexive matter that is felt by the individual.

Using these concepts, Goffman presents an analysis of group alignment and ego identity. Emphasis is placed on the dilemma of the stigmatized individual who finds that the "in" group and the "out" group each present an ego identity for him. Society tells him that he is a member of the larger group, which means that he is a normal human being, but also that he is "different" in some degree and that it would be foolish to deny this difference.

[8] *Ibid.*, p. 175.
[9] *Ibid.*, p. 41.
[10] E. Goffman, *Stigma* (Englewood Cliffs, N.J.: Prentice-Hall, 1963), p. 4.

Goffman proposes several solutions to the stigmatized black man: (a) to support a norm but be defined by himself as outside the relevant category, to realize the norm, and put it into practice personally; (b) to alienate himself from the community which upholds the norm, or refrain from developing an attachment to that community; or (c) to pass and cover as a member of the "in" group.

Goffman and Erikson deplore alienation and argue its faults for an integrated society; yet Goffman realizes that the support of such a norm shifts the burden from society to the victim.

> It is said that if he is really at ease with his differentness, this acceptance will have an immediate effect upon normals, making it easier for them to be at ease with him in social situations. In brief, the stigmatized individual is advised to accept himself as a normal person because of what others can gain in this way, and hence likely he himself, during face-to-face interaction.[11]

This line clearly absolves the wider society of any responsibility for the unfairness and pain of the society-imposed stigma; therefore, society can remain relatively uncontaminated by intimate contact with the stigmatized and relatively unthreatened in its identity beliefs. Consequently, the stigmatized black who cannot pass or cover must decide to assume responsibility for the sin or alienate himself from the community of the sinner.

In fact, Grier and Cobbs submit that it is necessary for a black man in America to develop a profound distrust of his country and of his white fellow citizens because he must be on guard against physical hurt. This condition promotes a cultural paranoia in which every white man is a potential enemy unless proved otherwise and every social system is set against him unless he personally finds otherwise. Adaptive devices are developed in response to this environment.

> They are no more pathological than the compulsive manner in which a diver checks his equipment before a dive or a pilot his parachute. They represent normal devices for "making it" in America, and clinicians who are interested in the psychological functioning of black people must get acquainted with this body of character traits which we call the Black Norm.[12]

The stigmatized black man fights for survival by synthesizing his personal and ego identities, weaving them into an "inner self" that is usually in

11 *Ibid.*, p. 119.
12 W. H. Grier and P. M. Cobbs, *Black Rage* (New York: Basic Books, 1968), p. 178. Reproduced by permission.

conflict with the external world, which can be fought only by the self-determination of his group.

Interestingly, Erikson argues that self-determination is an integral part of ego identity:

> For the American, group identity supports an individual's ego identity as long as he can preserve a certain element of deliberative tentativeness, as long as he can convince himself that the next step is up to him and that no matter where he is staying or going he always has the choice of leaving or turning in the opposite direction.[13]

Parsons states that a strong ego, secured in its identity by a strong society:

> . . . does not need artificial inflation for it tends to test what feels real, to master what works, to understand what proves necessary, to enjoy what's vital, to overcome the morbid, and to transmit its purpose to the next generation for the creation of a strong mutual reinforcement with others in the group.
>
> A weak ego does not gain substantial strength from being persistently bolstered.[14]

The choice of alternatives remains difficult for the black man in America. He is victim of a stigma which is so highly visible that passing or covering is almost impossible. If he supports the norm, he supports his own inferiority. In his separated status, he has created a black norm. This black norm has made the drive for integration impotent. This black norm may lead toward black nationalism.

The concept of nationalism has been discussed by Parsons (1965) in the framework of "societal community." Societal community refers to the total society as a system which forms a Gemeinschaft—a focus of solidarity or mutual loyalty of its members and a consensual base underlying its political integration. Such a Gemeinschaft may not exist for the total American society but only for the religio-ethnic-kinship groupings which form a network of associations. If so, it is necessary to establish a common core of values which Parsons discusses as follows:

> . . . the associational structure must be in accord with the common values of the society: members are committed to it because it both implements their values and organizes their interests in relation to other interests. In

[13] E. H. Erikson, *op. cit.*, p. 67.

[14] T. Parsons, "Full Citizenship for the Negro American?" in T. Parsons and K. B. Clark (eds.), *The Negro American* (Boston: Houghton Mifflin, 1965), pp. 709, 750. Reproduced by permission of *Daedalus,* Journal of the American Academy of Arts and Sciences.

the latter context it is the basis for defining rules for the play of interests which make integration possible, preventing the inevitable elements of conflict from leading into vicious circles radically disruptive of the community. It is also the reference base of the standards of allocating available mobile resources in complex communities.[15]

He argues that societal community is linked with political organization in all advanced societies but is also differentiated from it. However, that political organization (or government) is not identical with the community in American society today, and it is when the two are in conflict that revolutionary situations arise. Such a conflict exists at present between the political organization and that part of the black community which is not committed to the values of white supremacy and European superiority.

The central concept in Parsons' explanation of the emergence of nationalism is the differentiation of societal community. Three aspects of this emergence are: the differentiation of criteria for belonging to the nation in contrast to membership in the religio-ethnic-kinship group; the differentiation of the nation from its government; and the differentiation of the societal community as a nation from the integration of community, ascriptive bases and government to a synthesis of citizenship and territoriality.

Parsons defines inclusion as the process by which previously excluded groups attain full citizenship or membership in the societal community, and he classifies the components of citizenship as civil or legal, political, and social. Parsons feels that inclusion must be linked intimately with the process of differentiation to produce an increasingly pluralistic social structure. Inclusion should guarantee multiple roles and full participation with the maintenance of distinctive ethnic or religious identity.

Parsons analyzes the process of inclusion by using a model similar to the "supply and demand" paradigm of economics. With more control in the hands of those who are "in," there are demands for inclusion from the excluded group and from the elements already "in." In addition, there is a supply which operates from both sides of the exclusion line. Supply refers to the excluded groups' qualifications for membership, a matter of their cultural and social structures. Demand depends on the attitudes of both the group "wanting in" and important sectors of the group already "in." Much of the process occurs inconspicuously without much movement, but such movements gain strength as the strain of conflict between the normative requirements for inclusion and the actual limitations are translated into pressures to act. Parsons comments finally that the ultimate social grounding of the demand for inclusion lies in commitment to the values which legitimize it. However, the intensive strain to increase

[15] *Ibid.,* p. 710.

mobilization of such commitments encounters a problem deriving from the fact that value-commitment is only one of the factors necessary for successful inclusion. Parsons summarizes in this way:

> Strengthening this factor without likewise strengthening the others may lead not to promotion of the "cause" but to a disproportionate activation of the always-present factors of resistance, and hence to setbacks.[16]

Parsons' goal is inclusion, which needs value and association commitment and political power and influence for fruition. For excluded blacks, the reality base or starting point consists of the "always present factors of resistance," the absence or presence of a strong economic base, and the necessity for the excluded group to fight its way in. In assessing the alternatives available for decreasing the distance between the blacks and their goal of inclusion, there is a need for power. This presents a major problem for Parsons' inclusion paradigm, for he applies the principle of supply and demand to a situation demanding power.

Parsons strongly repudiates those who would achieve integration by power, emphasizing, instead, the mobilization of political and economic interests at the expense of value emphasis, acceptance, and willingness. He believes that only a balanced combination of ideal and real factors provides the formula for success. He indicates that the inclusion process is not synonymous with becoming white Anglo-Saxon Protestant. This process would hardly produce a new "in" group but rather a carbon copy of the group already "in." Consequently, the "in" group would continue to perpetuate itself because it constructs the qualifications for membership, restructures the institutionalized "slots," and rearranges the basic citizenship patterns. Such a condition would be rife with difficulties for a group whose major disqualifying factor is unchangeable.

The weaknesses in the "supply and demand" paradigm for the inclusion of black people seem numerous. The demands for inclusion from certain elements already "in" may be too small, silent, or powerless: the supply of those qualified for membership may be limited due to the unacceptability of blackness or of non-occidental values and cultures; the creation of institutional "slots" may be exclusively exploitative according to the basic citizenship patterns prevailing in the community; and the mobilization may rest almost entirely in the hands of the excluded group (the black people).

Assuming that the mobilization of factors for inclusion rests predominately with the excluded group, a model should afford that group with the initiative and the power. The black man needs a power model for many reasons. He is discriminated against because of color, which can never be altered to fit the requirements of the "supply" dimension. He

---

[16] *Ibid.*, p. 722.

has to fight for his legal-political rights. He has lost his religio-ethnic-kinship origins and heritage. He has rejected his adaptive and acquired plantation culture and lost the record of his gifts and contributions to the country. Parsons recognizes this condition:

> Even as the victim of the most radical discrimination of any group, the Negro has not only been forced to be subservient, but has also failed to develop, or bring with him from his southern rural past, sufficient ingredients for socially effective self-help. A question not merely of individual qualities and initiative, but of collective solidarity and mutual support at many levels, particularly the family and the local community.[17]

In fact, the "supply and demand" paradigm is much more suitable for individual mobility than for group inclusion because of the group's need for solidarity and collective support, power dimensions which spring from a separated condition. Although Parsons, Goffman, and Erikson discuss the dangers of separatism for America, they offer no viable alternatives which dignify blackness.

Erikson argues that the oppressor often has a vested interest in the negative identity of the oppressed because it is a projection of his own unconscious negative identity—a projection which makes him feel whole. It would seem highly likely, then, in view of this reality, that most excluded or stigmatized groups would actively adopt separatism.

But the decision to separate requires some degree of collective solidarity and mutual support. This has never occurred on a large scale in the black community. Grier and Cobbs explain:

> Thus the dynamics of black self-hatred are unique. They involve the child's awareness that all people who are black as he is are so treated by white people. Whatever hostility he mounts against white people finds little support in the weakness and the minority status of black people. As it is hopeless for him to consider righting this wrong by force, he identifies with his oppressor psychologically in an attempt to escape from his hopeless position. From his new psychologically "white" position, he turns on black people with aggression and hostility and hates blacks and, among the blacks, himself.[18]

Unity cannot be achieved because too many opportunists, who are anxious to be on the side of the winner, join the oppressor. Parsons suggests that the healthiest line of development for the black man would be toward group solidarity and cohesion and the sense that being a black man has positive value. Although he fears the danger of cultivating sepa-

[17] *Ibid.*, p. 740.
[18] Grier and Cobbs, *op. cit.*, pp. 198–199.

ratism, he feels that the pluralistic solution is "neither one of separatism, with or without equality, nor of assimilation, but one of full participation combined with the preservation of identity."[19]

One consideration from Carmichael and Hamilton, Cruse, Goffman, Parsons, and Erikson, then, is that group solidarity and cohesion may be best acquired from a separated condition or vantage point.

SEPARATISM: A POSSIBLE ROUTE TO INCLUSION

There are several explanations which support the assumption that separatism is a normal step up the sociological ladder to full participation in society. One argument compares black nationalism to the separatist approach of the early Christians, who tended to exaggerate their own importance and to reject all others. Carroll explores this proposition:

> . . . the early Christians by no means had the universal love for men that Christ spoke about. They appear to have gone through a definite phase; they had universal love for the *brethren*—and a universal pity for the rest of mankind. The brethren were the "in" group, the ones who knew Christ and His way and were on the road to salvation. The pagans were the "out" group, and the Christians pitied them and wished to convert them.[20]

The early Christians considered the lives of the pagans worthless, evil, and fit for damnation.

There is also a parallel between black separatism and the newly-arrived ethnic groups who were extremely nationalistic and entertained a contempt for all other groups, both racial and religious. Nationalism was used by the Irish in their attempts to participate more fully in American life:

> Irish nationalism was the cement, not the purpose of Irish American organization. Essentially they were pressure groups designed to defend and advance the American interests of the immigrant. Nationalism gave dignity to this effort, it offered a system of apologetics that explained their lowly state, and its emotional appeal was powerful enough to hold together the divergent sectional and class interests of the American Irish. This nationalism was not an alternative to American nationalism, but a variety of it. Its function was not to alienate the Irish immigrant but to accommodate him to an often hostile environment.[21]

[19] T. Parsons, *op. cit.*, p. 750.

[20] J. J. Carroll, "A Second Look at Black Nationalism," *America* (July 22, 1967), p. 84.

[21] T. N. Brown "Social Discrimination Against the Irish in the United States," in N. Glazer and D. P. Moynihan, *Beyond the Melting Pot* (Cambridge: MIT Press, 1963), p. 241. Reproduced by permission.

This nationalism, which gave structure to the Irish working class resentments, often produced political radicalism in other groups. In addition, the Irish "negative identity" operated in other ways during the Civil War:

> The divergence between liberal Protestant and Catholic views in New York grew when Catholics generally declined to support the movement for the abolition of Negro slavery. In July, 1863, the New York Irish rioted against the newly enacted draft. For four bloody, smoke-filled days the mobs ranged the city. They attacked Negroes everywhere, lynched some, and burned a Negro orphanage.[22]

Moreover, the Catholic Church was opposed to the issues of social reform during the post-Civil War period and alert to the perils of socialism.

A comparison also can be made between black separatism and the separation of colonial nations from the master countries. Clark (1965) first defined the dark ghetto as an economic colony, and Carmichael and Hamilton use this definition:

> At all times, then, the social effects of colonialism are to degrade and to dehumanize the subjected black man. White America's School of Slavery and Segregation, like the School of Colonialism, has taught the subject to hate himself and to deny his own humanity. The white society maintains an attitude of superiority and the black community has too often succumbed to it, thereby permitting the whites to believe in the correctness of their position.[23]

Nothing meaningful has been done about institutional racism because the black community has been the creation of, and dominated by, a combination of oppressive forces (imposed stigma) and special interests in the white community. Carmichael and Hamilton stress the need for the black community to redefine itself, to set forth new values and goals, and to organize around them (vis-à-vis Erikson's pseudospecies declaration).

In each of the three instances described above, an increase in group cohesion (pseudospecies declaration) seems to result in an increase in rejection of other groups (negative identity). Fanon describes this as follows:

> The naked truth of decolonization evokes for us the searing bullets and bloodstained knives which emanate from it. For if the last shall be first, this will only come to pass after a murderous and decisive struggle between the two protagonists. That affirmed intention to place the last at the head of things, and to make them climb at a pace (too quickly, some

[22] N. Glazer and D. P. Moynihan, *Beyond the Melting Pot*, p. 233.
[23] Carmichael and Hamilton, *op. cit.*, p. 31.

say) the well-known steps which characterize an organized society, can only triumph if we use all means to turn the scale, including, of course, violence.[24]

Fanon concludes that one cannot decide to turn any society upside down unless one decides from the start to overcome all obstacles that intervene. Fanon's ideas apply to any society where a group is excluded—in this case, the colonialism of the ghetto.

In order to overturn all obstacles, reality demands that black men deal effectively with negative identity, with their social identity, with their group identity, with their personal identity, and with their ego identity.

The Black Muslim movement endeavors to do exactly this. Elijah Muhammad continually emphasizes the need for group identity and unity. He urges black men to love one another and to pool their resources for the common good. This social identity is forged into the Community of Islam, an international brotherhood of Asiatics (since Africa is a part of Asia). The name "Negro" is discarded. A new name, given by Allah, is presented to each new member to replace his slave name. The quality of existence is enhanced by certain teachings. Arabic and the civilization and religion of the black man are taught in Muslim schools. The people are encouraged to obey rules and regulations that are more stringent than those of the Protestant Ethic, moral codes similar to those of the New England Puritans.

Muhammad's major critics arise out of the protest against racial and religious hate. They expect Negroes to be patient:

> White society assumes that the Negro will almost always act in accordance with the stereotypes of behavior which it has evolved. Thus, in its view, the Negro will always act as a paragon of almost supine patience and reasonableness; he will not be subject to the human emotions of hatred, anger and love, nor of personal and group pride.[25]

White society does not want the Negro to be bitter. White society does not want to feel responsible or guilty about its actions. The Negro is expected to take the punishment for an uncommitted crime and to love the criminal in return.

On the other hand, Elijah Muhammad does not expect his followers to shoulder the blame for their treatment in the larger society. He puts the blame squarely on the shoulders of white society, charging that such a society must be one of devils and beasts. This is his black norm. Having

---

[24] F. Fanon, *The Wretched of the Earth* (New York: Grove Press, 1963), p. 30. Translated from the French by Constance Farrington. Copyright 1963 by Presence Africaine.

[25] Eissen-Udom, *op. cit.*, p. 23.

freed his people of the burden of blame, the dilemma is resolved. They are free to decide what is to happen to them. He provides new identities and new motivations.

Although Erikson deplores the division of mankind into pseudospecies because it interferes with world identity and the oneness of mankind, it was such a division which promoted the cohesion of the black community and its concomitant rejection of whites. This shift toward separatism, led by Malcolm X through the teachings of Elijah Muhammad, is reflected now in the messages of nonviolent and violent Christian leaders.

In a plan outlined for the Chicago public schools, Rev. Jesse L. Jackson, [former] director of Operation Breadbasket, said:

> Black children, preyed upon psychologically, destroyed spiritually and confined physically, are victims of America's sickness bent upon devastating all hopes of innocent black boys and girls. . . . A new order is going to reign in the black community. Whites who remain in the ghetto schools will find it very hot. In fact, white principals must go. White engineers must go. White glaziers must go. White imagery must go.[26]

This position has been stated by others. The Inner City Parents' Council, under the leadership of Rev. Albert B. Cleage, Jr., presented a program to the Detroit Board of Education in 1967. Their report made the following recommendation for quality education in the inner city schools:

> We propose that all administrative vacancies (Counselors, Department Heads, Supervisors, Assistant Principals, Principals, Administrative Assistants and Junior Administrative Assistants, Assistant Directors, Divisional Directors, Assistant Superintendents and Field Executives) be filled with Afro-Americans until such positions have been filled with Afro-Americans in proportion to the number of Afro-American children and young people in the Detroit school population.[27]

This posture is not unlike the position of earlier ethnic groups. In his study of the Irish and Italian minorities of New Haven, Dahl (1961) called this nationalistic phase "the stage of socioeconomic homogeneity and ethnic solidarity." He hypothesized that an ethnic group passes through three stages on the way to political assimilation, from a highly homogeneous stage to a highly heterogeneous stage. He described an ethnic group member in the first stage as a ghetto resident, a member of a family with low and uncertain income, a victim of unemployment, a

---

[26] Rev. J. L. Jackson, *Chicago Defender* (March 8, 1968), p. 10.
[27] "Inner City Parents Present Program for Quality Education," a report of the Inner City Parents' Council, Detroit, July, 1967.

person of little prestige, or an object of discrimination by middle class Anglo-Saxon citizens.

Dahl explained that the public school system is an important instrument to the ethnic group. The acquisition of education provides the first step on the economic ladder, and the attainment of a teaching position affords a higher step.

> Jobs in the school system have been one of the main avenues of assimilation. When an ethnic group is in its first stage, some of its members become janitors in the schools. Later, as the ethnic group moves into its second stage, school teaching is a wedge that permits the group to expand its white collar segment. Then, in the third stage, members of the ethnic group begin to receive appointments as school administrators.[28]

Two prerequisites are necessary for this process of assimilation: (1) the training required for teaching must be inexpensive and easily available; and (2) teachers from immigrant backgrounds must be free to enter teaching without discrimination.

The petitions of Cleage and Jackson differ from those of the Irish and the Italians of New Haven in only one respect. The latter groups did not publicize their take-over.

Examples of separatism are abundant in the literature, but much ambiguity surrounds the concept because a confusion of bases exists. Separatism can be either a means or an end. When it is a means, the end is group mobility expressed as one of the following: assimilation, acculturation, inclusion, integration, or full participation in an open society. It is not within the scope of this chapter to discuss all ends. This chapter is concerned with integration and with inclusion or full participation, as discussed by Carmichael and Hamilton in this passage:

> The concept of Black Power rests on a fundamental premise: Before a group can enter the open society, it must first close ranks. By this we mean that group solidarity is necessary before a group can operate effectively from a bargaining position of strength in a pluralistic society. Traditionally, each new ethnic group in this society has found the route to social and political viability through the organization of its own institutions with which to represent its needs within the larger society.[29]

The Muslim community's attempt to deal with this goal may be prompted by the atavistic impulse to take the nationalistic tribal route. In this sense, as Carroll argues, nationalism in itself is a phase of growth common to all segments of mankind.

The maintenance of distinctive ethnic and religious identity may re-

[28] R. A. Dahl, *Who Governs?* (New Haven: Yale University Press, 1961), p. 153.
[29] Carmichael and Hamilton, *op. cit.*, p. 44.

quire separation in order to gain group solidarity and collective support to fight negative identities and stigma. Group solidarity and collective support are power dimensions which the "supply and demand" paradigm does not guarantee. The black man must have a power-inclusion model.

A POWER-INCLUSION MODEL

The power-inclusion model discussed here has been used by excluded groups for the achievement of group mobility and full citizenship in the American social order. This model has possibly five stages of progression toward inclusion. (See Figure 1).

The first stage is the *Separatist Stage* during which the excluded group defines its identity. This process includes the manifestation of the pseudo-species declaration, "We are the chosen people." It is during this stage that social or group identities are carefully delineated and religion is used to emphasize the "we" or "in" group feeling from which cohesion results.

The identity-separation phenomenon is difficult to analyze, for it is an ongoing process. The stages of identity formation probably occur before the inclusion process but provide the necessary impetus for movement into it. The process cannot begin until identity is defined; once this definition occurs, cohesion can develop.

The second stage is the *Nationalist Stage* in which the excluded group intensifies its cohesion by building a religio-cultural community of beliefs around its creation, history, and development. The history, religion, and philosophy of the nation from which the group comes dictates the rites, rituals, and ceremonies utilized in the proselytization of the old nationalism. Because of rejection by the white Anglo-Saxon Protestant and the ensuing exclusion from full participation in the social order, the excluded group rejects that social order and opts for its former nation. For the Irish Catholics, it was Ireland; for the Polish, it was Poland. This intense nationalistic involvement led to increased separation.

Accordingly, in the United States many groups are still separated. In some ways, the Jews are separated from gentiles; the Irish Catholics are separated from the Polish Catholics. Each ethnic, racial, social class, and religious group seeks voluntary association with its own members in one or more ways. Ethnic groups plug their form of nationalism into Americanism (the common core of myths and language provided by the white Anglo-Saxon ideal) and become Irish-Americans, Italian-Americans, German-Americans, and so forth. The nationalism of these groups is paraded annually on holidays such as March 17. So intense was the involvement of the nationalistic stage that such vestiges still remain. As group cohesion and solidarity increased, the development of negative identity occurred, resulting in the rejection of others.

The third stage of progression toward inclusion is the *Capitalistic Stage*.

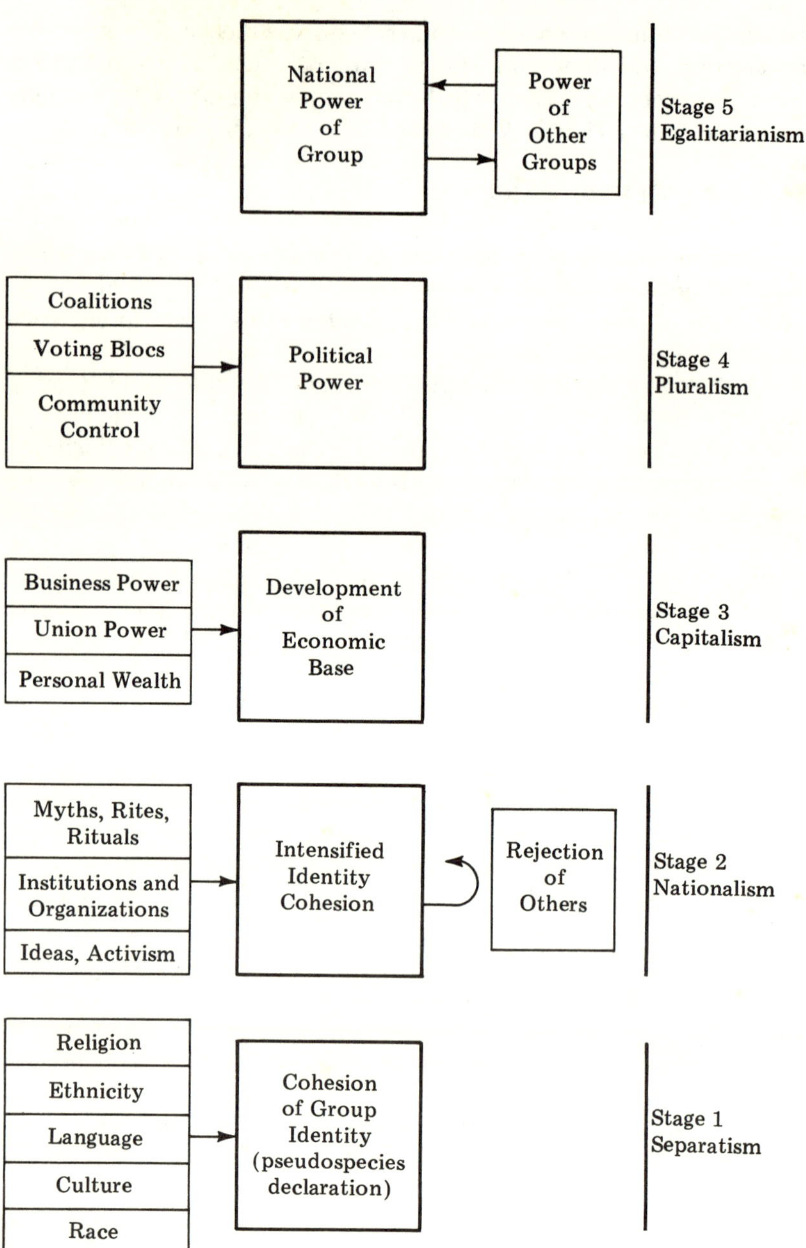

The cohesion developed in the Separatist Stage and magnified in the Nationalist Stage, added to the rejection of others created in the second phase, produces a need which can be developed into an economic base for the ethnic community founded on its active nationalism.

Such programs were discussed both by W. E. B. DuBois (1940) and Booker T. Washington. In fact, one of the accusations of the Kerner Report criticizes the "Booker T. Washington rhetoric" of the black separatist's economic programs. Glazer and Moynihan (1963) discuss the implications of the lack of a black business class, as proposed by Booker T. Washington, on job opportunities for black people.

Although there are many explanations for the lack of black businessmen, other ethnic groups obtained footholds in business by serving their own. This also provided jobs for their own people.

Glazer and Moynihan demonstrate that the best jobs demand skills and training which tend to be kept within the "in" group. Therefore, the problem is not simply discrimination against the blacks or any one group but against all outsiders. In other words, there are Irish and Italian skilled workers, in part, because Irish and Italians were prominent in contracting and construction and they dominated the unions. With other groups, then, nationalism and separatism have contributed toward an ethnic base for business and jobs.

The fourth stage is the *Pluralistic Stage* during which the group utilizes its cohesion-rejection powers to form a political bloc on its economic base in order to thrust its interests into the foreground of the political arena (Carmichael and Hamilton 1967). It is this stage which gives the illusion that integration is real.

For example, in the black man's drive for integration in housing, the white response was separation. At first sight, it would appear that whites were opting for separatism. On the other hand, since identity cohesion is an important variable in three stages of the power-inclusion model, the particular ethnic group involved in desegregation could be responding to the need for identity cohesion.

If an ethnic group is approaching or in the nationalistic phase when identity cohesion is great, the rejection of others will be intense. Resistance to desegregation may be fierce and violent. If the ethnic group is approaching or in the capitalistic phase, when identity cohesion and rejection have formed a strong economic base resistance may be immediate but nonviolent. In desegregation of housing, for example, this group could afford to relocate or to prevent the invasion.

When a group enters the pluralistic stage, desegregation may be a threat to their cultural institutions, but the group's high degree of participation in decision-making offers abundant opportunity for control of the rate of desegregation. Resistance might be delayed and nonviolent. Once in the egalitarian phase, the group has the power to control the conditions which provide impetus for desegregation. Bachrach and Baratz (1962) call this the silent face of power.

Carmichael and Hamilton indicate that coalitions are not viable when blacks are not equal partners. In this capitalistic society, no partner without capital is equal. In summarizing the experiences of the Mississippi Freedom Democrats, they write the following:

> The major moral of that experience was not merely that the national con-science was generally unreliable but that, very specifically, black people in Mississippi and throughout this country could not rely on their so-called allies. . . . Black people would have to organize and obtain their own power base before they could begin to think of coalition with others.[30]

In Carmichael's opinion at that time, it was imperative to form an independent base of political power *first*. The failure of the Lowndes County Freedom Organization in Alabama indicates the omission of a step in the progression—the economic base. Simply, candidates cost and need money. Any candidate who must be supported by another group has a bifurcated allegiance and can serve neither master.

The fifth stage is the *Egalitarian Stage,* sometimes called democratic, in which the interests of the group have as much chance of winning as those of other groups at this level of participation. This is utopian, yet in the American social order. For example, power is still held by white Anglo-Saxon Protestants but both Jews and Catholics are trying to get in. The Irish Catholics, through coalitions with other Catholics and blacks, managed to elect a president after some thirty years. Until recently, the Irish Catholics have been generally ineffective in gaining government assistance or support for their service programs, even though they save money for the taxpayers in educational facilities.

As Cruse says, this American world:

> . . . manages to reflect the social aspirations of the WASP, Catholic and Jewish groups above all others. . . . Among these three there is intense competition for recognition and group status, which, for political and propaganda reasons, is called fighting discriminatory practices. As long as the WASPs rule the roost, charges of discrimination will never cease until Catholics or Jews achieve more power and privileges than any "minority" could ever hope for in Rome or Israel.[31]

According to Cruse, American culture is sick because there is an American identity problem. If there is no American identity, what is the identity which is called American? If the so-called American identity is WASP, who are the people who are not WASPs? To solve these questions, Cruse calls for complete democratization of the national cultural ethos.

[30] *Ibid.,* p. 96.
[31] Cruse, *op. cit.,* pp. 451–452.

IMPLICATIONS FOR QUALITY EDUCATION

The ultimate goal of inclusion for excluded or stigmatized groups depends upon self-respect and identity. Wheelis (1958) says that identity is founded on value, specifically, on those values at the top: "beliefs, faiths and ideals which integrate and determine subordinate values." Any development of positive identities for members of excluded groups would require, then, a redefinition of Americanism in pluralistic terms and a revision of the common core values. For black people, stigma results from racism—the belief that race is the primary determinant of human traits and capacities and that racial differences produce an inherent superiority of a particular race. This belief may be firmly entrenched in the core values of American society. Separatists say that this value has destroyed the concept of the black man as homo sapiens. Wheelis suggests that modern man cannot recapture an identity out of the past because the old identity is not only lost but outgrown. He says that identity is not to be found but to be created and achieved.

Erikson prefers Vann Woodward's term "surrendered identity" because it does not assume total absence but something to be rediscovered. This must be emphasized because what is latent may become an actuality and a bridge to the future. He argues, moreover, that what is at stake is the realization of the fact and the obligation of man's genus. Separatists call this the struggle for survival.

As Grier and Cobbs say, there are no more psychological tricks that blacks can play upon themselves to make it possible to exist in dreadful circumstances. "No more lies can they tell themselves. No more dreams to fix on."[32]

With survival, then, as his goal, the separatist plans to rediscover his "surrendered identity" through black history, black literature, black myths, black models, black heroes and heroines, black teachers, black principals, and black religion. Such a process seems to repudiate the preservation of certain common core values. But to insure a pluralistic democracy, the common core of values should be common to each "nation" in this nation. Some common core values could be: love, peace, industry, honesty, democracy, humanity, and knowledge. Others, that are now common core values, could become alternates: property, western civilization, conformity, white male superiority, and Protestantism.

Donald A. Erickson (1968) explores this issue in his account of the struggles of the Amish people against the State of Iowa. They had been accused of violating the law by staffing their private schools with uncertified teachers. His research corroborated numerous other studies in

32 Grier and Cobbs, *op. cit.,* p. 213.

showing that the Amish educational approach had served the ethnic group well—and probably better than conventional schooling serves the larger society. The Amish ways are strange and their nonconformity is intransigent. Furthermore, they do not reinvest their earnings in the local economy because they are forbidden to purchase appliances and equipment, but they are skillful farmers, industrious, self-reliant, and humane. Erickson concluded that the action against the Amish was prompted not by the concern for the welfare of their children but by a bitter antagonism toward the Amish people and their common core values. He describes this Anglo-Saxon posture as "cultural arrogance."

The Community of Islam suffers from the same kind of religious discrimination. Muslim ways are also strange and their nonconformity is intransigent. In addition, they do not hide their conformance to the black norm.

Studies that have investigated separated groups with differing core values reflect some light on this difficult problem. Greely and Rossi (1966) found two ways by which Catholics could succeed markedly: the path of alienation from the Catholic community and the path of integration into the Catholic subculture. The latter was the most successful in leading to achievement, much more desirable from the Church's viewpoint and not dysfunctional for the larger society. The most likely explanation offered by Greeley and Rossi is that the religious community provides emotional support.

Erickson, in his review of the same study, observed that attending Catholic schools and participating in Catholic friendship cliques may promote well-being seldom experienced by adolescents who must function as members of a minority. He raised several provocative questions with regard to this observation.

> Will it turn out that the assimilationists are defeating their own purposes in attempting to outlaw Amish, Hutterite and Black Muslim schools? In the push for racially-integrated education, is the Civil Rights movement sometimes imposing a handicap on Negro youngsters by making them function as a minority at a time when they are most in need of emotional support?[33]

Being educated in the emotionally supportive setting of a school operated by one's own religious or ethnic group may promote more self-acceptance and security and render the individual more capable of full social participation. Erickson says it is possible:

> . . . despite folklore to the contrary, that if more Catholics were educated

[33] D. A. Erickson, "Contradictory Studies of Parochial Schooling," *School Review* (1967), 75, pp. 425–436.

in Catholic schools, more Lutherans in Lutheran schools, more Jews in Jewish schools and more Amish in Amish schools, there would be more national unity rather than less.[34]

Moreover, there is limited evidence to suggest that many graduates of Black Muslim schools continue their education in reputable colleges and universities and find niches in solid middle class vocations (Vontress 1965).

Other studies have been concerned with the core values of early ethnic groups. Handlin (1951) wrote much about the conflict between the public schools and the early ethnic groups. The schools were alien to the immigrants who thought of them as "sore spots" from which "might spread a hostile influence that could undermine the health of the whole immigrant community." One alternative was to devise voluntary schools that would serve to strengthen rather than weaken the coherence of the group. Although these attempts were judged unsuccessful by Handlin, the school was only one of several means of education utilized to build cohesion. The ethnic newspaper was another.

In addition to content, today's separatists are interested in the teaching-learning process and the use of school resources. Allison Davis (1948) pioneered the study of the effects of school resources and the teaching-learning process on children from different social classes. It was largely his work, and that of his colleagues, which changed the concept of intelligence and introduced the notion of cultural effects.

The Coleman Report (1966) also attempted to study the effects of school resources on the achievement of various ethnic groups. With some exceptions, mainly Oriental Americans, it found that the average minority pupil scored lower on tests at every level than did the average white pupil. However, the white group included many religio-ethnic-kinship groups. The Coleman Report might have yielded more information regarding the effects of ethnicity and religion had it separated Jewish, Catholic, and other ethnic groups from the white majority.

Stodolsky and Lesser (1967) have investigated this issue and confirmed the findings of Davis (1948) and Sexton (1961) that children from lower classes with less income do less well on tests than children from middle classes. But, the most striking finding of the study by Stodolsky and Lesser is that ethnicity does affect the pattern of functioning on intelligence tests, and once the pattern specific to the ethnic group emerges and is reinforced by the environment, social class variations within the ethnic group do not alter this basic organization. The other important finding is that social class influence is more powerful for the black group than for the other ethnic groups.

[34] D. A. Erickson, "Nonpublic Schools in Michigan," *School Finance and Educational Opportunity in Michigan* (Michigan Department of Education, 1968), p. 276.

The test scores of middle class children from various ethnic groups (Chinese, Jews, Negroes, Puerto Ricans, Irish Catholics) resembled each other more than the scores of different social classes within an ethnic group. For example, the verbal ability scores of middle class Negroes were more like the scores of middle class Jews than lower class Negroes. Significantly, the Irish-Catholic group failed to produce an ethnic group pattern:

> In short, there are at least two plausible explanations for the failure to replicate our results on other ethnic groups with the Irish-Catholic children: poor sampling of middle class and lower class Irish-Catholic families (due to their unexpected unavailability in Boston) or a real difference between Irish-Catholic children and those from other ethnic groups tested.[35]

A third explanation in terms of the power-inclusion model is that the Irish-Catholic group is now in the pluralistic stage of the inclusion process, vying for a place within the "in" group. Consequently, the original thrust has been dissipated by success.

Stodolsky and Lesser argue that providing a lower class family with what a middle class family has—better jobs, education, and housing—will produce levels of intellectual functioning resembling those of middle class children. This action will provide equal education and social opportunities for equal development. Then, since ethnic groups differ in patterns of ability, the problem becomes one of providing equal educational opportunity to all ethnic groups to maximize their development even at the expense of magnifying differences among the groups.

Stodolsky and Lesser conclude that recognizing the particular patterns of intellectual strength and weakness of various ethnic groups and maximizing the potential power of these patterns (by matching instructional conditions to them) will make the intellectual accomplishments of different ethnic groups more diverse and provide gains in pluralism within the society.

These findings chart directions for the development of separatism in the teaching-learning process. When the group is cohesive enough to create jobs from a strong economic base (which will change the milieu), additional income, education, and housing will lessen the effect of poverty on the learner. This will accelerate the process of equalization, for the disparity between the mental ability scores of middle class black children and lower class black children is greater than any other ethnic group tested.

A curriculum should be designed to expedite the maximum positive

---

[35] S. S. Stodolsky and G. Lesser, "Learning Patterns in the Disadvantaged," *Harvard Educational Review* (1967), 37,pp. 576–577.

development of any combination of individual strengths and weaknesses. Such a curriculum would need to support pluralistic values at the common core, and separatist values as alternates, in order to provide emotional support for all learners and to develop their personal, ego, and group identities. Necessarily, teacher-training institutions must be changed, and other social, governmental, and private agencies must be committed to correcting income deficiencies which prohibit learning in stigmatized groups.

Most minority groups in the United States desire full participation in American life. The majority of black people are not different. Grier and Cobbs believe that the black masses will rise with a demand that white Americans "get off our backs!" They argue that the solution will be to simply get off!

> This is no oversimplification. Greater changes than this in the relations of peoples have taken place before. The nation would benefit tremendously. Such a change might bring about a closer examination of our relations with foreign countries, a reconsideration of economic policies, and a re-examination, if not a redefinition, of nationhood.[36]

On the other hand, Elijah Muhammad and his followers do not share their faith in the white society. The black norm is far more evident in his approach:

> I have taught for years that you cannot demand the white man to accept you as his equal or as his brother, because he is intelligent enough to know that you are not his equal, that you are not his brother. Even if you go back to Adam—he is not the black man's father. We are not all compatible.[37]

Elijah Muhammad believes that the education of so-called Negroes has been a failure because it was designed by the slavemasters to keep Negroes in their place. He wants his people to acquire an education that will make them better able to use their knowledge for themselves.

Grier and Cobbs argue that the family prepares the child through its training to be free or slave and that "in spite of the yammering of naïve observers, education has never offered a significant solution to the black man's dilemma in America." But their solution is still dependent upon the white man's initiative, upon his decison to act on this problem. Elijah Muhammad insists that this is folly:

> One hundred years up from slavery. You still today feel that you have been schooled. You have a few diplomas and degrees. You can do little

[36] Grier and Cobbs, *op. cit.*, p. 203.
[37] Muhammad, *Message to the Blackman in America*, p. 233.

things educationally, but that does not yet even get you justice in America. You still suffer injustice with an armful of diplomas and degrees from colleges and universities . . .[38]

The objective of Muslim education, then, is to reeducate the so-called Negro: to attain his rightful place in the sun as a black man; to develop a feeling of dignity and appreciation of his own kind; to observe the daily Moslem duties; to learn Arabic; to observe the dietary laws; and to develop a sound moral character.

Elijah Muhammad directs his educational program toward group ends. This has not been the usual thrust of the educational institution in the United States. Janowitz explains that the American school system is adapted to facilitating the mobility of individuals rather than dealing with the problems of group mobility:

> But the contemporary requirements of social progress mean that the school system must also become concerned with group mobility, that is, with the transformation of the slums as a social entity.[39]

The option for separatism is neither new nor revolutionary. In fact, it seems to be the basic route to full participation chosen by excluded groups because it gives the initiative to the excluded group. For black people, this choice may be both a response to the failure of the whites in America to do anything and a reaction to their intransigence. But, more important, separatism has resulted from the acute awareness that this initiative must originate in the black community. This initiative may be beneficial to race relations in this country. The prospects are exceedingly good for the black people to "make it" but:

> . . . if this phase is inhibited by doting politicians or do-gooders, it may never come to be and a whole segment of mankind may be pushed deeper and deeper into immaturity.[40]

REFERENCES

Bachrach, Peter, and Baratz, Morton S. 1962. "Two Faces of Power," *American Political Science Review* **56**: 947–952.

Breitman, George (ed.) 1965. *Malcolm X Speaks.* New York: Grove Press.

Carmichael, Stokely, and Hamilton, Charles V. 1967. *Black Power.* New York: Random House.

Clark, Kenneth B. 1965. *Dark Ghetto.* New York: Harper and Row.

[38] Eissen-Udom, *op. cit.,* pp. 254–255.
[39] M. Janowitz, "Institution Building in Urban Education," in D. Street (ed.) *Innovation in Mass Education* (New York: John Wiley and Sons, 1969).
[40] Carroll, *op. cit.,* p. 85.

Coleman, James S., *et al.* 1966. *Equality of Educational Opportunity.* U.S. Office of Education. Washington, D.C.: U.S. Government Printing Office.

Cruse, Harold. 1967. *Crisis of the Negro Intellectual.* New York: William Morrow.

Dahl, Robert A. 1961. *Who Governs?* New Haven: Yale University Press.

Davis, Allison. 1948. *Social Class Influences Upon Learning.* Cambridge: Harvard University Press.

Davis, Allison, Gardner, Burleigh B., and Gardner, Mary R. 1965. *Deep South.* Chicago: University of Chicago Press.

DuBois, W. E. B. 1940. *Dusk of Dawn.* New York: Harcourt Brace Jovanovich.

Erickson, Donald A. 1968. "The Plain People and American Democracy," *Commentary* **45**: 36–44.

Erikson Erik H. 1968. *Identity, Youth and Crisis.* New York: W. W. Norton.

Glazer, Nathan and Moynihan, Daniel P. 1963. *Beyond the Melting Pot.* Cambridge: MIT Press.

Greeley, Andrew M. and Rossi, Peter H. 1966. *The Education of Catholic Americans.* Chicago: Aldine Publishing Co.

Grier, William H. and Cobbs, Price M. 1968. *Black Rage.* New York: Basic Books.

Handlin, Oscar. 1965. "Goals of Integration," in T. Parsons and K. B. Clark (eds.), *The Negro American.* Boston: Houghton Mifflin.

Handlin, Oscar. 1951. *The Uprooted.* New York: Grosset and Dunlap.

Muhammad, Elijah. 1965. *Message to the Blackman in America.* Chicago: Muhammad Mosque of Islam No. 2.

Myrdal, Gunnar. 1962. *American Dilemma.* New York: Harper and Row.

Parsons, Talcott. 1965. "Full Citizenship for the Negro American?" in T. Parsons and K. B. Clark (eds.), *The Negro American.* Boston: Houghton Mifflin.

Report of the National Advisory Commission on Civil Disorders. 1968. U.S. Riot Commission Report; also called Kerner Report. Washington, D.C.: U.S. Government Printing Office.

Sexton, Patricia C. 1961. *Education and Income.* New York: Viking Press.

Stodolsky, Susan S. and Lesser, Gerald. 1967. "Learning Patterns in the Disadvantaged," *Harvard Educational Review* **37**: 546–589.

Turner, Ralph H. and Killian, Lewis M. 1957. *Collective Behavior.* Englewood Cliffs, N.J.: Prentice-Hall.

Vontress, Clemmon E. 1965. "The Black Muslim Schools," *Phi Delta Kappan* **47**: 86–90.

Wheelis, Allen. 1958. *The Quest for Identity.* New York: W. W. Norton.

The Concept of Legitimacy in Black Psychology

CEDRIC CLARK

> You ache with the need to convince yourself that you do exist in the real world, that you're a part of all the sound and anguish, and you strike out with your fists. You curse and you swear to make them *recognize* you.
>
> —Author Ralph Ellison in
> *Invisible Man*

> All I'm asking for is a little *respect.*
>
> —Singer Otis Redding in
> "Respect"

The terms italicized in the above two quotations epitomize two major aspects of the Black Experience: feelings of not being *recognized,* and feelings of not being *respected.* These are not, of course, the *only* aspects of the Black Experience; there are many others, particularly those dealing with political, economic, and sociological concerns. And one cannot say that these other aspects are unrelated to processes involving recognition and respect. Indeed, as I shall suggest in the paragraphs below, feelings of recognition and respect are sometimes determined by these socio-economic-political factors.

From a psychological perspective, however, the single aspects of recognition (being paid attention to) and respect (having one's identity confirmed by others) seem critically important. This is not to say that concerns over recognition are unique to Black Americans in the sense of being restricted to them; these concerns are, however, more salient with regard to blacks. Moreover, these concerns have a long history. Marcus Garvey, founder of the Universal Negro Improvement Association, claimed as early as 1914 that:

> The only wise thing for us . . . Negroes to do, is to organize the world over, and build up for the race a mighty nation of our own in Africa. And this race of ours that cannot get *recognition and respect* in the country where we were slaves, by using our ability, power and genius, would develop for ourselves a nation that would get as much respect as . . . any other. . . .[1]

---

[1] Marcus Garvey, *Philosophy and Opinions of Marcus Garvey or Africa for the Africans* (London: Frank Cass and Co., Ltd., 1923), pp. 42–43. Emphasis added.

My purpose in this paper is to explore the theoretical significance of
these two elements of recognition and respect in an attempt to provide conceptual foundations for a Black Psychology which are rooted in an empirical reality common to large numbers of blacks. My discussion will
employ a theoretical construct which incorporates the social-psychological dynamics of both recognition and respect. I call this construct
legitimacy.

The concept of legitimacy is not foreign to the behavioral sciences. Parsons,[2] following Weber,[3] employs it in his analysis of general social
systems. Easton[4] uses it for his analysis of political systems. In anthropology, Swartz[5] uses the concept in his analysis of social change. Similar
uses of the concept are made by Kelman,[6] Flacks,[7] and Hollander and
Julian[8] in social psychology.

There are two basic propositions which are implicit in this paper. In the
interests of clarity it is perhaps beneficial to state these propositions explicitly here:

1. Legitimacy is an energy input required of all behavioral systems for
adequate functioning;

2. Black Americans have been denied legitimation, both from whites and
from other blacks.

Rather than attempt to explicate these two propositions in this context, I
will turn directly to a consideration of the concept of legitimacy, returning
in a later section of the paper to a more detailed consideration of these
and related propositions.

LEGITIMACY DEFINED

Legitimacy in this paper is defined as *the process whereby behavioral
systems are recognized and respected.*

A process involves the movement of elements through space and time.

[2] T. Parsons and E. Shils, *Toward a General Theory of Action* (Cambridge, Mass: Harvard University Press, 1951).

[3] Max Weber, *The Theory of Social and Economic Organization* (New York: Free
Press, 1964).

[4] David Easton, *A Framework for the Analysis of Political Systems* (Englewood Cliffs,
N.J.: Prentice-Hall, 1965).

[5] Marc Swartz, *et al.*, eds., *Political Anthropology* (Chicago: Aldine, 1966).

[6] H. Kelman, "A Social-Psychological Model of Political Legitimacy and Its Relevance
to Black and White Student Protest Movements," *Psychiatry* 33(2) (1970): 224–254.

[7] R. Flacks, "Protest or Conform: Some Social Psychological Perspectives on Legitimacy," *Journal of Applied Behavioral Science* 5 (1969): 127–150.

[8] E. Hollander and J. Julian, "Studies in Leader Legitimacy, Influence and Innovation," in *Advances in Experimental Social Psychology*, ed. L. Berkowitz (New York:
Academic Press, 1970).

The elements constituting the process of legitimacy are *symbols*—signs which represent, "stand for," or serve as the building blocks of, ideas. The meaning of symbols is acquired through the process of socialization or, more generally, cultural learning. Symbols which are transmitted across space and time represent a particular type of process, namely a communication process.[9]

A communication process can be further distinguished by three sets of elements which are present in the movement of symbols: (1) a symbol *source* or sender; (2) a *channel* over which the symbols are transmitted; and (3) a *receiver* which attempts to decode or interpret the symbols. The first and last of these elements constitute what are termed communication *systems*. The second—a channel—is the vehicle through which the elements of a communication process are transmitted. An example of a channel, in this sense, would be a television set. The two systems involved in this process might be (1) a particular network corporation (the source) and (2) a television viewer or group of viewers (the receiver). A communication process, then, involves the activities associated with the spatial and temporal transmission of symbols from a source to a receiver.

A *system*, therefore, is any set of elements which actively engages in the process of sending and receiving communication symbols. This includes, at one level, the set of elements which constitutes a human cell concerned with the transmission of DNA molecules and, at another level, the set of elements which constitutes a human being involved in the transmission of oral sounds (i.e., conversation).

As suggested earlier, the communication of legitimacy involves the transmission of a message which can be decoded (interpreted) in such a way as to accord recognition and respect to the receiver. The focus in the next two sections is on the activities of white psychological systems (message sources) which send messages to black psychological systems (message receivers). In the final part of this paper, an examination will be made of black systems communicating to other black systems.

RECOGNITION: THE FIRST STAGE OF LEGITIMATION

To recognize something or somebody means that I pay attention to it: I take it into account and acknowledge its existence. Recognition, in this sense, is related to but distinct from *awareness*. I can be aware of something, yet refuse to recognize it. The element of choice is thus implicit in the act of recognition.[10] Suppose, for example, an acquaintance of mine

---

[9] David Berlo, *The Process of Communication* (New York: Holt, Rinehart and Winston, 1960).

[10] Cedric Clark, "Social Change and the Communication of Legitimacy: The Case of Dispute Settlement," *Journal of the Developing Areas,* Vol. 5, No. 4 (July, 1971): 577–588.

enters a restaurant where I'm sitting. I may be fully aware of his entry, yet I may choose to ignore him. My acquaintance may, of course, impose his presence on me and, under such conditions, I may be forced to accord him recognition (but not necessarily respect). When I make this basic act of recognition I have provided the first (and necessary) condition for his eventual legitimation.

It is perhaps evident that recognition or non-recognition can operate as a form of social and political control. By not recognizing somebody, we can de-value his importance, and hence keep his behavior partly under our control, at least to the extent that the other person desires this recognition.

There are three aspects of the recognition act which deserve additional discussion. These are (1) the psychological *importance* of recognition; (2) the *form* the recognition takes; and (3) the *determinants* of recognition.

The Psychological Importance of Recognition

In a quotation similar to that presented by Ellison earlier, the psychologist William James observes that:

> A man's social "me" is the *recognition* which he gets from his mates . . . no more fiendish punishment could be devised than that one should be turned loose in society and remain absolutely unnoticed by all the members thereof.[11]

James goes on to emphasize that it is only through recognition by others that a person's sense of "self" is able to develop—a point stressed also by Mead.[12] This interaction with others enables a person to know himself as an object as well as an actor. If other people did not take one into account—i.e., recognize one's existence—it would be doubtful whether a healthy concept of the self would develop.[13] A person would not be able to differentiate himself from his environment. Such differentiation seems important if man is to avoid the kind of "ontological insecurity" described by Laing.[14]

The importance of being recognized is also epitomized in a statement by Martin Buber:

11 William James, *Psychology: The Briefer Course.* Ed. by Gordon Allport. (New York: Harper and Row, 1961).

12 George H. Mead, *Mind, Self, and Society* (Chicago: University of Chicago Press, 1934).

13 For a fuller discussion of this point, see Cedric Clark, "Competency and Legitimacy As Organizing Dimensions of the Black Self-Concept." Paper presented to the Self-Concept Work Group, *Social Science Research Council,* Chicago, Illinois (January 26–27, 1971b).

14 R. D. Laing, *The Divided Self* (Middlesex, England: Penguin, 1960).

Man wishes to be confirmed in his being by man, and wishes to have a presence in the being of the other. The human person needs confirmation, because man as man needs it. An animal does not need to be confirmed, for it is what it is, unquestionable. It is different with man: sent forth from the natural domain of species into the hazard of the solitary category, surrounded by the air of a chaos which came into being with him, secretly and bashfully he watches for a Yes which allows him to be and which can come to him only from one human person to another.[15]

This act of confirmation, it should be noted, says nothing about the manner in which one is confirmed. One could be a confirmed philosopher as well as a confirmed thief; the type of confirmation one receives is an important but quite different aspect of the legitimation process.

The Form of Recognition

How does one know if one is being recognized? Evidence of recognition appears to take two basic forms, depending upon whether the communication process is *interpersonal* (face-to-face) or *impersonal* (non-face-to-face or mass). In the first instance, recognition may occur in the form of verbal address: e.g., "John, how are you?" Through such direct or immediate communication, the existence of John is recognized (i.e., a necessary condition for legitimation has occurred). It is not always necessary, however, for the personal noun to be included in the address, since circumstances often indicate quite clearly that it is John who is in fact being recognized. However, to the extent that these circumstances do not occur and the use of the personal pronoun becomes less and less frequent, the situation of mass or *impersonal* communication begins to manifest itself.[16] If I pass John walking down the street and say "hello," or "what's happening, man?" I have recognized him in the form of verbal address, although it is possible for me not to recognize him (again, however, I may be aware of him). Thus, the statement, "I saw him, but I refused to recognize him" makes sense. It means that while I was aware of him, I *chose* not to let him know that I saw him. If enough people choose to ignore a person, that person would be unable to build and maintain a conception of himself.[17]

In a complex, industrialized society such as the United States, the most prevalent form of recognition occurs not through interpersonal or verbal address, but through impersonal and often symbolic representation.

[15] Martin Buber, "Distance and Relation," *Psychiatry* 20 (1957): 104.
[16] One of the peculiarities of the Black Experience is that many whites have employed a combined personal-impersonal label in much of their communication. This label is "boy."
[17] Clark, *op. cit.*, 1971b.

This representation is transmitted through the channels of mass communication and takes a variety of forms: television content, motion pictures, magazines, record albums, billboard advertisements, etc.

The impersonal form of recognition involves the portrayal of individuals who physically resemble the system and/or who share the values of that system. For example, white Americans have long been represented in such forms as Christmas cards; however, this is a relatively recent and still rare situation for Black Americans. Such pictorial representations communicate recognition to an individual and to his cultural system—a recognition communicated by physical resemblance (which is of course not the only type of recognition). Another example is the common postage stamp. While the black leader Frederick Douglass' picture appears on the twenty-five cent stamp, no Black American has yet appeared on the smaller denominations; i.e., on those which receive wide circulation, particularly among poorer people.

In a racially homogeneous society—a society in which there were no major physical differences among people—everyone could be recognized through pictorial or symbolic representation, because a single pictorial representation would resemble all concerned. It is obvious, however, that in a complex, multi-racial society, there are physical differences among people and, therefore, it is physically impossible to recognize all groups through a uniform non-verbal representation. Hence, some groups of people tend to be non-recognized or de-legitimated. That such non-recognition occurs, there can be little doubt. Its degree among the black population, and its reasons are, however, little understood and deserve careful research attention. While we can only speculate on the reasons here, the *effects* of this non-recognition of blacks are well-documented in psychological literature.[18] It is important to note, however, that pictorial modes of representation are not the only kind. As R. D. Laing observes:

> The need to be recognized is not of course, purely a visual affair. It extends to the general need to have one's presence endorsed or confirmed by the other, the need for one's total existence to be recognized.[19]

The Determinants of Recognition

What, then, may be suggested as determining whether one individual (A) accords recognition to another individual (B)? While there are perhaps numerous determinants, the most important appear to be (1) the *uniqueness* or informational value of individual B's actions, and (2) the

[18] See, for example, H. Proshansky and P. Newton, "The Nature and Meaning of Negro Self-Identity," in *Social Class, Race, and Psychological Development*, ed. M. Deutsch, *et al.* (New York: Holt, Rinehart, and Winston, 1968).
[19] Laing, *op. cit.*, p. 119.

perceived *relevance* of individual B's actions to the goals and values of individual A.

The notion of uniqueness is related to the distinction made earlier between awareness and recognition. We noted that to be aware of something does not necessarily mean that one recognizes it, in the sense of paying attention to it or taking it into account. By recognition it is not meant that the individual possesses the *ability* to make a differentiation of an object in his environment, but that he *exercises his option* to do so. Thus, we may assume some minimal level of awareness of individual B's actions by an observer A. Given this level of awareness, the question is what may determine whether A *chooses to pay attention* to B? One answer involves the extent to which these actions are unique or unusual.

Several authors have suggested that one of man's basic needs involves variety or novelty.[20] Hence, it is the unusual which frequently gains attention. The uniqueness of an action or event is no guarantee that it will be recognized and taken into account, however. The action must also be *relevant* if an observer is to pay attention to it. A clear case of relevancy occurs when a communication from one individual is addressed to another individual. Such an address singles out or differentiates an individual. Thus, in a group situation, I will pay attention to somebody if he calls (addresses) me. If he does not—i.e., if he speaks to the "group in general"—it is easy for me to ignore him.

When the form of recognition is mediated (impersonal) rather than immediate (face-to-face), relevancy is determined less by personal address than by the perceived effect of the actor's behavior on the goals or values of the observer or potential "extender" of recognition. Since a fundamental goal of all individuals involves the maintenance of a self-conception, actions viewed as affecting that self-concept are more likely to be recognized. Only in this way can threats to the self-concept be warded off. The reason why an action often has to be self-related if it occurs in impersonal forms is because the communication receiver has greater choice or "degrees of freedom" to ignore it.

What is true at the individual system level is also true at the social system level. For example, one of the reasons why most mass media systems do not take account of the activities of, say, the West African country of Mali might be because such media do not consider the actions of that political system relevant to their goals. More generally, one of the reasons why mass media systems do not pay attention to blacks is because blacks are often irrelevant to the goals and values of those (whites) who

[20] See, for example, D. Fiske and S. Maddi, *Functions of Varied Experiences* (Homewood, Ill.: Dorsey, 1961), and D. Berlyne, *Conflict, Arousal, and Curiosity* (New York: McGraw-Hill, 1960).

possess the means of mass communication. Only when the activities are perceived as directly related to the goals or interests of media systems, either positively or negatively (as were, for example, the riots of the sixties), are the activities of Black Americans taken fully into account.

To summarize: the process of legitimacy can be conceived of as a two-stage communication process. Recognition involves the first and necessary stage. Legitimation cannot occur without recognition; but recognition does not insure legitimation.

The importance of recognition was emphasized by noting that individual systems which are not recognized fail to develop and maintain adequate conceptions of self. The form of recognition was described as being either immediate (face-to-face) or mediated (impersonal). The former was considered descriptive of legitimation in normal conversation, while the latter was discussed in terms of the mass media. The determinants of recognition were defined in terms of the uniqueness or informational value of an action, and the relevance of this as perceived by an observer.

RESPECT: THE SECOND STAGE OF LEGITIMATION

As I suggested earlier, recognition is a necessary condition for legitimation to occur, but it is not a sufficient one. That is, without recognition, legitimation is impossible; but having it alone is no guarantee that legitimation will occur. A particular individual may, for example, recognize or take into account another individual but he may do so in a way which would communicate disrespect and thus de-legitimize him. This can occur by communicating in particular kinds of symbolic arrangements or by message content.

Message content which communicates respect is of three basic types. These are: (1) messages which share the *definition* of an actor's behavior; (2) messages which share the *assessment* of an actor's behavior; and (3) messages which share the *accountability* of an actor's behavior. To both anticipate and facilitate subsequent discussion, it is worth noting in this context that an individual who is "respected" (and subsequently legitimated) by an observer is one whose: (a) own definitions are employed by the observer in the interpretation of the actor's behavior; (b) own assessments are employed by the observer; and (c) own behavior, if favorable, is accounted for by attributing it to the actor's dispositions and, if unfavorable, is accounted for by attributing it to the individual's environment. These propositions are discussed in more detail below.

The three types of symbolic arrangements, together with the first stage of legitimation (recognition), are diagrammed in Table 1 below:

TABLE 1

The Process of Psychological Legitimation

Stage 1 (Recognition)	*Stage 2 (Respect)*
An individual *identifies the existence* of another by:	An individual *identifies with* another by:
1. Paying attention to him; by taking him into account	1. Sharing his *definitions* of his behavior 2. Sharing his *assessment* of his behavior 3. Sharing his *explanations* for his behavior

RESPECT AND BEHAVIOR DEFINITION

How a person's behavior is defined by another has important consequences for how both act in relationship to each other. When person A exhibits behavior X in the presence of person B, it is frequently the case that they will perceive (and hence define) it differently. This is because A and B bring different experiences and sets of expectations to the situation, often accompanied by different conceptual frameworks. There is thus always some variation between the ways in which any two individuals perceive and define an action. However, such variation can be minimal or maximal, and these limits often communicate "respect" and "disrespect," respectively.

Respect is communicated to a person when the observer's definition of that person's behavior shows minimal variance with the definition held by the person himself. The lack of agreement in definitions is itself often a sufficient condition for the communication of de-legitimation. That is, it is rare that a person is able to "identify with" or legitimate another person if that person and he do not define reality in similar ways. However, this is not to suggest that an *identity* of definitions is common or, perhaps, even desirable. There will always be some "error variance" which serves to protect the actor's own identity.

The Psychological Importance of Behavior Definition

What is suggested, then, is that not only is it important for a person to have his behavior recognized by observers, but it is equally important that his actions be defined by these observers in a way consistent with his own—at least to some minimal extent.

R. D. Laing writes in support of this proposition:

> . . . I expect that my own definition of myself should, by and large, be endorsed by the other person . . . when two sane persons meet, there appears to be a reciprocal recognition of each other's identity. In this mutual recognition there are the following basic elements: (a) I recog-

nize the other to be the person he takes himself to be and (b) He recognizes me to be the person I take myself to be.[21]

How an observer defines another person's behavior influences the sequence of actions (i.e., assessment, accountability) he takes with respect to him. Similarity of definition aids us in our desire to impose structure and consistency onto our environments. If I know that a person shares the same conception of the environment that I do, I am fairly certain that he will act within this environment the same way that I do or as I have done in the past. Such uniformity and confirmation of interpersonal expectations is what helps maintain systems of social interaction.[22]

Not only do shared definitions enable A to predict B's actions, but they also inform A as to how to behave in the presence of B. Shared definitions are, then, both *informing* and *maintaining*. Their importance is summed up in the recognition that psychological (and other) systems which lack either information (an informing function) or energy (a maintaining function) will disintegrate.[23] Computer systems, for example, require both data (information) and maintenance (electrical energy) for effective functioning. Similarly, man requires both information to deal with his environment, and support or maintenance for his conceptions of this environment.

An example of how definitions can extend or withhold legitimacy (respect) can be illustrated by the following example:

Suppose that after considerable work I produce a product X. While working I was more or less conscious of the goal of my activity and I had decided to define my product X as a 'musical composition.' Suppose an observer B recognizes product X. Suppose further that the observer, in his recognition of X, defines it as 'noise.'

What observer B has done is to de-legitimate or communicate disrespect to me by failing to share my conception of my activity. This was not done by ignoring it; i.e., the observer was aware of my product X and paid some attention to it. What he failed to do was to share my universe of definitions in his recognition of it.

The point here is that the concept "noise" defines a particular type of organization or structure in X; this structure is contrasted with that suggested by the concept "musical composition." While familiarity with both concepts (i.e., noise and music) on the part of me and an observer

<hr>

[21] Laing, *op. cit.*, p. 35.

[22] T. Newcomb, "An Approach to the Study of Communicative Acts," *Psychological Review* 60 (1953): 393–404.

[23] F. Berrien, *General Systems and Social Systems* (New Brunswick, N.J.: Rutgers University Press, 1968).

will make communication between us possible, the communication will be strained if we employ the concepts differently. It is the *differential* employment which is at issue, not the fact that one definition is "correct" and the other "incorrect." The "correctness" or "truthfulness" of definitions are philosophical issues which need not detain us in an analysis of functioning behavioral systems.

The Form of Behavior Definition

Like the process of recognition, the symbolic elements or messages which constitute a definition of a behavioral act can exist in either interpersonal or impersonal communication forms.

In interpersonal communication forms, behavioral definition may occur when the observer employs linguistic elements to encode some aspect of another person's behavior. Since encoding itself involves the more or less conscious choice of labels or concepts for the categorization of behavior, a process of definition is inherent to it. That is, to classify or to categorize is to define something as different from something else.

With respect to impersonal or mass communication forms, behavioral definitions occur when the observer (in this case a mass media system) encodes and exemplifies some aspect of another person's (or group's) behavior. As we noted earlier, it is rare that a person is himself presented in the mass media; he is usually represented by somebody else. These representations are often fictional and dramatic, particularly in the mass medium of television. Such dramatizations carry with them explicit definitions of actions. An example of what is meant here occurs with respect to the actions of Native Americans (or "Indians") as they have been defined by the mass media. A battle waged and won by Indians is frequently defined as a "massacre," while one won by the cavalry forces is usually defined as a "victory."

There are in fact very few English words, particularly those relating to significant social issues, which do not carry a double-meaning or which do not have a synonym which reflects a different impression. Why some words are chosen in preference to others (e.g., "riot" as opposed to "rebellion") is an interesting area for social research. At base, the only near-neutral classification is whether a certain quality or characteristic is "absent" or "present." But as soon as we begin to talk about what is absent or present or in what degrees it is absent or present we immediately enter into non-neutral or subjective territory—at least with respect to the description of psychological systems.

The Determinants of Behavior Definition

The essence of defining, then, involves the employment of concepts in the classification of social reality. Because concepts (and, hence definitions of behavior) have their origin in human experience, they are frequently peculiar to a given set of experiences. And to the extent that experiences differ substantially—like those of black and white Americans —the concepts derived from one set may be quite different from those derived from the other set, even when the behavioral actions observed are "identical." One observer looking at the family structure of Black Americans may see weakness, while another observer, from a different culture, may see strength.[24] Both observers may agree on the presence or absence of some quality, but may differ greatly in the value, or interpretation, made of it.

That people of different cultures perceive and define "reality" differently is suggested by the Sapir-Whorf hypothesis.[25] This hypothesis states that a person's language influences or determines his perception and classification of reality. And since language is a component of culture, the ultimate "determinant" is culture itself. A well-known example concerns the Native Canadian or "Eskimo" repertoire of concepts for what we label "snow." Because the phenomenon of snow is very important (has high relevancy) to the Eskimo, finer discriminations about it are made. If I, as a non-Eskimo external observer, were to discuss an Eskimo's actions in relationship to "snow" by using only one of the various labels, I could be de-legitimating his activity.

Similarly, if a person unacquainted with various aspects of the black culture were to suddenly find himself with the job of defining the complex of activities associated with, say, the production of black music, he may very likely employ definitions which are at variance with those supplied by the black cultural practitioners. And when the observer communicates to or about these practitioners it is likely that he will (albeit often unconsciously) communicate disrespect for them.

It should be noted, however, that simply because a person is born into one culture which has concepts different from another, this does not mean that he can never learn the conceptions and definitions of the other culture. This can be achieved, at least in part, via second language learning. It is perhaps clear, then, why voluntarily learning another person's language is often said to be one of the highest tributes (respect) one can give to that person. It represents a deliberate attempt to learn how another group of people perceive and define reality.

However, language learning may be a necessary, but not sufficient, condition for the acquisition of a person's definitional universe. One must also learn the *values* of the culture to which the person belongs; it is only through value learning that one can discern the appropriate situation for the application of learned concepts. This constitutes a rather

[24] Cf. Andrew Billingsley, *Black Families in White America* (Englewood Cliffs, N.J.: Prentice-Hall, 1968).
[25] Benjamin Whorf, *Language, Thought, and Reality,* Ed. John Caroll. (Cambridge, Mass.: M.I.T. Press, 1956).

serious problem for those who must study foreign languages only "by the book." The learning of a language independent of actual behavioral practices in the appropriate contexts does not equip one with the "world view" or what the Germans call the *Weltanschauung* of the people of that culture.

Applying these notions directly to the nature of black/white social interactions, it is easily recognized that most white Americans do not, for various reasons, learn "Black English" as well as blacks learn "White English."[26] Such a situation, even when occurring under programs of "racial integration," often leads to a process of de-legitimation of black behavior on the part of whites. Thus, even if there is sufficient recognition of aspects of the Black Experience (i.e., even if the first condition of legitimation is reached), many white Americans, unless they have both knowledge about and experience in the range of activities constituting Black American culture, are likely to de-legitimate black activities because they do not share the culture's definitions of reality. The extent to which this culture has been poorly recorded by blacks as well as poorly recognized by whites is a question for research.

RESPECT AND BEHAVIORAL ASSESSMENT

As I indicated earlier, concomitant with the process of defining an action is the process of evaluating it or assessing it. To the extent that "meaning" is derived through the manner in which we define phenomena, there is likely to be a strong evaluative component as part of this meaning.[27] In any case, it is clear that much of man's behavior involves the evaluation and assessment of other people. The assessment is often not manifest or, for that matter, conscious. While all aspects of human behavior partake of both conscious and unconscious elements, linguistic behavior—because it is so firmly rooted in a person's total cultural learning—is perhaps distinctive in the degree to which it is *wholly* unconscious.

The term "assessment" is perhaps preferable to "evaluation" inasmuch as the former tends to encompass a much wider range of judgments than simply "good" or "bad." Other dimensions used to classify behavior, while still strongly evaluative, are relevant in different contexts: e.g., "successful-unsuccessful," "competent-incompetent," "ambitious-non-ambitious." Which dimension is selected sometimes depends on the nature of the particular behavior which is manifested and the setting in which this behavior occurs. Also, however, the choice depends not on these factors

[26] Orlando Taylor, *Black English.* Unpublished manuscript, Center for Applied Linguistics, Washington, D.C., 1970.

[27] Cf. C. Osgood, *et al., The Measurement of Meaning* (Urbana, Ill.: University of Illinois Press, 1957).

alone, but also on the relationship between the assessor and the assessed. For example, an armed group of citizens might be termed "freedom fighters" or "guerillas," depending upon the relationship between the citizens and those doing the labelling.

The Psychological Importance of Behavioral Assessment

It is apparent that people want not only to be recognized as existing and have their actions defined in cognitively similar ways, but they also want to have their actions assessed in ways which generate self-respect. People want to be supported in their own classifications and evaluations of reality. Such support cannot be self-generated because an act of comparison is required. A single person's range of experiences is normally much too narrow to provide the kind of comparative analysis needed by cognitive systems. Such comparison can only be acquired through the process of interacting or communicating with others.[28]

Assessment also functions as "feedback" (positive and negative) for psychological systems. When positive, the behaving system is encouraged to retain its current mode of activity; when negative, it is encouraged to "adjust itself" to new exigencies. Such feedback is necessary for the successful functioning of all behavioral systems. Without adequate feedback, an individual will never know whether or not he is successful in the pursuit of his goals.

The Form of Behavioral Assessment

As was the case with other aspects of the legitimation process, assessment can occur through both interpersonal and impersonal forms. In the former case, an individual may simply say to another: "your behavior is good or competent."

Assessment may, however, take forms less obvious than this. If I wanted to negatively evaluate a person's actions, I might, for example, speak in a sarcastic manner of his achievements. Ridicule is, in fact, a quite common method of communicating de-legitimation. In this method, the linguistic symbols employed are arranged so as to communicate the following message: "This person or behavior is not to be taken seriously."

Assessments may be quite explicit, as, for example, a constitutional amendment declaring a Black American to be "three-fifths" of a man. They may, however, be quite indirect and mediated through impersonal or mass communication channels. In addition to labelling a particular action as "good" or "bad," the mass media may manipulate spatial and temporal dimensions. In terms of television presentation, for example, an individual's actions may be placed sequentially between actions which

28 Cf. Leon Festinger, "A Theory of Social Comparison Processes," *Human Relations* 7 (1954): 117–140.

are themselves labelled as "bad." By placing the reporting of a civil rights demonstration immediately after or immediately before presentation of some clearly labelled criminal activity, the event tends to be negatively assessed. Through the process of association, the viewer learns that the action in question is "bad."

Stylistic elements associated with spatial or pictorial representations are also important in the communication of respect. An example of delegitimation through pictorially produced assessment is the cartoon product known as a *caricature.* The exaggeration of the physical features of a person tends to influence one's judgment of his behavior in ways which are usually unfavorable. The TV images of blacks presented in such programs as *Stepin Fetchit, Tarzan,* and *Amos 'n Andy* represent such caricatures.

The Determinants of Behavior Assessment

How the actions of an individual or group are assessed depends on (1) the particular assessment *dimensions* possessed by the observer, (2) the *uniqueness* or visibility of the actor's behavior, and (3) the *relevance* of the actions to the observer.

Assessment requires the use of some dimensions or criteria in the process of evaluation. As was noted earlier, such dimensions often tend to be specific to the action displayed; e.g., the dimensions we use to judge how well a person plays football are different from those we use to assess how well he drives a car. While a physical skill is involved in both activities, it is likely that different dimensions associated with this "skill" will be employed. For example, we may talk of "agility" with respect to football playing and "care" with respect to driving a car. It is important to note, however, that inasmuch as dimensions are concepts, they are learned just as other concepts are learned. Thus, individuals who are observers of a culture distinct from their own, and in which they have not participated, may lack the dimensions relevant for the assessment of the behavior manifested in the observed culture.

Related to the availability of dimensions is the fact that the *uniqueness* of the actions taken by an actor may also affect the nature of behavioral assessment, just as it did the recognition of the actions in the first place. If behavior is to be assessed at all by an observer, it is necessary that the behavior fall within certain culturally-known boundaries. If the behavior is too unusual, it will be impossible for the observer to evaluate it, for he will be lacking the concepts necessary. A common occurrence of this is in the area of creative work. Many cases of creativity remain unappreciated because the requisite dimensions for assessment are unavailable to contemporary observers.

Thus, as was the case with the definitional component of "respect," an important determinant of behavioral assessment is the *culture* of the observing individual. Whereas, however, it was the concept component of culture which determined behavioral definition, it is the value component which determines the nature of assessment. Concepts heighten our attention to certain events, and values serve as standards of judgments.[29] Both are important in determining whether or not legitimacy is being communicated.

RESPECT AND BEHAVIOR ACCOUNTABILITY

The third component of respect, *accountability*, is closely associated with the process of assessment or evaluation. Accountability involves the attribution of blame or credit for the occurrence of an individual's actions. This tendency for man to search for causes of events—both social and non-social—is pervasive and may in fact be considered a fundamental psychological process.[30]

The Psychological Importance of Behavior Accountability

The tendency to attribute causality or accountability is important in the process of legitimation because it is intricately related to the parallel process of self-esteem maintenance.

In general, an observer either holds the individual himself accountable for actions or he holds that individual's environment accountable.[31] In other words, we tend to attribute responsibility or causality either *internally* or *externally*.[32] While people tend to use both external and internal cues for the attribution of causality, one orientation usually predominates with respect to a particular class of events and, as suggested below, with respect to a particular group of people.

The Form of Behavior Accountability

The form of accountability is, therefore, based on internal and external attributions of causality. That is, the primary element in the communication message is some stated cause for some action or sequence of actions. With respect to external attribution, this is sometimes done by placing the action in a temporal or spatial message sequence such that it is pre-

[29] Alfred Kuhn, *The Study of Society: A Unified Approach* (Homewood, Ill.: Dorsey Press, 1963).

[30] Fritz Heider, *The Psychology of Interpersonal Relations* (New York: John Wiley, 1957).

[31] H. Kelley, "Attribution Theory in Social Psychology," in *Nebraska Symposium on Motivation*, ed. D. Levine (Lincoln, Nebr.: University of Nebraska Press, 1967), pp. 192–238.

[32] J. Rotter, "Generalized Expectancies for Internal versus External Control of Reinforcement," *Psychological Monographs* (1966): 80.

ceded by some event or set of events. The antecedent action is thus interpreted as a cause.[33] For example:

"A banana peel lay on the sidewalk." "A man fell on the sidewalk."

This sequence of two sentences carries a meaning quite different from what would be conveyed if the second statement appeared alone. The appearance of the first statement enables one to "explain" (attribute causality to) the event described in the second.

Internal causality attribution cues, then, can be provided merely by having an absence of external attribution cues. Internal attributions may also be communicated by applying invariant trait descriptions to the acting individual. Stereotypes, for example, serve to "explain" the behavior of an individual in terms of his own internal state or dispositions. Thus, a person is considered "clumsy" if he falls down.

As will be suggested below, the causal-type thinking based on external and internal attributions enables us to excuse our own improper behavior (as being caused by events over which we have little or no control) and credit ourselves for proper behavior. Similarly, we can excuse or credit the behavior of others. The precise nature of this accountability through causal attribution describes whether the observer communicates respect (legitimacy) or disrespect (de-legitimacy) to the actor.

The Determinants of Behavioral Accountability

To appreciate the determinants of the specific form of accountability, consider the kinds of attributions a person would normally make for his own behavior. Whatever these are—either internal or external—they are likely to be consistent with a person's goal of maintaining a satisfactory self-concept. It is thus easy to see why the following types of attributions are probable: (1) internal accountability will occur when a person likes his actions or considers them "successful" and (2) external accountability will occur when a person dislikes his actions or considers them "unsuccessful."

For example, suppose I fall down while walking. An observer might witness this event and in some manner express *recognition* of it; he might agree with my *definition* of the act as a "fall"; he might further agree with me that the fall was an "unfortunate" event; i.e., he might *assess* it as "bad." When it comes to *accountability*, however, I, as an actor, may attribute causality differently from the observer. This may be because I am aware of more or different cues than the observer (who may be lo-

[33] Despite the revolution in modern physics, we still tend to think in Hume's terms of linear causality.

cated at some distance).[34] However, it is more likely that in order to maintain "face," I will attribute such incompetent behavior not to my own internal failings, but to some external force (e.g., a banana peel, or a "trip" by someone).

The relevant proposition which thus emerges is: the more negatively assessed the behavior, the less likely a person is to accept accountability (blame) for it; conversely, the more positively assessed the behavior, the less likely a person is to attribute causality (credit) to external forces.

In other words, we like to take credit for the good that we do and blame others for the bad that we do. The reason I slipped was because the sidewalk contained a banana peel, not because I was "clumsy." By making such attributions I am able to take account of my own behavior in a way which maintains my self-concept as a non-clumsy individual.

With respect to the process of legitimation, the important question concerns not only attributions of one's own individual behavior, but also the attributions one gives to others. Such other-attributions are fundamental to the communication of legitimacy. A proposition related to this would suggest that to the extent that individual A respects individual B, individual A will account for B's behavior in the same way as B would account for his own behavior.

Thus, again assuming a basic need for self-maintenance, good or positively assessed actions will be attributed to the internal characteristics of another, whereas bad or negatively assessed actions will be attributed to environmental forces. In other words, if we have respect for a person, we will blame his failures on things over which he has no control, and credit his successes to things intricately associated with him. This defines the extent to which we can *identify* with a person; to the extent that we do, we communicate respect or legitimacy to him.

Figure 2 below illustrates the types of accountability actions which are possible.

To summarize the discussion in this section: "respect," the second stage of the process of legitimacy, is viewed as involving three sub-processes— behavior definition, behavior assessment, and behavior accountability.

The *definition* of a person's behavior by an observer aids in the communication of respect to him. The extent to which a definition of a person's behavior is shared by both actor and observer determines the definition's entrance into a communication of respect. Consistency of definitions between interactants is important, for this permits predictability to exist in the interaction system. A desire for such predictability or consistency appears to be basic to man.

---

[34] R. Nisbett and E. Jones, "The Actor and the Observer: Divergent Perceptions of the Causes of Behavior," (Unpublished manuscript, Yale University, 1970).

ASSESSMENT OF ACTOR'S BEHAVIOR

	Competent *(Positive)*	*Incompetent* *(Negative)*
Internal *(Personal)*	RESPECT (High Identification)	DISRESPECT
External *(Environmental)*	DISRESPECT	RESPECT (High Identification)

SOURCES OF CAUSALITY (ACCOUNTABILITY)

FIGURE 2

*Conditions Under Which Second Stage of Legitimation
Is Fulfilled (Assuming shared "definitions")*

Definitions of behavior usually take the *form* of concepts which purport to describe some or all of an individual's activity. Much behavior occurs in mediated form, e.g., in books, on TV, etc. In such instances the behavior is sometimes defined by representative examples which may or may not maintain a receiver's conception of self.

The *determinants* of definition have their origin in the human experience of the definers (observers). These experiences are embodied in the concepts and values which constitute a person's culture. Definitions frequently differ as a function of the different cultures which reflect different sets of experiences within a society.

The second element in the communication of respect involves behavioral *assessment*—the act of applying a set of evaluative dimensions in judging an action or event. Such evaluation is important to man because he must use these judgments in steering his own goal-directed behavior. Through such judgments or assessments, a self-concept is created and maintained.

Assessment usually takes the *form* of labelling an action as "good" or "bad." This is sometimes done by the direct application of evaluative labels. Often, however, assessment occurs (1) through the sequencing of message units so as to create a "halo" effect through association, or (2) through a pre-structured form representing a caricature.

The nature of the assessment is *determined* ultimately by the culture of the assessor. His culture equips him with the dimensions by which he is able to judge another person. By the same token, an individual's culture often precludes him from making assessments which communicate respect to members of other cultures.

Behavior *accountability*, the third element of respect, is based in the apparent human need to "explain" or "seek causes" for events. Without an adequate base for lending predictability to his world, man would lose his own sense of belongingness or self-identity.

Behavior accountability takes the form of external or internal causality attributions. Respect is communicated to an individual when his "good" actions are attributed to the dispositions of the individual himself and his "bad" actions are attributed to the environment or to forces over which he has no control.

External and internal attributions of accountability are determined largely by the individual's need to maintain his own image or self-conception. This need creates a tendency to make attributions to others in a way consistent with his own self-attributions. However, man also desires to emphasize his own individuality or distinctiveness; this opposing tendency causes him to make attributions differently for others than for himself, which, in turn, often makes difficult the communication of respect and legitimacy.

PSYCHOLOGICAL LEGITIMACY AND THE CONTEMPORARY BLACK MOVEMENT

Implicit in preceding sections was a general concern with the relationship between black and white Americans, particularly as this relationship centers around communications or legitimacy (and de-legitimacy). In part, this focus was due to a belief that analysis of the Black Experience should not be restricted to the examination of black behavior. By emphasizing the *relationship* of blacks to whites we can remind ourselves that black behavior is still very much governed, if not controlled, by whites. The absence of blacks in control of the mass media virtually assures this fact.

However, over-emphasizing this point may tend to obscure the fundamental changes which are occurring in black relations with other blacks. The purpose of the present section is to discuss such changes in terms of the concept of legitimacy.

LEGITIMACY AND BLACK CONSCIOUSNESS: RECOGNITION FACTORS

"Black Consciousness" or "Black Awareness" can be viewed as cognitive-emotive-motoric responses involving a re-consideration of (a) the sources, (b) the form, and (c) the determinants of legitimation of black behavior.

Ralph Ellison's *Invisible Man*, whom we quoted in the introduction to this paper, is best described as a man having a need for recognition from white Americans. Perhaps the novel's popularity during the decades of the '50's and '60's is due to the fact that sources of black legitimacy (i.e., of recognition and respect) were, at that time, located within the white culture.

While the empirical evidence is yet sparse, it seems apparent that the decade of the '70's will be characterized by a substantial shift in the people whom blacks consider sources of legitimation. Specifically, greater numbers of Black Americans are likely to seek recognition from other blacks, and, in turn, communicate recognition to them. As is the case with most other dramatic social changes, the dominant interactants in this process are those who possess a relatively higher degree of education (not necessarily formal education or "schooling," however).

It is of course true that there are many blacks who have always communicated primarily, if not exclusively, with other blacks and who have transmitted and received legitimacy accordingly. Such a group, in fact, constitutes the largest proportion of Black Americans. However, a predominantly race-specific pattern of communication has not, historically, been characteristic of a smaller, yet more influential, group of educated blacks; i.e., those most likely to have read this article. It is the change among this particular group which is currently significant.

As indicated earlier, recognition takes both personal and impersonal forms. Increases in the former, where blacks are conversing with other blacks, seems evident, particularly on college campuses and in educational institutions in general. Calls for varieties of "Black Separatism" reflect this increasing willingness for blacks to pay attention to other blacks. While not yet extensive, there also appear to be changes occurring in the "mass" media. Subscriptions to black magazines and newspapers, for example, are increasing, while white subscriptions to the same appear to be decreasing. *Muhammad Speaks*, the official newspaper of the Nation of Islam (the "Black Muslims"), is now the largest-selling black weekly newspaper.

We discussed some of the determinants of recognition earlier in terms of the uniqueness and relevance of an individual's actions. In the context of the present Black Movement, actions by other blacks seem to have higher informational value and relevance than was true in previous decades. In other words, it now "matters" more or "makes more of a difference" to blacks what other blacks are doing, saying, and thinking. This is due largely to a belief in a "common fate" characterizing black behavior. This commonality is grounded not only on skin color but also on the basis of a *felt* (if not always described) history of experiences which distinguish the white and black populations of America. This common-fate belief acts as a sufficient condition to create the perception of greater relevance of black behavior to other blacks. Again, the "truth" of the phenomenon is irrelevant. As W. I. Thomas pointed out many years ago, "an event defined as real has real consequences."

LEGITIMACY AND BLACK CONSCIOUSNESS: RESPECT FACTORS

We have noted that recognition is a necessary, but not sufficient, condition for the process of legitimation to occur. What is also needed is the communication of respect: a sharing of definitions, behavioral assessments, and causal attributes. Currently, the communication of respect to blacks from other blacks appears less obvious than that of mere recognition. Nevertheless, one can point to an increasingly widespread emphasis on the sharing of "black" definitions, assessments, and attributions. Since, as we indicated earlier, all of these processes have their ultimate origin in human experience, there are more determined efforts to identify, articulate, and communicate the distinctive aspects of this experience. This appears to be one of the prime motivations behind the establishment of Black Studies programs across the country.

With respect to behavior *definitions*: perhaps the most dramatic form of concentrated effort in this direction is the change in self-definition; i.e., "Black" Americans define themselves differently than do "Negro" Americans. This re-definition of what or who one is is a kind of religious conversion; one is, in effect "reborn" into a new (black) society.[35] The terms "Black," "Nigger," "African," etc. take on new meanings and play an important part in both informing and maintaining black psychological systems.

Part of the new Black Awareness involves the *reassessment* as well as the re-definition of black behavior. Actions which were at one time assessed as "bad" are currently under reassessment and are being defined as "good" at best and, at worse, judgment is being suspended. The behavioral patterns of blacks which were previously denied or repressed are now openly displayed as evidence of a "new breed" of man. Having "nappy hair," "thick lips," or other visible signs of African descent are no longer viewed as stigmas; they are in fact assessed as positive aspects, if not the essential ingredients, of "Blackness." What was once ridiculed is now taken seriously.

[35] Cf. Charles Thomas, *Boys No More* (Berkeley, Calif.: Glencoe Press, 1971).

Concomitantly, there is now often a direct negative correlation postulated between what whites and blacks assess as positive or "good" behavior. James Brown rivals Johann Sebastian Bach for black recognition and respect. Such differential judgments lead to unpredictability in interracial encounters and, thereby, make social change possible, if not inevitable.

Changes in black *accountability* for black behavior are less evident than any other aspect of legitimation. Because a level of negative self-evaluation is still present among many blacks, there is often still an inability to identify with blacks. That is, society (largely through the mass media) has not taught blacks (nor, for that matter, whites) to recognize and respect black models. When black models are presented, they are frequently made to appear as villains or fools (at least in the eyes of the "high consciousness" blacks).

Thus, there is still a tendency for blacks to account for the success of other blacks in terms of an "enriched environment" (external attribution) and not "innate genius" (internal attribution). Conversely, black failures are often still accounted for by internal causality ("a bad nigger"), rather than in terms of external conditions ("forced unemployment"). This problem appears to have been recognized by some blacks; one of the aims of Black Studies curricula is to provide the environmental and nonenvironmental information necessary for generating patterns of accountability capable of eliciting greater black respect for black behavior.

Comprehensive Planning and Racism

WALTER W. STAFFORD and JOYCE LADNER

Unless future comprehensive plans for major urban areas in the U.S. are developed around a solid understanding of the implications of racism, they will not only be ineffectual but they may also be agents of disaster. Future black population majorities in thirteen major central cities will make old assumptions of "colorless" planning totally untenable.

For those planners who accept this premise, the first task is attempting to understand racism. Such an understanding should be based on social science and should afford a workable connection with planning cities. It should provide a framework for the changes necessary in urban political institutions if the cities of the future are not to become racial battlefields.

Our objective here is to offer working definitions of the two basic types of racism—*individual* and *institutional*—and to use them to analyze (1) some of the recent programs and plans devised to counter various urban crises and (2) some expected institutional alternatives such as black political majorities, metropolitan planning, and advocacy planning.

BACKGROUND

Unfortunately there is a real lack of systematic information on racism as related to urban planning. There have been many social science studies on race since the forties, but the majority do not relate racism to planning cities. Moreover, planning journals have shown little interest in the problems of black communities. This omission can be partially explained by the physical design bias which dominated planning in the early stages of its development. Another contributing factor is the failure of blacks— not only lower income groups but black intellectuals and scholars as well— to assign significant priority to planning. Black intellectuals, in a somewhat obvious attempt to relate colonialism to the U.S. racial crisis, should note the impact that culturally biased American and British planners have had on the development of Indian and African cities in countries that have achieved their independence. Major journals developed to study blacks— frequently begun by blacks because of segregation in scholarly circles—do not mention the impact of planning.

The divergence between planning and the black community is unfortunate, for there are interesting and important aspects in the history of both which are significant for the understanding of urban development in this country. Planners interested in utopian traditions should be interested in "organized Negro communities," such as Nashoba, founded by freed slaves during the period when utopian ideals were prevalent in American thought.[1] Blacks, on the other hand, should be aware of the history of urban form and transportation patterns that have limited their job accessibility.[2]

A history of exploitive political decisions in urban development has discouraged the black community. Blacks have not wished to build a body of knowledge upon former racist patterns, preferring to reject the decisions of white interest groups and decisionmakers on approaches to racial problems in urban areas and propose their own. Thus, the planner, responsible for even the simplest single function plans for black clients, faces a dilemma in what he can propose to crucial political decisionmakers.

Traditionally, planners have not been concerned with what blacks thought or how they perceived planning proposals. In our opinion, this occurred because of three basic factors:

[1] Jane and William Pease, "Organized Negro Communities," *The Journal of Negro History* 45, No. 1 (January 1962): 19–34.

[2] John Kain, *Commuting and the Residential Decisions of Chicago and Detroit Central Business District Workers* (Rand Corporation, April 1963).

1. Blacks have traditionally been excluded from decision-making roles;

2. As subunits of the pattern of political decision-making, blacks have had few resources with which to bargain;

3. Until recently, blacks have failed to see the important role of technicians who advise politicians.

Lower income blacks in Chicago's West side, Atlanta's "Bottom," or Pittsburgh's Homewood district are not likely to understand the technical proposals of planners, nor are they likely to be concerned. The exigencies of their day-to-day existence preclude concern with long-range comprehensive goals, but it does not follow that they are not concerned or interested in how planners and politicians manipulate their lives. The tendency toward inactivity in urban affairs within the black community stems from a lack of understanding of urban processes that resulted partially from migration of rural people to urban areas without an accompanying introduction to the complexities of urban administration. Rigid patterns of segregation maintained their lack of access to knowledge about important urban institutions.

One major change in this situation has been the recent emergence of new catalysts in the form of young black professionals loosely organized into coalitions—for example, the Afro-American Teachers Association. A major resource of these groups is the knowledge of urban culture and institutions their parents lacked. The new coalitions have been aided by: a decline of machine politics and the loss of power by old-line blacks who aligned themselves with the machine; increased security of status which is largely established within the black community; creation of lower level management jobs and federal positions; and most importantly, the inflexibility of large-scale organizations, such as school systems and welfare departments, which prevents them from meeting demands from the black community and from adjusting to their own internal frictions, without decentralizing their decision-making apparatus. These factors have helped to create a class of young professional blacks in decision-making positions.

The growth of such coalitions among professional blacks is of crucial importance to planning. These groups generally see themselves as having cultural roots within the black community but are cosmopolitan enough in outlook to link urban and national politics to their local goals. *In the future it is important for planners to understand that they are more likely to deal with these loosely organized coalitions than with individual blacks accorded political status.* The coalitions are more interested in changing and controlling the administrative apparatus of local government, than in attempting to persuade influential whites (usually by giving them status on boards of voluntary agencies such as the Urban League or NAACP) to act in proxy for them by manipulating key decisionmakers. Increasingly discontented with white policymakers in black affairs, the coalitions are interested in changing older political arrangements to become more responsive to black needs and demands.

What the planner will face is a complex set of black community strategies bearing on the administration and planning of central cities with racial problems. We contend that, because of the implications of these local strategies for national politics, federal requirements for comprehensive planning have already increased. Existing physical and social conditions in our cities determine the direction of the strategies. In racially tense urban areas there is usually little vacant land for residential expansion of the rapidly growing black population. Additionally, surrounding suburban communities with direct zoning and subdivision controls are maintaining segregated patterns which accentuate inner city problems. Planning decisions in many cases are reduced to decisions of which race gets what.

Planning decisionmakers cannot afford a narrow view of the consequences of their decisions. They must relate planning proposals to the needs of the black community and establish criteria for analyzing effects of planning programs. Twelve years ago Martin Myerson emphasized this approach to broader measures of comprehensive planning,[3] however, if it has been adopted within cities with large black ghettos, the effects have not been widely publicized. Moreover, and perhaps of equal importance, the *process* of comprehensive planning must become participatory in the broadest sense, especially where the black community is concerned.

WHAT IS RACISM?

The most serious problems that have confronted intellectuals and scholars attempting to study racism have sprung from ineffective and diverse definitions of the term. Unable to establish an operational definition of racism, students of race relations have been hampered in their efforts to formulate a viable methodology that would act to counter racism and its effects on the social system. Sociologists, psychologists, intergroup relationists, and race relations experts have assigned various meanings to racism, referring to it in the same vein as prejudice, discrimination, norm conflicts, and so on. No strong attempt was made to place it in the position of prominence it has recently been assigned: that of being our society's most destructive force which continues to systematically destroy an abundance of this nation's human potential. One of the primary reasons students of race relations were not more effective in formulating a viable theory and methodology of racism was their inability (or unwillingness) to treat racism as a very serious problem. They were willing to simultaneously

3 Martin Myerson, "Building the Middle Range Bridge for Comprehensive Planning," *Journal of the American Institute of Planners* 22 (Winter 1956): 59.

accept the "reality" of the abstract equality set forth in the Constitution along with the "normality" of institutional subjugation.

The most popular meanings assigned to racism generally revolve around the consequences of being black in the United States and the solutions that should be adopted to end the negative effects that accrue from the inferior social status to which black people are relegated. A broad definition taken from interdisciplinary approaches would be that racism is *an adaptive system of subjugation and exploitation based on a set of norms, roles, and expectations assigned by or to individuals, groups, or organizations.* Theoretically, the system can be divided into two patterns: *individualized racism* and *institutional racism.* However, this division somewhat oversimplifies the concept of racism since it is frequently difficult to separate individual and/or group attitudes from the institutions in which racism is incorporated. Under careful examination, one observes that attitudinal and institutional racism are intricately related since each depends on the other for sustenance. The individual racist must have an institutional framework for his behavior—for instance, he successfully fights integrated housing in his neighborhood because the local open housing ordinances are not enforced.

The adaptive nature of the system adjusts to individual practices and institutional norms which delineate between subordinate and superordinate positions, thus making it extremely difficult to distinguish class and racial implications. For example, individual practices or institutional policies which delineate subordinate positions may easily be substituted for stereotyped ideas about minority groups. Equally important for planners is the fact that some of the tools of planning—such as zoning, urban renewal, and subdivision controls—are not racist per se but are utilized to separate socioeconomic groups and thus adapt easily into the local racist framework and become de facto exclusionary measures.

The majority of the literature on racism is concerned with individual and, to a lesser degree, group prejudices. Attitudinal studies by social scientists have provided foundations for race relations policies of many social agencies in the United States. However, if there is any area in which social scientists have failed politicians, planners, and social agencies, it has been their lack of attention to institutional aspects of racism. The insistent emphasis upon small group behavior and group attitudes has forced a narrow focus on the implications of racism. As Irving Horowitz noted:

> My own belief is that the problem of sociology can be boiled down as follows: It has transformed the study of race into the study of small groups, hence moving sociology away from a wider appreciation of the socio-economic conditions of Negroes and toward a narrower psychological-introspective evaluation.[4]

4 Irving Horowitz, "Black Sociology," *Trans-action* 4, No. 9 (Summer 1967): 8.

Moreover, some of the assumptions utilized by planners have been based on early stereotyped views of such individuals as urban sociologist Robert E. Parks:

> The temperament of the Negro as I conceive it consists in a few elementary but distinctive characteristics, determined by physical organizations and transmitted biologically. These characteristics manifest themselves in a genial, sunny, and social disposition, in an interest and attachment to external, physical things rather than to subjective states and objects of introspection, in a disposition for expression rather than enterprise and action.[5]

More recently, the work of Nathan Glazer and Daniel P. Moynihan has been influential despite the fact that one of their major arguments is: "The Negro is only an American and nothing else. *He has no values and culture to guard and protect*"[6] (emphasis supplied). A sensitive and controversial dispute is currently underway between social scientists who support this position and black intellectuals who disagree.

Although sociologists have been singled out and perhaps indicted for their failure in this area, they are not alone. Other students of race relations have been just as ineffective. They have generally ignored the broader institutional framework which would relate to political policies. (For example, influencing abolition of racism in institutional and land use arrangements.) The clearest rationale for the attitudinal approach has been concern with conflicts and hostilities of races as groups, and hope that by understanding and eventually changing attitudes a benign relationship between races would be created. In proper perspective, attitudinal racism falls in a separate category of intergroup relations, which does not as a rule emphasize structural changes but instead devises within the system strategies that are designed to implement a "human relations" approach.

Institutional racism, on the contrary, can be defined as the operating policies, priorities, and functions of an on-going system of normative patterns which serve to subjugate, oppress, and force dependence of individuals or groups by: (1) establishing and sanctioning unequal goals, objectives, and priorities for blacks and whites, and (2) sanctioning inequality in status as well as in access to goods and services.

A profound revelation of the impact of institutional racism resulted from the research by social psychologist Kenneth Clark on the effects and consequences of racism in Harlem. Clark maintains that the ghetto ". . . is

---

[5] Robert Parks and Ernest Burgess, *Introduction to the Science of Sociology* (Chicago: University of Chicago Press, 1924), pp. 138–9.

[6] Nathan Glazer and Daniel Moynihan, *Beyond the Melting Pot* (Cambridge, Mass.: MIT Press, 1963), p. 53.

institutionalized pathology; it is chronic, self-perpetuating pathology; and it is the futile attempt by those with power to confine that pathology so as to prevent the spread of its contagion to the 'larger' community."[7] Presently, variations of institutional racism ranging from sophisticated to naïve are recurrent themes in "mainstream" America as well as in the black community. In some sense, it received an "official stamp of approval" as the root cause of urban disorders when the U.S. Commission on Civil Disorders assigned it top priority as an explanatory variable. Racism subsequently gained popular usage and, for the first time in American history, was placed in proper perspective.

In the black community, racism is considered to be the cause of the "powerlessness" of its residents. A strong emphasis is also placed on identifying and strengthening the culture of the black community, for it is here, its advocates maintain, that racism has taken a heavy toll by attempting to destroy the uniqueness of black culture. It is within this cultural context that the black community often attempts to relate to the broader urban institutional framework. Much of the impetus has arisen from the approach developed by Charles Hamilton and Stokely Carmichael in *Black Power: The Politics of Liberation*[8] and essays by Carmichael and other Black Power advocates. These authors assert that the powerlessness of black people is the primary reason for their inability to determine what course of action will be taken in their community on a given program, such as urban renewal. The theory of powerlessness can also be applied to a black community's inability to decentralize school boards and welfare assistance programs. An additional view draws analogies between American ghettos and colonial situations.[9] These analogies are espoused not only by black intellectuals but by many rank-and-file blacks. Finally, even white social scientists such as Banfield and Greer have so emphasized power relationships that seeking power among blacks has ceased to be viewed as abnormal and outside the range of their achievable goals.

This move toward themes of institutional racism, colonial analogies, and power relationships is important for planning, especially for supporters of an approach which purports to attack poverty of lower income blacks within the comprehensive planning framework. While the individual planner, professional, or technician responsible for the plan may or may not be prejudiced, the agencies and urban institutions which must implement the plan are under siege in the black community as being racist in how they define blacks and black community priorities. Today a proposed slum clearance program is prone to come under much more frequent at-

---

[7] Kenneth Clark, *Dark Ghetto* (New York: Harper and Row, 1965), p. 81.

[8] Charles Hamilton and Stokely Carmichael, *Black Power: The Politics of Liberation* (New York: Random House, 1967).

[9] Frantz Fanon, *The Wretched of the Earth* (New York: Grove Press, 1963).

tack by a wider range of black individuals and organizations than before the widespread acceptance of the racism concept.

CONFLICTS IN PROGRAMS

That large numbers of black people are rapidly becoming alienated from the dominant values of American society is attested to by the increasing emphasis that blacks place on: proving that the United States is a racist society; forming strong associational networks with other blacks to the exclusion of whites; and for many, Africanizing their cultural values. The alienation of the black community may also be witnessed in the manner in which the definitions of self, environment, and the goals of alleviating racism are used to define programs. The programs presently demanded in the black community are remarkably similar to those proposed in the emerging social welfare-physical planning approach. Most of the programmatic demands are not revolutionary but are closely aligned with the notion of democratic reformism. It is within this context that urban renewal plans can be assessed. For example, if the plans successfully accomplish the goal of providing standard low-income housing for poor people, then they are simply adhering to one of the premises of the welfare state—that every citizen is entitled to a decent standard of living. Beyond this premise is the most important issue of *which definitions of racism will be utilized in establishing guidelines for policy, personnel, utilization of skills, and goals of particular programs.*

A summary view of the most frequently used urban programs has been provided by Herbert Gans. The programs are typified as schemes for lower class *guided mobility,* or since 1964, *anti-poverty* programs. These schemes emphasize four major programmatic goals: "to extend the amount and quality of present social services to the hard-to-reach lower class population; to offer new methods of education, especially in the area of job training; to reduce unemployment by training and creation of new jobs; and to encourage self-help both on an individual and group basis, notably through community organization. In addition, programs in recreation, public health, delinquency prevention, and housing are often included in the plan."[10] But as Gans notes, the plans are not intended to deal with social structures but with neighborhoods and their residents.[11] For example, the Chicago and Denver comprehensive plans, as well as the Model Cities approach, illustrate the conflicts inherent in such programs. This disparity between the *need* to change social institutions and *programs* of individual and neighborhood improvement threatens to stalemate most of the programs.

[10] Herbert Gans, "Urban Poverty and Social Planning," in Paul Lazerfeld (ed.), *Uses of Sociology* (New York: Basic Books, Inc., 1967), p. 441.
[11] *Ibid.,* p. 440.

Given the definition of racism assumed by planners and social agencies, the guided mobility approach presents a specific danger. Both these comprehensive plans and the Model Cities program emphasize utilization of the existing (discriminatory) political framework to determine policy, and neither plan goes beyond broad abstract goals down to the level of program priorities. *Without programs to alter specific institutional frameworks, tensions will probably increase instead of decrease.* Moreover, the programs relay a false expectancy to the black community about citizen participation and decision-making on all levels, but the reality is that they are not intended to give blacks any significant power in determining planning priorities in their communities or in the overall social and physical planning framework. They are programs which are designed to fulfill the cities' vested interests not to solve the problems of poverty stricken communities. The mayors of large central cities have not been willing to compromise on this issue.

For example, the proposed Model Cities program in Chicago is dependent upon the Chicago Housing Authority's (conclusively racist) site selection policies and City Council decisions on racial balances among communities. Yet, organizations in the black community expect that utilization of the Model Cities program will enable them to shape policies and priorities of site selection for public housing. Specifically, many organizations are interested in low-rise walkups scattered throughout the city. However, the citizen participation arm of the Model Cities program is the local antipoverty program which in Chicago affords political patronage leverage with limited benefits for low-income blacks. In Atlanta, an acknowledged member of the Ku Klux Klan is a member of the Model Cities board of directors. It is difficult to see how the program will address itself to the needs of Atlanta's low-income black community when an acknowledged racist is voting on these programs.

Finally, the difficulties of structural changes in the black community are closely related to the established institutional network of urban social services—schools, hospitals, AFDC, and general assistance programs—of which many are racist in their structures and functions and can become meaningful only through a change in sociopolitical structure. Moreover, these programs are aimed only at aiding those individuals who are attracted to them. Many of the dispossessed never hear about the programs, and others have become so alienated through prior negative experiences with social service institutions that they no longer attempt to seek their services.

Thus, the social programs which would be the primary inputs in comprehensive plans for the black community remain basically a part of the larger institutional framework which maintains racism. The issues of racism have largely been defined as problems of attitudes, family disorganization, income, and so on, to give the programs local political feasibility and general acceptance. This is a dangerous game to play in angry black central cities . . . extremely dangerous.

CONFLICTS IN PLANS

The anger of blacks in the ghetto cannot be overemphasized. Given the oppressive political realities, the lack of systematic definitions of racism, and the realization that the professionals given responsibility for social and physical proposals are frequently either part of the oppressive structure or unconcerned with adequate definitions, blacks should be angry. Continuation of present trends in comprehensive planning and the social-welfare approach to ghettos will probably do little to alleviate this peculiar condition of urban bondage.

Many comprehensive plan proposals would only irritate problems in racially torn areas. The goals which offend influential whites are made abstract, without any programmatic means—perhaps indicating a lack of intention to carry out these goals. The goals which affect blacks are linked with specific means which have proven oppressive—such as urban renewal programs. These oppressive goals are supposedly legitimated by citations of citizen participation.

Some examples can be cited to document this serious criticism. *The Chicago Comprehensive Plan,*[12] faced with the possibility of a 41 percent black population and 900,000 or more blacks living in spatially restricted poverty areas by 1985, has placed the highest priority upon maintaining and attracting a white middle class, even though whites have been fleeing Chicago at a rate of 50,000 per year for the past five years. Urban renewal projects are proposed to accommodate middle-income whites remaining or returning to the city with public housing for lower income blacks. Over a fifteen year period, a total of 35,000 units of public housing will be built. Most of these units—unless blacks alter the established political pattern—will be built in the ghetto. Moreover, the public housing program combined with other clearance efforts will force the relocation of 7,500 persons a year, most of whom will be from the ghetto. This vicious cycle will only intensify welfare enclaves in other sections of the city, such as the West side—where some of the worst of the nation's riots have occurred, and living conditions defy imagination. Yet the *Chicago Comprehensive Plan maintains that its policies and priorities were established by citizen participation and public discussion.*

The General Plan of Boston,[13] with a smaller black population, utilized

[12] Department of Development and Planning, *The Chicago Comprehensive Plan* (Chicago: DDP, 1966).
[13] Boston Redevelopment Authority, *1965/1985 General Plan for the City of Boston* (Boston: BRA, 1964).

a similar approach to renewal within the overall policy framework. Yet both plans represent advances over other efforts. The Boston Plan is honest in its appraisal of the situation of blacks in the region, and the *Chicago Comprehensive Plan* is generally conceded to be a radical departure in its attempt to unify social, economic, and administrative factors with physical improvement programs.[14] Both go considerably further than the *Proposed Comprehensive Plan for the National Capital*.[15] This plan, released in 1967 when over 50 percent of the District of Columbia's population was black, fails to present a clear strategy or a coherent statement of policy and priorities related to the black majority population. The emphasis of the plan, like the Chicago plan, is to attract and retain more middle-income families. However, in fairness, one must note that some time ago integration ceased to be a relevant issue in Washington, and when the Chicago Plan was released, one criticism was that it did not give enough attention to integration.[16] The approach of the Washington Comprehensive Plan was "to produce a physical environment which will support the host of social activities which make up the life of a city. In other words, the physical plan serves social purposes. . . ."[17] Without this stated purpose the plan could have manipulated abstract social goals to cover its physical purposes. However, the danger of the approach is that only the middle class (in this case black *and* white) will directly benefit from shaping a physical environment proposed by middle class planners to support social activities. As we have previously indicated, many blacks consider their sociocultural outlook different from whites, and Washington, D.C. would certainly be an adequate example of our contention. Of equal importance, as other authors have pointed out, structuring physical goals to achieve social ends does not necessarily improve social ills and frequently has no positive effect.[18]

The overall social-physical effects cannot be taken lightly. Eunice and George Grier showed that in the *Policies Plan for the Year 2000*, developed in Washington in 1961 in anticipation of growth of the Washington region: three of the six proposed radial corridors would probably be segregated, and if "Negro expansion is cut off along the three corridors which are presently 'open,' the future population growth will be forced back into the city, thereby intensifying dangerous pressures which already

---

14 Phillip Wallick, "Comment" on Louis B. Wetmore, "The Comprehensive Plan of Chicago," *Journal of the American Institute of Planners* 33, No. 5 (September 1967): 354.

15 National Capital Planning Commission, *The Proposed Comprehensive Plan for the National Capital* (Washington, DC: NCPC, 1967).

16 Louis Wetmore, Stanley Hallet, Walter Stafford, Jerome Kaufman, *et al.*, *The Racial Aspects of Comprehensive Planning* (Chicago: Chicago Urban League, 1968).

17 *The Proposed Comprehensive Plan for the National Capital*, p. 12.

18 Gans, "Urban Poverty and Social Planning," p. 439.

exist."[19] The type of pressures that the Griers alluded to were evident in the April riots of 1968. While we do not propose that the Washington plan was a *direct* contribution to the riots, if our definition of "institutional racism" has any credence, the plan for the U.S. capital, with its unequal priorities for blacks and whites, represents an ideal type. It can be found in central cities all around the country. Integration is not the issue. Whether whites accept blacks is not nearly as relevant as the institutionalization of racism, either in the form of class or race biases, or in the severe limitations placed on the upward mobility of blacks.

The crucial question then is how to devise comprehensive plans in the face of the problems of massive lower income black populations. One answer is to obtain a greater knowledge of racism. It is clear that none of the plans previously mentioned adequately defined racism before proceeding to develop a comprehensive plan. The definition of racism was inadequate in approaches to both land use problems and program choices. *Another answer stems from the reality of the political process which confronts the planner. Once the planner adequately defines racism, will the city council, aldermen, or the interest groups who influence planning decisions accept the definition?* Or placed in a broader perspective, can planning, once it develops an approach to racism, equalize the priorities between blacks and whites without developing alternative approaches to the existing central city political situation? The answer to this question, as we perceive it, is *no*. New alternatives must be found and utilized.

SOME ALTERNATIVES

Black Majorities. The task of equalizing priorities in central cities will not be simple even if blacks obtain political majorities. The available planning tools are simply not effective in the face of widespread racism. Comprehensive Plans of Chicago, Denver, Boston, and Washington propose that stronger areawide open occupancy laws for housing and zoning be adopted to allow freedom of area residence and increased job availability. Such laws would have limited effectiveness. Evidence shows that open occupancy laws fail to provide any reasonable solution. Usually the passage of fair housing ordinances at the local or state level (twenty-two states have fair housing laws) have been innocuous to say the least, and only in rare instances have regulations been enforced. Additionally, where these ordinances exist there are usually zoning and subdivision controls which have so effectively boxed in lower income blacks that the ordinances are no more than moralistic gestures. An example of the great future effect of suburban zoning on central city problems has been presented by

[19] Eunice and George Grier, "Equality and Beyond: Housing Segregation in the Great Society," *Daedalus* 95, No. 1 (Winter 1966): 89.

the Regional Plan Association: "Right now about 2 million persons are living in municipalities which control the zoning and building codes determining where some 13 million will live in the year 2000. . . ."[20]

Furthermore, whites fail to grasp the fact that no one knows how many blacks want to suburbanize. Even if this was the consensus, the fact remains that the sheer numbers required for dispersal of the ghetto through suburbanization make the occurrence unlikely. For example, achieving the population level of 350,000 blacks outside the central city of Chicago by 1980, as projected by the *Chicago Comprehensive Plan,* would require a net migration plus natural increase of over 15,000 blacks per year for the next fifteen years.[21] This type of planning is not only politically unfeasible—it reflects wishful thinking!

Nor do the advocates of suburbanization specify the type of communities which would be advantageous for blacks, despite the fact that jobs are in the suburbs and blacks need employment. In the Chicago region, blacks in several suburban communities have been confronted with significant problems which planners have not been able to answer. For example, the black community in Joliet, Illinois, is having considerable difficulty because of an urban renewal project without an adequate relocation plan for the displaced persons. While this type of problem is also found in the central city, the likelihood of blacks raising a cry and being heard in the suburbs is significantly lessened. Moreover, many of the older suburbs where blacks are likely to eventually find housing are ineffectual political bodies with outstanding land use problems which for a politically isolated black population would be insurmountable. Most central cities are surrounded by communities of this type.

Metropolitan Planning. Another response to the problems of black central cities and exclusionary white suburbs has been the requirement of metropolitanwide planning as a condition of federal aid for metropolitan communities. Even if this requirement was strictly enforced, probably blacks would realize only minor gains. Officials in metropolitan planning agencies are more likely to be persuaded by influential whites than by blacks, who are loosely organized on a metro basis. The effect of metropolitan planning would be to usurp many of the rising political strengths blacks are likely to gain in central cities. Furthermore, response to demands even by regional offices of HUD will not necessarily favor blacks, especially since various federal program requirements are not interlocked. For example, in East Chicago, Indiana, the black community had been demanding that lower income housing be placed outside the ghetto, and the local city council refused. Blacks approached the regional

[20] Regional Plan Association, *Basic Issues of the Second Regional Plan* (New York: RPA, 1967).

[21] Stafford, *et al., The Racial Aspects of Comprehensive Planning,* p. 19.

office of HUD. According to newspaper accounts, the officials were sympathetic, however, they could not condition other federal program grants on refusal to select housing sites outside the ghetto. Finally, as Alan Altshuler has pointed out, metropolitan planning eventually approximates metropolitan government,[22] and blacks have been reluctant to endorse this political arrangement.[23]

Advocacy Planning. The limited alternatives that are available are forms of advocacy planning utilizing regional and national political alliances to further its causes. The political impetus in the black community closely approximates the format for advocacy planning. Both are basically concerned with *accountability* of political structures. For blacks, accountability concerns the relevance of organization or group definitions of racism, the layout of the decision-making apparatus, and what influence particular organizations have upon decisions which affect blacks. Planners seem to be concerned much more with the pluralistic democracy which advocacy planning affords. However, both approaches are concerned with the use of power, particularly how power is utilized to maintain and sanction oppressive patterns. Second, advocacy planning offers the possibility of analyzing the racial content of proposed planning programs and land use alternatives. Within this framework, advocacy planners would not only serve as technical advisors but would frequently become instigators of political reforms. Local leaders might even run for office on "technical" issues such as zoning or sewerage, thus bringing a new dimension to the political life of the ghetto while pinpointing the accountable elements in city government. A third possibility for advocacy planning is that blacks through increased political leverage will be able to secure demonstration grants from foundations and government sources to document the impact of social and physical planning proposals on racism. A fourth possibility for advocacy planning is suggesting institutional alternatives. Frieden has discussed the case of health service planning being extended into already established areas of social policy.[24] In this case, advocate planners with knowledge of the potential impact that particular policies are likely to have on black communities could suggest alternatives or propose new approaches. This, however, would require a new type of social-scientist-planner who could not only *propose* but *project* and *predict* patterns of change. Fifth, advocacy planning, through its emphasis upon political conflict as a desirable end, appears to lean toward decentralization of authority. Finally, an intermediate group of semiprofessional advocates could be trained in basic design, analysis

[22] Alan Altshuler, *The City Planning Process* (Ithaca, New York: Cornell University Press, 1965), p. 420.

[23] Scott Greer, *Metropolitics* (New York: John Wiley and Sons, Inc., 1963).

[24] Bernard Frieden, "The Changing Prospects for Social Planning," *Journal of the American Institute of Planners* 33, No. 5 (September 1967): 311–23.

of census tract data, surveys, and other primary techniques to build a semiprofessional planning staff in local black communities. Many black communities will not be able to provide adequate salaries to hire competent planners in the near future. Rather than settling for well-meaning planners without knowledge of racism, comprehensive planning, and politics, it would be better to train young blacks (including dropouts) who wish to learn art, drafting, community organization, and the like.

PLANS AND BATTLES

We have not presented all the ramifications of comprehensive planning and racism. It would take a book—which incidentally needs to be written —to document a systematic theoretical approach to racism and planning. All we are sure of at this point is that the approach needs further development and that blacks are not waiting for planners to develop it. Planners have to realize that they are very close to the urban battlefield, and on the urban battlefield one recognizes only the relevant. For the planner, an irrelevant understanding and definition of racism is worse than no definition at all.

Mayor Kenneth Gibson says—'Wherever the Central Cities Are Going, Newark Is Going to Get There First'

FRED J. COOK

Newark is a study in the evils, tensions and frustrations that beset the central cities of America. It is a city of 375,000, an estimated 61 percent Negro, 11 percent Puerto Rican. It is a city with an overall unemployment rate of 14 percent (25 to 30 percent among blacks and Puerto Ricans); around 25 percent of those who are employed work only part-time, and there are virtually no summer jobs and few programs for the city's 80,000 school children, who now roam the streets. As a result, one of every three Newarkers is getting some form of public assistance. There are, by conservative estimate, 20,000 drug addicts in the city, and only 7 percent of them are being treated. Newark has the highest crime rate of any city in the nation; the highest percentage of substandard housing; the highest rate of venereal disease, new tuberculosis cases and maternal mortality, and it is second in infant mortality. Most of these rates, like the crime rate, are still rising. In the Central Ward, perhaps the worst ghetto in the East, decent black families live as virtual prisoners in housing-authority projects, afraid to let their children outside even to play. The city's first black Mayor, Kenneth A. Gibson, often says: "Wherever the central cities of America are going, Newark is going to get there first."

There are at least two Newarks, separate and distinct, divided from each other, existing in an atmosphere of mutual suspicion and racial tension. There is the white-dominated, business-oriented Newark, and there are the densely populated sections where blacks and Puerto Ricans live. Business Newark looks almost as prosperous as ever. A new Gateway motel and business-office complex has been built opposite the old Pennsylvania Railroad Station. The gleaming white marble facade of the Prudential Insurance Company's national headquarters dominates the shining storefronts along Broad and Market. Bamberger's is still there; Ohrbach's is still there. Business Newark does $3.5-billion worth of retail trade annually. But out to the west and south, in the Central and the South Wards, it is a different story. "It is a jungle," says one cab driver, and another adds: "This city is dead."

The juxtaposition of white authority and the jungle strikes one with a forcible impact. The Essex County Courthouse and Hall of Records sit on a knoll along High Street, and chock-a-block with these symbols of governmental stability are the devastated structures of the Newark ghetto. Shattered, gaping, sightless windows stare out at the county buildings, and only a short jog away, where Springfield Avenue runs into High, one comes upon the still ghastly rubble of a war-ravaged Newark.

It was here, in the long hot summer of 1967, that mobs rioted, looted and burned in one of the nation's worst race riots; four years later, blackened ruins still stand as testament to that outburst. Wrecked and gutted buildings offend the eye; trash of all kinds befouls the gutters. One hulk stands out—a store that looks as if its entire front had been blasted away by mortar fire. One gazes into the cavernous emptiness of its interior, wondering what keeps it upright. Across the street an abandoned theater seems about to totter inward upon itself, the deep bay of its former entrance piled high with rubbish. Up and down the avenue for blocks, the same sights are repeated; the blackened, hollow shells of buildings stand, some boarded up, some closed off by iron gratings, all in ruin.

"The only new thing added on the street in three years is another bar— and, of course, we needed *that*," says one Negro leader. He shakes a gray head and adds: "I was in Germany, where the cities were all destroyed in World War II. Now they have been completely rebuilt, spanking new —and here we can't rebuild the Central Ward or Detroit or Watts."

Bad as the physical aspect of Newark is, the psychological and emotional factors are worse. The racial tensions inevitable in a city overwhelmingly black and Puerto Rican, but dominated for so long by a white minority, were intensified this winter by a record, 11-week teachers' strike. The strike closed about half of Newark's schools (the rest stayed open in an atmosphere of turmoil), and the black community reacted with outrage that at times exploded into fury. "The strike was eventually settled, but it is still with us," says a black leader. He explains:

"Parents whose children lost 11 weeks of school, and who perhaps couldn't graduate or who will be handicapped in the future, are frustrated and bitter. And the strike didn't settle the basic problem. Too many of Newark's teachers live in the suburbs; this is just a 9-to-3 job for them, and they are not concerned with the problems of black ghetto children. I taught in the Newark school system, and I know. Polarization? It couldn't be much worse. It was bad already, but now this is one of the worst polarized sections in the nation."

In this bleak picture there is just one ray of light and hope—the presence in City Hall of Newark's first Negro Mayor. Tour the city, talk to leaders of the black community, and you will hear the same phrases repeated over and over again. David Barrett, the bright, articulate 27-year-old president of the United Community Corporation, the community-service organization funded by the Federal Office of Economic Opportunity, perhaps expresses it best. His face lights up as he recalls the election of Mayor Gibson just one year ago.

"Expectations were very high," Barrett says. "You just expected that, overnight, things were going to be 10,000 times better. Now, of course, there is a gap between those high, perhaps quixotic, expectations and delivery. Still, the Negro and Puerto Rican communities feel that things are better, that there is a more sympathetic attitude, a better understanding at City Hall. This, as I see it, is the one great plus; Gibson's just being there is a positive plus."

Other community leaders agree. The Rev. Henry Cade, pastor of the Central Presbyterian Church, almost on the boundary line between the Central and South Wards, says: "There has been little positive movement since the riots of 1967. But there is a new kind of ethos, a new spirit in the community as the result of the last election." LeRoi Jones, who prefers to call himself Imamu Baraka—a short, bearded Negro poet who might weigh 120 pounds and who is one of the most controversial figures in Newark—concurs: "I think the biggest boost so far has been the feeling the community has that things are possible as the result of the election of Ken Gibson. People are not stifled and hopeless, as they were under the old, corrupt administration. Now there is someone in City Hall who gives them a feeling that things are possible."

But everyone recognizes that this hopeful mood cannot last unless there is positive action to change the sordid aspects of Newark. The Rev. Mr. Cade puts it this way: "What happens to a dream deferred? It can't be deferred too long, or it will turn into bitterness and rebellion."

The man on whom most of Newark pins its hopes sits in City Hall, boxed in on every side, unable to move toward the fulfillment of those hopes. Ken Gibson is not the typical politician. A short, chunky man, broad-shouldered, barrel-chested, with just the wisp of a mustache on his round face, he was trained as an engineer, and he weighs problems with an engineer's caution. He seems to lack dynamism on the public platform, abandoning the usual forms of political rhetoric to speak more drily about issues, but face-to-face he exudes a great deal of personal charm. No matter what the tensions of the day, he usually manages to seem calm, relaxed. Though slow to make up his mind, he appears confident and extremely sure of himself once he has arrived at a decision. And he is candid to a degree almost unheard-of among politicians. Shortly after he took office last year, he disclosed that one man had hinted he would pay $15,000 to name the police director and that another had suggested Gibson could have "10 percent off the top of everything," all city contracts, all public works. Gibson reported the offers to prosecuting authorities and concentrated on the task of trying to solve the massive problems of Newark.

Now, after a rough first year in office, he discussed the problems, the hopes that he knows repose in him and the frustrations he faces. "How long can you sustain this kind of hope without action?" he asked. "I don't think I should be used as a narcotic. I don't think that the power structure or the establishment or whatever you want to call it should think that just my existence here will keep things from happening."

But he acknowledged that he sees little prospect of being able to move forward in a dramatic way. When he took office, he found himself saddled with a $65-million deficit, the heritage of the scandal-studded regime of Mayor Hugh J. Addonizio. Property taxes in Newark were already at a virtually confiscatory level (taxes on a small $15,000 home run to $1,000 or more a year); the city lacked other sources of revenue; Federal funds were being cut back; there was just no money.

Gibson proposed a broad tax package. The key and most controversial feature was a 2 percent payroll tax to be paid by industry. The white business community was shocked. At one point, the Essex County Assembly delegation flatly refused to support the Mayor's proposals. But a compromise was eventually worked out: The State Legislature passed bills permitting Newark to collect a 1 percent payroll tax and six other new levies. Then the City Council, still controlled by adherents of the white political machine that had always run Newark, balked. The Council eventually approved the payroll levy and two minor new taxes, but that was as far as it would go. Gibson suggested dismissing 400 city employes as an economy measure, but the Council would not agree. Gibson, unable to economize, was left with a tax package that, it was estimated, would raise only $20-million instead of the $35-million his fiscal experts had calculated the city would need. Part of the gap was closed when the Council decreed that an $8-million accumulated surplus in the separate Water Department account should be used for current expenses.

"The money we need is just to maintain operations," Gibson says, "to pay the police, firemen, clerks, staff. What we are' talking about is just enough money to keep us afloat, enough money to let us live for another year. We aren't talking about changing things, improving things—just surviving." When the Water Department surplus was gone, the city was left with nothing to fall back on. "Now we have no surplus anywhere, absolutely nothing," Gibson says. "If anything extraordinary happens, if any crisis arises, this city is just going to be out of liquid."

On his first anniversary in office, Gibson was able to announce three new programs funded by the Federal Government (they would supply $50-million in mortgage funds to rehabilitate 2,500 dwelling units, provide for the appointment of one of the nation's first municipal ombudsmen and establish round-the-clock storefront centers in each of the city's five wards to help citizens with personal problems). But the Mayor intends to keep pressuring for more state and Federal aid, and he confesses: "I'm afraid the amounts we manage to spring loose will be small compared to our needs. We will probably have to cut down on staff and change our way of doing things even to provide the basic services the city has now. Next year, if we are still in the same situation, we will simply have to cut back on staff, and this means we'll have to cut services —the number of times you collect the garbage and clean the streets. I think this is going to have to happen before we get more money. People, you see, just don't believe us. The mayors of our central cities have been crying about the lack of funds for so long that many people seem to think we'll find the money somewhere. They seem to take the attitude: 'Die first, and when we come to your funeral, we'll believe you.'"

One Negro, a lifelong resident of Newark, says: "Ken has been catching hell from all sides, but there is little he can do. Somebody way up above is going to have to make decisions about priorities in this country."

Most of the criticism from Gibson supporters concerns two issues: the selection of a new police director and the handling of the school strike. Both grew out of the one fact that dwarfs all else in Newark—the polarization of the races.

When Gibson was elected, there was a strong demand in the black community that he name a black police chief. Black leaders emphasize such words as "humanity" and "sympathy" and "understanding"; they do not feel that the white man, however good his intentions, can really understand the black man and his problems. They believe that only black teachers can really teach black children. They believe that a white-controlled police force will always arrest blacks for offenses whites might commit with impunity. And they believe that, since they represent 70 percent of the population of Newark, they must have what they call "proportional representation" in all branches of municipal government— in other words, virtually complete control.

The first manifestation of this thrust for black power came in the pressure on Gibson to name a black police director. He disregarded it and appointed John L. Redden, who had joined the department in 1947 and had consistently scored highest on civil-service tests for advancement. In 1965 he was named deputy police chief, but he really came to prominence after the riots of 1967. He told the gubernatorial commission investigating the riots that gambling was rampant in Newark, and his testimony was one factor in leading the commission to conclude that there was "a pervasive feeling of corruption" at City Hall. To quiet the uproar, Redden was given command of a special gambling squad, and in a two-month crusade he cut such a swath that he was moved to a less sensitive job. He had an image of incorruptibility, but his appointment as police director satisfied no one. The blacks were displeased because Redden was white; the whites, because his record seemed to say he was the kind of man no politician could control. And so the City Council, black and white alike, voted 9-0 against Redden's confirmation.

Gibson was informed of the impasse half an hour before he was to take the oath of office on July 1, 1970, and even before he was officially Mayor he faced down the Council. He says he told the councilmen: "Listen, you are going to have a good relationship with the new Mayor or a bad one. Either Redden gets confirmed or I withdraw all my nominations here and now—and what's more I'm going to tell those people waiting outside just what it's all about." There were some 8,000 deliriously happy Gibson supporters waiting for the inaugural ceremony on the City Hall steps, and the Council could not face the reaction that would be provoked by the kind of speech Gibson threatened to make. Redden was confirmed.

Gibson has never regretted his choice. He had complete faith in Redden's honesty, he considered Redden the most capable man in the department and he thought a black police director would be sabotaged by his white department—and the black community would have to bear the onus for the failure.

"Those guys would have crucified a black director," he says. "At least Redden has some men he can work with. Redden is probably the only man in the department I have faith in as being able to do the kind of job that needs to be done. As far as Redden is concerned, I *know* I'm right."

Despite Gibson's assurance, though, this view is not accepted by the black community, not even by some of its more intelligent leaders. The Redden appointment was the first incident in a potentially dangerous trend, the tendency of the black community to want only black, to think that only black is right.

John Redden, who stepped into the bear pit at Gibson's urging, is stocky, round-faced, with thinning strands of sandy hair. He has a slow, sometimes wry smile, and is deliberate in his speech. He can also be tough. One of his first moves as police director was to shake up the department with wholesale transfers. His aim, he says, was "to improve the credibility of the department" by restoring public faith in it.

"In the nineteen-thirties the rackets took over this town," Redden says bluntly. "Longie Zwillman and Richie (the Boot) Boiardo and their kind ran it. It seemed to me that their object was to neutralize people who could hurt them. They paid off some people and neutralized others through fear or the desire that they just didn't want to be bothered taking the risk of bucking the system. The overall effect was that the rackets had their way."

Redden is convinced that "the vast majority" of policemen "really believed that oath when they held up their hands and took it," but the top-level political corruption was so bad that in the end many just gave up. Gibson, he believes, "is dedicated to breaking that tradition and providing an improved service. This isn't going to be accomplished overnight." The reason it isn't, he explains, is that many of the conditions that need changing have been ingrained in the department for more than a century. As long ago as 1857, a Newark Mayor called the department "defective" and "inadequate," and a Bureau of Municipal Research study in 1943 noted an "apathy on the part of successive administrations" and "an accumulation of hopelessness and indifference on the part of the community."

Between 1950 and 1960 some 100,000 of Newark's white residents moved out, and Negroes and Puerto Ricans moved in. The two-way migration continued during the sixties. "Society was changing while institutions didn't change," Redden says. Now he wants "to make the racial composition of the department closer to that of the city." Toward this end, he has launched several special campaigns to lure Negroes and Puerto Ricans into the force.

"We decided to do something that all police literature would say is unprofessional and impossible," Redden explains. "We decided to make every effort to recruit police personnel wholly within the boundaries of Newark. Now we have some straws in the wind which indicate we may be able to do this. In our present recruit class of 27 men, there are 16 black men, and they have all been recruited through the normal civil-service procedures. As a result of the recruiting drive we put on in April, we have a list of 77 potential recruits, the largest list since 1962, and about half of them are black."

The Newark force has an authorized strength of 1,225 patrolmen, and fewer than 200 of them are black now. In the past, it has often been difficult to recruit Negroes, for they have looked upon the department as a hostile white enclave. If Redden can continue 50 percent black recruitment, he hopes in time to break down some of this prejudice while bringing the composition of the force more nearly in line with that of the city.

Despite this campaign, there are still demands that Redden be replaced by a black police director. Such demands were especially prevalent during the explosive teachers' strike. The animosities aroused by that event were fierce, and Redden and his predominantly white force were caught in the crossfire.

It seems in retrospect that the strike, called by the Newark Teachers' Union, should never have happened. Mayor Gibson called it illegal, alienating some of his labor supporters, and he makes it clear that he thinks the black-controlled Board of Education was wrong to let the strike develop over peripheral issues, an attitude with which many black leaders strongly disagree.

Money was never a major factor in the stoppage because everyone realized the city had none. The strike erupted over two provisions in the previous contract, signed when the Addonizio forces controlled the Board of Education. The old contract called for binding arbitration of grievances and teacher exemption from so-called nonprofessional chores. The new board refused to honor these provisions, though it is axiomatic that when you try to rescind benefits won in a previous contract you are going to have a strike.

Gibson had appointed four black and Puerto Rican members to the school board—including Jesse Jacob, then its president—but he still did not have a majority of the nine members, and the board, once appointed, operates independently of City Hall. The Mayor, however, can exercise influence in times of crisis, and Gibson tried. He arranged a conference between board members and union leaders on the eve of the walkout, and he still believes the disagreement should have been settled then. But the new board members, joined by some of the old, stood fast, and their position was endorsed by the black community. David Barrett states the case this way: "The community's reaction was: 'Well, we didn't want that old contract in the first place, and it existed only because the previous Board of Education didn't represent *us*. Now we have a Board of Education that is representing the community, that is reflecting our will, and it should have the right to negotiate an entirely new contract.'"

Behind the stated strike issues was another, more basic prize: control of the schools. The black and Puerto Rican community saw the strike as an attempt by the teachers' union to dominate the schools, independent of community control; and community people, as Barrett says, became more determined than ever "to have some genuine say about what goes on in their schools, whether at the Board of Education level or the community level."

Barrett, who is now a computer programer, taught for one year at the Clinton Plaza Junior High School, and he draws on that experience to illustrate what he means about the white-black dichotomy in the schools of Newark. "I remember once we were in the teachers' room, and one teacher said: 'So-and-so's mother came in today. Why, you know, I didn't know she wasn't *married*.' In the Negro community, we accept these things; we know they exist—but we don't stigmatize the child because of it. Another time, another teacher. 'So-and-so's father came in today,' she said. 'He was the *dirtiest* man I ever saw!" It never seemed to occur to her that he was dirty because he was working at a dirty job to make a living; that he had to take time off from that job to come to school to see about his child; that all of this showed some kind of concern on his part, for which he should have been praised. The fact that this man came to school dirty from his job never would have made any impression on me at all.

"We're talking about attitudes and characteristics—about sensibilities. There is even a difference between white teachers who have been reared in Newark and live in Newark, and those from the suburbs. Those who live here are much closer in understanding of the students—not so close as black teachers, but much, much closer than some of the suburban teachers who have a tendency to misunderstand black kids on the human level."

There are 89 schools in the Newark system, staffed by 4,405 teachers. The school population is 85 percent black and Puerto Rican; the teaching staff is almost two-thirds white. The racial balance among teachers is reversed in one of Newark's key schools, the Robert Treat Elementary School, in the Central Ward ghetto. Out of 1,100 students there, all are black except for five whites and about 20 Puerto Ricans, but the teaching staff of 65 is three-quarters black. During the strike, only four of the staff joined the strikers, and afterward the community refused to have them back.

Eugene Campbell, a tall, slender 33-year-old Negro with a full beard and mustache, is principal at Robert Treat. Born in Newark, educated in the city's schools and at Newark College, he is alert, quick and decisive in his movements. He is sometimes called an "ultra-militant," a term at which he bridles. Campbell sees the controversial provisions of the old teachers' contract as "ludicrous, absurd, downright ridiculous." To him, there is no such thing as a "nonprofessional chore." He explains: "Children who come in here have to be taught how to use the lavatory, how to use the cafeteria. The only place they've eaten is at home; they have to be taught the routine of the cafeteria, how to eat in a mess hall of 100 or more and to get out promptly when they're finished because we are crowded here." The old contract relieving teachers of such chores provided, Campbell says, "for the training of 252 aides to fill tasks being performed by 2,000 teachers." He snorts in derision. "One emotionally and culturally adjusted teacher is worth eight aides. Only the teacher has the respect of the students. Only the teacher knows how to control situations that may develop."

One of the more turbulent scenes during the strike occurred when 70 unionists picketed Robert Treat. "That caused a lot of bad feeling as far as the community went and as far as the students were concerned," Campbell says. "The students heard people on the picket lines calling their teachers scabs, whores, cursing them in vile language. One of our striking teachers was on the line, and I just got a barrage of phone calls from parents who were angry and upset by the whole performance."

All Newark seethed as the strike dragged on. One tumultuous meeting in Symphony Hall resulted in a small riot after the Board of Education voted to turn down a proposed strike settlement. The black community, enraged at the teachers when the strike was called, now cheered, shouted and applauded the school board's action insuring a prolongation of the shutdown. The reaction can be understood only if one understands what was at stake once the strike started: control of the schools, with race a fundamental issue.

The disturbance in Symphony Hall sorely tried Redden's men. They attempted, without success, to keep the aisles cleared, and in the midst of the fracas arrested the Rev. Dennis Westbrooks, a Negro councilman from the Central Ward, and four juveniles, accusing them of obstructing an aisle. The audience turned in fury upon the policemen, who used nightsticks to quell the uproar. The arrest of the Rev. Westbrooks provoked a furious backlash. David Barrett sums up community feeling: "Would they have arrested a *white* councilman for blocking an aisle? We considered this an outrage, and the whole black community demanded Redden's resignation."

Redden, unwilling to stir up emotions over old issues, prefers not to talk much about the incident now. It is known, however, that a delegation of blacks demanded that he suspend nine white policemen for their actions at the Symphony Hall riot. Redden flatly refused. "For what?" he is said to have demanded. "For trying to do their duty and maintain order?" It is also known that Redden offered to resign and let Mayor Gibson appoint a black police director. Gibson wouldn't hear of it. As tempers mounted, LeRoi Jones called Redden "a racist turkey," and Redden, having had enough, took a weekend for cogitation and then on his own authority issued a press release so blunt that it made some of Gibson's advisers quail. He denounced the inflammatory rhetoric used during the strike and suggested that the black community examine itself. He said:

"Reference has been made to police brutality. Admittedly, there have been instances of police brutality, but let us view it in the context of the display of violence and brutality in the community. In 1950 there were 24 criminal homicides in this city; in 1970 there were 143. This year promises to outstrip last year. Let us view it also in the context of the violence displayed and advocated . . . at public meetings . . .

"The present tensions parallel the conditions that existed before the riots in 1967. At that time a public issue, not of the police department's making, was used to inflame emotions. At that time the same type of demagogic rhetoric and violent conduct at public meetings was used to inflame passions. At that time, persons loaded the guns which were used to take the lives of 23 people. The blood of those persons is on the hands of those who loaded the guns more so than those who squeezed the triggers. The guns are being loaded again by those who would plunge this city into the same type of apocalyptic convulsions it experienced in 1967."

In the aftermath of this confrontation, Mayor Gibson moved forcefully. It is no secret in Newark that he used all his influence to end the strike. Though the manner of it pleased few, he settled it on the only possible terms, ratifying the arbitration and nonprofessional-chores clauses in the old contract and promising the black community that he would appoint a task force on education and that the Board of Education would set up a curriculum committee to study school programs.

(Since then Gibson has appointed to the board Lawrence Hamm, a 17-year-old black high school senior who led the Newark Student Federation in its demands for a greater voice in school affairs during the teachers' strike. In the board reorganization, Jacob was replaced as president by Mrs. Helen Fullilove.)

The resumption of classes brought no end to the polarization in Newark, for the black community saw the strike as just one incident in its drive for power. At the heart of this thrust is the slight, challenging figure of LeRoi Jones. He heads the Committee for a Unified Newark, which solidified Gibson support in the 1970 mayoralty election. He operates out of a headquarters at 502 High Street, a barren, dilapidated storefront at the intersection with Springfield Avenue. The door of his headquarters is plastered with the kind of slogans that raise the hackles of Newark's white residents. The most prominent placard begins: "Young Brother!! It's Nation Time!! Help Build a Black Nation. Become a Simba, a Young Lion . . ." It urges "innovations for revolution." Another placard shows a muscular black man grabbing a white arm holding a revolver and shoving it aloft so that the white man cannot shoot. It describes the goals of the black man in America as "freedom and independence," and declares: "NOTHING WILL STOP US FROM BECOMING MASTERS OF OUR OWN DESTINY."

Jones, when one meets him, seems more moderate than his slogans suggest. He does not rant, but talks quietly, reasonably, as if arguing the undeniable logic of his case. Though he insists that he is not the violent racist whites have pictured, there is the quality of steel behind his deceptive mildness. And some of the things he says in his unemotional way are bound to shock white traditionalists.

"These slogans," he explains, waving to the placards on the wall, "are made to seem violent and racist because many people benefit by our not being in control. We've worked hard with preschool programs. We try to teach our children pride in our race. That's what these slogans mean. We try to build up a sense of pride and identity. It may shock white people, but it's sometimes easier for black children to identify with Stokely Carmichael than George Washington. After all, George Washington was a slaveholder. That's not to say anything against him, for that was the custom of his time. But the fact remains.

"Then take the situation in Newark. Most of the 20,000 narcotics addicts are in the black community, and the white community hasn't done much about it. How do you expect us to respond to George Washington and 'The Star Spangled Banner' when a situation like this is permitted to exist? If there was a situation like this in the white community, we could see President Nixon threatening to bomb the Turkish heroin growers or cut off trade with France because of its heroin refineries, but with us we don't have the power to deal with it that way. We can't go to a Congressman and say, 'If you don't vote economic sanctions against France and Turkey until this stops, we will see to it that you don't get re-elected.' We don't have that kind of power today. But we must get it."

Jones declares flatly—and it is a sentiment one hears throughout the black community—"There will have to be black control of the City Council in 1974. This neocolonial situation must end. This city does $3.5-billion worth of retail business every year, and our percentage of it is less than six-tenths of 1 percent. That is all that remains here. There's a Gold Coast here that surrounds the worst ghetto in the East. Nobody is asking for anything but equity, the kind of equity Americans have always believed in. But this will have to come in time from our own inner creativity."

Given the quality of the Newark schools, which have for years been graduating what Eugene Campbell calls "functional illiterates," does the black community in Newark have the resources to take over completely?

"No," Jones answers. "We are not totally able to run the city at this point. But we know that we have enough black men here now who have the kind of imagination and creativity that, given the opportunity, can be trained to take over these jobs. We certainly know we couldn't do it any worse than the way things were run by the past administration, which was not only racist but corrupt."

Capturing control of the City Council in the 1974 election will take some doing. Four of the nine members are elected at large; the other five represent the city's five wards. In the "at-large" election, the vote in the outlying, almost wholly white North Ward and other white residential districts is a heavy factor. And then there is the Byzantine nature of Newark politics. The old Italian-dominated white political machine maintained power for years by running council candidates who would split the black vote, and the Rev. Mr. Cade says there are rumors that the same tactic will be tried in the next contest. There is also an effort to try to drive a wedge between Mayor Gibson and the blacks led by LeRoi Jones. David Barrett recalls that after the school strike was settled some newsmen tried to get black leaders to say they were disenchanted with the Mayor, but he argues that this isn't so. "We may disagree on an issue or two, like the appointment of Redden and the school strike," he says, "but that doesn't mean we are going to split with the Mayor."

It all requires a delicate juggling act by Mayor Gibson. A true moderate, he must neither alienate his black support nor surrender to it, for he would never have been elected without a sizable white vote. His opponents in 1970 raised the cry that in office he would be the tool of Jones. Obviously, he hasn't been. If he had, Redden wouldn't be police director and the teachers' strike might have been allowed to continue to an ultimate showdown. But Gibson makes no secret of the fact that he tries to work with Jones because Jones does, in truth, represent powerful segments of the black community. Jones, he stresses, "is very good with young people, with high-school and college students especially. He provides them with a strong image they look up to and respect. And he's very dedicated to the things he believes in. He'll work seven days a week, sometimes 24 hours a day, and a lot of those who oppose him want to work a seven-hour day and a five-day week. I say to them, 'You aren't going to beat a man like LeRoi Jones that way.'"

Gibson pauses, smiles his slow, soft smile, and advances another argument: "I say to them, 'If he's as radical as you think he is, isn't it better to have him working within the political structure to get it changed rather than saying, "Let's blow it up"?' When I use that argument with people, there isn't any answer. They have to agree; they say, 'You're right.'"

There is, of course, another side of Newark, the powerful and important business community. Its principal spokesman has been Donald S. McNaughton, chairman and chief executive officer of Prudential Insurance. McNaughton is one of a growing breed of executives who believe that business must concern itself not just with balance sheets, but with the welfare of communities in which it thrives. He recognizes all the massive problems of Newark, but is still optimistic about the long-range future. He points out that Newark is the hub of Northern New Jersey, "the nation's fourth-largest market"; that it is a great sea, air, rail and highway center; that it is the third-largest financial center in the nation; that it is developing "a huge complex of higher educational institutions." In a recent speech before the U.S. Chamber of Commerce, he cited Newark's problems as symbolic of those of the central cities in which "we are living in a puzzling paradox: poverty and prejudice standing side by side with prosperity and plenty." McNaughton argued that the nation cannot go on this way and survive, and he perceived as "a basic difficulty" the fact that "we have no good system, in fact little system at all, for determining national priorities." He exhorted businessmen to recognize that the Federal Government must establish a sound, long-range priority schedule and to lend their talents to devising it. On this, he said, "the survival of democracy might depend."

Under McNaughton's leadership, Prudential has tried to act on this philosophy in Newark. It helped bankroll the new Gateway motel-business complex, which was needed, McNaughton says, because the demand for office space in Newark is steadily growing. It invested in the University Gardens housing project as a partner of the state under an arrangement to furnish low-income and middle-income housing. It invested more than $1-million in loans with low interest rates to restore three-family and four-family homes. McNaughton explains that the same could not be done for one-family homes "because they cannot afford to pay the taxes."

McNaughton hailed Gibson's election, saying, "Every indication is that he is a paragon of honesty." He assigned Prudential experts to work with the new Mayor in studying the city's finances and trying to get it on a sound operating basis. When the city could not afford the salary that would attract the best business administrator it could find, McNaughton induced the Newark Chamber of Commerce to contribute. The black community reacted with suspicion and hostility; it feared that white business was buying influence in the new regime at City Hall. McNaughton wrote a letter insisting that no one connected with the chamber should try to take advantage of the situation. Later, speaking of black resistance to the salary subsidy, he asked: "Would they rather we didn't do anything? What do they want from us? Do they want us to help the Mayor or don't they want us to help the Mayor?"

Such are the personalities and issues that dominate Newark. The men themselves, whatever their race, whatever their intentions or capabilities, are trapped in a situation that defies solution with the resources at hand.

A social worker says: "A couple of our workers got mugged in broad daylight in one of the housing projects. The women in that area of the Central Ward are scared to go out on the street, even in the daytime. I know one woman who has five children. She drives them to school in the morning, picks them up in the afternoon and takes them right into her apartment. She's afraid even to let them out to play."

A cab driver who works out of Penn Station says: "I'm lucky I don't work the streets. Some cab drivers have been mugged right on the street in broad daylight in the Negro section. They wait until the fare's been paid, then they come at you from both sides. It's like they come right out of the ground, it happens so fast. They wrench open the doors and take the money."

On April 1, Willie Gibson, the 60-year-old father of the Mayor, was on his way to a wake when he was punched, stomped and beaten by a gang of youths. He suffered serious head injuries and was taken to Beth Israel Medical Center, where he spent a week recovering.

Crime and violence hold much of Newark in thrall. Police Director Redden says: "There is a growing demand in the black and Puerto Rican community for better police services. I hear this wherever I go, whether among people who own their own homes or those who live in housing projects—wherever I go in the city there is this basic feeling that people want greater security."

Yet the police alone cannot deal with crime unless social conditions can be changed. And the changes needed are in those areas that have been stressed again and again in every central city of America: jobs, housing, health.

Housing in Newark is a special disaster. One social worker says that landlords in the Central Ward ghetto charge $150 to $160 a month for apartments in tumble-down buildings. The social worker himself had to move from an apartment in which the roof leaked so badly that the kitchen ceiling collapsed. "Every time it rained, you couldn't cook for the flood," he said, "and when you tried to get to the bathroom, you got a shower bath on the way." He searched, and the best apartment he could find—it rented for $125 a month—was in another tottering structure that had only one thing to recommend it: "It was clean."

The health problem staggers the imagination. Mayor Gibson says: "The number of people who die needlessly in heart-attack or accident cases from the lack of instant treatment must be fantastic." No doctor dares go into the Central Ward. No ambulance will go there unless the police have gone to the scene and summoned it. If the police are busy or the ambulance is tied up, the patient often dies.

"I remember a case we had last winter," Gibson says. "I was listening to the calls on the police radio. There was a bad accident near Newark Airport. The policeman on the scene kept calling and calling for the ambulance. 'Where's the bus?' he finally asked. 'It's on a heart-attack case,' he was told. 'This guy's bleeding to death. Can't you do something?' the policeman pleaded. He was told: 'The only ambulance we have is on the way to the hospital with the heart case.' The next morning, I read in the newspapers that two persons had died in that crash.

"We spend all kinds of money for space technology," he says, "but we can't put ambulances on the streets of Newark. And then there's this: Before I took office, Martland Hospital was trying to raise $5,000 for a cardiac machine to treat heart patients. They still haven't been able to raise the $5,000; they still don't have the machine. Now what is $5,000 in this country?"

Perhaps the frustrations that erode the human soul in Newark are best caught in an anecdote told by a black leader about a confrontation game developed by Federal experts and called "Urban Dynamics." Its object is to make different groups in a community aware of one another's problems. Black leaders from the ghetto are put in the position of the white power structure and confronted with its problems: the white, establishmentarian types take the roles of ghetto residents. The black leader who participated in this educational exercise says:

"You know, we reacted just the same way the white establishment class does—*the very same way!* Faced with big tax increases, we took our money and moved our plants to the suburbs. Crime went up in the city —we moved out. We reacted just the way the white power structure does —*the very same way!*

"But what was amazing was to see the representatives of the white power class playing the game from the standpoint of the minorities. For the first time, they were really brought face to face with the problems of the black man in the central cities. No job. No decent place to live. Afraid of being mugged. Trapped. It was just too much. Some of them couldn't stand it. They'd just get up and walk out, saying, 'I'm not going to play *that* game any more.' And one became so frustrated and angry that he jumped up and cried out: 'Right on! Burn the city down!'"

Just so desperate is the situation in Newark.